WARRANTIES IN MARINE INSURANCE

Second edition

WARRANTIES IN MARINE INSURANCE

Second edition

Barış Soyer, LLB, LLM, PhD
Senior Lecturer in Law
University of Wales Swansea
Institute of International Shipping and Trade Law

Cavendish
Publishing
Limited

London • Sydney • Portland, Oregon

Second edition published in 2006 by
Cavendish Publishing Limited, The Glass House,
Wharton Street, London WC1X 9PX, United Kingdom
Website: www.cavendishpublishing.com

Published in the United States by Cavendish Publishing
c/o International Specialized Book Services,
5804 NE Hassalo Street, Portland,
Oregon 97213-3644, USA

Published in Australia by Cavendish Publishing (Australia) Pty Ltd
45 Beach Street, Coogee, NSW 2034, Australia
Website: www.cavendishpublishing.com.au

First edition published in 2001

British Library Cataloguing in Publication Data
Soyer, Barış
Warranties in marine insurance. – 2nd ed.
1. Insurance, Marine – Great Britain 2. Warranty – Great Britain
I. Title
346.4'10862

Library of Congress Cataloguing in Publication Data
Data available

ISBN 10: 1-85941-943-7
ISBN 13: 978-1-85941-943-4

1 3 5 7 9 10 8 6 4 2

To my family: specially my son Özgür-James (OJ)

FOREWORD TO THE SECOND EDITION

My predecessor as foreword-writer, Mrs Yvonne Baatz, rightly called the first edition of this book both readable and thought-provoking. Now comes the second edition which continues that tradition. Its readability speaks for itself and, in the absence of any positive proposal for reform of the law of insurance warranties, wishes for that reform continue to be provoked by Dr Soyer's apt and illuminating criticisms. It is a tribute to the author that, in spite of many additions, the text is overall more succinct than the previous edition. This has been largely achieved by excision of the discussion of general defence to claims of breach of warranty in order to concentrate on the book's main theme of evaluating the current state of marine insurance warranties and proposing its reform.

History does not relate how common it is for a mere reviewer (118 LQR 647) to be promoted to foreword-writer; it will not surprise the reader to learn, however, that it is not only a less arduous, but an infinitely more pleasant task to wish the second edition even more success than the first.

Lord Justice Longmore
Court of Appeal
Royal Courts of Justice
Strand
London
June 2005

PREFACE TO THE SECOND EDITION

The principal objective of the first edition was to review the law in respect of marine insurance warranties, as concisely as possible, and identify any existing and potential difficulties in this area. It was also intended to put forward some viable proposals, towards the resolution of such difficult issues that are still inadequately dealt with by the present legal regime. This objective remains unchanged for the second edition, but the scope of the book has been extended to cover international developments and market responses to some of the problematic aspects of the warranty regime. To this end, in this edition, attention has been devoted to the reform proposals put forward by the Australian Law Reform Commission. Also, there is a systematic discussion of the potential impact of the International Ship and Port Facility Security Code on the implied warranty of seaworthiness and other relevant sections of the Marine Insurance Act 1906. By the same token, implications of the International Hull Clauses 2003 on various aspects of the current legal framework regime have been considered.

For any common law subject, four years is a long period during which one might reasonably expect intensive judicial activity. This was certainly the case for insurance law and judgments handed down by British courts shed some light on various aspects of the warranty regime. In this edition, I have made an attempt to incorporate these decisions into the text and to provide a commentary on them.

Some authors are of the opinion that the process of updating should be restricted to bringing existing material up to date by weaving in material that has come into existence since the completion of the previous edition. This approach, which might be appropriate for a textbook, is not, in my opinion, one which should be followed in a research monograph. I took the opportunity not only to update the text, but also to rearrange the structure of the book in the light of my increased understanding of the subject and valuable comments received from legal scholars. I have, therefore, decided to remove the part which evaluated the interrelation between various defences available to a marine insurer, such as breach of utmost good faith, wilful misconduct of the assured and sue and labour clauses, and breach of warranty defence. I still believe that this part was a useful one, but rapid developments in those areas would have required more detailed analysis and there was a danger that the main gist of the book might have been diluted.

The book is, therefore, divided into two main parts. The first part, Chapters 1 to 6, evaluates the current law, highlighting the potential problems and offering some solutions. In the second part, Chapters 7 and 8, the scope and nature of a possible reform in this area are discussed, in the light of a comparative study and recent developments in the marine insurance market.

The road to the second edition has been a tiring and, at times, stressful one. Along the way I have incurred numerous debts of gratitude. In particular, I would like to thank my family, especially my partner (Jean), my son (Özgür-James), my mum and dad (İlkay and Özgür), my sister (Banu) and my grandmother (Hatíce), for their love and support. I would also like to mention the support and assistance I received from my colleagues at Swansea and to thank Prof Iwan R Davies for doing his best to create a productive research environment within the Department. I am also greatly indebted to Prof Rhidian D Thomas, the Director of the Institute of International Shipping and Trade Law, for being accommodating and responsive to my inquiries on the subject. It would be a material non-disclosure (!) on my part if I failed to mention how inspirational he has been in my development as an academic lawyer. I also have to mention the support and assistance of colleagues from other institutions. In that respect, Mrs Yvonne Baatz, the Director of the Institute of Maritime Law, Dr Susan Hodges, Cardiff University, and Professor Robert Merkin, University of Southampton, deserve particular mention as their suggestions and comments have been very valuable, as always. Last, but not least, I wish to express my thanks to the staff of Cavendish Publishing Limited for their assistance and understanding throughout the production process of the second edition.

Needless to say, any infelicities remain my own.

The law stated is on the basis of materials available to me on 1 February 2005.

Dr Barış Soyer
May 2005
Swansea

CONTENTS

TABLE OF CASES

TABLE OF STATUTES

TABLE OF STATUTORY INSTRUMENTS

TABLE OF OVERSEAS LEGISLATION AND STANDARD INSURANCE CONDITIONS

TABLE OF EUROPEAN AND INTERNATIONAL LEGISLATION

TABLE OF ABBREVIATIONS

ABI	Association of British Insurers
AC	Appeal Cases
ADS	Allgemeine Deutsche Seeversicherungs-Bedingungen
A & E	Adolphus & Ellis' Reports (1834–40)
AMC	American Maritime Cases
ANZ Ins Cas	Australia and New Zealand Insurance Cases
aff'd	affirmed
All ER	All England Law Reports
App Cas	Appeal Cases
Art	Article
AG	Attorney General
BCLC	Butterworths Company Law Cases
BCLR (3d)	British Columbia Law Reports, Third Series
BILA	British Insurance Law Association
B & Ad	Barnewall & Adolphus' King's Bench Reports (1830–34)
B & Ald	Barnewall & Alderson's King's Bench Reports (1817–22)
B & C	Barnewall & Cresswell's King's Bench Reports (1822–30)
B & S	Best & Smith's Queen's Bench Reports (1861–65)
bdi	both days included
Beav	Beavan's Rolls Court Reports (1838–66)
Bos & P (BP)	Bosanquet & Puller's Common Pleas Reports (1796–1804)
Br & B	Broderip & Bingam's Common Pleas (1819–22)
Burr	Burrows' King's Bench Reports (1757–71)
CB	Common Bench Reports by Manning, Granger & Scott (1856–65)
CCLI	Canadian Cases on the Law of Insurance
CLC	Commercial Law Cases
CLR	Commonwealth Law Reports
CMI	Comité Maritime International
CSO	Company Security Officer
C Rob	Christopher Robinson's Admiralty Reports (1799–1808)
Camp	Camp Reports
Ch	Chapter/Chancery Law Reports
Ch App	Chancery Appeals Law Reports (1865–75)
Ch D	Chancery Division Law Reports (1876–90)
cif	cost, insurance and freight
Cl & F	Clark & Finnelly's House of Lords Cases (1831–46)
Co	Company
Com Cas	Commercial Cases (1896–1941)
Conn	Connecticut Reports
Corp	Corporation
CPR	Civil Procedure Rules
Cowp	Cowper's King's Bench Reports (1774–78)
Cromp & M	Crompton & Meeson's Exchequer Reports (1832–34)
DGM & M	De Gex, Macnaghten & Gordon's Chancery Reports (1851–57)
DLR (3rd)	Dominion Law Reports (3rd series)
DM	German Mark

DOS	Declaration of Security
Dod Adm R	Dodson's Admiralty Reports (1811–22)
Doug(l) (KB)	Douglas' King's Bench Reports (1778–85)
Dow	Dow's House of Lords Cases (1812–13)
DTV	Deutscher Transport-Versicherungs-Verband
EB & E	Ellis, Blackburn & Ellis' Queen's Bench Reports (1861–69)
EC	European Community
ER	East's Term Reports, King's Bench (1801–12)
EWCA Civ	Court of Appeal Civil (England and Wales)
EWHC (Comm)	Divisional Court/Commercial Court (England and Wales)
E & B	Ellis & Best Queen's Bench Reports (1861–69)
East	East's Term Reports, King's Bench (1801–12)
Eng Rep	English Reports Full Print (1210–1865)
edn	edition
ed	editor
et al	*et alii* (Latin) – and others
Ex	Exchequer Reports (1847–56)
Ex D	Exchequer Division Law Reports (1875–80)
Exch	Exchequer Law Reports (1865–75)
Exch Ct	Canada Law Reports, Exchequer Court
F	Federal Reporter
F 2d	Federal Reporter, Second Series
F 3d	Federal Reporter, Third Series
FCA	Federal Court of Australia Reports
fc&s	free of capture and seizure
FLR	Federal Law Reports (Australia)
FTLR	Financial Times Law Reports
F Supp	Federal Supplement (USA)
F & F	Foster & Finlason's Nisi Prius Reports (1858–67)
Fed Cas	Federal Cases (USA) (1789–1880)
Fed Rep	Federal Reporter (USA)
fob	free on board
fn	footnote
GEIP	General Establishment of Iraqi Ports
HL Cas	House of Lords Cases (Clarke's) (1847–66)
ICA	Insurance Contracts Act (Norway)
ICC	Institute Cargo Clauses/Institute Container Clauses
ICR	Industrial Court Reports
IHC	International Hull Clauses
IOB	Insurance Ombudsman Bureau
ILR	Insurance Law Reporter (Canada)
ILRA	Insurance Law Reform Act (New Zealand)
IMF	International Monetary Fund
IMO	International Maritime Organisation (formerly IMCO)

IR	Irish Reports
ISMC	International Safety and Management Code
ISPSC	International Ship and Port Facility Security Code
ISSC	International Ship Security Certificate
ITCF	Institute Time Clauses (Freight)
ITCH	Institute Time Clauses (Hull)
ITLQ	International Trade Law Quarterly
ITR	Irish Term Reports (1785–95)
IVCH	Institute Voyage Clauses (Hull)
IYT	Institute Yacht Clauses
ibid	*ibidem* (Latin) – in the same place
Inc	Incorporated
Ir Ch R	Irish Chancery Reports (1850–66)
Ir Cl R	Irish Common Law Reports (1866–78)
JIML	Journal of International Maritime Law
KB	King's Bench Law Reports (1901–52)
LJPC	Law Journal Reports, New Series Privy Council (1865-1946)
LJ QB	Law Journal Reports, New Series Queen's Bench (1831–1946)
LMCLQ	Lloyd's Maritime and Commercial Law Quarterly
LR	Law Reports (Canada)
LR CP	Law Reports Common Pleas (1865–75)
LR Ex	Law Reports Exchequer (1865–75)
LRLR	Lloyd's Reinsurance Law Reports
LR PC	Law Reports Privy Council (1865–75)
LR QB	Law Reports Queen's Bench (1865–75) (1891–)
LSA	London Salvage Association
LT	Law Times Reports (1859–1947)
LlL Rep	Lloyd's List Law Reports (1919–50)
Lloyd's Rep	Lloyd's List Law Reports (1951–)
Lloyd's Rep IR	Lloyd's Law Reports Insurance and Reinsurance
Ltd	Limited
MA	Marine Act
MIA	Marine Insurance Act
MSA	Merchant Shipping Act
M & S	Manning & Scott's Common Bench Reports (1845–56)
M & W	Meeson & Welsby's Exchequer Reports (1836–47)
Man & Gr	Manning & Granger's Common Pleas Reports (1840–44)
Man R	Manitoba Reports
Mason	US Circuit Court Reports
Moo & M	Moody & Malkin's Nisi Pleas Reports (1826–30)
Moo PC	Moore's Privy Council Cases (1862–73)
NBR	New Brunwick Reports (Canada) (1825–1929)
New JL Rev	New Jersey Law Review

Ont SCJ	Ontario Supreme Court Judgments
P(D)	Probate, Divorce & Admiralty Division Law Reports (1875–90)
P&I	protection & indemnity
PFSA	Port Facility Security Assessment
PFSO	Port Facility Security Officer
PFSP	Port Facility Security Plan
Peake's Add Cas	Peake's Additional Cases (1795–1812)
plc	public limited company
QB	Queen's Bench Law Reports
QBD	Queen's Bench Division Law Reports (1875–90)
Qd R	Queensland Reports
R	The Reports (1893–95)/Rex, Regina (Latin) – King, Queen
RR	Revised Reports (1785–1866)
Re LR	Reinsurance Law Reports
rev'd	Reversed
r	rule
SA	South African Law Reports
SC	Quebec Official Reports, Superior Court (Canada)
SCR	Canada Supreme Court Law Reports
SI	Statutory Instrument
SIFL	Solicitors Indemnity Fund
SLT	Scots Law Times Reports
SMS	Safety Management System
SOGA	Sale of Goods Act
SR	New South West State Reports (Australia)
SS	Steam Ship
SSO	Ship Security Officer
SSP	Ship Security Plan
Selw NP	Selwyn, Law of Nisi Prius, 13th edn, 1869
So 2d	Southern Reporter, Second Series
TLR	Times Law Reports
TR	Durnford & East's Term Reports (1775–1800)
Taunt	Taunton's Common Pleas Reports (1808–19)
UCR	Upper Canada Reports
US	US Supreme Court Reports
viz	*videlicet* (Latin) – namely
WLR	Weekly Law Reports
Wils	Wilson's King Bench Reports (1742–74)

BIBLIOGRAPHICAL ABBREVIATIONS

Arnould   *Arnould's Law of Marine Insurance and Average* (16th edn, Vols I and II by Sir M Mustill and JCB Gilman), London, 1981. (Vol III by JCB Gilman and NV Smith), London, 1997) (earlier editions of this book have also been cited throughout the text)

Clarke   *The Law of Insurance Contracts* (4th edn, by MA Clarke), London, 2002 (earlier editions of this book have also been cited throughout the text)

Carver   *Carver's Carriage by Sea* (13th edn by R Colinvaux), London, 1982

Chalmers and Archibald   *The Marine Insurance Act 1906* (3rd edn, by MD Chalmers and JG Archibald), London, 1922

Hurd   *Marine Insurance* (by HB Hurd), London, 1922

Huybrechts, Hooydonk and Dieryck   *Marine Insurance at the turn of the Millenium* (Vols I and II by M Huybrechts, EV Hooydonk and C Dieryck), Antwerp, 1999

Ivamy   *Law of Marine Insurance* (8th edn, by ERH Ivamy), London, 1988

MacGillivray   *MacGillivray on Insurance Law* (10th edn, by N Legh-Jones, J Birds and D Owen), London, 2003 (earlier editions of this book have also been cited throughout the text)

Park   *A System of the Law of Marine Insurances* (8th edn, by F Hilyard), London, 1832

Thomas   *The Modern Law of Marine Insurance* (by DR Thomas), London, 1996. (Vol II by DR Thomas), London, 2002

Wilken and Villiers   *The Law of Waiver, Variation and Estoppel* (2nd edn, by S Wilken), Oxford, 2002

CHAPTER 1

WARRANTIES IN GENERAL

I – MEANING OF THE TERM 'WARRANTY'

(A)   The term 'warranty' in contract law

1.1   The term 'warranty' has been described as 'one of the most ill used expressions in the legal dictionary'.[1] This is particularly the case in the law of contract where it has been used in various senses. In its most traditional non-insurance sense, it is understood as meaning a term of the contract, the breach of which entitles the aggrieved party to damages, but not a right to treat the contract as repudiated.[2] Accordingly, the injured party is still under an obligation to perform the contract, despite the fact that the contract is breached by the other party. Apart from warranties, contracts might include two other terms, namely conditions and innominate (intermediate) terms. Breach of a term classified as a 'condition' entitles the innocent party either to elect to terminate the contract, with the consequence that both parties are discharged from further performance, or affirm the contract and claim damages. Whether breach of a term that is classified as an 'innominate term' by the courts would entitle the injured party to elect to terminate the contract depends upon the nature of the event to which the breach gives rise. The injured party can elect to terminate the contract for breach of an innominate term if, but only if, the requirement of substantial failure is satisfied; otherwise, he can only claim damages.[3]

1.2   Sometimes, the term 'warranty' is used to indicate that the injured party, in case of breach of a condition, has chosen to affirm the contract and claim damages. In such a case, the injured party is said to sue on a 'warranty *ex post facto*',[4] although this expression is somewhat misleading, since the breach is still that of a condition of the contract.[5]

1.3   The term 'warranty' is also used to refer to certain guarantees given by a retailer under a sale contract. For instance, in a contract for sale of a television set, the seller might agree to supply parts free of charge for a period of one year. This kind of guarantee is, usually, called a 'warranty' and is binding on the part of the seller since it will form part of the sale contract.

1.4   It has become common in recent years for retailers to offer their customers, particularly those who buy technical equipment, the opportunity of buying a so-called

---

1   *Finnegan v Allen* [1943] 1 KB 425, p 430, *per* Lord Greene MR.
2   See s 11(4) of the the Sale of Goods Act (SOGA) 1979, for the definition of the term 'warranty' for contracts that are within its scope.
3   *Hong Kong Fir Shipping Co Ltd v Kawasaki Kisen Kaisha Ltd* [1962] 2 QB 26. For a detailed analysis of conditions, warranties and innominate terms, see, *The Law of Contract*, 11th edn, (by GH Treitel) London, 2003, pp 788–805.
4   *Wallis, Son & Wells v Pratt and Haynes* [1911] AC 394.
5   Note that in many older cases the term 'warranty' has been used in the same sense as the term 'condition' and this has led to a considerable degree of complexity. See, eg, *Behn v Burness* (1863) 3 B & S 751.

'extended warranty'. This will commonly give the customer, in return for payment, a guarantee that the cost of repairs will be covered for a certain period of time.[6] Although these types of schemes are often called 'warranties', they are, in fact, a sort of insurance against mechanical breakdown and this is the better way of describing them. The way such a scheme generally operates is that the retailer is associated with a company offering mechanical breakdown insurance. If the retailer has a franchise in relation to the mechanical breakdown insurance from the manufacturer, it may be with a company with which the manufacturer has an agreement, or it may be through the scheme operated by the retailer, or it may be through the retailer's own contracts. Whatever the case is, the role of the retailer will generally be as an agent for the company operating the scheme and the actual contract of 'insurance' is between the consumer and the operating company. This inevitably means that the retailer is not liable himself and cannot use the scheme to avoid any of his liabilities under the contract of sale.[7]

(B)   The term 'warranty' in insurance law

1.5   Unlike general contract law, the use of the term 'warranty' is rather restricted in insurance law. The term is, occasionally, used in some exclusion clauses that intend to limit the liability of the insurer under the contract. For instance, in a clause which is worded as '... warranted free from capture and seizure', the term 'warranty' means that the insurer is not liable for the perils of capture and seizure.[8]

1.6   However, the word 'warranty', in a technical sense, is used to refer to a certain term of an insurance contract, breach of which has particular legal consequences. With a warranty, one party of the insurance contract, the assured, undertakes certain obligations that need to be complied with within a certain period of time and the liability of the insurer, under the insurance contract, depends on the assured's compliance with these obligations.[9] In this respect, warranties are used by the insurer as a shield against liability.[10]

1.7   Warranties are said to serve a very significant function in the law of insurance, that is, determining the scope of the cover agreed by the insurer. A contract of insurance is described as: 'A contract whereby the insurer undertakes to indemnify the

---

6   This kind of 'extended warranty' is quite commonly offered by second-hand car dealers and stores that sell domestic appliances.

7   In order to harmonise legal rules in Member States and ensure a uniform minimum level of consumer protection, in the context of the internal market, on certain aspects of the sale of consumer goods and associated guarantees, an European Community Directive (99/44/EC) has been made on Certain Aspects of Sale of Consumer Goods and Associated Guarantees. All types of guarantees given by retailers are subject to Art 6 of this Directive. The Directive has been implemented into English law by The Sale and Supply of Goods to Consumers Regulations 2002 (SI 2002/3045).

8   See *Morgan v Provincial Insurance Co Ltd* (1932) 148 LT 385, where Scrutton LJ said: '... but it must be remembered that in contracts of insurance the word "warranty" does not necessarily mean a condition or promise the breach of which will avoid the policy. A warranty that a marine policy is free from particular average certainly does not mean that, if there is a partial loss to the insured ship, the whole policy is avoided. It merely describes the risk and means that the only risk being insured against is the risk of a total loss and that a partial loss is not the subject of the insurance.'

9   See s 33(1) and (3).

10   In the law of contract/sales, warranties are generally used as a sword to impose liability on one party to the contract.

assured, in manner and to the extent thereby agreed, against certain losses in return of a payment known as premium.'[11] Accordingly, from the insurer's point of view, the extent of the risk is crucial, as his liability will largely depend on it. The warranties incorporated into the contract play an essential role in assessing the risk. For example, a warranty to the effect that the insured vessel will not navigate in a certain area gives an idea to the insurer about the extent of the risk he has agreed to provide cover for. If this obligation is breached, the risk initially agreed is altered and that is the reason why the insurer is allowed to discharge himself from further liability in such a case.

1.8   Warranties are quite commonly used in marine insurance and the Marine Insurance Act (MIA) 1906 has provided the legal framework.[12] However, this does not mean that the use of such terms is unique solely to marine insurance contracts. Warranties also appear in all types of non-marine insurance contracts.[13] Generally speaking, the rules laid down by the MIA 1906 for marine warranties could also be applied to non-marine warranties. It has, in fact, been observed on numerous occasions that the judges refer to marine insurance principles, or the provisions of the MIA 1906, when a non-marine warranty is involved.[14]

There are certain differences that exist between marine and non-marine warranties. First, implied warranties that have been incorporated into marine insurance contracts by the MIA 1906, for example an implied warranty of legality, do not exist in non-marine insurance.[15] The main reason for this distinction is that non-marine insurance lacks the additional element of marine adventure. Accordingly, in non-marine insurance, warranties must be created with express wording.

Secondly, in marine insurance, it is a statutory rule that an express warranty must be stated in the policy, or incorporated into it by words of reference appearing in the policy itself.[16] This does not, however, appear to be the general rule in non-marine insurance where it is sufficient for an insurer to obtain the signature of the applicant to a declaration saying that, 'This proposal is to serve as the basis of the contract', whereupon the warranty is an effective term of the contract, even though not expressly mentioned in the policy when that is issued.[17] The solution adopted by non-marine

11 See s 1.
12 See ss 33–41.
13 For instance, a warranty, which requires the insured use to be the only use throughout the cover, is quite commonly incorporated into property policies. Similarly, it is not unusual in fire policies to see a warranty, which requires the assured to keep the fire-fighting equipment in a working condition throughout the policy.
14 For example, in *Thomson v Weems* (1884) 9 App Cas 671, p 684, Lord Blackburn, *obiter dictum*, said: 'In my opinion, as regards the effect of breach of warranty, the same principles apply whether the insurance be marine or not.' Paragraph 2(b) of the Statement of General Insurance Practice 1986, which applies to insurance contracts apart from marine and aviation, provides that, unless fraud is involved, the insurers will not rely on a breach of warranty defence where the circumstances of the loss are unconnected with the breach. The existence of this provision does not mean that a difference between marine and non-marine warranties as to the effect of breach has been created. From a legal point of view, the same rule applies to both; however, non-marine insurers with this voluntary code, which has no legal effect, have restricted their right to rely on this defence on certain occasions. The nature and effect of a Statement of Practice will be discussed later in the final chapter of this book (Chapter 8).
15 It was expressly stated by the Court of Appeal, in *Euro-Diam Ltd v Bathurst* [1990] 1 QB 1, that there was no implied warranty of legality in non-marine insurance.
16 See s 35(2).
17 See *Duckett v Williams* (1834) 2 Cromp & M 348; *Joel v Law Union & Crown Insurance Co* [1908] 2 KB 863; *Rozanes v Bowen* (1928) 32 LIL Rep 98; *Unipac (Scotland) Ltd v Aegon Insurance Co* 1996 SLT 1197.

insurance could be harsh for the assured since, in cases where a copy of the proposal form is not kept by the insured, there is a danger of him forgetting what he had warranted in it.[18]

Finally, it has been observed that the courts have a tendency to construe non-marine warranties narrowly so that the scope of the undertaking is restricted.[19] However, in marine insurance, despite the potential applicability of similar interpretation rules, the courts are reluctant to interpret warranties in favour of the assured. One possible reason behind this could be the fact that the marine insurance market is a place where the demand side is made up of professional people, for example, shipowners, charterers, cargo-owners, and they are expected to have a certain amount of knowledge regarding commercial rules and practices.

(C)   Warranty needs to be distinguished from misrepresentation

1.9   Section 20 of the MIA 1906 stipulates as follows:

> Every material misrepresentation made by the assured or his agent to the insurer during negotiations for the contract, and before the contract is concluded, must be true. If it be untrue the insurer may avoid the contract.[20]

Accordingly, if during negotiations, the assured, in response to a question, states that the majority shareholders of the insured company are German citizens, but this is not the case, the insurer might be entitled to avoid the contract for misrepresentation. In some representations, like the one above, the assured affirms the existence of a certain fact. Since with a warranty the assured either undertakes to do an act or affirms/denies the existence of certain facts,[21] it could appear that there is a similarity between express warranties and representation. However, the distinction between these two concepts is a fine one and was drawn by Lord Mansfield more than 200 years ago.[22] The case commonly cited to illustrate one aspect of this distinction is *Pawson v Watson*,[23] where Lord Mansfield emphasised that a warranty 'makes a part of written policy', whereas a representation is made outside the written contract.[24] Eight

---

18   For a general criticism of the 'basis of the contract' clause, see Law Commission, 1980, paras 7.1–11.

19   See, eg, *Havelock v Hancill* (1789) 3 TR 277; *Dobson v Sotheby* (1827) Moo & M 90; *Sillem v Thornton* (1854) 3 E & B 868; *Australian Agricultural Co v Saunders* (1875) LR 10 CP 668; *Yorke v Yorkshire Insurance* [1918] 1 KB 662; *Winicofsky v Army & Navy, etc, Insurance Co* (1919) 35 TLR 283; *Simmonds v Cockell* [1920] 1 KB 843; *Glicksman v Lancashire & General Assurance Co Ltd* [1927] AC 139; *Provincial Insurance Co v Morgan and Faxon* [1933] AC 240; *Woolfall & Rimmer Ltd v Moyle* [1942] 1 KB 66; *Sweeney v Kennedy* (1948) 82 LIL Rep 294.

20   For the definition of the term 'material' and the application of 'actual inducement test', which need to be satisfied in order to avoid the policy, see the decision of the House of Lords in *Pan Atlantic Insurance Co Ltd v Pine Top Insurance Co Ltd* [1995] 1 AC 501; [1994] 2 Lloyd's Rep 427.

21   See s 33(3).

22   Whether a statement is a representation or warranty could be quite crucial as the legal remedy afforded for a misrepresentation is radically different than the one for breach of a warranty. Accordingly, s 20 allows the insurer to avoid the contract *ab initio* in cases where a material misrepresentation is made, while, in case of breach of a warranty, the insurer is discharged from liability automatically by virtue of s 33(3).

23   (1778) 2 Cowp 785.

24   *Ibid*, pp 787–88. In fact, by virtue of s 35(2), an express warranty must be included in, or written upon, the policy, or be contained in some document incorporated by reference into the policy.

years after he delivered the above judgment, Lord Mansfield clarified the distinction further in *De Hahn v Hartley*[25] *where he said that:*[26]

> There is a material distinction between a warranty and a representation. A representation may be equitably or substantially answered; but a warranty must be strictly complied with.[27]

1.10 There is another difference between these concepts, which has been highlighted by Lord Eldon LC in *Newcastle Fire Insurance Co v Macmorran & Co*,[28] as follows:[29]

> It is a first principle of the law of insurance, on all occasions, that where a representation is material it must be complied with – if immaterial, that immateriality may be inquired into and shown; but that if there is a warranty it is a part of the contract that the matter is such as it is represented to be. Therefore, the materiality or immateriality signifies nothing.

II – WARRANTIES IN MARINE INSURANCE

(A) Historical development of the warranty regime in marine insurance

1.11 Although certain studies[30] suggested that Babylonians in the third millennium BC had advanced a form of marine insurance,[31] it is generally accepted that the earliest form of marine insurance was developed in the eastern Mediterranean during the Middle Ages.[32] The earliest types of marine insurance were bottomry and *respondentia* loans. Under a bottomry agreement, the owner of a vessel raised funds by pledging his ship for the repayment of the loan on her arrival at her destination, together with the interest on the bond. If the ship was lost and never reached her destination, there was no liability on the owner to repay the loan. In such a case the lender would have lost the money lent under the bond. The money lent on the security of the cargo was called a *respondentia* loan.

1.12 Marine insurance contracts, which intended to provide indemnity against marine risks upon the payment of a price, known as a premium, originated with the Hanseatic merchants and with the Lombard merchants in Northern Italy in the late 12th and early 13th centuries. Hence, the term 'policy' which is clearly derived from the Italian *polizza*, meaning a promise or undertaking.[33] The law and practice developed were later imported to England when Lombard merchants (who were

---

25 (1786) 1 TR 343.
26 *Ibid*, p 345.
27 Section 20(4) and (5) of the MIA 1906, stipulates: 'A representation as to matter of fact is true, if it be substantially correct, that is to say, if the difference between what is represented and what is actually correct would not be considered material by a prudent insurer ... A representation as to a matter of expectation or belief is true if it be made in good faith.'
28 (1815) 3 Dow 255.
29 *Ibid*, p 262.
30 See, *Shipping Law and Admiralty Jurisdiction in South Africa*, (by J Hare) Kenwyn, 1999, p 650.
31 The Code of Hammurabi (2250 BC) is generally quoted as the earliest recorded example of a maritime loan incorporating a risk 'premium', though more in the form of bottomry.
32 Hurd, 1922, p 10.
33 *O'May on Marine Insurance and Practice*, (by J Hill) London, 1993, p 1.

forced to migrate to England in the 13th century by the Kaiser of Germany, Friedrich II) persuaded Henry IV to grant them a section of the City of London where they could build their homes and carry on their trade in safety.[34] The usages of Lombard merchants have crystallised into a universal body of rules, and these rules, as the basis of a long series of interpretations and of judicial decisions, have become a part of English law.[35] It is, therefore, accurate to suggest that English and European marine insurance law have common roots. Early English marine insurers, in other words, Italian practitioners operating in England, were practising the marine insurance that had been advanced in Europe. However, starting from the 17th century, significant divergences between English and European insurance systems occurred, mainly due to different approaches adopted by English judicial authorities.

1.13   In the policies drafted by these Italian practitioners, it was quite common to see provisions requiring the assured to do something, or refrain from doing something, during the currency of the policy. While breach of such a term was treated in the same way as breach of any other contractual term in the European systems, breach was required to go the root of the contract and be causative of the loss for the insurer to avoid liability,[36] English law developed a different approach on this matter. Such a provision was regarded as a condition on which the insurer's promise of cover was dependent. Accordingly, the insurer was given an opportunity to repudiate the policy, in case of breach of such a provision. The first reported case in this area appears late in the 17th century. In *Jeffries v Legandra*,[37] the insurers undertook to insure against perils of sea, pirates, enemies, etc, from London to Venice, and the assured warranted to depart with a convoy. It was held that the words to 'depart with convoy' extended to sailing with the convoy for the whole voyage, but this undertaking would have been satisfied in cases where the ship was forced to separate from the convoy for reasons other than the wilful default of the master. In the judgment, it was acknowledged that compliance with this undertaking was a condition precedent to the liability of the assured, but the warranty was held not to be breached since the insured vessel's separation from the convoy was purely accidental. In two further cases that were decided in the late 17th and mid-18th centuries, a similar approach was adopted.[38] The courts, in both cases, accepted the underwriters' analysis of dependent condition, but construed the warranties involved, according to what was customary among merchants, holding that the warranties were not breached by minor discrepancies, and the assureds recovered.[39]

1.14   The law on such undertakings was later developed and clarified in the second part of the 18th century by Lord Mansfield, who became Chief Justice of the King's Bench in 1756. Lord Mansfield had a profound knowledge of commercial law and could be regarded as a figure who laid the foundations of the modern English law of

---

34 For a detailed analysis on the development of marine insurance in England, see *The History of Lloyd's and of Marine Insurance in Great Britain,* (by F Martin) London, 1876.

35 See *Lohre v Aitchison* (1878) LR 3 QBD 558.

36 *The Development and Principles of Insurance Law in the Netherlands from 1500 to 1800,* (by V Nickerk) Kenwyn, 1999, p 957.

37 91 Eng Rep 1171.

38 *Lethulier's Case* (1692) 91 Eng Rep 384 and *Gordon v Morley* 93 Eng Rep 1171.

39 It should be noted that, in *Gordon v Morley* 93 Eng Rep 1171, the jury was composed of merchants and this could be the main reason for such an assured-friendly interpretation adopted.

marine insurance. His method of dealing with marine insurance cases was to ascertain the customs from merchant men engaged in the business and with due regard to the Continental Codes, especially to the Marine Ordinance of 1681, to assimilate those customs into the general principles of English law.[40] He developed a similar approach for marine warranties and dictated the rules that still govern the warranty regime in the 21st century. Highly influenced by mercantile practice, he ruled, in *Kenyon v Berthon*,[41] that materiality of breach to the loss is not relevant in relying on breach of warranty defence. In that case, insurance upon a vessel described in the policy as 'in port 20th of July, 1776', was held to be defeated on proof of the fact that she had sailed two days earlier. Lord Mansfield, in deciding this case, declared that, '... though the difference of two days may not make any material difference in the risk, yet as the condition has not been complied with, the underwriter is not liable'. Also, considering the significance of such an undertaking for the underwriter in insurance practice, in another case[42] he adopted the rule that breach of warranty cannot be excused. A couple of years after, in *De Hahn v Hartley*, clarifying the scope of this undertaking further, he held that the validity of the insurance contract depended on the compliance with the warranty and exact (literal) compliance was required to satisfy this requirement.[43] One of the questions that occupied the law courts most, in all early insurance trials, and which, like others, was not definitely settled until the judicial reign of Lord Mansfield, was of seaworthiness. It was acknowledged that the insurers should not be responsible for any loss arising from insufficient or defective quality, or condition, of the insured vessel, but the way to protect the interest of the insurer was not developed. Lord Mansfield, in *Eden v Parkinson*,[44] getting inspiration from the Marine Ordinance 1681,[45] laid down the doctrine of implied warranty of seaworthiness, in the most concise manner, as follows:

> By an implied warranty, every ship insured must be tight, staunch, and strong; but it is sufficient if she be so at the time of sailing. She may cease to be in 24 hours after departure, and yet the underwriter will continue liable.

Following earlier cases in this regard,[46] Lord Mansfield also equated marine warranties with conditions in general contract law and ruled that a breach of warranty entitled the insurer to repudiate the contract prospectively as from the date of breach.[47]

---

40 Hurd, 1922, p 15.
41 (1778) 1 Dougl 12(n).
42 See *Hore v Whitmore* (1778) 2 Cowp 784.
43 He laid down this rule with the following wording: 'It is perfectly immaterial for what purpose a warranty is introduced; but being inserted, the contract does not exist unless it be literally complied with.'
44 (1781) 2 Dougl KB 732.
45 Section 12 of the Ordinance reads as follows: 'However, if the merchant prove that when the ship put to sea she was unfit for sailing, the master shall lose his freight, and pay the other damages and losses.' It must be noted that this provision affords the injured party (usually, cargo-owner) compensation, regardless of the negligence on the part of the shipowner. The effect of this Ordinance on the development of the implied warranty of seaworthiness will be examined later, in Chapter 3.
46 See *Pordage v Cole* (1669) 83 Eng Rep 403.
47 See *De Hahn v Hartley*, (1786) 1 TR 343, where he said: 'Now, in the present case, the condition was the sailing of the ship with a certain number of men; which not being complied with, the policy is void.' Despite the use of the term 'void', when one considers the judgment as a whole, it is obvious that what Lord Mansfield intended to say was that the contract is repudiated as from the date of breach of a marine warranty.

1.15   Almost all the rules adopted by Lord Mansfield regarding marine warranties have been drafted into the MIA 1906[48] by Sir Mackenzie Chalmers, the drafter of the first Bill of the Act. This practice is not extraordinary considering that the intention of the Act was to codify the existing law without making any alterations. The only change adopted by the Act was the remedy available to an insurer in case of breach of a warranty. Section 33(3) of the Act stipulates that breach of a warranty discharges the insurer from liability as from the date of breach. It has been clarified by the House of Lords, in *Bank of Nova Scotia v Hellenic Mutual War Risks Association (Bermuda) Ltd (The Good Luck)*,[49] that this section has the effect of discharging the insurer from further liability automatically and breach of warranty does not entitle the insurer to repudiate the contract as from date of breach. There is evidence to suggest that Sir Mackenzie Chalmers intended to follow Lord Mansfield's approach and equate marine warranties to conditions in general contract law.[50] Also, at one stage during its chequered passage to the statute book, which took just over 12 years, the second sentence of s 33(3) of the Bill read '... if it be not so complied with, the insurer may avoid the contract'. However, the first committee of lawyers, shipowners, underwriters and average adjusters appointed by Lord Herschell in 1894 and the second committee, which considered the draft Bill by order of the Lord Chancellor, Lord Halsbury, adopted the remedy known as 'automatic discharge' in case of breach of a marine warranty, by changing the sub-section initially drafted, and, in this way, a new contractual term with a completely new remedy for its breach was created in marine insurance.

(B)   Classification of marine warranties

1.16   A marine warranty is defined by s 33(1) as follows:

> ... a promissory warranty, that is to say, a warranty by which the assured undertakes that some particular thing shall or shall not be done, or that some condition shall be fulfilled, or whereby he affirms or negatives the existence of a particular state of facts.

It is crystal clear from this definition that the MIA 1906 has regarded all marine warranties as 'promissory'. Put another way, all marine warranties are, in a general sense, 'promissory' since they include a 'promise' of the assured in relation to certain matters. Some authorities, while classifying non-marine warranties, use the term 'promissory' for warranties that relate to a future event.[51] Such an approach is confusing and contradicts the wording of s 33(3). Accordingly, the phrase 'promissory warranty' should be regarded as a collective expression for all warranties, at least as far as marine warranties are concerned, and promissory warranties be categorised according to different criteria.

---

48 See ss 33–41.

49 [1992] 1 AC 233; [1991] 2 Lloyd's Rep 191, hereinafter referred to as *The Good Luck*.

50 In all editions of books written by Sir Mackenzie Chalmers, the drafter of the MIA of 1906 (*A Digest of the Law Relating to Marine Insurance*, 1901 and 1903, and *The Marine Insurance Act 1906*, 1907, 1913, 1922 and 1932), the following commentary appears: 'It is often said that breach of a warranty makes the policy void. But this is not so. A void contract cannot be ratified, but a breach of warranty in insurance law appears to stand on the same footing as the breach of a condition in other branches of contract.'

51 See, eg, *Bird's Modern Insurance Law*, 6th edn, (by J Birds and NJ Hird) London, 2004, pp 148–49.

(a) Classification of promissory warranties according to the time of undertaking

1.17 Certain warranties relate in time to the circumstances at the inception of the risk. For instance, a warranty whereby the assured declares that the ship-managers have a certain citizenship is a warranty of this type. In cases where such a warranty is breached, the insurer never comes on risk[52] and, accordingly, the premium is refundable due to total failure of consideration, unless the breach of warranty is, in fact, fraudulent.[53]

1.18 Some warranties, on the other hand, undertake that a given state of affairs will be satisfied or avoided at some time after the inception of the risk. This kind of warranty could also be referred to as a 'warranty as to future events'. A navigation warranty which requires the insured vessel not to navigate in certain areas during the currency of the policy is a warranty of this type. By virtue of s 33(3), the breach of such a warranty does not prevent the risk from running and leaves untouched any right that has already vested in the assured at the time of the breach. Accordingly, the assured may still claim for a partial loss which has occurred before the breach. Whether the assured could recover part of the premium paid depends on the divisibility of the risk insured against.[54]

1.19 Finally, an assured with a warranty might undertake that a given state of affairs will not only exist at the inception of the risk, but also during its continuation. It is appropriate to refer to warranties of this type as 'continuing warranties'. The implied warranty of legality that requires the insured adventure to be a lawful one and, so far as the assured can control the matter, be carried out in a lawful manner, is a good example of warranties of this type. In cases where the warranted state of affairs does not exist at the inception of the risk, the insurer is not liable for any loss which occurs during the currency of the policy. On the other hand, if the warranted state of affairs ceases to exist at any point during the continuation of the policy, the insurer is discharged from further liability from that moment, but any right which has already vested in the assured before the time of breach remains untouched.

(b) Classification of promissory warranties according to the nature of undertaking

1.20 Depending on the nature of undertaking, warranties may be divided into affirmative warranties and warranties which need to be satisfied by a positive/negative act. The affirmative warranty, to borrow from s 33(1), affirms or negatives the existence of a particular state of facts. For instance, a warranty in which the assured warrants that the flag of the insured vessel has always been British, is a warranty of this type. The warranties of the latter type, according to s 33(1), undertake that some particular thing shall or shall not be done, or that some conditions shall be fulfilled. The implied warranty of seaworthiness, which requires the insured vessel to

---

52 *Thomson v Weems* (1884) 9 App Cas 671.
53 See s 84(1).
54 See s 84(2).

be seaworthy at the commencement of voyage, could be given as an example of a warranty of this latter type.

1.21   In cases where the assured affirms or negatives the existence of a certain fact with a warranty and the affirmation/the negative is proven to be inaccurate, the insurer never comes on risk. The reason for this is that affirmative warranties relate to a period before the attachment of the risk. Conversely, in the case of breach of a warranty of the latter type the insurer is discharged from liability, since the warranted event relates to a period after the attachment of the risk. In this respect, it is clear that there is an overlap between affirmative warranties and warranties examined under the previous heading, warranties which relate in time to the circumstances at the inception of risk. Accordingly, it can be suggested that affirmative warranties are warranties that relate in time to circumstances at the inception of the risk, and vice versa. The same is true for warranties which need to be satisfied with a positive/negative act and warranties as to future events.

(c)   Classification of promissory warranties according to their structure

1.22   According to their structure, warranties could be express or implied. In fact, this is the classification on which the warranties regime in the MIA 1906 is based.[55] Express warranties appear in the policy, or are incorporated therein by reference to them. Under the principle of freedom of contract, the number and extent of express warranties depend on the consensus of the assured and insurer. Implied warranties, on the other hand, are incorporated into certain marine policies by the MIA 1906 and, accordingly, their number and scope is determined by the Act.[56] Provisions of the MIA 1906 apply equally to express and implied warranties, for example, exact (strict) compliance is required for both of them. When examining the legal situation in relation to marine warranties in the following chapters of this work, this distinction will be taken into account.

---

55   See s 33(2).
56   There are only four implied warranties: implied warranties of seaworthiness, portworthiness, cargoworthiness and legality. The nature and scope of these warranties will be examined in Chapters 3 and 4.

CHAPTER 2

EXPRESS WARRANTIES

I – FORMATION OF EXPRESS WARRANTIES AND NECESSITY FOR INCLUSION IN POLICY

2.1   Section 35(1) of the Marine Insurance Act (MIA) 1906 clearly provides that no formal or technical wording is required for the creation of an express warranty. An express warranty can be created with any kind of wording, provided that the parties' intention is to give warranty status to the clause in question. The words 'warranty' or 'warranted' are, therefore, not essential in order to create an express warranty.[1] Accordingly, in *Aktielskabet Greenland v Janson*,[2] a clause worded 'No mining timber carried' was held to be an express warranty. Similarly, in *Sea Insurance Co v Blogg*,[3] the court did not hesitate to afford warranty status to a clause that, without using the word 'warranted', required the insured vessel to sail on or after a specific date.[4]

2.2   To determine whether there was a common intention to create an express warranty is not an easy task. Until the judgment of the Court of Appeal in *HIH Casualty & General Insurance Ltd v New Hampshire Insurance Co and Others*,[5] there was speculation as to which factors were to be taken into account by courts during the process of assessing the common intention of parties. In this case, the insurers subscribed to two slips for the insurance of banks against the risk that the films that they had funded would not produce sufficient revenue to repay the loans (pecuniary loss indemnity policy). The insurers, then, obtained reinsurance cover from a group of underwriters. The reinsurance contract was subject to all terms, clauses and conditions as the original insurance contract and to follow that placement in all respects. The underlying contract was a slip policy and against the word 'interest', it was stated that the producers would produce and make six made-for-TV films.

The required number of films was not made, and the reinsurers refused to indemnify the insurers on the basis that these terms amounted to warranties, breach of which brought the risk under the direct policies to an end, so that the insurers could not be under any liability to make payment to the assured and, accordingly, the reinsurers could be under no liability to provide an indemnity. Affirming the judgment

---

1   However, it must not be thought that the use of these words is of no importance. They may be good evidence of the parties' intention to create an express warranty. As was stated in *Ellinger & Co v Mutual Life Insurance Co of New York* [1905] 1 KB 31, the use of the word 'warranted' shows *prima facie* that the parties understood that a breach of it should be a permanent or temporary bar to the insurer's liability.
2   (1918) 35 TLR 135.
3   [1898] 2 QB 398.
4   The parties have liberty in giving a warranty status to any variety of terms of contract. In *Overseas Commodities Ltd v Style* [1958] 1 Lloyd's Rep 546, for example, where a cargo of canned pork was insured, the assured warranted that all tins were marked by the manufacturer with a code for verification of date of manufacture.
5   [2001] EWCA Civ 735; [2001] 2 Lloyd's Rep 161.

of the trial judge, David Steel J,[6] the Court of Appeal held that the term was a warranty. Rix LJ proposed that a term is a warranty: (a) if it goes to the root of the contract; (b) if it is descriptive of the risk or bears materially on the risk of loss; and (c) if damages would be an inadequate or unsatisfactory remedy for breach.[7]

2.3   While two of these tests, namely (a) and (c), determine new yardsticks which a term alleged to be a warranty should be tested against, it has traditionally been the case that any statement of fact bearing upon the risk undertaken is, if introduced into the written policy, to be construed as a warranty. In *Baring v Clagett*,[8] for example, a policy was effected on goods that were qualified with the words 'on board *The Mount Vernon*, an American ship'. It was held that this description of the vessel contained a warranty that the goods were carried on board an American ship.[9]

In cases where the words describing the subject matter of insurance contain a statement of intention as to certain things rather than a statement of fact bearing upon the risks undertaken, such words cannot be construed as an express warranty. In *Grant v Aetna Insurance Co*,[10] a steamship was described in a policy of fire insurance as '... now lying in Tait's Sock, Montreal and intended to navigate the St Lawrence and lakes from Hamilton to Quebec, principally as a freight boat, and to be laid up for the winter in a place approved by the company'. The ship never left the dock and, approximately 11 months later, was destroyed by fire. The words qualifying the subject matter of insurance were not construed as an express warranty by the Privy Council, but merely as an expression of the assured's intention to remove her for the purpose of navigation in the manner described. Accordingly, the assured was not precluded from recovery.[11]

2.4   The new guidelines put forward by Rix LJ have been instrumental in assessing the legal status of terms in dispute in two recent cases. In *Paul Toomey of Syndicate 2021 v Banco Vitalicio de Espana SA de Suguros y Reaseguros*,[12] the insurers agreed to insure a Spanish football club in respect of the economic loss that might arise from the team being relegated from the First Division of the Spanish Football League. They then turned to the London market for reinsurance where they obtained cover for 32% of

---

6   [2001] 1 Lloyd's Rep 378.
7   [2001] EWCA Civ 735, [101].
8   (1802) 3 B & P 201.
9   See, also, *Lothian v Henderson* (1803) 3 Bos & P 499; *Baring v Christie* (1804) 5 East 398; *Barnard v Faber* [1893] 1 QB 340.
10   (1862) 15 ER 589.
11   *Ibid*, p 594. Lord Kingdown, of the Privy Council, gave the opinion of the court as follows:
     Their Lordships are of the opinion that the question depends entirely on the meaning to be attached to these words. If they import an agreement that the ship shall navigate in the manner described in the policy, there being an engagement contained in the policy, they must be considered as a warranty; and the engagement not having been performed, whether the engagement was material or not material, the insurers are discharged. But their Lordships think that this is not the true meaning of the words used. They consider that the clause in question amounts only to this: the assured says, my ship is now lying at Tait's Dock; I mean to remove her for the purpose of navigation in the manner described, and if I do, the policy shall still be in force; but, in that case, I engage to lay her up in winter in a place to be approved by the company. This construction which implies no contract to navigate, seems to their Lordships the natural meaning of the words used, and imputes a reasonable interpretation to the parties to the policy.
12   [2004] EWCA Civ 622.

their liability. Even though the underlying policy issued by the insurers to the assured was a valued policy as a matter of Spanish law, in the reinsurance slip policy it was defined as an indemnity policy. The consequence of the underlying policy being a valued policy is that the reinsurers would be liable for their proportion of the pesetas 2.9 billion, irrespective of the possibility that the actual loss suffered by the Club would be less.

Having indemnified the assured, the insurers turned to their reinsurers in London. However, their claim was rejected, *inter alia*, on the ground that the clause in the reinsurance contract as to the description of the interest was to be construed as a warranty and as the term was breached at the inception the reinsurers were not liable. In the light of the guidelines set out by Rix LJ, the Court of Appeal held that the term was indeed a warranty as it went to the root of the transaction and was descriptive of and bore materially on the risk. Thomas LJ noted also that damages would have been an unsatisfactory remedy due to the inherent difficulty in their assessment.[13]

2.5   A similar decision was reached in *GE Reinsurance Corporation v New Hampshire Insurance Co*,[14] where the reinsurers of a film finance policy included in the policy a term to the effect that the film production company would maintain the employment of its creative inspiration, Steve Stabler, throughout the duration of the policy. In fact, Mr Stabler left the production company soon after the reinsurance risk was incepted. Before the expiry of the insurance policy, the producers had become insolvent and there was little prospect of them repaying the principal sum of US $100 million. The reinsurers contended that they were entitled to deny liability as the term in question was a warranty. On the application of the *HIH* criteria, Langley J held that the term was a warranty as Mr Stabler's role was a material factor in defining the extent of the risk due to his role and involvement in the production company. It was also taken into account that if reinsurers were to be limited to a claim for damages for breach that would be an unsatisfactory and inadequate remedy as it would never be possible to assess how Mr Stabler's departure had affected the producer's ability to repay the loan.

2.6   Apart from these guidelines, Thomas LJ seems to suggest, in *Toomey v Vitalicio*, that the draconian effects of breach of an insurance warranty, in that it discharges the insurer even if the breach is not causative of the loss, should be taken into account when evaluating whether a term is a warranty or not. It is inevitable that the legal consequences of any breach would spring to the minds of judges in the process of reaching a decision on the matter. However, the crucial thing is that they do not extend their deliberations to analysis of the facts surrounding a loss with a view to determining whether there is a substantial relationship between the warranty and the loss incurred.[15] A post-mortem analysis to identify the relationship between the warranty and the loss requires that the cause of loss be resolved before the legal nature

---

13 *Ibid*, [46].
14 [2003] EWHC 302 (Comm); [2004] Lloyd's Rep IR 404.
15 *Elkhorn Developments Ltd v Sovereign General Insurance Co* (2001) 87 BCLR (3d) 290, British Columbia Court of Appeal, reversing the decision of the chambers judge (2000) 18 CCLI (3d) 203.

of the clause in question is determined. This is not at odds with the wording of the Act, which defines warranties by reference to the conditions and circumstances undertaken by the assured.[16]

2.7   Despite the fact that no specific form is necessary to create an express warranty, s 35(2) requires a warranty to be included in, or written upon, the policy, or contained in some document incorporated by reference into the policy. Necessity for inclusion of an express warranty in the policy is unique to marine insurance and has no application in non-marine insurance where the answers in the proposal form can be included in the contract as express warranties by a 'basis of the contract clause'.[17] Answers to questions contained in slips or proposal forms can only become warranties in marine insurance if they are inserted or incorporated, either directly or indirectly by way of reference, into the policy.

2.8   In practice, in the Lloyd's market, a slip procedure is used for almost all marine insurance policies. Accordingly, a Lloyd's broker prepares a slip containing all the particulars of the proposal necessary to allow underwriters to make a decision whether or not the risk is acceptable and, if it is acceptable, at what premium. The broker submits the slip to the leading underwriter. If the leading underwriter is willing to provide cover, he writes his firm's name on the slip and further states on the slip the amount of liability that is to be undertaken. The slip is presented to various underwriters by the broker until the requisite level of subscription is obtained. On full subscription, the broker prepares policy wording that is submitted to the assured and to leading underwriter for approval on behalf of the following market. The wording is then presented to the Lloyd's Policy Signing Office, renamed In-Sure in 2001, which issues a single policy on behalf of all the contributing underwriters, and which represents the terms and conditions set out in the slip.

2.9   A warranty may be written in any part of the policy, either at the top or bottom,[18] or transversely on the margin,[19] or on the back.[20] In Lloyd's Marine Policy (MAR 91), a separate section has been allocated for the insertion of special conditions and express warranties and it has been stated that they form part of the policy. Therefore, no dispute arises in modern policies as to whether the warranty has been inserted into the policy or not.

---

16 See, s 33(1) of the MIA 1906.

17 The Law Commission Report (1980) evaluated the present law as to the legal effect of 'basis of the contract' clauses, Pt VII, pp 90–92, and concluded that the current situation creates injustice for the assured and it is in need of reform. Accordingly, insurers have volunteered not to use 'basis of the contract' clauses in insurances of individuals. (See para 1(b) of the Statement of General Insurance Practice and of the Statement of Long Term Insurance Practice 1986.) It is also submitted that clauses of this nature are open to challenge under the Unfair Terms in Consumer Contracts Regulations 1999 SI 1999/2083 as amended by SI 2001/1186; SI 2001/3649; SI 2003/3182 and SI 2004/2095.

18 *Blackhurst v Cockell* (1789) 3 TR 360.

19 *Bean v Stupart* (1788) 1 Dougl 11; *Kenyon v Berthon* (1788) 1 Dougl 12(n).

20 If written on the back, it should be referred to on the face of the policy, since, if the policy is apparently complete on the face of it, the assured's attention might never have been directed to the back and he would be entitled to accept what appeared on the face as constituting the whole contract between the parties.

Despite the existence of a number of decisions by Lord Mansfield to the contrary,[21] it is settled by modern authorities, which have been accepted by appellate courts, that warranties attached to the policy, or contained in a slip pasted onto the policy, can be considered as being included in the policy.[22]

2.10   On some occasions, dispute as to the existence of an express warranty could arise simply due to a discrepancy between the wording of a slip and policy. What happens if an express warranty, despite the fact that it appears in the slip, has not been referred to in the policy? It is vital to evaluate the legal relationship between these two documents in order to be able to provide an answer to this question. The issue has been considered at some length by the Court of Appeal in *HIH Casualty & General Insurance Ltd v New Hampshire Insurance Co and Others*.[23] The facts of the case were summarised earlier. The relevant question was whether the requirement to make six films as mentioned in the slip policy, a warranty, was a part of the reinsurance agreement even though this obligation was not expressed in a similar language in the reinsurance policy. In the end, the decision did not turn on this point as the Court of Appeal was convinced that the words which appeared in the policy 'six revenue generating entertainment projects', were another way of saying that the assured was under an obligation to make six films.

2.11   Rix LJ, however, *obiter dictum*, considered what the position would have been had the term, which required six films to be made, appeared only in the slip. His Lordship dismissed the suggestion that the slip should not be admissible to act as an aid to the construction of the policy.[24] The court's task should be to identify what the intention of the parties was: either that the slip is superseded by the policy or that both documents live together. In the latter case, if it is not possible that both documents live together it may be proper to regard the policy as superseding the slip simply because it is the latter contract.

In the present case, Rix LJ was of the opinion that the parties' intention was that both documents live together to the extent that was possible. The fact that the policy wording was incomplete played a significant role in the conclusion reached. As certain essential aspects of the cover, for example the maximum cover for each film and the amount of premium, were not referred to in the policy wording, the insurance cover made sense only if the slip was taken as the basis of the agreement. Therefore, the term requiring the production of six films could have been regarded as a term of the insurance contract by virtue of the slip, even though it had not appeared in the policy wording.

2.12   On the other hand, in cases where the slip is superseded by the policy, an express warranty contained in a slip can only be considered as being incorporated into the agreement if the reference to it in the policy is clear. In *Doak v Weekes and*

---

21   See *Pawson v Barnevelt* (1778) 1 Dougl 12, where it was held that a separate document, even if delivered with the policy, cannot form part of it. Lord Mansfield also held, in *Bize v Fletcher* (1778) Dougl 12n (4), that even where the document was wafered on the policy, it cannot be a part of it.

22   *Bensuade v Thames & Mersey Marine Insurance Co* [1897] AC 609; *Cordogianis v Guardian* [1921] 2 AC 175; *Rozanes v Bowen* (1928) 32 LIL Rep 98. This approach is consistent with s 35(2), which employs a broad term – 'to be included'.

23   [2001] EWCA Civ 735; [2001] 2 Lloyd's Rep 161.

24   *Youell v Bland Welch and Co Ltd* [1992] 2 Lloyd's Rep 127, pp 140–41, per Beldam, LJ and *Punjab National Bank v De Boinville* [1992] 1 Lloyd's Rep 7, pp 12 and 13.

Commercial Union Assurance Co plc,[25] in the proposal form it was expressly warranted that the vessel was 19.90 m in length, whereas it was over 20 m. The only reference to the proposal form in the policy was as follows:[26]

> It is hereby understood and agreed that this insurance is subject to the following signed declaration and warranty which appears in the proposal form: non-operating owners must ensure that the details provided in this form in respect of the vessel's operator(s) are correct in every respect. Notice of change of the operator(s) together with full details of his/their experience must be given immediately.

The Australian first instance court rejected the insurer's submission that there had been a breach of warranty on the owner's part in relation to the statement of the length of the vessel. Ryan J said that:[27]

> I do not read this clause as having the effect of incorporating the proposal in the policy. It operates at most to incorporate into the policy warranties about certain matters which have nothing to do with the length of the vessel ... In my opinion there is nothing written upon the policy or contained in a document incorporated by reference in the policy which amounts to an express warranty that the vessel was 19.90 m in length.

2.13   Finally, it must be borne in mind that an express warranty does not exclude an implied warranty, unless inconsistent therewith. This rule, which is incorporated in s 35(3), merely reflects the common law situation. In *Sleigh v Tyser,*[28] the policy provided that the fittings of the vessel to carry cattle were to be approved by a Lloyd's surveyor and they were, in fact, approved. During the voyage a large number of cattle died, partly due to insufficiency of appliances for ventilation and partly due to an insufficient number of cattlemen to manage them. The ship was held to be unseaworthy in both respects and the implied warranty was not excluded by the approval of the fittings by the surveyor.[29]

II – CONSTRUCTION OF EXPRESS WARRANTIES

(A)   Necessity for construction and significance of precedent

2.14   Even if the words used are sufficient to allow an express warranty to be inferred, in some cases there remains the difficulty of interpretation of the actual words used. Such a situation arises either because the parties fail to make their intentions clear in the words that they adopt, or because the inherent ambiguities of language may make it impossible to state the parties' intentions in such a way that no misinterpretation is impossible.

---

25   (1986) 4 ANZ Insurance Cases 60.
26   *Ibid,* p 74.
27   (1986) 4 ANZ Insurance Cases 60, p 74.
28   [1900] 2 QB 333.
29   See, also, *Quebec Marine Insurance Co v Commercial Bank of Canada* (1870) LR 3 PC 234, to the same effect.

2.15   Whatever the reason is for interpretation of an express warranty, the object is to ascertain the extent of the express warranty precisely. If express warranties are construed very broadly and against the assured, the function of insurance in seeking to prevent loss supersedes the primary function of loss distribution. Similarly, adopting a narrow construction of express warranties might lead to results that contradict the main principles of insurance. From the insurer's point of view, risk prediction is one of the main elements of insurance and the premium is adjusted according to the extent of the risk undertaken. Since express warranties serve a function of determining the extent of the risk, construing them narrowly will, though unintentionally, make the insurers undertake a risk which they would not have accepted, or would have accepted by charging a higher premium, had they known that such a construction of the express warranty would have been adopted.

2.16   Where the court has already decided the meaning of words used in an express warranty, the same interpretation can be adopted by means of the application of the doctrine of precedent, if the meaning of the words is an issue in a later case.[30] There are, however, some dangers of applying the doctrine of precedent in a strict sense when construing express warranties. First, as was expressed by Atkin LJ,[31] where the wording differs in important respects from that used in earlier formulations, it is dangerous to construe it by analogy with the earlier provisions since it may well be that the wording has deliberately been altered for the purpose of overcoming the original decision. Secondly, it must be borne in mind that the words appearing in an express warranty might mean different things in marine and non-marine insurance.

(B)   Rules adopted by courts for construction of express warranties

2.17   Since marine insurance law is a part of contract law, the rules and principles adopted by general contract law for the construction of contractual terms can also be employed for the construction of marine policies.[32] The guidelines developed by courts over the past years, in relation to the construction of marine warranties, are evaluated in this part of the chapter. During this analysis, the case law will be referred to intensively, and some illustrations given, using the standard Institute Clauses published by the Institute of London Underwriters. It must, however, be borne in mind that this process is a rather complicated one, which does not invite easy generalisation, and the judges could rely on various different interpretation rules and techniques even when evaluating different parts of the same warranty.[33]

---

30   The importance of the doctrine of precedent in insurance law was highlighted by Parke B, in relation to construction of a term of the policy in *Glen v Lewis* (1853) 8 Exch 607, p 618, in the following way: 'If a construction had already been put on a clause precisely similar in any decided case, we should defer to that authority.'

31   *Re Calf and Sun Insurance Office* [1920] 2 KB 366, p 382.

32   Brett LJ highlighted this point in the Court of Appeal, in *West India & Panama Telegraph Co Ltd v Home & Colonial Marine Insurance Co Ltd* (1880) 6 QBD 51, p 58: 'An English policy is to be construed according to the same rules of construction, which are applied by English Courts, to the construction of every mercantile instrument.'

33   For instance, see the judgment of Aikens J in *Brownsville Holdings Ltd and Another v Adamjee Insurance Co Ltd (The Milasan)* [2000] 2 Lloyd's Rep 458, hereafter referred to as *The Milasan*.

(a)   Literal construction

2.18   In case of a dispute as to the meaning or extent of an express warranty, the court's starting point is to interpret the intention of parties by looking at what the parties have, in fact, said in their contract. To this end, the words used in a warranty are construed in their plain, ordinary and popular sense, that is to say, in accordance with their dictionary meaning.[34]

2.19   When assessing the ordinary meaning of words or phrases, courts will always consider the immediate context in which those words and phrases appear. Therefore, traditional cannons of interpretation, such as *ejusdem generis* and *expressio unius est exclusio alterius*, might assit courts in their attempt to discover literal meaning of words. The meaning and possible applications of these rules to some standard marine insurance warranties will be considered next.

(i)   Ejusdem generis

2.20   The *ejusdem generis* rule, which is laid down with reference to the construction of statues – namely, that where several words preceding a general word point to a confined meaning, the general word shall not extend in its effect beyond subjects of the same class[35] – applies in the construction of contracts.[36] This rule was expressed in relation to a marine insurance policy by Lord Birkenhead LC as follows:[37]

> Where specifications of particular things belonging to the same genus precede a word of general signification, the latter word is confined in its meaning to things belonging to the same genus, and does not include things belonging to a different genus.

2.21   If this is applied to the interpretation of express warranties, it can be concluded that, if particular words used in a warranty have a generic character, more general following words must be construed as having the same character. The standard Institute Fishing Vessels Clauses,[38] for example, sets out a disbursements warranty as follows:

> Warranted that no insurance is or shall be effected to operate during the currency of this insurance by or for account of the Assured, owners, managers or mortgagee on: disbursements, commissions or similar interests ...

---

34   Lord Watson observed, in a general sense, in *Thomson v Weems* (1884) 9 App Cas 671, p 687, that: 'The [matter] must be, in my opinion, interpreted according to the ordinary meaning of the words used if that meaning be plain and unequivocal and there be nothing in the context to qualify it.' See, also, *Robertson v French* (1803) 4 East 130 and *Stanley v Western Insurance* (1868) LR 3 Ex 71.
35   *Sendiman v Breach* (1827) 7 B & C 96; *R v Nevill* (1846) 8 QB 452; *AG v Brown* [1920] 1 KB 773.
36   *Cullen v Butler* (1816) 5 M & S 461; *Harrison v Blackburn* (1864) 17 CB 678.
37   *Stoomvart Maatschappij (Sophie H) v Merchants Marine Insurance Co Ltd* (1919) 122 LT 295, p 296.
38   (20/7/1987), drafted by the Institute of London Underwriters.

When applying the *ejusdem generis* rule to ascertain the extent of this warranty, it can be concluded that the words 'or similar interests' will have the same character as the words 'disbursements and commissions' and would, probably, include an insurance policy on profits, or excess or increased value of hull and machinery, but not protection and indemnity (P&I) cover, which has a completely different character.

(ii) Expressio unius est exclusio alterius

2.22   According to this rule, express mention of one thing may imply the exclusion of another related thing.[39] The rule can be applied in marine insurance where an express warranty might have covered a number of matters, but in fact mentions only some of them. Unless these are mentioned merely as examples, the rest are considered to be excluded from the proposition. The standard Institute Warranty on Indian Coal is worded: 'Warranted not to sail with Indian Coal as cargo ...' The application of *expressio unius est exclusio alterius* rule suggests that, since it is not expressly excluded, the warranty does not cover Indian coal, if any, carried as fuel.

(b) Construction of words in commercial context

2.23   Although determining the ordinary meaning of the words and phrases is the starting point in construing express warranties, it is an accepted canon of construction that a commercial document, such as a marine insurance policy, should be construed in accordance with sound commercial principles and good business sense so that it receives a fair and sensible application. Therefore, commercial understanding of the words and phrases used in an express warranty could qualify their literal meaning.[40] In *Bean v Stupart*,[41] the court had to construe the meaning of an express warranty, which required the vessel to carry '30 seamen besides passengers'. In fact, 26 mariners had signed the ship's register and, to make up the number 30, the assured reckoned the steward, cook, surgeon and some boys. The court held that boys were included under the term 'seamen' by mercantile usage and accordingly the warranty was satisfied. The commercial understanding as to 'seamen' meant persons employed in navigation as distinct from passengers. Similarly, in *Hart v Standard Marine Insurance Co Ltd*,[42] where there was a warranty stating '... warranted no iron or ore exceeding the net registered tonnage ...', it was held that an ordinary businessman would consider that the term iron includes steel and, accordingly, the warranty was breached when a quantity of steel in excess of such tonnage was shipped.

---

39   *Blackburn v Flavelle* (1881) 6 App Cas 628, p 634.
40   Nield J remarked, in *Lowenstein (J) & Co Ltd v Poplar Motor Transport (Lymm) Ltd (Gooda, Third Party)* [1968] 2 Lloyd's Rep 233, p 238 that: ' I am satisfied that ... I should construe the words according to the understanding of business people so as to make their meaning realistic and such as to give business efficacy to the agreement between the parties.' Lord Diplock made this point more vigorously, in *Antaios Compania Naviera SA v Salen Rederierna AB (The Antaios (No 2))* [1985] AC 191, p 201, as follows: '... if detailed semantic and syntactical analysis of words in a commercial contract is going to lead to a confusion that flouts business common sense, it must be made to yield to business common sense.'
41   (1788) 1 Dougl 11.
42   (1889) 22 QBD 499.

2.24   In similar vein, when construing the ordinary meaning of words in question, one might also have to admit evidence as to whether those words had any special meaning to the individuals in the area. In other words, the meaning of words used in an express warranty may also be qualified by usages of trade that are known, or presumed to be known, in any locality.[43] In *Dolbec v US Fire Insurance Co*,[44] a vessel was securely moored at a dock in Montreal, with her engine removed, when she was destroyed by fire. The marine policy stipulated an express warranty that during the winter months, the yacht was to be 'laid up and out of commission'. Against the insurer's allegation as to breach of warranty, the assured argued that the yacht was securely moored with her engine removed and, therefore, the warranty was satisfied. The Canadian Court of Appeal held that the words 'laid up and out of commission' had to be interpreted in accordance with the usual practice followed in laying up boats in the area where the loss occurred. The court found that the practice in the Montreal region was to remove boats from the water during winter months and, accordingly, the warranty was breached, as this was not done.

2.25   Another consequence which flows from the principle of construing words and phrases from the perspective of commerce and trade is that in construing an express warranty, the commercial object or function of the clause and its apparent relation to the contract as a whole should be taken into account.[45] This was the case in *The Milasan*,[46] where the court was asked to construe an express warranty in a yacht policy that required 'professional skippers and crew' to be 'in charge at all times'. The insurers contended that the warranty required that the assured employed at all times a person who was professionally qualified to be a skipper of this type of motor yacht. Aikens J decided that the rationale for the warranty was to ensure that the vessel was properly looked after all the time, both winter and summer, and wherever she was – whether cruising, or in a marina for the winter months. Accordingly, he held that the words 'professional skipper' referred to a person who had some professional experience that qualified him to be regarded as skipper and this did not necessarily mean that he had to pass formal examinations.[47]

A similar finding was made in two recent cases. In *Agapitos v Agnew (The Aegeon) (No 2)*,[48] the insured vessel, the *Aegeon*, became a total loss as a result of a fire that commenced on 19 February 1996 while the ship was undergoing repairs with a view to be converted to a passenger cruise ship. The initial cover agreed on 9 August 1995 contained a warranty to the effect that the *Aegeon* had London Salvage Association's (LSA) approval of location, fire fighting and mooring arrangements. At the inception there was a valid certificate of approval from the LSA, but two weeks later it expired and was not renewed. The assured sought to argue that the warranty was to be construed as a warranty confined to the state of affairs existing at the date of the contract and not as requiring the assured to obtain the further approval of the LSA

---

43 See the remarks made by Henry J, in *Provincial Insurance Co of Canada v Connoly* [1879] SCR 258, p 269.

44 [1963] BR 153.

45 *Lake v Simmonds* [1927] AC 487, p 508, per Viscount Sumner; and *Morley v United Friendly Insurance plc* [1993] 1 Lloyd's Rep 490, p 495, per Beldam, LJ.

46 [2000] 2 Lloyd's Rep 458.

47 *Ibid*, p 467. It is clear from the judgment that, while construing the other parts of the express warranty, Aikens J adopted a literal construction.

48 [2002] EWHC 1558; [2003] Lloyd's Rep IR 54.

after the current certificate expired on 30 August. Moore-Bick J suggested such a construction failed to take into account of the commercial context in which the insurance was written. It is well known in marine insurance practice that the LSA's approval is given for a limited period and it does not make commercial sense to impose a warranty of this kind at the date of inception, but be willing to allow the protection it provides to lapse within a matter of weeks.

In *Eagle Star Insurance Co Ltd v Games Video Co SA and others (The Game Boy)*,[49] there was a warranty requiring the assured to comply with all recommendations of the LSA prior to attachment. The assured failed to install appropriate telephones and appoint security watchmen, contrary to the ongoing recommendations of the LSA. However, it was agreed by the assured that the recommendations of the LSA had to be complied with prior to attachment of the risks so there was no breach for not fulfilling ongoing recommendations. Simon J held that the warranty in question was a continuing warranty and that adopting the construction put forward by the assured would have rendered it commercially meaningless. The learned judge construed the phrase 'prior to attachment' not as referring to the duration of the warranty, but rather to the date upon which the promise was made by the assured.

(c) Factual Matrix

2.26   In their attempt to ascertain the meaning of words and phrases used in an express warranty, courts might seek assistance of other factors, such as the background knowledge (factual matrix) that would reasonably have been available to the parties in the situation in which they were at the time of the contract.[50] The 'factual matrix' is a wide concept and extends to anything that would have affected the way in which the language of the document would have been understood by a reasonable man.[51]

2.27   In the insurance context, factual matrix might also include consideration of the entire policy as a whole.[52] As indicated earlier, if not superseded by the policy, the slip can constitute background when interpreting the meaning of a warranty which

---

49   [2004] EWHC 15; [2004] 1 Lloyd's Rep 238.
50   *Investors Compensation Scheme Ltd v West Bromwich Building Socity* [1998] 1 WLR 896, p 912, per Hoffmann LJ.
51   In *BCCI v Ali (No 1)* [2001] UKHL 8, [2002] 1 AC 251, [39], Hoffmann LJ attempted to qualify this statement:

> When ... I said that the admissible background included 'absolutely anything which would have affected the way in which the language of the document would have been understood by a reasonable man' I did not think it necessary to emphasise that I meant anything which a reasonable man would have regarded as *relevant*. I was merely saying that there is no conceptual limit to what can be regarded as background. It is not, for example, confined to the factual background but can include the state of the law (as in cases in which one takes into account that the parties are unlikely to have intended to agree to something unlawful or legally ineffective) or proved common assumptions which were in fact quite mistaken. But the primary source for understanding what the parties meant is their language interpreted in accordance with conventional usage: 'we do not easily accept that people have made linguistic mistakes, particularly in formal documents'. I was certainly not encouraging a trawl through 'background' which could not have made a reasonable person think that the parties must have departed from conventional usage.

52   *Cornish v Accident Insurance Co* (1869) 23 QBD 453; and *Hamlyn v Crown Accidental Insurance Co* [1893] 1 QB 750.

appears in the policy.[53] Similarly, extrinsic evidence is admissible if the words can, on ordinary principles of construction, have more than one meaning.[54]

(d) Contra proferentem rule

2.28   It is possible that the rule of interpretation expressed in the latin maxim, *verba caratum fortius accipiuntur contra proferentem*, could be relied on when construing express warranties. The meaning of this rule in insurance context was explained by Staughton LJ, in *Youell v Bland Welch & Co Ltd* as follows:[55]

> ... in case of doubt, wording [in a contract] is to be construed against the party who proposed it for inclusion in the contract: it was up to him to make it clear.

Since most of the warranties have been drafted by the insurer, this rule requires warranties to be construed against the insurer in the case of a dispute as to meaning of the warranty. Put another way, in cases where this rule is adopted, the insurer is penalised for not making the extent of the warranty clear.

2.29   However, it should not be automatically assumed that the *contra proferentem* rule requires all express warranties to be construed against the assured. In some cases, the broker of the assured could be the source of an ambiguous wording in the policy. In a number of cases it has been expressed that, where the ambiguous wording is contained in a slip put forward to the insurer by the assured's broker, the wording should be construed as having that meaning least favourable to the assured.[56] Colman J, in *The Zeus V*,[57] expressed his doubts as to such a rule.

> Although there may be many cases in which where the broker puts forward the ambiguous wording, it should be construed against the assured, this is not, in my judgment, an invariable rule. If the wording is exclusively for the protection of the insurer, *albeit* put forward in the broker's slip, it will usually be as inappropriate to construe the words against the assured as against the insurer. In such a case, the underwriter can be expected to correct the wording if he does not like it. That expectation at least neutralises the inference to be drawn from the fact that the wording is put forward by the assured's broker. Each case must be construed on its own facts and having regard to the nature and contractual function of the wording.

Bearing in mind the nature and role of express warranties, it is probably a right conclusion that they should not be construed against the assured, even in cases where his broker is the guilty party in the ambiguous wording. Otherwise, the insurer is put in a very strong position, despite the fact that he is to a certain extent, by not examining the wording in the slip thoroughly, responsible for the ambiguous drafting.

---

53 *HIH Casualty & General Insurance Ltd v New Hampshire Insurance Co and others* [2001] EWCA Civ 735.
54 *Zeus Tradition Marine Ltd v Bell (The Zeus V)* [1999] 1 Lloyd's Rep 703, reversed on different grounds [2000] 2 Lloyd's Rep 587, hereafter referred to as *The Zeus V*.
55 [1992] 2 Lloyd's Rep 127, p 134.
56 *A/S Ocean v Black Sea & Baltic General Insurance Co Ltd* (1935) 51 LlL Rep 305; *Barlett & Partners Ltd v Meller* [1961] 1 Lloyd's Rep 487; *Denby v English and Scottish Maritime Insurance Co Ltd* [1998] Lloyd's Rep IR 343 (CA).
57 [1999] 1 Lloyd's Rep 703, p 718.

2.30   In order to apply this rule the existence of ambiguity must be identified first. In *J Kirkaldy & Sons Ltd v Walker*,[58] the assured unsuccessfully argued that there was an ambiguity as to the meaning of an express warranty, which required the insured drydock to be surveyed as to its condition. In that case, the marine policy provided 12 months' cover for a drydock that was bought by the assured. At the commencement of the insurance period, the drydock was in Sweden and it was about to be towed to Portland. One of the clauses in the policy provided that:

> Towage of the vessel to be undertaken by TSA Tugs Ltd. Towage approval survey – applies to both tows – and condition survey to be performed by Surveyor Peter Curtis and all recommendations complied with prior sailing.

In fact, Mr Curtis surveyed the drydock before the towing. However, this was not a detailed survey and did not determine whether it was seaworthy for a 12 months' port risks cover. In his evidence Mr Curtis said that he had considered that the assured's instructions amounted to a requirement for an inspection for towage approval only. The towing began on 12 August 1997 and the drydock arrived in Portland on 21 August 1997. On the weekend of 8–9 November 1997, there was stormy weather. On the morning of 10 November 1997, one of the drydock's cranes fell from the top deck onto the pontoon deck, causing the drydock to sink at its moorings. The assured claimed £1 m for wreck removal expenses. The insurer denied liability on the ground that there had been a breach of warranty in that no condition survey had been performed and the risk had come to an end no later than the sailing of the drydock in August 1997. The assured argued that the term 'condition survey' had no fixed or uniform meaning and it could mean: (a) that the condition of the dock was to be surveyed for the purposes of tow; (b) that a survey of the condition of the dock (including its machinery and equipment) was to be carried out as far as possible; (c) that the condition of the dock was to be surveyed and the surveyor was to exercise a judgment as to whether the dock was fit to operate as a floating drydock. The assured requested Longmore J to take this ambiguity into account, to construe the warranty *contra proferentem* and to hold that condition survey warranty required the assured to have the drydock surveyed only for the purposes of tow (the interpretation which is most in favour of the assured). Longmore J held that there was no such ambiguity, as alleged by the assured, in the wording of the express warranty. The wording of the warranty made clear that the requirement of the condition survey was a requirement in addition to the purposes of towage approval and Mr Curtis' understanding of the express warranty was not relevant.[59]

2.31   Despite the existence of evidence that the *contra proferentem* rule is relied on extensively by judges in non-marine insurance, the rule has not found the same degree

---

58 [1999] Lloyd's Rep IR 410.
59 For a similar finding see *Cole v Accident Insurance Co Ltd* (1889) 5 TLR 736; and *Capital Coastal Shipping Corp & Bulk Towing Corporation v Hartford Fire Insurance Co (The Cristie)* [1975] 2 Lloyd's Rep 100.

of support in marine insurance.[60] The possible reason for this might be the fact that, in non-marine insurance, the assured is usually a non-professional in the sense that he is not a person whose everyday business dealings involve the making and carrying out of insurance contracts, while this is not the case in marine insurance. The assured in marine insurance usually operates in a market governed by long-standing and well-known rules of law and practices and, for this reason, he can reasonably be expected to be aware of the niceties of insurance law and the extent of terms of the contract he has signed.[61]

III – STANDARD EXAMPLES OF EXPRESS WARRANTIES

2.32   As examined earlier, the parties are given a wide range of discretion, not only to create an express warranty on any point, but also to determine its extent. Simply for this reason, an attempt to describe all the different types of express warranties that can be employed in a marine policy is a futile exercise. It is, however, possible to examine the main express warranties that are used in the market and the ones that have been specially mentioned in the MIA 1906 – namely, warranty of good safety, nationality and neutrality – for the purpose of illustration.

(A)   Express warranties as to future events

(a)   *Warranties as to geographical limits (locality warranties)*

2.33   It is the general understanding of the assured and insurer that the ship may navigate in any navigable waters, unless there are contrary restrictions in the policy. The position is acknowledged in the Institute Clauses, which state that:[62]

> The vessel is covered, subject to the provisions of this insurance, at all times and has leave to sail with or without pilots to go on trial trips and to assist and tow vessels or craft in distress ...[63]

2.34   When it is intended to restrict the movement and operation of the insured vessel, this is usually achieved by employing express warranties. These kind of warranties are called navigation (locality) warranties, where the assured undertakes either that the insured vessel will navigate within the confines of a specified area, or

---

60 The rule, eg, has been adopted in construing non-marine warranties in: *Havelock v Hancill* (1789) 3 TR 277; *Australian Agricultural Co v Saunders* (1875) LR 10 CP 668; *Yorke v Yorkshire Insurance Co Ltd* [1918] 1 KB 662; *Simmonds v Cockell* [1920] 1 KB 843; *Glicksman v Lancashire & General Assurance Co Ltd* [1927] AC 139; *Provincial Insurance Co v Morgan and Faxon* [1933] AC 240; *Woolfall & Rimmer Ltd v Moyle* [1942] 1 KB 66; *Sweeney v Kennedy* (1948) 82 LlL Rep 294.

61 The same justification was given by the Law Commission for excluding marine insurance contracts from a potential reform on breach of warranty in insurance law. See Law Commission, 1980, s 2.8, p 14. Note, however, that in *Richard Henry Outhwaite v Commercial Bank of Greece SA (The Sea Breeze)* [1987] Lloyd's Rep 372, p 377, Staughton J said that the word 'accepted', which appears in standard Institute Disbursements Warranty, for example, Institute Time Clauses (Hulls) (ITCH) 1995, cl 22.2, is a vague word and could be interpreted *contra proferentem*.

62 The Institute Time Clauses (Hulls) (ITCH) 1995, cl 1.1.

63 The same wording has been adopted by the 1983 version of the ITCH.

she will not navigate in specific waters or beyond a specified point. There are five sets of locality warranties designed by the London Market Joint Committee and they are published by the Institute of London Underwriters.[64] One of these Institute warranties, which provides restrictions on proceeding voyages in north Russian waters, for example, is worded as follows:

Warranted no North of 70 degree North Latitude other than voyages direct to or from any port or place in Norway or Kola Bay.

The common feature in all five sets of Institute warranties as to navigation of the insured vessel is that the assured undertakes that the vessel will not proceed to specific areas, or beyond a specified point. These are the areas where there are numerous dangers for navigation, such as poor visibility, icebergs and arctic weather conditions. Apart from these standard Institute warranties as to locality, the parties have liberty to create any type of express warranty restricting the assured vessel to proceed to areas where, for example, there is war or similar hazardous situations, such as a possible pirate attack.

2.35 Arnould has advocated that a clause restricting the navigation of vessels to certain geographical limits is not a warranty in its strict sense, but a term that defines the risk covered by the policy.[65] Arnould's point is that clauses of this nature have been traditionally given a warranty status without being given any vigorous judicial consideration.

2.36 It was first in *Colledge v Harty*,[66] where the court was asked to determine whether a clause restricting the geographical limits of navigation of a vessel was a warranty or an exception in legal terms. The clause in question stated that the ships were '... not to sail from any port on the east coast of Great Britain to any port in the Belts between 20 December and 15 February'. After hearing arguments from both sides, it was held that such a term was a warranty. Later, in *Birrell v Dryer*,[67] where the policy contained the clause: 'Warranted no St Lawrence between 1 October and 1 April', the House of Lords considered the clause as a warranty and in so doing relied on the precedent.[68]

Arnould cited the statement of Scrutton LJ, in *Re Morgan and Provincial Insurance Co*,[69] to support the argument that clauses of this nature are not warranties. Although the case was not concerned with marine insurance, Scrutton LJ observed that:[70]

... if a time policy contains a clause 'warranted no St Lawrence between 1 October and 1 April', and the vessel was in the St Lawrence on 2 October, but emerged without loss, and during the currency of the policy in July a loss happens, the underwriters

---

64 Under reference cl 26 (1/7/1976).
65 Arnould, 1981, para 698.
66 (1851) 6 Exch 205.
67 (1884) 9 App Cas 345.
68 See, also, *Provincial Insurance Co of Canada v Leduc* (1874) LR 6 PC 224 and *Simpson SS Co Ltd v Premier Underwriting Association Ltd* (1905) Com Cas 198, where the clauses restricting the navigation of the insured vessel were held to be warranties.
69 [1932] 2 KB 70.
70 *Ibid*, p 80.

cannot avoid payment on the ground that between 1 October and 1 April the vessel was in the St Lawrence (*Birrell v Dryer*). That is an example of a so called warranty, which merely defines the risk insured against.

2.37   With all respect to Arnould, it is believed that the status of the clauses in question in the above mentioned cases was correctly identified. In both cases, the assured undertook to fulfil an obligation, in other words he affirmed that a certain event (entering the specified areas) would not occur during the currency of the policy. This was done by using the phrase 'the vessels shall not sail' in *Colledge v Harty*, and 'Warranted no St Lawrence' in *Birrell v Dryer*. Therefore, the intention in incorporating the said clauses was not to bring the insurer off risk during the period when the assured does not comply with them, and again on risk when he does. If the intention was to create a clause to that effect, this could have been done with a different wording that did not impose any obligation on the assured. For example, the following wording would be ideal for such a purpose: 'The insurer is not to be on risk while the vessel sails in the areas specified …'

2.38   However, Arnould's view as to clauses restricting the navigation of the insured vessel has recently found judicial support in the Supreme Court of British Columbia. In *Federal Business Development Bank v Commonwealth Insurance Co Ltd (The Good Hope)*,[71] there was a clause in the policy which stated that:

> Warranted vessel laid up at the north foot of Columbia Street with permission granted to demonstrate within Vancouver Harbour for the purpose of sale.

The trial judge found as a fact that, for a short period of time, the vessel had been outside the geographical limit specified in the clause. It was held that the clause in question was not a warranty, but only a provision delimiting the risk. The decision was based on the fact that it could not be the intention of the parties to preclude the assured from liability for breach of that clause, especially in cases where the situation was restored later on.[72]

2.39   Undoubtedly, with appropriate wording, a legal effect other than warranty can be given to a clause that restricts the navigation of the insured vessel.[73] It is, however, not appropriate to generalise the issue by arguing that the clauses of this kind are not warranties, but clauses delimiting the risk. The legal status of the clause in question depends on its wording. It can be argued, by relying on the House of Lords' decision

---

71   [1983] 2 CCLI 200.

72   Such reasoning is the same reasoning adopted by the British Columbia Court of Appeal, in *Case Existological Laboratories Ltd v Foremost Insurance Co et al (The Bamcell II)* (1980) 133 DLR (3d) 727; aff'd by the Supreme Court of Canada [1983] 2 SCR 47 (*sub nom Century Insurance Co of Canada v Case Existological Laboratories Ltd*), hereafter referred to as *The Bamcell II*. This case and its justification will be discussed below [2.86–2.88]. The same approach was adopted in another case in Canada. In *Britsky Building Movers Ltd v Dominion Insurance Corp* [1981] 7 Man R (2d) 402 (Co Ct), the Manitoba County Court held that the clause, 'Warranted confined to the navigable waters of the Province of Manitoba' was not a warranty, but a clause delimiting the risk.

73   In the International Hull Clauses (IHC) 2003, geographical limits imposed on the movement and operation of the insured vessel by the Institute Warranties (1/7/1976) have been retained, but it is clearly stated in cl 11 that in the event of breach of these provisions the insurers shall not be liable for any loss, damage or liability or expense arising out of, or resulting from, an accident or occurrence during the period of breach.

in *Birrell v Dryer*, that the standard Institute Clauses as to locality are warranties.[74] On the other hand, the courts would not hesitate to give a different legal status to a clause restricting the navigation of the insured vessel that, with clearer terms, manifests an intention not to warrant. In *Navigators and General Insurance Co Ltd v Ringrose*,[75] for example, a clause worded as 'the vessel is insured whilst within the UK' was held by the Court of Appeal to be a clause delimiting the risk, rather than a warranty.[76]

(b)   Institute warranty as to towage and salvage services

2.40   Towage and salvage services are operations that involve increased risks for the vessels engaged in them. In order to restrict the engagement of the insured vessels in such operations, an institute warranty has been employed in hull policies.[77] This warranty provides that the insured vessel will not be towed any time after the inception of the risk. Customary towage and towage to the first safe port or place when in need of assistance are excepted from the scope of the clause and, therefore, are not covered by the warranty. It is possible to determine the extent of the warranty by evaluating the scope of these exceptions.

Whether a towage service is customary or not, will be identified according to the practice and customs in the trade for the vessels concerned. For instance, it is likely that a towage service engaged whilst the insured vessel is manoeuvring in restricted waters (for example, in a harbour, canal or river) will be considered as a customary towage. Similarly, if towage services are engaged by a professional tower for the safety of the insured ship, the warranty in the policy does not prejudice the assured. In order to grasp the scope of the exception some hypothetical situations will now be taken into account and, in each case, whether the towage services are engaged for the safety of the insured vessel will be discussed.

The warranty will not be barred in cases where the insured vessel is in distress at sea and her master enters into a contract with a passing ship, whereby the other ship undertakes to tow her to safety subject to payment for towage services whether or not they are successfully completed. The same is true if the master of the insured vessel

---

74   The law on locality warranties, however, has shown dramatic changes in America during recent years. In *La Réunion Française SA v Halbart* [1999] AMC 14, a locality warranty, which limited the operation of the insured vessel to the Atlantic Coast of the USA and a defined area in the Bahamas and the Caribbean, was subject to judicial examination. The Federal District Court held that any locality warranty, which could confine an insured to a coastal region, such as the east coast of the United States, or west coast of Mexico, and which did not express itself in a numeric figure, was utterly without meaning or effect. The court's judgment read, p 23, that: 'The language of an insurance policy must be accorded its plain meaning. The plain meaning of the navigational Limits Warranty does not comprehend a mileage limitation. Without such limitation in the Policy, [the assured] could not have breached it.' *Cf La Réunion Française SA v Christy* [1999] AMC 2499, delivered by the Middle District Court of Florida.

75   [1962] 1 WLR 173; [1961] 2 Lloyd's Rep 415.

76   See the decision of the Supreme Court of New South Wales in *Wilson v Boag* [1956] 2 Lloyd's Rep 564, to the same effect.

77   See cl 1.1 of ITCH and Institute Voyage Clauses (Hull) (IVCH) (both the 1983 and 1995 versions) which provides: ' ... it is warranted that the vessel shall not be towed, except as is customary or to the first safe port or place when in need of assistance, or undertake towage or salvage services under a contract previously arranged by the assured and/or owners and/or managers and/or charterers.'

accepts a salvage from a salvage tug while she is in distress at sea, verbally agreeing to base the operation on the Lloyd's 'no cure – no pay' salvage agreement and, accordingly, the insured vessel is towed to a safe port. Similarly, the warranty will still be satisfied if the insured vessel has been reasonably abandoned by her master, officers and crew and an independent vessel finds her drifting and tows her to a place of safety.[78] Such towage services are, however, acceptable only until the first safe port or place. Therefore, the warranty is barred in cases where the assured enters into a towage contract for the towage of the insured vessel from a port of distress to a repair port.

2.41   The second obligation imposed on the assured is not to undertake towage or salvage services under a contract previously arranged. The logic behind such a restriction is crystal clear. Undertaking salvage services as salvor, or towage services as tower, increases the risk insured against and the insurers do not wish the insured vessel to be exposed to unnecessary peril simply to afford the assured the opportunity to benefit from a salvage award or towage fee. Accordingly, the warranty is breached in cases where the insured vessel enters into a contract to tow or salve another vessel which is not in distress from one place to another in return for a benefit. The extent of this second obligation has, however, been narrowed to give the assured an opportunity to undertake salvage or towage services in cases where there is no contract previously arranged. The reason for this exception is not to discourage the master of the insured vessel from taking a distressed vessel in tow where human life may be in danger, or where the distressed ship is drifting and no other salvage services are available. Therefore, there is no breach of warranty if the master of the insured vessel agrees within the terms of Lloyd's 'no cure – no pay' salvage agreement to take a distressed ship in tow to a safe port.

2.42   It should be noted that the legal nature of this clause has been transformed into a suspensory provison under the International Hull Clauses (IHC) 2003. By virtue of cls 10.2 and 11, if the insured vessel is towed (excluding customary towage and towage to the first safe port or place when in need of assistance) or undertakes towage or salvage services under a previously arranged contract, the insurer is not liable for any loss or damage, liability or expense arising out of or resulting from an accident or occurrence during the period of breach. The cover is reinstated as soon as the breach is over.

(c)   Warranties as to the cargo carried

2.43   It is a common practice, especially in time hull policies, to incorporate a warranty that restricts the type of cargo the ship may carry, or sometimes the way in which cargo shall be carried. There is a standard Institute warranty to this end, in relation to Indian coal, that provides that:[79]

---

78   This is a pure salvage service and the salvor is entitled to an award up to the value of the salved property under the International Convention on Salvage 1989 which has been given force of law in the UK by s 224 and Sched 11 of the Merchant Shipping Act 1995.
79   Warranty 6 of cl 26 (1/7/1976) drafted by the Institute of London Underwriters.

Warranted not to sail with Indian coal as cargo:

(a) between 1 March and 30 June, bdi [both days included];

(b) between 1 July and 30 September, bdi except to ports in Asia, not West of Aden or East of or beyond Singapore.

Indian coal is a form of lignite, which is particularly subject to spontaneous combustion if carried in a damp condition during the hotter parts of the year. The aim of this warranty is to reduce the risk of fire on board the insured vessel by preventing the assured from carrying Indian coal as cargo during the main monsoon season (March to June) and to limit the distance for carrying such coal as cargo during the later monsoon season (July to September).

2.44   Apart from this standard Institute warranty in respect of Indian coal, any kind of cargo warranty restricting the carriage of specific cargo may be incorporated in the policy. For example, in *Aktielskabet Greenland v Janson*,[80] a warranty was incorporated into the policy prohibiting the insured vessel from carrying mining timber. Similarly, it was warranted, in *Hart v Standard Marine Insurance Co Ltd*,[81] that no iron or ore in excess of the registered tonnage would be carried.

(d)   Laid up and out of commission warranties

2.45   Some hull policies, especially the ones effected to provide cover for yachts, incorporate warranties that require the insured vessel to be laid up and out of commission at a specific time of the year. With cl 4 of Institute Yacht Clauses,[82] for example, it is warranted that the assured yacht will be laid up out of commission as stated in the schedule to the policy. Similarly, due to ice conditions, which make navigation impractical in winter months, the Canadian Board of Marine Underwriters Great Lakes Hull Clauses (1/9/1971) contain a warranty to this effect.[83]

2.46   It is clear that the practice and custom at the place where the insured vessel is located will play a crucial role in construing the scope of a warranty of this nature.[84] In any case, a reasonable interpretation must be adopted when examining the meaning of a warranty of this type. In *MacDonald v Liverpool and London Globe Insurance Co Ltd et al*,[85] a policy of insurance warranted that the yacht insured was to be laid up and out of commission from 1 October at noon until 1 April at noon. The assured had removed all of the navigational lights and equipment, unplugged the stove and fridge, sealed some windows and filled the fresh water tanks with antifreeze. The vessel was destroyed by fire on 6 October while moored awaiting to be hauled out of water for the winter. The Canadian first instance court found for the assured and Richard J summarised the judgment in the following way:[86]

---

80   (1918) 35 TLR 135.
81   (1889) 22 QBD 499.
82   (1/11/1985) drafted by the Institute of London Underwriters.
83   Lines 87–88 read as follows: 'Warranted that the Vessel be properly moored in a safe place and under conditions satisfactory to the Underwriter's Surveyor during the period the vessel is in winter lay-up.'
84   See the Canadian cases *Daneau v Laurent Gendron Ltée: Union Insurance Society of Canton Ltd (Third Party)* [1964] 1 Lloyd's Rep 220 (Exch Ct Can) and *Dolbec v US Fire Insurance Co* [1963] BR 153.
85   [1978] 22 NBR (2d) 172.
86   *Ibid*, p 181.

In large measure, the defence is a technical one. It is the equivalent of saying that if the boat had burnt one minute past 12 noon of 1 October 1976, that it would not have been covered by the insurance. Upon a consideration of all the evidence before me, I would find it most reasonable to interpret the warranty clause as meaning that sailing of the boat must terminate on the specified day and that retrieval from the water must be carried out within a reasonable time thereafter.

(e)   Survey warranties

2.47   As they suffered severely from numerous losses caused by sub-standard vessels during late 1980s, marine underwriters have since adopted the practice of insisting on warranties that require the insured vessel to be surveyed, ideally before the attachment of the risk, but in any event within a short period after the commencement of the policy. In order to meet the needs of the market an express warranty was produced in 1993 by the Joint Hull Committee in the following terms:[87]

> Warranted vessel be subject to a Condition Survey, at owner's expense, by the Salvage Association within 30 days and all recommendations complied with.

> It being understood that the surveyor's recommendations may include the necessity that this survey be upgraded to a Structural Condition Survey (JH 722) as per warranty attached.[88]

This warranty requires the assured not only to have a condition survey by the Salvage Association done within 30 days, but, also, to comply with all the recommendations made by the surveyor. It is acknowledged in the warranty that the surveyor could request the condition survey to be upgraded to a structural condition survey. The condition survey required is a detailed and technical one and the Salvage Association produced a set of guidance notes for their own surveyors, specifying the method by which this survey should be carried out.

Nowadays, survey warranties for hull policies are used quite often in the market and a warranty of this kind, worded in a similar fashion, has recently been subject to judicial examination, in *J Kirkaldy & Sons Ltd v Walker*.[89]

2.48   A similar express warranty was produced in 1995, as a result of consultation with the Salvage Association, for cargo policies. This warranty provides that:

> Warranted the Salvage Association or its appointee, at the assured's expense, shall in respect of the items listed below:

> 1   Approve vessel(s), tug(s), barges(s), towing arrangements, all other carrying conveyances and all fitting equipment including cranes required or loading/unloading operations.

---

87 Condition Survey Warranty (JH 115).

88 This form of warranty was then amended, in March 1994, to enable underwriters to receive a copy of the Salvage Association's recommendations and/or reports (JH 115A). For a voyage policy, the underwriter may not want copies of recommendations and reports. However, for a time policy, he will probably wish to monitor progress and gain greater insight into the operation of the vessel, generally.

89 [1999] Lloyd's Rep IR 410: the scope of this warranty has been evaluated earlier during the analysis of *contra proferentum* doctrine. In practice, in cases where an older vessel is concerned usually a condition survey is made condition precedent to the attachment of risk. See *The Zeus V* [2000] 2 Lloyd's Rep 587.

2   Approve all packing, loading, stowage, securing and unloading arrangements.

3   Attend and approve all stages of handling during transhipment.

4   Approve all transport operations including transport to vessel, voyage arrangements and transport from vessel to site.

5   Approve prevailing weather conditions or stipulate acceptable weather criteria for handling and transit operations.

And all recommendations complied with ...

This warranty has not been as popular as the Condition Survey Warranty for hull policies. Perhaps the market is not hard enough to assist underwriters to insist on such a warranty. It is submitted that such a warranty will provide mutual benefit both for underwriters and assureds. The benefit of the warranty survey for the underwriters is the approval of all the proposals for handling and transportation by a marine professional, whose sole purpose is to determine whether the venture presents any unreasonable risk to the underwriter. The assured has the benefit of the surveyor's assistance in providing quality control for the handling and transportation. No assured would want severe damage or loss to occur, which might result in heavy contractual penalties or the loss of future business.

2.49   Another form of survey warranties is the one which is commonly used when the vessel is insured for the period whist she is undergoing repairs in a shipyard. This type of warranty would usually require the approval of the vessel's lay-up arrangements by the Salvage Association and compliance with its recommendations. There is no standard wording for this type of warranty, but it is usual that the assured undertakes to obtain the approval of the Salvage Association not only for lay-up arrangements, but also for fire-fighting provisions and all movements in the shipyard. This type of warranty is normally supplemented with another warranty requiring the assured to keep Salvage Association's certificate updated during the currency of the risk.[90]

(f)   Premium warranties

2.50   In recent years, express warranties that require the assured to pay the premium within a certain period have been in common use. Without doubt, such warranties are used in time policies. These warranties are, usually, drafted in the following way: 'Warranted each instalment of premium paid to underwriters within 60 days of due dates.'[91]

A premium warranty usually follows a clause that permits premiums to be paid in instalments. A typical instalment clause is worded as follows:

If the premium is to be paid by instalments, the instalments have to be paid as following: one-fourth to be paid as a first instalment due and payable when insurance attaches; one-fourth due and payable at three months from inception; one-fourth due and payable at six months from inception; one-fourth due and payable at nine months from inception.

---

90   See, eg, *Agapitos v Agnew (The Aegeon) (No 2)* [2002] EWHC 1558; [2003] Lloyd's Rep IR 54.

91   This period is extended to 75 days in some policies.

(g)   Warranty of good safety

2.51   In earlier days, when communication was not so advanced, it was quite important for the assured, for the purpose of accessing the risk, to know the exact position and state of the vessel on a certain date. For this reason, warranties that declared the whereabouts or condition of the vessel on a date named were quite frequently inserted into marine policies. It is not, therefore, surprising that there is a special section in the MIA 1906, which was drafted early in the last century, that regulates this type of express warranty. Section 38 provides that where the subject matter is warranted 'well' or 'in good safety' on a particular day, it is sufficient for it to be safe at any time during that day. The origins of this section could be traced to *Blackhurst v Cockell*,[92] where a policy on a ship contained a warranty stating that : '... lost or not lost. Warranted well on 9 December.' The policy was subscribed between 1 pm and 3 pm on 9 December. The vessel was, in fact, lost at about 8 am on that day. It was held that the warranty was complied with by the fact that the vessel was safe at some time on the day when the underwriters subscribed the policy, although she was not safe at the particular hour when they subscribed it. The use and significance of warranties of this type have been reduced dramatically in modern marine insurance practice, as a result of developments in communication.

(B)   Continuing express warranties

(a)   Warranty of nationality

2.52   Section 37 expressly states that there is no implied warranty as to the nationality of the vessel, or that her nationality shall not be changed during the risk. A warranty of this kind can, however, be created by agreement in a marine insurance contract. It is not uncommon to see express warranties as to the nationality of the insured vessel and a continuing warranty status is usually afforded to them; that is to say, the assured not only warrants that the ship has a specific nationality at the inception of the policy, but he also warrants to keep her in the same nationality throughout the risk.[93]

2.53   In cases where such a warranty has been created, the vessel must carry the usual documents and other things that are necessary to prove her nationality. These are the flag, the certificate of registry, logbook, certificates of origin, etc.[94]

(b)   Warranty of neutrality

2.54   It often happens in time of war that the assured warrants the insured ship or goods to be neutral. Such a warranty is referred to as a 'warranty of neutrality', and it is the only express warranty that has been both qualified and described by the MIA 1906. After affording a continuing warranty status, s 36 imposes certain obligations on the assured and requires him to comply with these obligations, unless otherwise

---

92 (1789) 3 TR 360.
93 *Eden v Parkinson* (1781) 2 Dougl KB 732 and *Tyson v Gurney* (1789) 3 Term Rep 477.
94 *Geyer v Aguilar* (1898) 7 Term Rep 681; *Rich v Parker* [1798] 7 Term Rep 705; *Baring v Clagett* (1802) 3 B & P 201.

expressly stated in the warranty. Therefore, in cases where a warranty of neutrality has been created in respect of the ship or goods and no qualification is made, the warranty of neutrality is subject to these provisions.

2.55   According to s 36, the property must have a neutral character at the commencement of the risk and, so far as the assured can control the matter, its neutral character must be preserved. If the vessel is warranted neutral, she must be wholly owned by neutrals. In this respect, the nationality of the person or persons who own the vessel must be identified to see whether they are the subjects of a neutral state or not. As to what establishes nationality, Lord Kenyon LCJ held, in *Tabbs v Bendelack*,[95] that persons residing in a country and carrying on a trade by which both they and the country were benefited were also considered as the subjects of that country. Therefore, a person can be considered as the subject of a state if he resides and carries out his business in that state, even though he is not citizen of that state.

In cases where the goods carried are warranted neutral, again, the test adopted by Lord Kenyon has to be applied to determine the nationality of the people who own them. If the goods carried on the vessel are in different ownerships and are covered by separate insurance policies, only the goods warranted neutral must be so. It is not necessary that the whole cargo be neutral owned.[96] However, in cases where goods warranted neutral are loaded upon an armed vessel of a belligerent, or the ship on which they are loaded sails under convoy, or in company of an armed belligerent force, or under licence of a hostile government, this is a breach of the warranty of neutrality of the goods.[97]

2.56   The warranty of neutrality will have a continuing effect only as far as the assured has control over the matter. It will, for example, be no breach of warranty if property warranted neutral is really owned by neutrals, but the parties become belligerents by the subsequent breaking out of hostilities between the state of which they are subjects and another state.

2.57   Section 36(2) imposes an implied condition that the insured vessel shall be properly documented as far as the assured can control the matter. That is to say that she will carry the necessary papers to establish her neutrality, and that she will not falsify or suppress her papers, or use simulated papers.[98] In a case of breach of this obligation, the insurer can only deny liability in the event of loss occurring through the breach. Therefore, breach of this condition does not discharge the insurer from liability automatically as does the breach of neutrality warranty or other warranties.

(c)   Institute disbursements warranty

2.58   The disbursements clause,[99] in the standard Institute Hull Clauses, lists certain hull insurable interests, such as disbursements, managers' commissions and profits, in respect of which the assured is permitted to effect insurance policies to run

---

95   (1801) 3 Bos P 207n.
96   *Barker v Blakes* (1808) 9 East 283.
97   *The Fanny* (1814) 1 Dodson's Adm R 443.
98   Note that there is no such obligation imposed by s 36(2), when the goods are warranted to be neutral.
99   See cl 21.1 of the ITCH 1983; cl 22.1 of the ITCH 1995; cl 1901 of the IVCH 1983; cl 20.1 of the IVCH 1983; cl 24 of the IHC 2003.

additionally and concurrently with the hull and machinery policy to which the disbursements clause attaches. The second part of the said clause introduces a warranty in which the assured warrants not to effect insurances on these ancillary interests in excess of the amounts stated in the first part of the clause, either at the inception of the hull and machinery policy or during its continuation. For example, the disbursements clause permits the assured to effect an insurance policy on disbursements in addition to the hull and machinery policy up to a sum not exceeding 25% of the value stated therein. With the disbursements warranty, the assured warrants that he will not effect an insurance policy in respect of disbursements in excess of the amount (25%) stated in the hull and machinery policy.[100]

2.59   A warranty of this kind has been introduced in standard Institute Hull Clauses following the case of *Thames & Mersey Marine Insurance Co v Gunford Ship Co*.[101] In this case, the vessel was insured on a valuation that was in excess of the insurable value, and the freight was insured under a valued policy for a sum in excess of the gross amount at risk. In addition, the shipowners had effected a valued policy on disbursements. In examining the list of payments, which were alleged by the assured to be the subject matter of the disbursements policy, the court found that they were items which were already covered by either the freight or the hull and machinery policies. It was, accordingly, held that the disbursements policy constituted an over-insurance, by double insurance, and the assured was not entitled to any sum in excess of the indemnity provided by law.

2.60   Furthermore, there are some sound underwriting reasons for introducing a disbursements warranty. In the absence of any restrictions upon the amount of additional insurances allowed, it would be possible for an assured to cover his vessel on full conditions for a valuation which he held sufficient to cover most partial losses and he could then arrange additional cover on 'total loss only' conditions at a lower rate of premium in order to bring the cover up to the full value required. Such an insurance programme would result in the first insurance becoming a first loss policy and would distort the premium loss ratio figure.

(d)   Institute classification warranty

2.61   The 1995 version of Institute Hull Clauses[102] (both time and voyage) impose an obligation on the assured, owners and managers to ensure, throughout the period of insurance, that: (a) the vessel is classed with a classification society 'agreed by the insurers' and that her class is maintained; and (b) any recommendation or restriction imposed by the society, relating to the vessel's seaworthiness or maintenance of it, should be complied with by the dates required by that society.[103]

---

100 It must be noted that, although breach of this warranty discharges the insurer from liability in respect of the hull and machinery policy, it has no direct effect on the additional policies.
101 [1911] AC 529.
102 See sub-cls 4.1 and 4.2 of the ITCH 1995, and sub-cls 3.1 and 3.2 of the ITVH 1995.
103 Introduction of this clause can be considered as a reaction of the market towards the numerous bulk carrier (and tanker) losses in the 1980s and early 1990s.

Although the word 'warranted' has not been employed in the said clause, it is submitted that it creates a continuing warranty as an intention to warrant can be inferred from its language and the specified remedy.[104] It is further expressly stated in the clause that breach of such duties will discharge the insurer from liability from the date of breach. The harsh consequences of breach of this warranty are curbed if the vessel is at sea at the time of breach. In such a case, the date of discharge from liability will be deferred until her arrival at the next port.

2.62   The assured is put under a similar obligation under the IHC 2003.[105] Whether this obligation could still be regarded as a continuing warranty is, however, debateable. This is because by virtue of cl 13.2 of the IHC 2003, the effect of breach of this provision is stated to be automatic termination of insurance at the time of such breach. One might wonder whether it is intentional that the remedy is stated to be automatic termination of the contract rather than automatic discharge from liability. It should be noted that cl 4.2 of the ITCH 1995 makes reference to the latter.

IV – DISTINGUISHING OTHER EXPRESS TERMS OF THE MARINE INSURANCE CONTRACT FROM WARRANTIES

2.63   An express warranty is not the only express term of a marine insurance contract. There are some other express terms, which either determine the extent of the cover or set up the rights and obligations to the parties of an insurance contract. The law has not, however, treated these different terms in the same way and, accordingly, different legal consequences have followed when they are breached. Since the remedy afforded for breach of warranty is draconian from the assured's point of view – in the sense that it discharges the insurer from further liability, automatically, and can be enforced irrespective of whether the breach is material to the loss or not[106] – it is not uncommon to see an attempt by the assured to convince the court to classify the provision in question as a term other than an express warranty. Thus, it is necessary, not only to identify the structure of express warranties, but also to distinguish them clearly from other express terms of a marine insurance contract. The object of this part of this chapter is to examine the other main express terms of a marine insurance contract and compare them with express warranties. The place of express warranties in the ranks of contractual terms can be clarified and a clearer view of the overall situation be obtained, as a result of such an analysis.

---

104 This clause was originally drafted as: 'Warranted that: the vessel is classed with ... and existing class maintained.' See the document of Joint Hull 131 (30/6/1989).
105 See cl 13 of the IHC 2003.
106 These issues will be discussed in Chapter 5.

(A) Conditions in marine insurance contracts

2.64   Marine insurance contracts consist of terms known as 'conditions', on the fulfilment of which the validity of the policy or the liability of the insurer depends.[107] In the insurance context, conditions are classified in two main categories and these will now be evaluated.

(a) Condition precedent to the attachment (commencement) of the risk

2.65   Certain conduct of the assured – that is, payment of the premium and survey of the insured subject matter – are so fundamental for the insurer that he might not wish to be on risk until they are fulfilled. This could be achieved by making such conduct condition precedent to the attachment of the risk.[108] The safest forms of policy wording required to create a condition precedent to the attachment of risk involve either the use of the phrase 'condition precedent' or a statement that, in the event that the condition is not complied with, the insurer is not to be on risk. However, on some occasions parties might intend to create a condition precedent without using this traditional wording. For instance, in *The Zeus V*,[109] a clause worded as 'subject to survey including valuation by independent qualified surveyor' was held to be a condition precedent to the attachment of the risk.[110]

2.66   An express warranty, which relates to a period after the attachment of the risk, can be distinguished from a condition of this type in two respects. First, breach of an express warranty of this nature does not prevent the contract from coming into existence, while breach of the latter does. Secondly, in case of non-fulfilment of a condition precedent to the attachment of the risk, the assured is entitled to return of his premium for total failure of consideration.[111] However, when an express warranty, which relates to a period after the attachment of the risk, is breached the assured could be entitled to the return of the premium only if the risk and the adventure insured is divisible into stages.[112]

On the other hand, in terms of their effect, there is no significant difference between a warranty that relates to a period before the attachment of the risk and a condition precedent to the attachment of the policy.

---

107 In *W & J Lane v Spratt* [1970] 2 QB 480, p 486-7, Roskill J defined conditions in respect of transit insurance with the following words: 'By a "condition" I mean a contractual term of the policy, any breach of which by the assured in the event of a loss arising otherwise payable under the policy, affords underwriters a defence to any claim irrespective of whether there is any causal connection between the breach of the contractual term and the loss.' It is submitted that this description can also be used for marine insurance conditions.

108 Conditions of this nature have been described by the Supreme Court of New South Wales, in *Kodak (Australasia) Pty Ltd v Retail Traders Mutual Indemnity Insurance Association* (1942) 2 SR 231, p 234, as '... a condition going to the operation of the policy as a binding document ... [such a term] is intended to entitle the insurer to treat the policy as a document which never became binding on him.'

109 [1999] 1 Lloyd's Rep 703, aff'd in [2000] 2 Lloyd's Rep 587.

110 However, in the present case the Court of Appeal held that the condition had not been broken as there had been two surveys, which taken together, met the requirements of the clause.

111 See s 84(1).

112 See s 84(1) and (2).

(b)   Condition precedent to the liability of the insurer

2.67   Such conditions usually relate to matters arising after a loss under the policy and define the circumstances in which the liability of the insurer is to arise.[113] They are generally concerned with the claims process. A condition of this type can be created either by the use of the phrase 'condition precedent to the liability of the insurer', or by spelling out the consequences of breach of such a condition.[114]

Clause 43.1 of IHC 2003, for example, is a condition of this kind and requires the assured to give notice to the leading underwriter(s) as soon as possible in the event of an accident or occurrence whereby loss, damage, liability or expense may result in a claim under the current policy.[115] It is stipulated in cl 43.2 that, if notice is not given within a specified time, no claim is recoverable under the current insurance in respect of such loss, damage, liability or expense.

2.68   Express warranties are distinct from conditions precedent to the liability of the insurer in the sense that, in a case of breach of an express warranty, the insurer is discharged from further liability automatically as from date of breach. However, where a condition precedent to the liability of the insurer is breached, the validity of the policy itself is unaffected, unless the policy itself provides to the contrary, and, in this way, the insurer's potential liability for future claims is preserved.

2.69   In some instances, a court might read a condition precedent as discharging the insurer from all liability under the policy thereafter. This is likely to arise only if the wording employed is clearly to that effect,[116] and also the obligation is one which goes to the root of the contract.[117]

2.70   In terms of their legal effect, there is a similarity between an express warranty and a condition precedent of this nature: both discharge the insurer from further liability. However, it has to be stressed that in marine insurance practice it is not so common to see conditions of this nature.[118] A possible reason for this could be the fact that obligations of a serious nature have traditionally been given the warranty status.

(B)   Innominate (intermediate) terms in marine insurance contracts

2.71   In *Hong Kong Fir Shipping Co Ltd v Kawasaki Kisen Kaisha Ltd*,[119] the Court of Appeal recognised the existence of a further contractual term, namely innominate (intermediate) terms. These innominate terms differ from contractual conditions in that their breach does not itself rise to a right to be discharged from the contract; and from contractual warranties in that the injured party's remedy is not *prima facie* restricted to damages. The injured party can only be discharged from the contract if the

---

113 *London Guarantee Co v Fearnley* (1880) 5 App Cas 911, p 915, *per* Lord Blackburn.
114 In *Richardson v Roylance* (1933) 47 LlL Rep 173, eg, a condition of this type was created by the use of the wording that: 'No claim shall attach to this policy unless the terms of this condition have been complied with.'
115 See, also, cl 13.1 of the ITCH and cl 11.1 of the IVCH 1995, to the same effect.
116 *Kazakstan Wool Processors (Europe) Ltd v Nederlandsche Credietverzekering Maatschappij NV* [2000] Lloyd's Rep IR 371.
117 *Welch v Royal Exchange Assurance* [1939] 1 KB 294, p 312, *per* Mackinnon LJ.
118 *Cf* the new Recomissioning Condition in the IHC 2003, cl 34.
119 [1962] 2 QB 26.

consequences of breach of an innominate term are serious. In the context of insurance law, it was Hobhouse J who first indicated the possibility that certain undertakings are likely to be regarded as innominate. In *Phoenix General Insurance Co of Greece SA v Halvanon Insurance Co Ltd*,[120] having implied a term into a facultative/obligatory reinsurance contract to the effect that the reassured should conduct his business in accordance with market practice and due diligence in certain respects including the maintenance of records and accounts, he made the following observation in relation to the nature of such terms:[121]

> The term or terms are all innominate and therefore the consequence of any breach for any particular cession or any individual claim or indeed for the contracts as a whole, must depend on the nature and gravity of the relevant breach or breaches.[122]

2.72   The innominate term analysis, in the insurance context, has fairly recently found application in *Alfred McAlpine plc v BAI (Run-Off) Ltd*.[123] In that case, the nature of a clause that required the assured to give notice in writing, as soon as possible, with full details in the event of any occurrence which may give rise to a claim under the policy, formed the subject matter of judicial analysis. The facts of the case can be summarised as follows: an accident on a construction site in May 1991 led to serious injury to a worker, O'Malley. He was employed by Moss, who was acting as subcontractor for RC Construction Ltd (RCCL), who were in turn subcontractors for Alfred McAlpine Ltd. RCCL had contracted with the insurer, BAI (Run-Off) Ltd, to provide indemnity against all sums that RCCL shall become legally liable to pay as compensation arising from accidental bodily injury to any person who was not an employee of RCCL The policy also contained the notification clause mentioned above. RCCL did not notify the insurer immediately after the incident. In fact, the event was not notified until 4 June 1992. O'Malley sued Moss and McAlpine as co-defendants. He recovered £254,000 from McAlpine in February 1996.[124] McAlpine had RCCL joined as a third party on the basis of the common law duty of care, the Occupiers' Liability Act 1957 and the Civil Liability (Contribution) Act 1978. McAlpine later obtained an uncontested judgment in their favour for a sum of £243,000 against RCCL, although this could not be satisfied as RCCL had been wound up in March 1992. McAlpine therefore sought to enforce the contract of insurance entered into between RCCL and BAI, as the statutory assignees of RCCL under the Third Parties (Rights Against Insurers) Act 1930. BAI defended the claim on the basis that RCCL had failed to provide both adequate and prompt notice of the potential claim. Since, under the 1930 Act, McAlpine had no better rights than those of RCCL, BAI were *prima facie* entitled to raise any defence against McAlpine that could have been established against RCCL The basis of BAI's defence was that the notification clause was a condition precedent to their liability.

The first instance judge, Colman J, rejected this argument. According to him, in practice a failure to satisfy notification clauses may have little or no prejudicial effect

---

120 [1985] 2 Lloyd's Rep 599.

121 *Ibid*, p 614.

122 See, also, the judgment of Hirst J in *Black King Shipping Corporation & Wayang Panama SA v Mark Ranold Massie (The Litsion Pride)* [1985] 1 Lloyd's Rep 437, hereinafter referred to as *The Litsion Pride*.

123 [2000] 1 Lloyd's Rep 437 (CA), affirming [1998] 2 Lloyd's Rep 694.

124 On the basis of, *inter alia*, the Construction (Working Places) Regulations 1996 SI 1996/94.

on the insurer. This was considered as potentially inconsistent with the common intention that breach of the clause would entitle the insurer to deny any liability for the claim.[125] Colman J stated that, '... such draconian effect would not be necessary to give insurers the protection they deserve'.[126] Furthermore, Colman J held that the insurer, as drafter of the contract, was under a duty to make it clear that the term was to be classified as a condition precedent if that was the desired intention.

Delivering the judgment of the Court of Appeal, Waller LJ held that there may be conditions that cannot be classified from the outset as fundamental or minor and such provisions may be regarded as falling into the 'innominate' category recognised by the Court of Appeal in *Hong Kong Fir Shipping Co Ltd v Kawasaki Kisen Kaisha Ltd*.[127] The notification clause, which was discussed above, according to Waller LJ, belonged to this category. When reaching this decision, Waller LJ, relied on the judgment of the New South Wales court, in *Trans-Pacific Insurance Co (Australia) Ltd v Grand Union Insurance Co Ltd*,[128] where a similar point had been considered. In that case, Giles J had decided that the claims co-operation clause in the policy before him was not a 'condition', but a clause which, if breached, could entitle the insurers to reject the claim then under consideration. Following this reasoning, Waller LJ concluded that, in a liability contract of insurance, the obligation of the insurers to pay individual claims were severable obligations. A breach by the assured of his obligation to give notice in relation to one claim could mean, if breach had sufficiently serious consequences for the insurers, that this would entitle the insurers to reject that claim, but the contract of insurance as a whole would remain intact. It naturally follows that a breach by the assured of his obligation to give notice in relation to a claim would entitle the insurer to damages only, if breach did not have serious consequences for the insurers. On the facts before them – where a claim had not been made for several months, and only after the assured had ceased trading – the Court of Appeal held that there had been no repudiation as the insurer had ultimately been given sufficient information to investigate and deal with the claim. The assured was, nevertheless, in breach of the clause, but, as the insurer had abandoned any claim for damages and rested upon the right not to make payment at all, it followed that the assured was entitled to recover.

2.73   A similar legal analysis has been adopted in *K/S Merc-Scandia XXXXII v Certain Lloyd's Underwriters (The Mercandian Continent)*[129] where an obligation in a liability policy to keep underwriters fully advised in the event of an occurrence that might result in a claim[130] was regarded as being a clause the serious breach of which entitled the underwriters to reject the claim. In the circumstances of the case, as the breach of the clause had not affected the underwriters position or liability, they were not allowed to reject the claim.[131]

---

125 In this respect, reference was made to *Cehave NV v Bremer Handelsgesellschaft mbH (The Hansa Nord)* [1976] QB 44.
126 [1998] 2 Lloyd's Rep 694, p 700.
127 [1962] 2 QB 26.
128 (1989) 18 NSWLR 675.
129 [2001] EWCA Civ 1275; [2001] 2 Lloyd's Rep 563, affirming [2000] 2 Lloyd's Rep 357, hereinafter referred to as *The Mercandian Continent*.
130 The notification clause was worded as follows: '... in the event of any occurrence which may result in a claim ... the assured shall give prompt notice ... and shall keep underwriters fully advised.'
131 More recently, the Court of Appeal decided in a similar fashion in *Glencore International AG v Adrian Peter Ryan (The Beursgracht)* [2001] EWCA Civ 2051; [2002] Lloyd's Rep IR 335.

2.74   One should not lose sight of the fact that in both *Alfred McAlpine* and *The Mercandian Continent*, it was a notification requirement that was regarded as an innominate severable obligation. There remains a number of unanswered questions. First, is the reasoning adopted in these cases confined to notification clauses or should the severable innominate term analysis apply to other clauses relating to the making of claims under insurance policies, such as claim co-operation clauses, clauses requiring the assured to take reasonable steps to avert or minimise a loss? The answer to this question is possibly an affirmative one, but it remains to be seen how the case law will evolve on this point. Furthermore, are there innominate terms which are not severable? If so, how will it be possible to distinguish them from severable ones?

2.75   Even though there are several question marks surrounding this recently discovered concept, it is fair to suggest that the distinction between severable innominate terms and express warranties is clear cut. The former usually relates to ancillary duties relating to the making of claims under insurance contracts, whilst the latter one deals with undertakings of a significant nature made by an assured. Furthermore, breach of a severable innominate term can, at most, deprive the assured from a particular claim. However, breach of a warranty discharges the insurer from further liability automatically.

(C)   Exclusion clauses in marine insurance contracts

2.76   In all types of insurance contracts, it is possible to see clauses that define the extent of the policy by cutting down the scope of the cover. Since express warranties operate in a similar manner by defining the essence of the risk covered, one might find it difficult to draw a distinction between the two. Unlike an express warranty, the intention when incorporating an exclusion clause is not to warrant, but to exclude liability. Exclusion clauses can be classified in two categories by reference to the way they come into operation. The types of exclusion clauses and their interrelation with express warranties will now be examined.

(a)   *Clauses that exclude the insurer from liability for a particular risk*

2.77   Clauses of this kind exclude the liability of the insurer under the policy for certain risks. Therefore, the insurer has no liability in cases where the loss is caused or the peril brought into operation by clauses specified in the exclusion clause. The occurrence of such a peril, unlike breach of an express warranty, does not discharge the insurer from liability. The insurer remains liable for losses outside the exclusion clause, whether arising before or after the events which constitute the excluded peril. Here, causation plays a distinct role. If the risk excluded by the exclusion clause is the *proximate* cause of the loss within the meaning of s 55, then the insurer has no liability for such a loss.

2.78   Although there is a clear distinction between an exclusion clause and an express warranty, some confusion might arise due to the traditional wording employed for exclusion clauses in some marine policies. It is, for example, not uncommon to encounter an exclusion clause worded as: 'Warranted free from capture and seizure.'[132] Such a clause simply means that the insurer is not liable for the perils of capture and seizure, and there is no intention to create an express warranty.[133]

(b)   Clauses delimiting (describing) the risk (suspensory provisions)

2.79   Some exclusion clauses operate not by excluding liability for certain events and risks, but by setting out the circumstances in which the insurer is to be on risk. An exclusion clause of this type is referred to as a term 'delimiting (describing) the risk' or, sometimes, a 'suspensory provision'. The effect of such a clause is that the operation of the policy is suspended for the period when the circumstances specified in the clause are not satisfied. Accordingly, the insurer is not liable for any loss which occurs during this period, but, unlike breach of an express warranty, the validity of the insurance contract is not affected and the cover reattaches as soon as the original position is restored.

2.80   Whether a provision is an express warranty, or a clause delimiting the risk, can be ascertained by construing the language used. A provision is a warranty if it puts the assured under an obligation to do something or refrain from doing something. On the other hand, a provision which determines the physical scope of the cover, should be considered as a clause delimiting the risk. For example, in *Riverside Landmark Corp v Northumberland General Insurance*,[134] where a policy of marine insurance contained the words '... covering whilst being towed in tandem by Irving Tug TBA from Quebec City to Tampico, Mexico', it was the view of the Canadian court that the words were descriptive of the risk and the policy was not invalidated, but the cover was suspended during the period when the vessels in question were not towed in tandem.

2.81   Clause 9 of Institute Container Clauses (Time)[135] is as an example of clauses of this type. This clause stipulates that each container is covered, including whilst on deck, within the sea and territorial limits specified in the schedule. This means that the cover is suspended when the container is in port, or at sea, but outside the territorial limits specified in the schedule and, if it is damaged while in these areas, the insurer is not liable at all. The cover, however, reattaches as soon as the container is at sea and in the territorial limits specified in the schedule.[136]

2.82   Even though the distinction between an express warranty and a clause delimiting the risk seems to be a fine one on paper, in practice mapping the boundaries between these terms has proven to be difficult. This is because clauses delimiting the

---

132 Such a clause appeared in the policy in *Department of Fisheries and Oceans, Fishing Vessel Insurance Plan v Lec Tulloch* (1989) unreported, 6 February, decided by the Federal Court of Appeal of Canada. The clause in question was worded as follows: 'Warranted free from any claim for loss, damage or expense when anyone other than the assured is master of the insured vessel named in cl 1 herein without prior approval of the plan. On approval the plan may charge an additional premium as a condition thereof.'

133 In *The Good Luck* [1992] 1 AC 233, pp 261–62, Lord Goff distinguished between '... those warranties which simply denote the scope of the cover (as in the familiar fc&s clause – warranted free of capture and seizure) and those which are promissory warranties, involving a promise by the assured that the warranty will be fulfilled.'

134 [1984] 8 CCLI 118 (Ont SCJ).

135 (1/1/1987), drafted by the Institute of London Underwriters.

136 See cl 6 of the Institute War and Strikes Clauses Containers (Time), to the same effect.

risk and warranties share a functional similarity: each provides against the possibility that the risk is or will be different from the risk expected.

Clauses delimiting the risk concern a temporary difference between the actual risk and risk expected. An express warranty, on the other hand, might concern both a temporary and regular possibility of such a change. Thus, distinction between these two clauses could be easily marked when an express warranty intends to deal with a change or difference of a permanent nature. For instance, it would be very difficult for an assured to argue that a clause that warrants that the insured vessel shall sail on 1 January is a clause delimiting the risk, not a warranty. Similarly, where the assured undertakes to have the cargo surveyed by a certain date, this intends to deal with a permanent change in the risk and cannot be remedied at a later stage. However, if a warranty deals with changes of temporary nature, which are capable of being restored after a period of non-compliance, it is possible that problems might arise as to its legal nature.

2.83   There is a series of non-marine insurance cases where courts decided to classify the clause in question as a clause delimiting the risk rather than a warranty simply in order to avoid harsh consequences from the assured's point of view. As indicated above, this can happen only in cases where it is intended that the clause prevents a temporary increase in the risk undertaken by the insurer. In *Farr v Motor Traders' Mutual Insurance Society Ltd*,[137] the assured ran a taxi business using two taxis. On applying for insurance for the use of these vehicles, he warranted in the proposal form that each vehicle would be driven for only one shift each day. The policy was issued in February 1918 and the statement remained true until August 1918, when one of the taxis was driven for two shifts for one day, or a little longer. Later, after this practice had ceased, an accident occurred. It was held that the term in question was a term delimiting the risk and not an express warranty, so that the assured was entitled to recover for an accident happening at a time when the term was being complied with. Similarly, in *Provincial Insurance Co Ltd v Morgan and Faxon*,[138] the proposal form contained a clause, which warranted that the insured lorry was to be used only for carrying coal. It was, in fact, occasionally used to carry timber, instead of, or as well as, coal. The lorry had an accident shortly after offloading a quantity of timber. The Court of Appeal, the conclusion of which was upheld by the House of Lords, held that the clause was not a warranty, but a clause delimiting the risk. Accordingly, the insurers were held liable, as the lorry had not been carrying timber when damaged.[139]

2.84   It is submitted that in both cases, the provisions in question were designed to define the cover not by physically describing the limits of cover, but by putting the assured under specific obligations: namely, not to drive each vehicle for more than one shift each day in the former, and not to use the vehicle to carry anything apart from coal in the latter. Perhaps the fact that the provisions in question were breached occasionally during the currency of the policies and the potential injustice to the assured who would lose a claim for breach of a policy term unconnected with the loss played a crucial role in the courts' decision.

---

137 [1920] 3 KB 669.
138 [1933] AC 240; (1932) 44 LlL Rep 275.
139 See, also, *Roberts v Anglo-Saxon Insurance Co* (1927) 27 LlL Rep 313.

2.85   A similar attempt to protect one party of the contract from a severe consequence, this time the insurer, could also be observed in a more recent case. In *CTN Cash & Carry Ltd v General Accident Fire & Life Assurance Corp Ltd*,[140] the assured's burglary policy contained the following provision:

> It is warranted that the secure cash kiosk shall be attended and locked at all times during business hours.

A robbery took place during business hours when the kiosk was not attended. If the clause in question had been regarded as a warranty, the insurer would not have been able to bring a defence on the grounds of waiver. For that reason, the insurer argued that the term was, despite its express title, a clause delimiting the risk. Macpherson J, relying mainly on the *Farr v Motor Traders* case, decided that the clause in question was a clause delimiting the risk.

2.86   It looks like this trend has found support in the context of marine insurance in Canada in *The Bamcell II*.[141] *The Bamcell II* was a converted chip barge, which was used in oceanographic experiments. She was operated by compression of air, which could be admitted or released through valves on deck. Raising or lowering the air pressure caused the stern of the barge to rise or fall, thus allowing *The Bamcell II* to float or float off certain modules used in experiments. The vessel sank during daytime as a result of the negligence of an employee who opened the air valves and failed to close them later. The marine policy in the case contained the following clause:

> Warranted that a watchman is stationed on board *The Bamcell II* each night from 2200 hours to 0600 hours with instructions for shutting down all equipment in an emergency.

Such a watchman was never stationed on board *The Bamcell II* from the day after the inception of the policy until the accident. The underwriters gave evidence at the trial that this clause was intended to be a warranty and the risk was accepted on the basis that the assured would strictly comply with it. Accordingly, they contended that, since the assured never placed a watchman on board from the first day after the inception of the risk, the warranty was breached and the insurer was discharged from liability under the policy from that moment, even if the loss was unconnected with such a breach.

In the British Columbia Court of Appeal,[142] Lambert JA concluded that the clause was a suspensory provision and not a warranty. The assured was, accordingly, allowed to recover under the policy as the loss occurred during daytime and not between the hours stated in the clause. When reaching this decision, he cited the following passage from *MacGillivray and Parkington on Insurance Law*:[143]

> Clauses of this nature are sometimes referred to as 'warranties descriptive of the risk' or 'delimiting the risk'. This usage is not an accurate one, but it serves as a remainder that a court may be prepared to construe a clause as one descriptive of the risk even though the word 'warranty' or 'warranted' appears in it, as where a car was 'warranted used only for the following purposes'. That case illustrates the point that

---

140 [1989] 1 Lloyd's Rep 299.
141 (1980) 133 DLR (3d) 727, aff'd [1983] 2 SCR 47.
142 133 DLR (3d) 727.
143 6th edn, 1975, pp 263–64.

there is no magic in the word 'warranted' which is frequently used with considerable ambiguity in policies.

2.87 The primary cases relied upon by the editors of *MacGillivray and Parkington* in the above passage concerning suspensive provisions are the cases of *Farr v Motor Traders' Mutual Insurance Society Ltd* and *Provincial Insurance Co Ltd v Morgan and Faxon*, both of which have been discussed above. It is submitted that *The Bamcell II* can be distinguished from both these cases. The common feature in two former cases is the fact that the provisions in question were breached only for a short period of time. By contrast, in *The Bamcell II*, the assured was in breach of the clause in question from the beginning of the insurance period until the date of loss. In fact, he had never complied with the provision and had no intention of complying with it.

2.88 Furthermore, in the Court of Appeal, Lambert JA suggested that, in order to determine the status of the clause in question, the intention of the parties when incorporating the clause into the policy must be observed. He, accordingly, said that:[144]

> The parties cannot have intended that if the watchman was late one night, or even missed a night, then the insurers should be discharged from liability for the remainder of the term of the policy ... It is my opinion that the clause in this case under the heading of 'special conditions' is a clause which limits the risk and not a true warranty which discharges the insurer. The limitation on the risk has no effect in this case.[145]

This observation, which makes sense in the first instance, is subject to some severe objections. Lambert JA has not cited any authority, or given any explanation, to support this statement. With all respect, the author is of the opinion that the presumed intention of parties cannot be ascertained simply by judging the fairness of the clause in question. As was stated by Hobhouse J in *Cooke and Arkwright v Hayden*:[146]

> It is not the courts' function, by process of construction, to make for the parties a reasonable contract which they have not made for themselves.

The assured, in *The Bamcell II*, was in a position to bargain the conditions of the insurance he was purchasing. If he had had genuine doubts regarding the fulfilment of the obligations stated in the contract, he should not have agreed them in the first place. Besides, he was in breach of that particular clause from the outset and never had any intention of complying with it. Thus, defining the clause in question as a clause delimiting the risk would mean awarding the assured, who had not judged his position accurately.

Finally, some judicial support can be drawn from various authorities to show that the interpretation adopted by the Supreme Court of Canada in *The Bamcell II* in relation to the status of the 'watchman clause' was inappropriate. In *Perryman Burns Coal Co Inc v Northwestern Fire & Marine Insurance Co (The Harlem)*,[147] a clause worded as

144 (1980) 133 DLR (3d) 727, pp 740–41.
145 Richie J, in the Supreme Court of Canada, concurring with the findings of Lambert JA said, [1983] 2 SCR 47, pp 55–56, that: 'The clause would only have been effective if the loss had occurred between 2200 hours and 0600 hours, and it was proved that there was no watchman stationed aboard during these hours. To this extent, the condition contained in the clause constituted a limitation of the risk, but it was not a warranty.'
146 [1987] 2 Lloyd's Rep 579, p 582.
147 [1927] AMC 1089.

'Warranted that a watchman is to be on board at all times when loaded', was held to be an express warranty and breached when the watchman left the barge for two hours to get his supper.[148]

For all the arguments advanced above, it could be concluded that the watchman clause in *The Bamcell II* was an express warranty and not a provision delimiting the risk. It is believed that, if a clause worded in the same way as that in *The Bamcell II* is considered by English courts, under the light of the authorities cited, it will be regarded as an express warranty.[149]

2.89   Unfortunately, neither of the courts involved in *The Bamcell II* litigation laid down a convincing, or indeed any, test as to how express warranties should be distinguished from clauses delimiting the risk. To date, the test put forward by Donaldson J in *De Maurier (Jewels) Ltd v Bastion Insurance Co Ltd*[150] remains the main legal measurement in this area. He suggested that breach of a clause delimiting the risk does not affect the nature or extent of the risks falling outside its terms; breach of a promissory warranty may, however, affect such risks. No doubt there is force in this approach. However, it is an overstatement to suggest that breach of a clause delimiting the risk has no impact on the nature or extent of the risks falling outside its terms. Take the clause in *Bamcell II*, for example, where the assured warranted that a watchman would be stationed on board each night from 2200 to 0600 hours. Imagine that a group of armed men boarded the vessel at night at a time when there was no watchman and at 0700 in the morning, after the cover is reinstated, by using force they stole the vessel's equipment. In this example, how accurate would it be to suggest that breach of watchman requirement had no impact whatsoever on the extent of the risks falling outside its terms?

2.90   It is submitted, therefore, that the most significant element in mapping the legal nature of a clause is to consider in which manner it attempts to define the risk. It would be regarded as a clause delimiting the risk if it describes the instances or circumstances when the cover will or will not be available. In contrast, it is an express

---

148 See, also, *Lean G Bukwalter v Aetna Insurance Co (The Dauntless)* [1928] AMC 1430; *Elizabeth B Briody v Northwestern Fire & Marine Insurance Co (The Silk)* [1931] AMC 1348; *Tacoma Oriental SS Co v JF Tallant* [1931] AMC 1351.

149 The Supreme Court of Canada had reached another contradictory decision on a similar issue long before *The Bamcell II*. In *James Staples v Great American Insurance Co New York* [1941] SCR 213, a clause in a yacht policy that provided that the vessel was warranted to be used for pleasure purposes only, was held to be a clause delimiting the risk and not warranty. Kerwin J said: 'I cannot read the statement as a condition that, upon the yacht being used for other than private pleasure purposes, the policy would be avoided, even though at the time the loss was suffered, the yacht was not being so used.' Again, no authority was cited for this statement. It is submitted that such an approach is beyond the scope of English marine insurance law. Accordingly, there is no dispute as to the warranty status of Institute Yacht Clauses, cl 3.2 ((1 November 1985) drafted by the Institute of London Underwriters) which has been worded exactly in the same manner: 'Warranted to be used solely for private pleasure purposes.' However, it should be noted that in non-marine insurance, occasionally, *The Bamcell II* has been referred to by English courts in order to justify that a certain clause is a suspensory provision and not an express warranty. Recently, in *Kler Knitwear Ltd v Lombard General Insurance Co Ltd* [2000] Lloyd's Rep IR 47, by citing *The Bamcell II*, Morland J held that the following clause in the assured's policy covering its business was a suspensory provision: 'Sprinkler Installations Warranty – It is warranted that within 30 days of renewal 1998 the sprinkler systems at the Jellicoe Road/Gough Road/Spalding Road locations must be inspected by a LPC approved sprinkler engineer with all necessary rectification work commissioned within 14 days of the inspection report being received.'

150 [1967] 2 Lloyd's Rep 550, p 559.

warranty if it sets out the conditions that the assured promised to exist or not to exist or identifies circumstances that the assured has undertaken to perform or not to perform.

2.91   To avoid any inconvenience that may arise in future as to the status of an express warranty, it is advisable to draft express warranties in such a way that the effect of any breach is stated expressly. Alternatively, the parties can state in the policy that the clause in question is to be construed as a warranty within the terms of the MIA 1906. In the wake of the dubious decision in *The Bamcell II*, it is not surprising to see that in Canada the insurers have attempted to express themselves in the clearest possible terms. Clause 1 of the British Columbia Builders' Risks Clauses[151] reads as follows:

> This policy contains warranties and general conditions none of which are to be interpreted as suspensive conditions. The Underwriters have agreed to accept the risk of insuring the Vessel on the condition precedent that the Assured will comply strictly and literally with these warranties and conditions. If the Assured breaches any of these warranties or conditions, the Underwriters at their option will not pay any claims arising thereafter, regardless of whether or not such breach is causative or in any way connected to such claim.

(D)   Cancellation clauses in marine insurance contracts

2.92   Under ordinary circumstances, a marine insurance contract remains in force until the expiration of the insurance period.[152] In some cases, however, an express term of the contract may enable either the assured or insurer to determine the policy before it expires. Such clauses are called cancellation clauses. They are contained in almost all marine insurance contracts[153] and require the party who wishes to operate them to give notice to the other party. In cases where such a clause is operated, the insurance comes to an end on the stipulated date and any loss happening after the date of termination is not covered.

2.93   There is no interrelation between clauses of this nature and express warranties, as they are directed to different aspects. A cancellation clause gives the parties to an insurance contract the right to terminate it by giving notice and there is no breach of contract if they are operated. Some obligations, on the other hand, are imposed on the part of the assured by an express warranty and the insurance contract is breached if they are not complied with.

---

151 (1/1/1989).
152 This period is a specific period of time in time policies, while it is a certain marine adventure in voyage policies.
153 See, eg, Institute Containers Clauses (Time) (1/1/1987), cl 11.

CHAPTER 3

IMPLIED WARRANTY OF SEAWORTHINESS

3.1   As examined in the previous chapter, the express warranties are actually expressed in the policy or incorporated therein by reference. They have in fact been made a part of the insurance contract and are known by both parties to the contract. The implied warranties, on the other hand, do not appear in the policy, but are tacitly understood by the parties to be present. They are implied by law from the circumstances in which the bargain was effected.

3.2   Implied warranties are not present in any areas of insurance law except marine insurance.[1] The reason for this lies in the unique nature of the marine adventure. When a vessel is engaged in a marine adventure, apart from the shipowner, numerous interests, such as crew, buyer or, in some cases, seller of the cargo carried on board,[2] are exposed to maritime perils; however, neither the assured nor the insurer is in a position to ascertain the condition of the insured vessel during the period when she performs the voyage. In order to balance the conflicting interests of contracting parties and minimise the pitfalls of the marine adventure, marine insurance law has imposed certain implied warranties into marine insurance contracts.

There are four warranties implied by the Marine Insurance Act (MIA) 1906, namely: warranty of seaworthiness (s 39(1), (3) and (4)); warranty of portworthiness (s 39(2)); warranty of cargoworthiness (s 40(2)); and warranty of legality (s 41). The object of this chapter is to evaluate the implied warranty of seaworthiness from different angles. Other implied warranties will form the subject matter of Chapter 4.

I – ORIGINS OF THE DOCTRINE OF SEAWORTHINESS

3.3   When the history of law is observed, it can be clearly seen that each legal rule or institution has been created in order to meet different needs of the social or commercial life. The situation is exactly the same in maritime law. For instance, the

---

1   There is, for example, no implied warranty in life insurance that the life is in good health or free from disease and, similarly, there is no implied warranty in fire insurance that the premises are well built and incorporate fire precautions. Similarly, it was held in *Trickett v Queensland Insurance Co* [1936] AC 159, that there was no implied warranty of roadworthiness in motor insurance. In *Euro-Diam Ltd v Bathurst* [1990] 1 QB 1, it was stressed by the Court of Appeal that there was no implied warranty of legality in non-marine insurance.

2   The person who effects the insurance in relation to the cargo carried on board is determined according to the type of the sales contract. If the sale is on so called fob (free on board) terms, the seller's part is performed when he puts the goods free on board the ship. In that case, the contract of carriage and insurance for the cargo shipped will normally be effected by the buyer. On the other hand, when the sale is cif (cost, insurance and freight), the seller bears the cost of insurance and freight and the buyer takes the delivery abroad at the end of the transport. Here, it is usually the seller who contracts with the shipowner for the conveyance of goods and engages in effecting the insurance for the cargo carried.

legal principles on general average were created around 500–600 BC,[3] in order to protect the interest of parties who were involved in, or affected by, a sacrifice to preserve both the vessel and the rest of the cargo in a case of emergency. The doctrine of seaworthiness was formed and developed for a similar reason, namely, to protect the different interests exposed to a marine adventure from the possible hazards of that marine adventure. In connection with the developments in maritime law, the doctrine was advanced further and received a different legal character in marine insurance.

3.4   Provisions relating to seaworthiness of a vessel first appeared in charterparties and carriage of goods by sea contracts in the 5th century. According to Ashburner, Byzantine charterparties contained a seaworthiness provision. This provision did not, in fact, afford a legal consequence. It only recommended that the merchants, who wished to load great and valuable cargoes, determine whether the vessel had a complete set of tackles, a sufficient number of sailors and was watertight.

3.5   The Laws of Oleron, which were proclaimed in about 1150 AD by Eleanor Duchess of Guienne,[4] contained several provisions relating to seaworthiness.[5] These provisions, unlike the clause in Byzantine charterparties, regulated seaworthiness as an obligation and afforded some legal consequences in case of its breach. By virtue of Art X, for example, the master of a ship, when chartering a vessel to merchants, had to show them the vessel's cordage, ropes and slings with which the cargo was to be hoisted abroad or ashore. If the master of the ship omitted to show the equipment to the merchants and there was an accident, as a result of a defect in that equipment, he would be held liable for damages. Article XIII of the same codification set out the master's obligation to provide a sufficient crew. If he failed to do so, the shipowner would be liable for damages. Similar provisions are to be found in the Laws of Wisbuy, published in the 13th century.[6]

---

3   It was expressed by a Roman lawyer of the third century AD, Paulus, in his famous book *Sentence of Paulus*, that Rhodian sea law contained the following provision as to general average: 'If, for the sake of lightening a ship, a jettison of goods has been made, what has been given for all, shall be made up by the contribution of all.' For a detailed analysis on Rhodian sea law, see Ashburner, 1909.

4   These rules take their name from the Ile d'Oleron off the southwestern coast of France and they are admitted to be the foundation of all the European maritime codes. The earliest French edition, published in 1485, bears a title *Jugemens de La Mer, des Maisters, des Mariniers, des Merchants, et de tout leur estre*, a literal translation of which is the title of the earliest English edition, published in the reign of Henry VIII – *Judgments of the Sea, of Masters, of Mariners, and Merchants, and All Their Doings*. A version appears in 30 Fed Cas 1171.

5   In these provisions, the term 'seaworthiness' is not expressly mentioned. However, when they are examined carefully, it can be seen that they contain rules about the categories to which seaworthiness extends. This issue will be discussed in detail later in this chapter, [3.16]–[3.44].

6   See 20 Fed Cas 1180. Wisbuy, on the island of Gothland, in the Baltic Sea, was the great maritime and commercial port of the north of Europe in the 13th century and its maritime code was then known as *Das Hogeste und das Oldeste Water Rechte von Wisbuy* (*The Ancient and Supreme Water Law of Wisbuy*). In parallel to Art X of the Laws of Oleron, Art XXII of the Laws of Wisbuy stipulated that the master of the ship and the mariners were obliged to show the merchant the cordage that was used for hoisting the cargo in and out of the ship. If they omitted to do so, they would be liable for damages in case of an accident. A provision similar to Art XIII of the Laws of Oleron, which dealt with sufficiency of the members of the crew, can be found in Art XXV of the Laws of Wisbuy.

3.6 In 1681, a comprehensive body of Marine Ordinances was published by Louis XIV under the discretion of his celebrated minister of finance, Colbert.[7] The Ordinances included a provision which, very likely, formed the foundation of the commercial warranty of seaworthiness.

> However, if the merchant prove that when the ship put to sea she was unfit for sailing, the master shall lose his freight, and pay the other damages and losses.[8]

The significant feature of this Ordinance was that it afforded the merchant a right to indemnity, solely upon proof of the vessel's unfitness, independent of any fault or negligence on the part of owner or master. This, apparently, was the interpretation of Valin RJ, whose commentary on the Marine Ordinances, published in 1766, was accepted as authoritative in Europe.[9] Charles Abbott, the author of the most popular English admiralty text of the early 19th century,[10] writing in 1802, seems to credit the Marine Ordinances and Valin's interpretation with being the source of the commercial warranty of seaworthiness. Abbott further declares that a contract of marine insurance is clearly void if the ship, at the commencement of the voyage, is not seaworthy, although the person who has effected the insurance is ignorant of that circumstance.[11] Abbott's text leaves no doubt that the origin of the commercial warranty of seaworthiness was the Marine Ordinance 1681 and an absolute warranty of seaworthiness implied by law prevailed in England at the turn of the 19th century as to contracts of affreightment and marine insurance contracts.

3.7 As can be observed, the law on seaworthiness has been developed gradually, but dramatically, over the last 2,500 years. Initially, a provision regarding seaworthiness used to be inserted into charterparties in order to warn the merchant who would have loaded cargo on a vessel. This provision did not impose any obligation on the part of the shipowner and it was simply advising the merchant to inspect certain aspects of the vessel's structure before the commencement of voyage. Early in the 13th century, seaworthiness gained a legal meaning in carriage of goods by sea contracts, in the sense that a merchant who loaded cargo on a vessel was afforded a legal remedy (damages) in case of breach of this obligation as a result of the negligence of the master. Finally, parallel to the increasing concerns of safety at sea and the importance of marine transport, the legal remedy that was afforded to the merchants loading cargo on board a vessel was altered, towards the end of the 17th century, and the merchants were afforded a right of indemnity, solely upon proof of the vessel's unseaworthiness, independent of any fault or negligence on the part of the owner or master. The implication of this development on marine insurance was immediate. Due to the distinct nature of the marine adventure, seaworthiness obligation has been implied into marine insurance contracts as a warranty with severe legal consequences from the assured's point of view of course. Whether this warranty status afforded in marine insurance creates a fair regime for the assured, will be discussed at the end of this book.

---

7 30 Fed Cas 1203.
8 Section 12 of the Marine Ordinances of Louis XIV.
9 See, *Treatise of Law Relative to Merchant Ships and Seamen*, 2nd edn, (by C Abbott) Newburyport, 1810, p vi.
10 *Ibid*, pp 251–52. Abbott later became Lord Chief Justice of the King's Bench and is frequently referred to in texts and opinions as Lord Tenterden.
11 As analysed in Chapter 1, despite the use of the term 'void', the effect of breach of warranty of seaworthiness at that period was to repudiate the contract prospectively as from the date of breach.

II – MEANING, NATURE AND EXTENT OF SEAWORTHINESS IN MARITIME LAW

(A)   Lack of unique definition of seaworthiness in maritime law

3.8   'Seaworthiness' is a rather strange term for the non-jurist. It can be defined as 'ability to withstand ordinary stress of wind, waves and other weather which the vessel might normally be expected to encounter'.[12] The marine insurance definition of seaworthiness can be found in s 39(4), which stipulates as follows:

> A ship is deemed to be seaworthy when she is reasonably fit in all respects to encounter the ordinary perils of the seas of the adventure insured.[13]

3.9   The crucial element in the definition of seaworthiness is, therefore, the ability of the vessel to encounter 'ordinary perils' of the intended voyage. In assessing which perils will be regarded as 'ordinary', reference should be made to the decision of Mustill J, in *JJ Lloyd's Instrument Ltd v Northern Star Insurance Co (The Miss Jay Jay)*,[14] where he categorised weather conditions under three headings: (i) 'abnormal bad weather' – here the weather lies outside the range of conditions which the assured could reasonably foresee that the vessel might encounter on the voyage in question; (ii) 'adverse weather' – namely, weather that lies within the range of what could be foreseen, but at the unfavourable end of that range – in effect, the weather is worse than could be hoped, but no worse than could be envisaged as a possibility; and (iii) 'favourable weather' – namely, weather that lies within the range of what could be foreseen, but is not bad enough to be classed as 'adverse'. He concluded that in order to be regarded as seaworthy, the vessel must be fit to deal adequately with adverse as well as favourable weather.

3.10   Being a broad and general definition, this is not the only legal definition of seaworthiness in maritime law. In *McFadden v Blue Star Line*,[15] Channel J employed a different definition of seaworthiness in respect of contracts of carriage contained in charterparties or bills of lading. According to Channel J, to be seaworthy a vessel '... must have that degree of fitness which an ordinary, careful and prudent owner would require his vessel to have at the commencement of her voyage, having regard to all the probable circumstances of it'.

3.11   Marine insurance definition, therefore, determines seaworthiness of a ship by her ability to encounter the ordinary perils of the sea; whereas the common law criterion uses the standard of the ordinary, careful and prudent shipowner. When considering these definitions, one might probably think that the meaning of seaworthiness is different in marine insurance from its meaning in other areas of

---

12   *Black's Law Dictionary*, 6th edn, St Paul, 1990.
13   This definition is derived from the celebrated case of *Dixon v Sadler* (1839) 5 M & W 405, aff'd (1841) 8 M & W 895, where Baron Parke defined 'seaworthiness' in the following terms: '... it is clearly established that there is an implied warranty that the vessel shall be seaworthy, by which it meant that she shall be in a fit state as to repairs, equipment, crew and in all respects to encounter the ordinary perils of the voyage insured, at the time of sailing upon it.'
14   [1985] 1 Lloyd's Rep 264, p 271; hereafter referred to as *The Miss Jay Jay*.
15   [1905] 1 KB 697.

maritime law. However, that seaworthiness means the same thing with reference to a policy as it does with reference to a contract of carriage by sea, was held by Bateson J, in *The Firemen's Fund Insurance Co v Western Australian Insurance Co Ltd and Atlantic Insurance Co Ltd*.[16] Although the emphasis of interest is different in marine insurance and carriage of goods,[17] the approach adopted by Bateson J, in the *Firemen's Fund* case, is, in a general sense, accurate. The same word should mean the same thing when used in a mercantile contract, whether that contract be of one description or another. Furthermore, despite the fact that they approach the point from different angles, both definitions are in harmony and, in fact, complete each other. A vessel that is not able to encounter the ordinary perils of the voyage she is engaged in, is surely not a type of vessel that will be sent to sea by a prudent shipowner. By the same token, a vessel which will be sent to sea by a prudent shipowner, is probably a vessel which can encounter the ordinary perils of the voyage she is engaged in. It can, therefore, be concluded that the term 'seaworthiness' means the same thing when used in an insurance contract or carriage contract. In this respect, when examining the scope and nature of the seaworthiness, not only the insurance cases, but the carriage cases can be taken into account.[18] A combined application of both definitions was used by Erle J, in *Gibson v Small*,[19] as follows:

> [Seaworthiness] expresses a relation between the state of the ship and the perils it has to meet in the situation it is in; so that a ship before setting out on a voyage is seaworthy if it is fit in the degree which a prudent owner uninsured would require to meet the perils of the service it is then engaged in, and would continue so during the voyage unless it met with extraordinary damage.

(B)   Nature of seaworthiness

3.12   A few points emerge from a careful examination of the definition of the concept of seaworthiness stipulated in s 39(4). First, the duty to supply a seaworthy ship is not equivalent to a duty to provide one that is perfect and such as cannot break down except in extraordinary circumstances. It is sufficient if the ship has that degree of fitness which an ordinary careful and prudent owner would require his vessel to have at the commencement of her voyage, having regard to all probable circumstances of it.[20] In the same sense, it has been held in the USA that it is not the best and most skilful form of the construction that is required to meet the warranty of seaworthiness, but only a sufficient construction for vessels of the kind insured and the service in which they are engaged.[21] Moreover, the warranty does not imply that the assured of

---

16   (1927) 28 LILRep 243.

17   If a ship is insured for a voyage from A to B, the insurer's primary concern is whether she is reasonably fit at the commencement of the voyage to carry that sort of cargo, which a vessel of her type might be expected to load, over that part of the world's oceans, at that time of the year. On the other hand, a cargo-owner with a particular cargo to load on board that vessel, at that time, is specially concerned that the ship is reasonably fit to carry this particular cargo.

18   See, for example, Arnould, 1981, para 738, citing contract of carriage cases as relevant to unseaworthiness in the context of marine insurance. Similarly, see Carver, 1982, paras 147–57, citing marine insurance cases as relevant to unseaworthiness in the context of carriage of goods by sea.

19   (1853) 4 HL Cas 353, p 384.

20   (1853) 4 HL Cas 353, p 384, *per* Lord Erle.

21   *Moores v Louisville Underwriters* 14 Fed Rep 226.

the vessel undertakes that she will be free from suspicion of unseaworthiness. It is enough if she is seaworthy in fact.[22]

3.13   Secondly, the implied warranty of seaworthiness is very far reaching. As will be examined later in this chapter, it does not just cover the structure of the vessel, but extends to the smallest details on board, such as the adequacy of stores and accuracy of the charts. According to the drafter of the Act, Sir Mackenzie Chalmers, the words 'in all respects' in s 39(4) include 'manning, equipment and stowage', but these additional words were cut out in the Lords, being regarded as unnecessary and probably restrictive.[23] In this way, an opportunity was given to courts to extend the definition of seaworthiness in parallel with the developments in shipping.

3.14   Finally, it is a question of fact, having regard to all the circumstances, whether the ship when she sailed was fit to encounter the ordinary perils reasonably expected on that voyage.[24] Each case has to be examined in the light of surrounding circumstances and, for this reason, the concept does not lend itself to easy application or absolute definition. In other words, the concept is relative in a number of respects.[25] For instance, seaworthiness varies according to the voyage to be undertaken. A ship seaworthy for inland navigation or coastal voyages might be unseaworthy for an ocean voyage. In *Cohen (G) Sons & Co v Standard Marine Insurance Co Ltd,*[26] a ship without steam power was held to be seaworthy for a tow from England to Germany. In an Australian case, *Oleo Pty Ltd v Vonguard Insurance Co Ltd,*[27] following the decision in the *Cohen* case, it was held that seepage of water through the wooden hull of a vessel did not necessarily render the vessel unseaworthy for the purposes of the MIA 1909 (Cht).[28] In this case, the assured sent the fishing vessel from Geraldton to Fremantle for repairs to her wooden hull, which had begun to take in water at a steady, but controllable rate. *En route* from Geraldton to Fremantle, the vessel began to take in water faster than the bilge pumps could pump it out and she sank. The insurer declined liability under the marine insurance policy, on the ground that the assured had sent the vessel to sea in an unseaworthy condition with privity to such unseaworthiness. Anderson J held that the assured was entitled to recover under the contract. Although the wooden hull of the vessel was leaking when she left Geraldton, this did not necessarily mean that she was unseaworthy. The trial judge was of the opinion that unseaworthiness must be judged relative to the nature of the voyage to be undertaken and the evidence indicated that, on leaving Geraldton, the vessel was fit for the voyage to Fremantle.

The extent of the seaworthiness obligation may also differ for the same voyage at different seasons. A ship, for example, may be seaworthy for a summer voyage, but unseaworthy for the same one undertaken in winter, as she is not in a condition to overcome perils to be anticipated on a winter voyage, such as light ice. Similarly, a

---

22   *Towse v Handerson* (1850) 4 Exch 890.
23   See Chalmers and Archibald, 1922, p 64.
24   *Steel v State Line SS Co* (1877) LR 3 App Cas 72.
25   In *Foley v Tabor* (1861) 2 F & F 663, Erle CJ, in his direction to the jury, said that: '... seaworthiness is a word which the import varies with the place, voyage, the class of the ship and even the nature of the cargo.'
26   (1925) 30 Com Cas 139.
27   (1991) Supreme Court of Western Australia, unreported.
28   In Australia, the MIA 1906 was incorporated into local legislation by means of the MIA 1909.

greater supply of bunkers is required for a winter North Atlantic voyage than for one in summer, as ice may be encountered. Thus, a ship which is not provided with more bunkers for a winter voyage than for the same summer one, might be considered as unseaworthy in this respect.

The extent of the obligation can also be different for the same voyage at the same season. In one American case[29] it was held that, although the vessel was seaworthy for that voyage in ordinary weather at that season, she was unseaworthy as she left the port without being fitted to cope with the hurricane that was announced to be approaching. Moreover, the extent of the warranty may vary for the same voyage at the same season, according to whether the ship is loaded with one kind of cargo or another. A celebrated case decided towards the end of the 19th century[30] could be the best example to illustrate this point. In this case, a cargo of wet sugar was provided for the vessel, called *The Isle of Wight*, by her charterer. A great deal of moisture drains from the wet sugar and, when the cargo had been nearly all shipped, it was found that there was an accumulation of water in the hold, the result of drainage from the sugar mixing with the ordinary leakage of the ship which the pumps were unable to deal with because of the nature of the material, and which rendered the ship unseaworthy for the voyage. The ship was perfectly seaworthy, except with respect to this particular kind of cargo, and the pumps were quite sufficient for all purposes. It was held that the nature of the cargo loaded rendered her unseaworthy.

Seaworthiness may also vary with the class of the ship insured. The classical example on this point is *Burges v Wickham*.[31] In this case, the vessel had been built for river navigation and, on this account, was generally unfit for ocean navigation. However, everything was done that could possibly be done by temporary appliances, to render a vessel of its type as strong as it could be made to withstand the perils of the voyage insured and the underwriters were so notified. The court held that the warranty must be taken to be limited to the capacity of the vessel and, therefore, was satisfied if, at the commencement of the risk, the vessel was made as seaworthy as it was capable of being made, although it might not make the vessel as fit for the voyage as would have been usual and proper if the venture had been one of sending out an ordinary sea-going vessel. In this respect, a ship will be considered seaworthy if she is made as seaworthy as is reasonably practicable by ordinary available means. Accordingly, a steamer of light construction, built for inland navigation, was held to be unseaworthy for an ocean voyage as it was not strengthened by putting in temporary strengthening in *Turnbull and Others v Janson*.[32]

The required standard of seaworthiness is not absolute, in the sense that it is 'relative', among other things, to the state of knowledge and the standard prevailing at the material time.[33] Therefore, seaworthiness also develops over time to reflect evolving knowledge and standards of ship construction. The improvements and changes in the means and modes of navigation frequently require new equipment, or

---

29 *Texas & Gulf SS Co v Parker* 263 Fed Rep 864.
30 *Stanton v Richardson* (1874–75) LR 9 CP 390. See, also, *Daniels v Harris* (1874) LR 10 CP 1.
31 (1863) 3 B & S 669.
32 (1877) 36 LT 635.
33 *Burges v Wickham* (1863) 3 B & S 669; *Barldey & Sons Ltd v Federal Steam Navigation Co* (1926) 24 LlL Rep 446; *Western Canada SS Co Ltd v Canadian Commercial Corp* [1960] 2 Lloyd's Rep 313.

new forms of old ones; and these, though not necessary at first, become so when there is an established usage that all ships of certain quality, or those to be sent on certain voyages, or used for certain purposes, shall have them. For example, when science produces new means to increase safety of vessels and their use becomes standard practice, a vessel becomes unseaworthy if the new means are not employed, or kept in effective condition. On the other hand, if there is an international convention or statute requiring the vessels to be fitted with these new means, then the absence of them will render the ship unseaworthy even though their usage has not become general practice.[34] However, in the absence of a standard practice or statutory provision, seaworthiness need not be maintained at the cost of always introducing the latest, best appliances.[35]

3.15   This relative nature of the term, that the standard of seaworthiness required varies depending on the scientific developments, raises another question. What would the situation be if a degree of equipment and preparation is deemed essential in some countries, whereas it is considered superfluous in others? It has been held in the USA that, in such cases, seaworthiness is to be measured by the standard in the ports of the country to which the vessel belongs, rather than by that in the ports of the country where the insurance was made.[36] Arnould considers this rule as full of good sense and equity and worthy of adoption in English jurisprudence.[37] On the other hand, such an adoption seems to be inconsistent with the wording of s 39(4). This sub-section clearly declares that the standard of seaworthiness required will be determined according to the voyage insured. Therefore, if this rule is adopted, the standard of seaworthiness required will be different for the same voyage for one ship flying the flag of a country that is not party to any safety convention, and for an English flagged ship. This situation can be made clearer with a specific example. Let us imagine that two sister ships, one English and one Cyprus flagged, are insured separately under the Institute Voyage Clauses (Hull) (IVCH) 1995 for a voyage from Southampton to Vancouver. If both ships, at the commencement of the voyage, are not provided with the navigational equipment required by an International Convention to which England is party, the English ship will be considered unseaworthy (and the insurers could be discharged from liability), while the Cyprus flagged ship will be considered seaworthy if Cyprus is not party to the same Convention and the required equipment is considered as superfluous in Cypriot ports. This hypothetical example shows that the adoption of the American rule would cause the standard of seaworthiness required for the same voyage to change; this situation is contrary to the wording of s 39(4).

---

34 As far as English ships are concerned, these regulations will be examined below, [3.24] and [3.25].

35 *Virginia Cardina Chemical Co v Norfolk SS Co (No 2)* (1912) 17 Com Cas 277, p 279. For instance, one of the recent developments in ship design is centralised navigation control, which comprises a set of instruments that display on several screens all the data and commands needed to oversee and navigate the ship. This system is intended to allow the ship to be controlled by a single seaman. Presence of a system of this type has neither been a common practice, nor been made compulsory by any international convention or national legislation, therefore, it is not, at the current moment, a standard in determining the seaworthiness of the vessel. It might, however, be regarded as a standard in the near future, depending on the general acceptance of the system in the shipping world.

36 See *Tidmarsh v Washington Ins Co* (1827) 4 Mason 439, where Story J said that: 'It seems to me that where a policy is underwritten on a foreign vessel, belonging to a foreign country, the underwriter must be taken to have a knowledge of the common usages of trade in such country as to equipment of vessel of that class, for the voyage in which she is destined.'

37 Arnould, 1981, para 732, fn 31.

As was admitted by Arnould,[38] there is not any English marine insurance case that can be cited in support of this rule. Nor is there any English decision where the standard of the shipowner's obligation to the owners of the cargo, with regard to seaworthiness, has been held to vary according to the nationality of the ship or her owners. The cases are, in reality, all to the opposite effect.[39]

(C)   Categories of matters to which seaworthiness extends

3.16   It has been demonstrated in the previous part of this chapter that the term seaworthiness is relative in many respects and varies according to the voyage undertaken, the class of the ship, and, finally, developments in ship construction. This relative nature of the term makes it nebulous and comprehensive. For this reason, to a certain extent, we must compromise in the definition of seaworthiness; although the concept is an ancient one and utilised in shipping law to attach or deny liability. It is also not sensible to attempt to define seaworthiness by listing the conditions that are necessary for the fitness of all ships, for all possible voyages, at all times. However, at least the areas of attention that are likely to be important in the decision as to whether a particular ship is fit for a particular voyage may be indicated. It is, therefore, the basic object of this part of the book to examine general aspects in which a vessel must be seaworthy.[40] During this process mainly the case law and the statutes which impose obligations relating to seaworthiness will be taken into account.[41]

The intention of Diagram 1 is to show the main categories of matters to which seaworthiness extends and it will be followed by a detailed examination for each category.

(a)   Structure and other technical equipment of the vessel

(i)   The hull

3.17   To be considered seaworthy, a vessel's hull must be tight, staunch and strong to safely encounter the ordinary action of the wind and waves to which she will be exposed. In this respect, bulkheads, plating and rivets in older ships must be in good condition. In *Aktieselskabet de Danske Sukkerfabrikker v Bajamar Compania Naviera SA (The*

---

38 Arnould, 1981, para 732, fn 31.
39 As discussed earlier, the carriage of goods by sea cases can be cited as relevant to seaworthiness in the context of marine insurance.
40 As indicated by Cresswell J in *Papera Traders Co Ltd v Hyundai Merchant Marine Co Ltd (The Eurasian Dream)*, hereinafter referred to as *The Eurasian Dream*, [2002] EWHC 118 (Comm), [2002] 1 Lloyd's Rep 719, [150], there is a possibility that these categories might overlap in an individual case.
41 It should be borne in mind that it is not necessary to identify the precise defect in the ship to establish unseaworthiness: *Eridania SpA and Others v Oetker and Others (The Fjord Wind)* [1999] 1 Lloyd's Rep 307, aff'd [2000] 2 Lloyd's Rep 191. There is, however, an 'inevitable presumption of fact' that a vessel is unseaworthy 'if there is something about it which endagers the safety of the vessel or its cargo or which might cause significant damage to its cargo': *Athenian Tankers Management SA v Pyrena Shipping Inc (The Arianna)* [1987] 2 Lloyd's Rep 376, p 389, *per* Webster J.

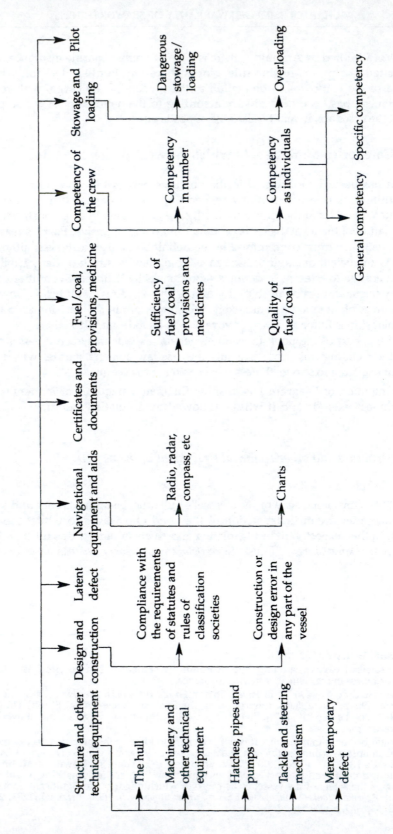

Diagram 1: Categories of matters to which seaworthiness extends

Torenia),[42] the ship was held to be unseaworthy as her hull structure was seriously weakened by corrosion. In *The Toledo*,[43] damage of the plating as a result of deformation of the brackets and frames in the internal structure of the ship, which exposed her to much greater stresses than provided for when she was built, rendered the ship unseaworthy. Similarly, loose rivets,[44] a crack in one of the ship's hull plates[45] and corroded cap screws in the hull[46] might render a ship unseaworthy.

(ii) Machinery and other mechanical equipment

3.18   Under the implied warranty of the assured as to seaworthiness, it is necessary, not only that the hull of the vessel be tight, staunch and strong, but also that the vessel's engines, boilers and generators be in good working order. Thus, in *Quebec Marine Insurance Co v Commercial Bank of Canada*,[47] the ship was held to be unseaworthy as her boilers were defective. In a similar fashion, in *Project Asia Line Inc v Shone (The Pride of Donegal)*,[48] defects in the generators, which amounted to a real risk that the ship might have been left without power during the course of the voyage, was a factor rendering her unseaworthy.[49]

The fact that the vessel is not properly equipped to fight an engine room fire could render her unseaworthy.[50] Similarly, a cut pipe that makes the emergency fire pump of the vessel useless also constitutes unseaworthiness.[51] Mechanical damage to the insulation of the vessel's electrical wiring is another reason for a ship to be considered unseaworthy.[52]

It has recently been established, in *The Eurasian Dream*,[53] that lack of a technical equipment, which is not physically attached to the vessel, but significant in establishing connection between the master and the rest of the crew, for example a walkie-talkie, could be a factor rendering the ship unseaworthy.

---

42   [1983] 2 Lloyd's Rep 210.

43   [1995] 1 Lloyd's Rep 40.

44   *Southwestern Sugar & Molasses Co Insurance v Artemis Maritime Co Insurance* [1950] AMC 2054.

45   *Huilever SA v The Otho* [1943] AMC 210.

46   *CCR Fishing Ltd v British Reserve Insurance Co* [1990] 1 SCR 814; [1990] AMC 1443; [1991] 1 Lloyd's Rep 89 (Supreme Court of Canada).

47   (1870) LR 3 PC 234. See, also, *Hong Kong Fir Shipping Co v Kawasaki Kisen Kaisha Ltd* [1962] 2 QB 26 and *The Amstelsot* [1963] 2 Lloyd's Rep 223.

48   [2002] EWHC 24 (Comm); [2002] 1 Lloyd's Rep 659.

49   Corrosion of the turbo charger was another factor rendering the vessel unseaworthy in this case.

50   *Asbestos Corp Ltd v Compagnie de Navigation Fraissinet et Cypri en Fabre* [1972] AMC 2581. Also, corrosion of the main valve for the CO2 system and the practice of securing fire hydrants with a rope, a practice that had an adverse impact on the utility of the hydrant, were factors which rendered the vessel unseaworthy in *The Eurasian Dream* [2002] EWHC 118 (Comm), [2002] 1 Lloyd's Rep 719.

51   *Manifest Shipping & Co Ltd v Uni-Polaris Insurance Co Ltd & La Réunion Européene (The Star Sea)* [1995] 1 Lloyd's Rep 651, hereafter referred to as *The Star Sea*, later reversed on different grounds by the Court of Appeal, [1997] 1 Lloyd's Rep 361. The Court of Appeal's judgment has recently been affirmed by the House of Lords, [2001] UKHL 1; [2003] 1 AC 469; [2001] Lloyd's Rep 389.

52   *The Subro Valour* [1995] 1 Lloyd's Rep 509.

53   [2002] EWCH 118 (Comm); [2002] 1 Lloyd's Rep 719.

(iii)   Hatches, pipes and pumps

3.19   Hatches should be tight enough not to allow water in if there is to be seaworthiness. The poor condition of hatch boards in the tween decks, which prevents proper stowage and endangers the ship's safety, could render the ship unseaworthy.[54] Similarly, the poor condition of the pipes can lead to the vessel's unseaworthiness in some cases. For example, the vessel was rendered unseaworthy in a case where the absence of a rose at the end of the pipe in the ballast tanks allowed a stick to pass through the pipe and jam the ballast tank valve.[55] In *Seville Sulphur & Cooper Co v Colvis Lowden & Co*,[56] steam pipes clogged with muddy water rendered the vessel unseaworthy.[57] A defect in the pumps or breakdown of a centrifugal pump during severe, but expectable, weather also rendered a vessel unseaworthy.[58]

(iv)   Tackle and steering mechanism

3.20   The ship must be furnished with ground tackling that is sufficient to encounter the ordinary perils of the seas. The House of Lords, in *Wilkie v Geddes*,[59] held a vessel to be unseaworthy where her bow anchor and the cable of the small bow anchor were defective. In the same way, failure of an electric steering system,[60] a defect in steering gear[61] and leakage in telemor steering apparatus[62] would also render a vessel unseaworthy.

(v)   Mere temporary defect

3.21   A temporary defect in the ship's structure or technical equipment due to some negligence at the time of sailing also constitutes a breach of the implied warranty of seaworthiness, provided that it is not capable of easy remedy. Thus, in *Dobell v Rosemore*,[63] a ship was held to be unseaworthy where a porthole was insecurely fastened and the fault could not be remedied without removal of the cargo, which was not practical at the time. Conversely, a temporary defect which, in the ordinary course of the voyage, could and would be remedied by the crew does not constitute unseaworthiness. In such a case, the ship will be regarded as seaworthy despite the defect and it is immaterial whether the defect is put right or not. If not, there is then negligence on the part of the crew, but unseaworthiness of the ship is not going to be an issue. Thus, in the case of *Steel v State Line SS Co*,[64] it was stated by Lord Blackburn, *obiter*, that failure to close a porthole securely, even though it was readily accessible, did not constitute unseaworthiness if the sea water entered and damaged the cargo in

---

54   *Demsey & Associates Inc v SS Sea Star* [1970] AMC 1088.
55   *The Brilliant* 138 F 743.
56   (1888) 15 R 616.
57   This decision was, however, not followed in *Cunningham v Colvis Lowden & Co* (1888) 16 R 295.
58   *The Vizcaya* [1946] AMC 469.
59   (1815) 3 Dow 57; 3 ER 988.
60   *M/V Republica de Colombia (Complaint of Flora Mercante Grancolombian, SA)* 440 F Supp 704.
61   *Haracopos v Mountain* (1934) 49 LlL Rep 267 and *Ionian SS Co v United Distillers of America Inc* [1956] AMC 1750.
62   *Erie & St Lawrence Corp v Bernes-Ames Co* [1931] AMC 1995.
63   [1895] 2 QB 408.
64   (1877) LR 3 App Cas 72, pp 90–91.

heavy weather. It was also held, in *Hedley v Pinkey & Sons SS Co*,[65] that, negligence of the master in having stanchions and rails fixed did not constitute unseaworthiness.[66]

(b)   Design and construction of the vessel

3.22   A vessel must comply with the requirements of statutes[67] and rules of classification societies[68] in the course of its construction and design. Failure to do so renders the ship unseaworthy. These rules and regulations are principally concerned with the strength of the ship and reliability of the machinery and equipment. In *The Marine Sulphur Queen*,[69] for example, a vessel which was converted to a molten sulphur carrier, from a T-2 tanker, was held to be unseaworthy as it did not comply with American Bureau of Shipping standards on transverse bulkheads. In some cases, construction or design error in any part of the vessel could be adequate to render her unseaworthy if it impinges upon her ability to encounter the ordinary perils of the seas. In *USA v Charbonnier*,[70] for example, defective construction of vent pipes, which caused excessive internal pressure, was held to be sufficient to render the vessel unseaworthy. Similarly, in *The Miss Jay Jay*,[71] a design error, namely, using materials during design which were quite unfitted for the purpose of navigation, was held to render the vessel unseaworthy.

(c)   Latent defect in hull or machinery

3.23   A latent defect was defined in an American case as one which '... a reasonably careful inspection would not reveal. It is not a gradual deterioration but rather a defect

---

65   [1894] AC 222.
66   See, also, *Gilroy & Sons Co v Prince & Co* [1893] AC 56, p 64, *per* Lord Hershell; and *Ajum Goolam Hossen & Co v Union Marine Insurance Co* [1901] AC 362.
67   The required standard, which needs to be met during the construction and design of vessels, varies according to the type and purpose of the vessel in question. For instance, cargo ships, passenger ships, fishing vessels and tankers each have their particular rules. The main current UK regulations dealing with ship construction are as follows: Merchant Shipping (Cargo Ship Construction) Regulations 1997 SI 1997/1509, which give effect to the Safety of Life at Sea (SOLAS) Convention 1974, as amended and implemented, in part, in Council Directive (94/57/EC); Merchant Shipping (Passenger Ship Construction: Ships of Class I, II and IIA) Regulations 1998 SI 1998/2514, as amended by SI 2002/1650; Merchant Shipping (Passenger Ship Construction: Ships of Classes III to IV(A)) Regulations 1998 SI 1998/2515 as amended by SI 2002/1650; Fishing Vessels (Safety Provisions) Rules 1975 SI 1975/330, made under the Fishing Vessels (Safety Provisions) Act 1970, s 1, as amended by SI 1975/471, SI 1976/432, SI 1977/313, SI 1977/498, SI 1978/1598, SI 1978/1873, SI 1991/1342, SI 1996/2419 and SI 1998/928; the Merchant Shipping (Prevention of Oil Pollution) Regulations 1997 SI 1997/1910, which apply to oil tankers.
68   Ships may be built in any country to a particular classification society's rules, and ships are not restricted to classification by the relevant society of the country where they are built. Classification is not compulsory, but the shipowner with an unclassed ship will be required to satisfy the governmental regulating bodies that it has sufficient structural assignment of a load line and issue of a safety construction certificate.
69   [1973] 1 Lloyd's Rep 88.
70   [1930] AMC 1875.
71   [1987] 1 Lloyd's Rep 32 (CA).

in metal itself.'[72] There is a substantial amount of case law to support the proposition that a latent defect in hull or machinery would render a vessel unseaworthy if it impinges upon her ability to encounter the ordinary perils of the seas. The defect, therefore, has to be in relation to a matter which affects her capability to combat ordinary sea perils. A latent defect in loading equipment would not render a vessel unseaworthy, as it would not affect her ability to encounter the ordinary perils of the seas. In *Mills v Roebuck*,[73] a French built vessel was fastened with iron bolts liable to rust, causing her to decay without any visible warning. She sprang a leak and was condemned. The precise inquiry was whether the assured could recover upon a ship which had a latent defect unknown to parties. Without hesitation, the learned Chief Justice ruled that as the ship was unseaworthy the insurer was exonerated from liability.[74] In *The Hellenic Dolphin*,[75] the ship was held to be unseaworthy because of an undetected defect in her basic plating.

(d)   Navigational equipment/aids

3.24   In order to be regarded as seaworthy, apart from being sound in structure, a vessel must be supplied with means whereby she may be safely navigated. Therefore, she must have on board devices and systems that will improve the safety and efficiency of maritime navigation, such as a reliable compass,[76] radio,[77] foghorn[78] and other equipment that a ship cannot do without, so to speak, for navigation.

---

72 *Sipowicz v Wimble and Others (The Green Lion)* [1974] 1 Lloyd's Rep 593. To determine whether a defect is latent or not is not an easy task. In cases where the design defect causes damage to the machinery or hull that, in turn, is responsible for physical loss, it is accepted that the loss is occasioned from a latent defect; see *Prudent Tankers SA v Dominion Insurance Co Ltd (The Caribbean Sea)* [1980] 1 Lloyd's Rep 338. On the other hand, the loss is not occasioned from a latent defect if the defect in design itself brings about physical injury due to the unfitness of the machinery or hull for its purpose; see *Jackson v Mumford* (1904) 9 Com Cas 114. The Court of Appeal, in *Promet Engineering (Singapore) Pte Ltd v Sturge (The Nukila)* [1997] 2 Lloyd's Rep 146, evaluated the meaning of latent defect that appears in Inchmaree Clauses in standard hull policies. This case concerned a marine platform on an accommodation platform. In 1987, serious fatigue cracks were found in the 'spud cans' for each of the three legs of the platform, which, if left unrepaired, would have led to the imminent collapse of the platform. The cracks had resulted from defects in the welding of the spud cans and the subsequent ordinary effects of the sea on them. Repairs were effected at the cost of Singapore $903,148, and a claim was made under a Lloyd's policy that provided cover for latent defects under the Inchmaree Clause. There is authority that suggests that, in a case where a latent defect simply becomes patent, the loss cannot be held to be occasioned from a latent defect; see *Oceanic SS Co v Faber* (1907) 13 Com Cas 28 and *Hutchins Bros v Royal Exchange Insurance Corp* [1911] 2 KB 398. The Court of Appeal distinguished the present case from *Oceanic SS Co v Faber* and *Hutchins Bros v Royal Exchange Insurance Corp*. According to the analysis of the Court of Appeal, at the outset there was a latent defect in the spud cans, however, this defect had not simply become patent, but had caused additional damage to the insured matter. Accordingly, it could be concluded that, if a piece of machinery suffering from a latent defect breaks down, causing additional damage to the machinery itself, or to other subject matter, the loss is one within the policy. However, the loss is not within the policy when a piece of machinery which suffers from a latent defect, rendering it valueless, breaks down. See, the solution adopted by cl 2.2.2 of the IHC 2003 in order to overcome the effect of the Court of Appeal's judgment in *The Nukila*.
73 Reported in Park, 1832.
74 See, also, *The Glenfruin* (1885) 10 PD 103 and *The Caledonia* (1894) 157 US 124.
75 [1978] 2 Lloyd's Rep 336.
76 *Paterson SS Ltd v Robin Hood Mills Ltd (The Thordoc)* (1937) 58 LIL Rep 33.
77 *The TJ Hooper* [1932] AMC 1169.
78 *The Niagara* [1898] 84 Fed Rep 902.

Equipment of this type is referred to as 'navigational equipment/aids'.[79] Certain international conventions that aim to achieve higher standards of safety at sea, such as the SOLAS 1974, have made provisions regarding the navigational equipment that must be carried on board a vessel.[80] Chapter V, reg 12 of SOLAS 1974 requires a vessel to have the following navigational equipment, in working condition, during a marine voyage: compass (magnetic and gyro compass), radar (two installations for vessels of more than 10,000 gross tonnes), automatic radar plotting aid, echo-sounding device, speed and distance indicator, indicators to show the rudder angle and the rate of revolution of each propeller, and radio direction finder. SOLAS 1974 has been implemented into the domestic law of the UK and there is a tendency to adopt SOLAS Codes (amendments to the existing Code) as they appear.[81] Therefore, to commence a voyage in violation of these regulations, at least as far as British ships are concerned, will constitute unseaworthiness.[82]

3.25   To be able to navigate safely, apart from the above requirements, ships must also be equipped with adequate and up to date charts,[83] light books and notices to mariners. By virtue of Chapter V of the SOLAS 1974, state parties must ensure that ships flying their flags '… carry adequate and up to date charts, sailing directions, list of lights, notices to mariners, tide tables and all other nautical publications necessary for the intended voyage'. In order to satisfy this requirement imposed on the British government, the Merchant Shipping (Safety of Navigation) Regulations 2002[84] have been made by the Secretary of State using the power delegated by ss 85 and 86 of the MSA 1995. These rules require ships and hovercrafts registered in the UK (other than those less than 12 m in length), and fishing vessels, and other ships and hovercraft while in UK waters, subject to certain exceptions specified, to carry such up to date charts of sufficient detail and other nautical publications as are necessary for each part of the intended voyage.[85] If a British flagged ship commences a voyage in violation of these regulations, there is little doubt that the vessel will be regarded as unseaworthy.

---

79   This term must be distinguished from the term 'aids to navigation', which is used to define the equipment or services that are intended to facilitate the conduct of ships and, usually, are situated ashore, or along the coast, such as maritime signals and beacons.

80   The SOLAS is designed as a standing code on ship safety. Article III contains rules for the amendment of the SOLAS through the Maritime Safety Committee of the IMO, in whose deliberations all states party to SOLAS 1974 may participate. Thus, as problems appear and technology and solutions change, the Code can be developed with all the necessary speed.

81   For instance, the Merchant Shipping (Radio Installation) Regulations 1998 SI 1998/2070, as amended by SI 2001/1638 give effect to the amendments to Chapter IV of SOLAS 1974, which were adopted at the conferences on Global Maritime Distress and Safety Systems in 1988, 1992 and 1995.

82   For the definition of British and UK ship, see s 1 of the Merchant Shipping Act (MSA) 1995.

83   *The Steel Scientist* [1936] AMC 387; *The Maria* [1937] AMC 934; *The Irish Spruce* [1976] Lloyd's Rep 63.

84   SI 2002/1473 as amended by SI 2004/2110.

85   The publications and relative publishers so specified are: *International Code of Signals*, HMSO; *Merchant Shipping Notices*, Department of Transport; *Mariners' Handbook*, Hydrographer of the Navy's; *Notices to Mariners*; *Navigational Tables*; *List of Radio Signals*, Hydrographer of the Navy's; *List of Lights*, Hydrographer of the Navy's; *Sailing Directions*, Hydrographer of the Navy's; *Tide Tables*; *Tidal Stream Atlas*.

*(e)   Certificates and documents necessary for the protection of the vessel
        and cargo*

3.26   To be considered seaworthy, the ship must also have on board all certificates
and documents necessary for the protection of the ship and cargo, that is to say those
which may be required by the law of the vessel's flag or by the laws, regulations or
lawful administrative practices of governmental or local authorities at the vessel's port
of call.[86] In a sense, safety certificates are pieces of secondary, rather than primary,
regulation since they are documents that declare that other specific safety rules have
been complied with. For instance, Sched 3 of the MSA 1995[87] requires all UK ships,
ships registered in a country which is a party to the International Convention on Load
Lines 1966, ships flying the flag of a Convention country, except warships and
fishing/pleasure vessels, to hold a load line certificate when they depart from a UK
port. This certificate, in fact, declares that the ship is deemed to have been surveyed in
accordance with the load line rules. Similarly, a cargo ship departing from UK ports
must carry a radio certificate that declares that the vessel, among other matters,
complies with the Rules for Direction Finders, as contained in the amended form of
SOLAS 1974.[88] Again, under the International Safety Management (ISM) Code, which
has been implemented as part of SOLAS 1974,[89] the vessels must have a valid safety
management certificate and document of compliance showing that the management
system in respect of that vessel complies with the requirements of the ISM Code. In
similar vein, the International Ship and Port Facility Security (ISPS) Code, which has
been implemented into English law,[90] requires vessels to carry a valid International
Ship Security Certificate that verifies compliance of the ship's security plan with the
regulations of the ISPS Code.[91]

3.27   Furthermore, some provisions might make it compulsory for vessels to carry
certain documents. For instance, the Merchant Shipping (Code of Safe Working
Practices for Merchant Seamen) Regulations 1998[92] require every UK ship to carry
copies of the Code of Safe Working Practices for Merchant Seamen.[93] Similarly, the
Merchant Shipping (Carriage of Cargoes) Regulations 1999[94] necessitate all sea-going
UK cargo carrying ships and non-UK sea-going cargo carrying ships, while they are
within the UK or the territorial waters thereof, to have appropriate documentation on

---

86 *Alfred C Toepfer v Tossa Marine Co Ltd (The Derby)* [1985] 2 Lloyd's Rep 325, p 331, *per* Kerr LJ.
87 This schedule gives effect to the International Convention on Load Lines signed in London
    on 5 April 1966.
88 These rules were adopted into English law by the Merchant Shipping (Safety of Navigation)
    Regulations 2002 SI 2002/1473, as amended by SI 2004/2110.
89 This code has been implemented into English law by the Merchant Shipping (International
    Safety Management (ISM) Code) Regulations 1998 SI 1998/1561.
90 The Ship and Port Facility (Security) Regulations 2004 SI 2004/1495.
91 The impact of these international instruments on provisions relating to seaworthiness will be
    discussed at the end of this chapter.
92 SI 1998/1838.
93 The Code of Safe Working Practices is obtainable from the Stationery Office Publications
    Centre.
94 SI 1999/336; these regulations give effect to the amendments to Chapter VI of SOLAS 1974,
    adopted by the Maritime Safety Committee of the International Maritime Organisation (IMO)
    at its 66th session.

cargo stowage and securing.[95] Such documentation may consist of one or more of the specified Codes of Safe Practice.[96]

Commencing a voyage without the certificates or document specified by the above regulations will, therefore, render a vessel unseaworthy.[97] However, the absence of a document, such as a certificate of stowage given at the port of loading, which is not a necessary document, or a foreign measurement certificate, which is not shown to be a usual document,[98] does not render a vessel unseaworthy.[99]

(f) Sufficiency of fuel/coal, provisions and medicines

3.28   Besides being competent in hull, machinery and other technical equipment to resist the ordinary perils of the voyage insured, the ship must be provided with sufficient fuel, stores, provisions and all other things that the custom of trade or statutes have made requisite for the voyage. Otherwise it cannot be considered as seaworthy. It was held in numerous cases that insufficiency of fuel/coal for the entire voyage rendered the ship unseaworthy.[100] It has been held, in one American case, that to be adequate the bunkers should be 20–25% greater than the tonnage of bunkers that it is estimated will be consumed on the contemplated voyage under normal conditions.[101] Having sufficient amount of bunkers may not be enough to render a vessel seaworthy in some cases. The ship will still be considered unseaworthy, if the quality of the bunkers is low. Thus, in *Fiumana Società di Navigazione v Bunge & Co Ltd*,[102] the vessel was held to be unseaworthy where she was provided with low grade coal that was liable to spontaneous combustion during the voyage.

3.29   Similarly, the vessel must have sufficient provisions[103] and medicine[104] on board for the intended voyage, in order to be considered seaworthy. As far as British

---

95 These regulations do not apply when the cargo carrying ship loaded, or intended to load, liquids in bulk, gases in bulk and cargoes that are classified as dangerous goods.

96 The Codes of Safe Practice so specified are: (1) the Code of Safe Practice for Cargo Stowage and Securing, adopted by the IMO by resolution A 714 (17) 1992 edn; (2) the Code of Safe Practice for Ships Carrying Timber Deck Cargoes, adopted by the IMO by resolution A 715 (17) 1992 edn; (3) the Code of Safe Practice for Solid Bulk Cargoes, adopted by the IMO by resolution A 434 (XI) 1991 edn; (4) International Code for the Safe Carriage of Grain in Bulk, adopted by the Maritime Safety Committee of the IMO by resolution MSC 23 (59), 23 May 1991.

97 See *Cheikh Boutros v Ceylon Shipping Lines (The Madeleine)* [1967] 2 Lloyd's Rep 224, where the documentation for the voyage was inadequate and this was held to render the vessel unseaworthy.

98 *Chellew Navigation Co Ltd v AR Appelquist Kolimport SA* (1933) 45 LlL Rep 190, p 193.

99 *Wilson v Rankin* (1865) LR 1 QB 162 and *Apex (Trinidad) Oil Fields Ltd v Lunham & Moore Shipping Ltd* [1962] 2 Lloyd's Rep 203.

100 *Thin v Richards & Co* [1892] 2 QB 141; *The Vortigern* [1899] P 140; *McIver & Co Ltd v Tate Steamers Ltd* [1903] 1 KB 362; *Greenock SS Co v Maritime Insurance Co Ltd* [1903] 2 KB 657; *Timm & Son Ltd v Northumbrian Shipping Co Ltd* [1939] AC 397. See, on the other hand, *Walford de Baedemaecker & Co v Galindez Bros* (1897) 2 Com Cas 137, where insufficient coal was held not to amount to unseaworthiness.

101 *The Willdomino* [1927] AMC 129. American cases are parallel to English ones in this area. See, eg, *The Edgecomb* [1933] AMC 421; *The Caledonier* [1929] AMC 69; *The Waalhaven* [1930] AMC 27; *The Glymort* [1933] AMC 1293.

102 [1930] 2 KB 47.

103 *The Wilhelm* (1866) 14 LT 636.

104 *Woolf v Claggett* (1806) 3 Esp 257.

ships are concerned, the Secretary of the State has made some regulations regarding these issues. The Merchant Shipping and Fishing Vessels (Medical Stores) (Amendment) Regulations 1996[105] require every UK ship and government ship, other than a ship employed in inland navigation, a pleasure vessel used for non-commercial purposes and not manned by professional crew, or a tug not operating in harbour areas, to carry on board prescribed medical stores. The Merchant Shipping (Provisions and Water) Regulations 1989[106] require every sea-going UK ship, other than a ship under 24 m in length, a pleasure vessel, a submersible vessel, or an offshore installation whilst on or within 500 m of its working stations, to be provided with adequate water and provisions. A UK vessel, therefore, commencing a voyage in violation of these regulations, will be considered unseaworthy.

(g)   Efficiency/competency of the crew

3.30   The human factor plays a vital role in seaworthiness of any vessel. It has been submitted that, while a good master may save a poor ship, a poor master may lose a good one. The fact that the term 'seaworthiness' includes a crew sufficient generally in number and skill for the proper navigation of the vessel was first stated in *Wedderburn v Bell*,[107] at the beginning of the 19th century.

3.31   While in the *Wedderburn v Bell* case, the term 'efficiency' was used to define this concept, in some similar cases the term 'competency' was employed.[108] Although the terms competent and efficient do seem to be used interchangeably in practice, it is submitted that there is a slight difference in their meanings. In *The Makedonia*,[109] Hewson J held that efficiency was a better word as it covers situations where (say) an officer is generally competent, but through lack of sleep, drink or illness may be inefficient. This approach seems accurate, since lack of application in the use of skill and knowledge does not seem to be within the ambit of 'competence'. As stated before, since the terms are used interchangeably in practice the same approach will be followed in this book.

3.32   Before considering the forms of incompetence/inefficiency, it is vital to draw the distinction between them and the concept of 'negligence', because a ship will be considered unseaworthy if her crew is incompetent, but not if her crew is merely negligent.[110] Therefore, if the vessel, crew and equipment were originally sufficient and the master and crew were persons of competent skill, the warranty of

---

105 SI 1996/2821. These regulations amend the Merchant Shipping (Medical Stores) Regulations 1995 SI 1995/1802. They implement Council Directive (92/29/EC) 31 March 1992, on the minimum safety and health requirements for improved medical treatment on board vessels, so far as that Directive relates to the carriage of medicines and other medical stores.

106 SI 1989/102, as amended by SI 1993/1072.

107 (1807) 1 Camp 1. This case was later followed by *Holdsworth v Wise* (1822) 7 B & C 794.

108 See, eg, *Hong Kong Fir Shipping Co v Kawasaki Kisen Kaisha Ltd* [1962] 2 QB 26; *The Star Sea* [1995] 1 Lloyd's Rep 651.

109 [1962] 1 Lloyd's Rep 316.

110 This being the general situation, in some cases gross or severe negligence may be traceable to incompetence and, thus, can amount to unseaworthiness. In *The Roberta* (1937) 58 LIL Rep 159, Greer LJ commented that: '... he was a man who was incompetent to be an engineer of this vessel whether he had or had not been negligent. It seems to be inconceivable that a fully competent engineer should have failed to discover that this cock was open or, indeed, he should have left it open.'

seaworthiness is satisfied and, although such master and crew by their acts or omissions brought the ship in the course of the voyage, and at the time of loss, into an unseaworthy state, the underwriter is liable for all loss which is *proximately* caused by the perils insured against.[111]

The distinction between incompetence/inefficiency and negligence is simply the distinction between general capability and incapability. If a seaman is not capable of carrying out a task, he is incompetent. In other words, a seaman is incompetent, if he does not possess the level of capability or skill to be reasonably expected of an ordinary seaman of his rank. Basic incompetence has also been defined in the terms of 'disabling want or skill'.[112] Negligence, on the other hand, arises where a seaman has the basic ability to perform his duties properly, but fails to carry them out to a reasonable standard on a particular occasion.[113]

3.33   First, the crew on board a vessel must be competent in number. Most of the maritime nations have regulations governing the manning of ships of their flags. The UK is not an exception to this general rule. Accordingly, the Merchant Shipping (Safe Manning Hours of Work and Watchkeeping) Regulations 1997[114] require the manning of all ships sailing from a UK port to be maintained at all times to at least the levels specified in the safe manning document.[115] If a ship proceeds to sea with a crew less in number than her document requires, she is unseaworthy in this respect.[116] It is submitted that the crew may also be considered collectively inefficient or incompetent if they cannot efficiently communicate in a common language amongst themselves.[117] Despite the lack of case law on this point, this approach is quite sensible. Lack of communication between the officers and crew may be extremely dangerous for the safety of the ship and other ships and may even turn a ship into a floating danger.

3.34   The crew on board a vessel must also be competent as individuals. They must hold the necessary certificates that are required by the provisions of the relevant statutes. As far as the UK is concerned, these statutes are: Merchant Shipping (Training

---

111 In *Walker v Maitland* (1821) 5 B & Ald 171, p 175, Bayley J said that: 'It is the duty of the owner to have the ship properly equipped and, for that purpose, it is necessary that he should provide a competent master and crew in the first instance; but having done this he has discharged his duty.'

112 *Standard Oil Co of New York v Clan Line Steamers (The Clan Gordon)* [1924] AC 100, p 121, *per* Lord Atkinson.

113 *Norris v William Moss & Sons Ltd* [1954] 1 WLR 346; *Braizer v Skipton Rock Co Ltd* [1962] 1 WLR 471; *Blackfriars Lighterage & Cartage Co Ltd v RL Hobbs (The Lander)* [1955] 2 Lloyd's Rep 554.

114 SI 1997/1320, as amended by SI 2002/2125; SI 2003/3049; SI 2004/1469 and SI 2004/1713.

115 The safe manning document means a document issued, in the case of a UK ship by the Secretary of the State, and in the case of any other ship, by or on behalf of the government of the state whose flag the ship is entitled to fly. This document shows the numbers and grades of the personnel required to be carried by the ship.

116 It was held in many cases that undermanning rendered a vessel unseaworthy. See *Forshaw v Chabert* (1821) 3 Br & B 158 and *Burnard & Alger Ltd v Player & Co* (1928) 31 LlL Rep 281. In Australia, however, breach of a regulation of this type was held to amount to illegality of the adventure insured, rather than unseaworthiness of the vessel. See *Doak v Weekes & Commercial Union Assurance Co plc* [1986] 82 FLR 334 and *Switzerland Insurance Australia Ltd v Mowie Fisheries Pty Ltd* [1997] FCA 231. This issue will be discussed later in the following chapter, during the examination of the implied warranty of legality. It is sufficient to say, at this stage, that these Australian decisions go beyond the English law.

117 Roger, 'Human factor in unseaworthiness claims' (1993) *LMCLQ* 345.

and Certification) Regulations 1997;[118] Merchant Shipping (Local Passenger Vessels) (Master's Licences and Hours, Manning and Training) Regulations 1993;[119] Merchant Shipping (Certification of Ships' Cooks) Regulations 1981;[120] Fishing Vessels (Certification of Deck Officers and Engineer Officers) (Amendment) Regulations 1998;[121] Merchant Shipping (Vessels in Commercial Use for Sport or Pleasure) Regulations 1998.[122] Manning a ship in violation of these statutory provisions renders her unseaworthy.

3.35   The fact that the master or the officers of a ship hold the required certificates of competence does not automatically mean that they are competent. There is still a possibility that they might be regarded as incompetent due to lack of ability, knowledge or training on a specific issue. In other words, a distinction must be drawn between general and specific competence. An example of this situation can be seen in *The Star Sea*.[123] An engine room fire occurred on board *The Star Sea*. *The Star Sea's* engine room fire-fighting system included four banks of CO_2 cylinders. The safety plan of the vessel stipulated that all the cylinders should be discharged into the engine room simultaneously, in the event of fire. The master did not know that all the CO_2 cylinders had to be discharged at once in the event of such a fire. He was also unaware of the importance of introducing CO_2 as soon as it became apparent that a fire in the engine room could not be extinguished in another way. Tuckey J held that the vessel was unseaworthy, as the master was incompetent, notwithstanding his long service. This demonstrates that the courts are prepared to categorise a seaman as technically incompetent if he lacks knowledge or training on specific issues, even though he has performed adequately for years. The decision of Tuckey J on this point was later affirmed by the Court of Appeal and House of Lords both of which reversed the first instance decision on other grounds.[124]

It should be borne in mind that directing the master or crewmen to read all the literature on board will not be treated as the provision of sufficient information on the part of the owner or manager, specially if the documentation on board is too voluminous and includes irrelevant and/or obsolete information.[125]

3.36   Similarly, although the master or officer is properly certificated, yet, by reason of the nature of the ship or her equipment, further instruction ought to have been provided by the owners. Lack of further instruction may render the ship unseaworthy.

---

118 SI 1997/348, as amended by SI 1997/1911. These regulations give effect to the Convention on Standards of Training Certification and Watchkeeping for Seafarers (STCW) 1978, as amended on 7 July 1995.
119 SI 1993/1213, as amended by SI 2003/3049.
120 SI 1981/1076.
121 SI 1998/1013.
122 SI 1998/2771 as amended by SI 2002/1473.
123 [1995] 1 Lloyd's Rep 651.
124 [1997] 1 Lloyd's Rep 361 (CA); [2001] UKHL 1; [2003] 1 AC 469; [2001] 1 Lloyd's Rep 389 (HL). A similar decision was delivered in a more recent case. In *The Eurasian Dream* [2002] EWHC 118 (Comm); [2002] 1 Lloyd's Rep 719, despite their long-standing service the crew were held to be incompetent as they were improperly or inadequately trained in fire fighting. Also, the master, who was new to car-carriers, was described as a 'car-carrier novice' by Cresswell J.
125 *Ibid, The Eurasian Dream.*

In *Standard Oil Co of New York v Clan Line Steamers (The Clan Gordon)*,[126] a ship's ballast tanks were emptied and she capsized. Vessels of that construction, turret ships, were likely to do that if the tanks were emptied when they were carrying homogeneous cargoes, but not if they were carrying a variety of goods. The master, although generally competent and experienced in turret ships, had not been specifically instructed of this particular risk. The House of Lords held the vessel to be unseaworthy because of the master's incompetency. In the same sense, the vessel was considered unseaworthy in *The Schwan*,[127] as her engineer was not warned of the unusual and dangerous character of a three-way valve.

3.37   A disinclination on the part of the crew or master to perform their contractual duties properly might also be regarded as a form of incompetency. In *The Eurasian Dream*, ignorance of the master and crew as to the peculiar hazards of car carriage and car-carriers and the characteristics and equipment of the vessel was sufficient to render the vessel unseaworthy.

3.38   Even where the master or officer does hold the necessary certificate, there is always the fact that such competence as he once possessed may have been eroded by the ravages of time. In *Moore v Lunn*,[128] the drunken state of the master and chief engineer when they started the voyage was held to be sufficient to render the vessel unseaworthy. Another good example might be an officer who has become lazy in relation to the techniques of navigation and seeks, in the time honoured phrase, to 'cut corners'.

3.39   There is one further factor to be investigated. If temporary incapacity, such as illness or tiredness, renders the master incapable of performing his duties at the commencement of the relevant voyage, he can be considered as incompetent. A ship which proceeds to sea in this condition will be considered as unseaworthy. It must, however, be borne in mind that there is no warranty that the state of the master's health will be perfect. It is enough if he is in reasonably good health.[129]

(h)   Stowage and loading

3.40   The cargo may be so badly stowed as to affect the seaworthiness of the vessel. In *Kopitoff v Wilson*,[130] iron armour plates were so badly stowed that, as a consequence, during heavy weather, they went through the side of the ship, causing loss of the ship, which was found to be unseaworthy by reason of bad stowage. Similarly, in *The Standale*,[131] a cargo of grain was stowed in the hold without adequate protection having been taken against its shifting, and this kind of stowage rendered the ship unseaworthy.[132] It must be borne in mind that bad stowage does not always render the ship unseaworthy. Bad stowage, which affects only the cargo damaged by it and

---

126 [1924] AC 100.
127 [1909] AC 450.
128 (1923) 15 L1L Rep 155.
129 *Rio Tinto Co Ltd v Seed Shipping Co* (1926) 24 L1L Rep 316.
130 (1876) 1 QBD 377.
131 (1938) 61 LIL Rep 223.
132 See, also, *Steel v State Line SS Co* (1877) LR 3 App Cas 72 and *Firemen's Fund Insurance Co v Western Australian Insurance Co and Atlantic Insurance Co* (1927) 28 L1L Rep 243.

nothing more, still leaves the vessel seaworthy for the venture. In *The Thorsa*,[133] chocolate was stowed in the same hold as gorgonzola cheese, on arrival the chocolate was tainted with cheese. The stowage of chocolate and cheese in the same hold could not constitute a breach of warranty of seaworthiness, as the stowage did not endanger the safety of the vessel, but was simply bad stowage.[134] The ship shall again be considered unseaworthy if she carries on deck goods that, having due regard to the safety of the ship, ought not to be carried there.[135]

3.41   Seaworthiness requires that a vessel be safely loaded. If a vessel is loaded so heavily that she cannot safely sail on the voyage contracted for, she is unseaworthy. In *Foley v Tabor*,[136] a vessel was held to be unseaworthy as a result of the ship being overloaded to such extent as to increase her danger and difficulty in navigation.[137] Similarly, a vessel was held to be unseaworthy when she was inherently unstable, having loaded an excessive deck cargo when she sailed.[138] The load lines, fixed in the International Convention on Load Lines 1966,[139] must not be submerged at any time. If, at the commencement of the voyage, the load lines are submerged, this will render the ship unseaworthy.[140]

Similarly, loading a vessel in contravention of the international rules, which are adopted for different types of vessels, might render a vessel unseaworthy. For instance, in *Transocean Liners Reederer v Euxine Shipping Co Ltd (The Imvros)*,[141] a carriage case, the vessel was held to be unseaworthy where a cargo of timber was loaded on deck in contravention of the IMO Code of Practice for Ships Carrying Timber Deck Cargoes. In *Northern Shipping Co v Deutsche Seereederei GmbH (Kapitan Sakharov)*,[142] the vessel was rendered unseaworthy due to the fact that dangerous cargo was loaded under deck in contravention of the International Maritime Dangerous Goods Code and SOLAS 1974.

(i)   Pilot

3.42   It has been advocated, by Ivamy,[143] that, if at any part of the voyage, a pilot is required, the vessel will be considered unseaworthy unless she obtains one. When the case law and the wording of the MIA 1906 is examined, it can be seen that the situation is not as straightforward as suggested by Ivamy. Whether the lack of a pilot renders the vessel unseaworthy will be examined by considering various possibilities.

---

133 [1916] P 257.
134 See, also, *Elder Dempster Co Ltd v Paterson Zochonis & Co* [1924] AC 522, in which bad stowage crushed casks of palm oil, but did not render the vessel unseaworthy.
135 *Daniels v Harris* (1874) LR 10 CP 1.
136 (1861) 2 F & F 663.
137 See, also, *Laing v Boreal Pacific* (2001) 25 CCLI (3d) 189, affirming (1999) 12 CCLI (3d) 66 (Federal Court of Appeal Canada).
138 *Smith, Hogg v Black Sea & Baltic Insurance* [1940] AC 977. See, also, *Biccard v Shepherd* (1861) 14 Moo PC 471.
139 This Convention was implemented into English law by Sched 3 of the MSA 1995.
140 Overloading a vessel in contravention of the load line rules is a statutory offence, exposing the master or owner to criminal prosecution and the ship to detention under s 4 of Sched 3 of the MSA 1995.
141 [1999] 1 Lloyd's Rep 848.
142 [2000] 2 Lloyd's Rep 255.
143 Ivamy, 1988, p 376.

3.43   If a vessel sails from a port where a pilot may be procured and the nature of the navigation requires one, she will probably be unseaworthy without one unless the master himself has competent knowledge of the navigation.[144] Similarly, if a vessel sails from a port where pilot has been made compulsory by a statute,[145] she will be considered unseaworthy without one. One might consider whether, sailing in violation of a statutory provision like this, would render the voyage illegal and, thus, constitute a breach of the implied warranty of legality, instead of breach of seaworthiness. This can be extremely important as, unlike the breach of the implied warranty of seaworthiness, the breach of the implied warranty of legality cannot be waived by the insurer. Although this issue will be examined in detail in Chapter 4, it is appropriate to offer a brief explanation at this stage. The general rule established by the case law is that a breach of a safety regulation does not render the voyage illegal, but instead renders it unseaworthy.[146]

3.44   The situation is more complicated if a pilot is required at any stage or at the end of the voyage. If the usage requires a pilot at any stage or at the end of the voyage and the vessel does not get one, she cannot be considered unseaworthy. This approach, adopted in *Phillips v Headlam*,[147] is consistent with the wording of s 39(4), since, according to this section, the ship is required to be seaworthy at the commencement of the voyage and, as will examined later in this chapter, there is no continuing warranty of seaworthiness. Accordingly, the state of unseaworthiness, which occurs at a later stage either as a result of the negligence of the crew or any other reason, does not constitute breach of this implied warranty. In this case, the insurer might only argue that the master is incompetent, as he does not know or consider the importance of the pilot for that specific part of the voyage. An argument like this can succeed depending on the facts of each case, but the burden, which is on the shoulders of the insurer, is a heavy one.

In *Hollingworth v Brodrick*,[148] it was suggested by Patterson J that if usage requires that at a particular stage of the voyage a ship should take a pilot on board, such part of the voyage is to be treated as a separate stage for the purpose of the warranty of seaworthiness. This approach, which seems plausible at first glance, requires the application of the doctrine of stages in cases where usage requires a pilot for a particular stage of the voyage. Accordingly, the ship will be considered unseaworthy if she is not provided with a pilot for that stage. Such an approach, however, is inconsistent with the wording of s 39(3). According to this sub-section, an insured voyage can be divided into stages if only the ship requires different kinds of, or further, preparation or equipment. Since the ship does not require such preparation or

---

144 *Dixon v Sadler* (1839) 5 M & W 405; and *The Framlington Court* 69 Fed Rep 300 (1934).

145 Article II of the Convention on the Regime of Maritime Ports 1923 recognises the right of each state to organise and administer pilotage services as it thinks fit. The state is free to impose a compulsory service, providing that it respects the principle of equality in the charges made; it may also exempt its own citizens from mandatory use of a pilot provided they meet certain technical conditions. In the UK, pilotage was originally the responsibility of independent individuals. Later, it was administered by the Corporation of Trinity House, in certain districts, and by local pilotage authorities, elsewhere. Since the Pilotage Act (PA) 1987, it has been provided by competent harbour authorities.

146 See *St John Shipping Corp v Joseph Rank Ltd* [1957] 1 QB 267.

147 (1831) 2 B & Ad 380.

148 (1837) 7 A & E 40, p 48.

equipment for the part of the journey for which usage requires a pilot, the doctrine of stages should not be applied in this case. Moreover, such an extension to the doctrine of the stages will be inconsistent with the logic behind it. The doctrine of stages has been developed to protect the assured. Under this doctrine, if a ship is insured for an adventure which contains both a sea and a river voyage, she will not be considered unseaworthy from the moment she sails for the sea voyage, without the necessary equipment for the river voyage. She can be provided with this equipment before the river voyage starts and, in this way, the implied warranty of seaworthiness is satisfied. If the doctrine of stages, however, is extended to cover this particular issue, this will create a great disadvantage for the assured and a powerful weapon will be given to the insurer to discharge himself from further liability.[149]

It was held, in *Law v Hollingworth*,[150] that failure to take on board a pilot at any stage, or at the end of the voyage, rendered a vessel unseaworthy if pilotage was made compulsory by means of a statute. In that case, the ship at the time of loss did not have a pilot on board as required by Act of Parliament.[151] It was made clear, by the cases decided later, that the breach of a duty imposed by an Act could only render a vessel unseaworthy, if it was a duty relevant to the commencement of the voyage. Here, the duty imposed, taking a pilot on board, was a duty relevant to the final stage of the voyage. Its breach, therefore, should not constitute unseaworthiness. As discussed above, since it is not possible to apply the doctrine of stages in situations like this, it can be safely concluded that *Law v Hollingworth* was wrongly decided. It was later overruled by *Dixon v Sadler*.[152]

The standard Institute Hull Clauses contain a clause giving leave to sail or navigate with or without pilots.[153] It is submitted, with approval of Arnould,[154] that the effect of this clause is to preclude the underwriters from avoiding the policy merely on the ground that the vessel was unseaworthy by reason of her lack of a pilot, which was necessary at the end or during the continuance of the voyage.

(D)   An attempt to extend the doctrine: ships subject to arrest and seaworthiness

3.45   In *Morrisey v SSS & J Faith*,[155] the American judge, Connell JC, extended the meaning of seaworthiness dramatically, and held that the term should not be limited to merely the physical facilities of the vessel. In this case, a contract of affreightment was concluded between the Pakistan Government and the defendant company for the carriage of a certain cargo by the company's vessel named *Faith*. *Faith*'s crew was poorly fed and underpaid. Moreover, sister ships of *The Faith*, owned by the defendant company, had already been embroiled in litigation. There was a multitude of

---

149 The application of the doctrine of stages to voyage policies will later be discussed in this chapter, [3.57]–[3.61].
150 (1797) 7 TR 160.
151 The then PA of 5 Geo 2, c20.
152 (1839) 5 M & W 405.
153 Clause 1.1 of the ITCH and IVCH 1983 and 1995 stipulates that: 'The vessel is covered subject to the provisions of this insurance at all times and has leave to sail or navigate with or without pilots ...'
154 Arnould, 1981, para 726.
155 [1966] AMC 71.

unsatisfied creditors, including the crew of *Faith*, and any of them could arrest the vessel. In a case of arrest, the owners lacked the resources to free her from the arrest process, either by satisfaction of the claims or the posting of a bond. The judge, taking these facts into account, held the vessel to be unseaworthy. In delivering his judgment, Connell JC said that:[156]

> If the owner leaves the vessel unprotected against the foreseeable seizure by creditors, she is just as liable to be stopped short of her destination as if she were left unprotected against the ordinary perils of the navigation.

Considering the objective of the doctrine of seaworthiness, to enable the insured vessel to complete the intended voyage successfully, one can argue that this is a fair and sensible judgment. Such an interpretation is, however, inconsistent with the definition of 'seaworthiness' stipulated in the MIA 1906. By using the words 'to encounter the ordinary perils of the seas', the draftsman intended to limit the scope of seaworthiness to the physical ability of the vessel in question. The other factors, such as the possibility of arrest and lack of facilities to free her from arrest, should not play any role in determining a vessel's seaworthiness. It seems that English courts, at least in cases where the MIA 1906 applies, will hold a vessel to be seaworthy in a situation like this, under the restrictive wording of s 39(4).

III – IMPLIED WARRANTY OF SEAWORTHINESS IN MARINE INSURANCE

3.46   Being an ancient concept, the doctrine of seaworthiness is quite significant in several different legal contexts of maritime law. It is utilised in maritime law to attach liability for certain consequences and it operates both as a defence mechanism and, also, liability imposing doctrine. For instance, apart from marine insurance, the doctrine plays a crucial role in carriage of goods, towage contracts, general average, seamen's contract of employment,[157] limitation of liability, carriage of passengers[158] and, even, in public maritime law.[159] It is beyond the scope of this book to discuss the impact of the doctrine on these areas.

3.47   The implied warranty of seaworthiness plays a crucial role in the law of marine insurance as it is one of the most effective defences used by insurers. In many cases, its breach causes the insurance cover to be lost, even though there is no causal relationship between the breach and the loss and, in this respect, it can be regarded as the 'instant death' of the assured. The MIA 1906 implies a warranty of seaworthiness only in a voyage policy, but not in a time policy.[160] The aim of this part of the chapter is to examine the application of the doctrine of seaworthiness in different aspects of

---

156 *Ibid*, p 77.
157 See s 42 of the MSA 1995.
158 See Arts 3, 13 and 18 of the Convention Relating to the Carriage of Passengers and their Luggage by Sea 1974 (Athens Convention). This Convention was implemented into English law by Sched 6 of the MSA 1995.
159 See ss 94, 95 and 98(3) of the MSA 1995.
160 The rationale for this difference will later be examined at [3.66] to [3.69].

marine insurance. The legal problems that may arise and the position in practice will be considered. The case law and standard Institute Clauses will generally be referred to for the purpose of clarifying or explaining the legal position in this area. Before considering the legal aspects, the need to regulate seaworthiness as a defence in marine insurance will first be discussed.

(A)   The need to regulate seaworthiness as a defence in marine insurance

3.48   Marine insurance contracts are designed to provide indemnity for the assured for losses which are incidental to a marine adventure.[161] Marine adventure is unique in the sense that once it has commenced, the assured has very limited control over his vessel and this situation needs to be taken into account when the balance between the parties to the contract is adjusted. In order to maintain the balance between the parties, English law has implied a seaworthiness warranty in voyage policies and a somewhat lesser provision in respect of seaworthiness for time policies. Other legal systems have made an effort to keep the balance between the assured and insurer, either in a way similar to English law or in an entirely different framework. The type and form of the defences afforded to marine insurers in other jurisdictions in case of unseaworthiness will be evaluated and compared to English law later in this book in Chapter 7. As a result of such an examination, it is expected to reach a conclusion as to whether the warranty status afforded in respect of voyage policies and seaworthiness provision in respect of time policies serves the needs of the insurance market for the new millennium. In this part, however, the reasons for regulating seaworthiness as a defence for the insurer in marine insurance contracts will be examined.

3.49   The main reason for the existence of provisions relating to seaworthiness in marine insurance contracts is simply a reflection of the general shape of the contract to insure. 'Uncertainty' (either as to whether the event happens at all or as to when it happens)[162] is the characteristic property of insurance contracts and underwriters are not expected to insure against certain events or inevitable losses. If the ship is sent to sea in an unseaworthy state, it is exposed to greater risk than normal and the probability of a loss is very high. In other words, the event in such a case is one which can be, in a way, determined by the assured and it is not totally 'uncertain'. Without such an obligation in marine insurance, underwriters would be expected to insure the assured against inevitable losses, which is not the function of insurance in any circumstances. Furthermore, in an insurance contract, the insurer agrees to indemnify the assured against a risk in return for a payment called a premium. The risk, therefore, is the distinguishing factor of an insurance contract. An underwriter conducting business in the marine market must be taken to possess sufficient experience and sources of information to rate the risk that the vessel will suffer loss by the perils of the seas, etc, during the voyage. What he cannot rate is the possibility that the shipowner will not try, or will try and fail, to make the ship seaworthy before the

---

161 Section 1 reads as follows: 'A contract of marine insurance is a contract whereby the insurer undertakes to indemnify the assured, in manner and to the extent thereby agreed, against marine losses, that is to say, the losses incident to marine adventure.'

162 The former refers to indemnity insurance, whereas the latter to contingency insurance, eg, life insurance.

risk ever commences. Imposing a seaworthiness warranty into voyage policies and a similar obligation as to seaworthiness in time policies, therefore, helps the insurer to rate the risk properly and adjust the premium accordingly.

3.50   Secondly, the rule is disciplinary in nature. It is designed to protect the innocent freighter and crew against the consequences of owner's cynical act of sending the ship on its way in a condition that puts all the interests at risk. Lord Mustill, however, did not find this justification convincing and criticised it on two grounds.[163]

First, he argues that, in the case of cargo insurance, a claim under the policy will fail if the carrying vessel was unseaworthy at the start of the voyage even though the assured has no means of knowing whether the ship was seaworthy or not. Although this argument seems attractive at first sight, it is open to a fatal objection. Being an implied warranty in each voyage policy, seaworthiness is not conclusive in nature. That is to say, it can always be neutralised by means of a waiver clause. Thus, in all cargo policies this implied warranty has been waived on the condition that the assured, or their servants, are not privy to such unseaworthiness.[164] In this way, the harsh consequences of the breach of this implied warranty for the cargo-owner are in practice disregarded.

Moreover, Lord Mustill is of the opinion that to impute a regulatory function to marine insurance law is inconsistent with its private law character. In pure theory, freedom of contract is the main principle dominating private law. In this sense, contracts are created only by agreement; that is, an agreement creating at least one obligation is, in principle, both necessary and sufficient for the contract. In the real word, however, pure theory is soon in tatters; the obligation creating agreement may be necessary and sufficient, but, for a number of reasons, it is not conclusive. In other words, the principle dominating private law, freedom of contract, is not unlimited and its border lines are drawn by the law itself. For example, the main content of many contractual relationships is compulsory.[165] Similarly, the obligation to make a contract may be created by common law,[166] by statute[167] or by Arts 81 and 82 of the European Community (EC) Treaty.[168] The concept of public policy may also play an important role in determining the borders of the freedom of contract principle. All these examples show that, despite the fact that freedom of contract is the main principle of the private law, the contract between parties may be interfered with and some duties or obligations may be imposed on one or both parties by express or implied terms of the law. In this sense, to impose rules regulating the relationships between the contracting parties does not render the private law character of the marine insurance and the wider interests of the public have a part to play in this area of the law, just as in other areas of private law.

---

163 See Mustill 'Fault and marine losses' (1988) *LMCLQ* 310, p 345.
164 See cl 5.2 of the Institute Cargo Clauses (ICC) (1982) (type A, B, C).
165 See Dock Work Regulations Act 1976.
166 For the common innkeeper or carrier.
167 For example, s 12 of the Employment Act 1982, which was repealed, used to impose an 'actionable' duty not to refuse a contract with non-union suppliers.
168 *Garden Cottage Foods Ltd v Milk Marketing Board* [1984] AC 130.

(B)   Voyage policies

(a)   Extent of the implied warranty of seaworthiness in voyage policies

3.51   Section 39(1) declares, in general terms, that:

> In a voyage policy there is an implied warranty that at the commencement of the voyage the ship shall be seaworthy for the purpose of the particular adventure insured.

As can be observed, this provision does not distinguish the nature of the subject matter insured. This means that the warranty of seaworthiness is equally implied in a voyage policy,[169] whatever the subject of insurance. The warranty, therefore, applies whether the policy is on ship, goods, freight, or any property exposed to a maritime peril.[170] Similarly, in cases where the cargo insurance contracts are effected on an 'open cover' basis,[171] the implied warranty of seaworthiness would still apply to each overseas shipment embraced within the open cover because each adventure relates to a separate voyage. Thus, each certificate of insurance issued under an open cover will be subject to s 39(1).

3.52   Section 39(1) requires the ship to be seaworthy 'at the commencement' of the voyage. What is exactly meant by this wording? The voyage may be considered as commenced when the ship sails, or alternatively, when she leaves the port and proceeds to open sea. 'Sailing' in marine insurance cases, where there is a warranty to sail before a particular day, has been held to be 'breaking ground' leaving her moorings ready for sea, though not leaving port.[172] The significance of this discussion becomes clear in a case where a ship, which has sailed from her moorings, becomes unseaworthy as a result of negligence of the crew while she is still in port. If the time of sailing is the time when the voyage commences, the assured may argue that there is no breach of the warranty of seaworthiness, as unseaworthiness, which occurs after the commencement of the voyage has no significance.[173] On the other hand, if the voyage commences after the ship leaves the port and proceeds to sea, then the insurer may rely on breach of warranty defence.

Since the phrase 'at the commencement of the voyage', and not the word 'sailing', is used in s 39(1), one might consider that there is a difference in their meanings and something else, other than sailing, is meant in this sub-section. A literal construction reveals that this is not the case. One of the dictionary meanings of 'commencement' is 'sailing'.[174] Therefore, there is no doubt that the phrase 'at the commencement of the voyage' means the same thing as 'at the time of sailing'. If the draftsman's intention was to give a different meaning to s 39(1), this could have easily been achieved by

---

169 For the definition of voyage policy, see s 25(1).

170 See ss 1 and 3.

171 An open cover is an agreement whereby the underwriter undertakes to insure all shipments or interests of the assured for certain voyages or trades, either at specified rates of premium, or at rates to be arranged. The underwriter is notified by the assured, when the shipments are made, of the interests attaching to the cover.

172 *Roelandts v Harrison* (1854) 9 Ex 444, p 465.

173 'The assured makes no warranty that the ship shall continue seaworthy throughout the voyage', *per* Lord Mansfield in *Berman v Woodbridge* [1781] 2 Dougl 781. This point will later be examined at [3.62]–[3.64].

174 See, *The Concise Oxford Thesaurus,* (by B Kirkpatrick) Oxford, 1995.

wording the sub-section differently. For example, the sub-section could have been worded as that: 'In a voyage policy there is an implied warranty that when the ship leaves the port, she shall be seaworthy ...'

3.53   This outcome can also be supported by case law. The meaning of the phrase 'commencement of voyage' was considered four years after the enactment of the MIA 1906, in *Mersey Mutual Underwriting Association Ltd v Polland*.[175] Accordingly, the voyage commences when the vessel, which is being fitted and equipped for sea, is possessed of her clearances, crew and, if necessary, cargo commences to navigate upon her voyage and no longer remains moored in the course of preparing. The commencement of a voyage, as distinguished from the termination of lying in port, is determined by that which purports to be done at the time of the act of quitting the actual mooring. This judgment clearly states that the voyage is considered as being commenced as soon as the ship sails, therefore, s 39(1) in fact takes the time of sailing into account when determining the time which the warranty starts to bite. It must, however, be borne in mind that, in some cases, the sailing of the ship may not be enough for the commencement of the voyage. If there is no intention of commencing the voyage, merely the movement of the ship cannot be considered as an act that commences the voyage. This issue was discussed in *Sea Insurance Co v Blogg*,[176] and this case is still good law by virtue of s 91(2). In this case, there was a sailing warranty requiring the ship to sail on or after 1 March. It appeared that the ship in question had finished loading her cargo before 10 pm on 29 February and, having previously cleared the custom house, was then ready to proceed to sea; but by a regulation of the port, ships were not permitted to go out to sea after dark. At 10 pm, the master, with the object of keeping his crew on board, moved the ship away from the wharf, about 500 yds out into the river, and there anchored. In moving the ship thus, he placed her in a slightly more advantageous position for starting than she would have been if she had remained at the wharf. The gaining of that advantage was the only motive of the master in moving her. On the following morning, 1 March, she proceeded on her voyage and it was held that the ship had sailed on 1 March.

3.54   There is one final point that has to be addressed regarding the extent of the warranty of seaworthiness in voyage policies. Section 39(1) refers only to the seaworthiness of the 'ship'. Accordingly, it can be considered whether the warranty of seaworthiness is implied for lighters, crafts and the like employed for the conveyance of the cargo from the ship to the port of discharge. This question was raised in the case of *Lane v Nixon*.[177] In that case, the goods were damaged while being carried from the ship to the port of discharge by means of a lighter. The insurers were held liable as a result of a cover clause worded as '... until the goods be safely landed in the port of discharge, including all risks to and from the ship'; but the implied warranty of seaworthiness was held not to be attached to the lighters so used. This judgment is sound and consistent with the wording of s 39(1) as the seaworthiness is required only at the commencement of the voyage. Unless the process of landing of cargo by means of lighters can be considered as a separate stage of the voyage, the implied warranty does not apply after the voyage has commenced. The judges could not regard it, in any sense, as a stage of the voyage.

---

175 (1910) 26 TLR 386.
176 [1898] 2 QB 398.
177 (1866) LR 1 CP 412.

Even if landing of cargo had been regarded as a separate stage of the voyage, this time a further problem would have occurred. Can the lighters and other crafts employed for the conveyance of the cargo be regarded as a 'ship'? This issue was not considered in *Lane v Nixon*, and the judgment was based on the fact that s 39(1) applies only at the commencement of the voyage and conveyance of cargo from the ship to the port of discharge is not a separate stage of the voyage.

The general definition of ship can be found under s 313 of the MSA 1995, which has defined 'ship' as including every description of vessel used in navigation. This definition laid particular emphasis on two points. First, it is not the form, the construction, the rig, the equipment, or the means of propulsion that is determinative in deciding whether a structure is a ship or not. Accordingly, a hopper barge, with no means of propulsion, was held to be a vessel in *The Mac*.[178] Secondly, any structure which is, in fact, used in navigation is a vessel.[179] The term navigation has been described, in *Steadman v Schofield*,[180] as 'a planned or ordered movement from one place to another'. Therefore, any structure that is capable of making a planned or ordered movement from one place to another and, in fact, does such make a movement, is regarded as a vessel, regardless of its size, shape and source of power.[181] In the light of the criteria expressed in s 313 of the MSA 1995 and the relevant case law, it is highly probable that an English court in the case of a dispute would hold that the definition of 'ship' in the MSA 1995 applies to lighters and crafts used for similar purposes. It is obvious that they do navigate, in the sense that they make a planned or ordered movement from one place to another and perform their duties in this way. However, the fact that there is no case law regarding the position of lighters or other crafts used for navigation, and the conservative and descriptive view of English courts regarding the definition of a vessel, must be borne in mind.[182]

3.55   *Lane v Nixon* has made it clear that there is no implied warranty of seaworthiness for lighters, crafts and the like employed for the conveyance of the cargo from the ship to the port of discharge. Is, however, the situation the same for crafts employed for the conveyance of the cargo to the ship at the beginning of the

---

178 (1882) 7 LR PD 126. In that case, whether a hopper barge was a ship or not was decided by taking into account s 2 of the MSA 1854 (in force at that time): 'Ship shall include every description of vessel used in navigation not propelled by oars.' As can be seen, the present definition of a ship in s 313 of the MSA 1995 is quite similar to the definition in s 2 of the MSA 1854. In this respect, it is not wrong to conclude that the outcome of this case would be the same under s 313 of the MSA 1995 and that *The Mac* is still good law. *The Mac* was later followed in *The Mudlark* [1911] P 116, where a sea-going steel hopper barge, 90 ft long and 19.5 ft wide, without means of propulsion, was held to be a vessel under s 742 of the MSA 1894, which was worded in exactly the same way as s 2 of the MSA 1854.

179 The definition of a vessel under American federal law lays a particular emphasis on the expression 'transportation', instead of 'navigation'. Section 3 of 1 USC (originally enacted as Act of 30 July 30 1947, Ch 388, s 3, 61 Stat 633) defines the word vessel as: '... including every description of watercraft or other artificial contrivance used, or capable of being used as a means of transportation on water.'

180 [1992] 2 Lloyd's Rep 163, p 166.

181 For example, in *The Titan* (1923) 14 LlL Rep 484, limitation of liability was allowed for a floating crane, which had broken down in the River Tyne hitting several ships. Similarly, in *The Harlow* [1922] P 175, a dumb barge had been held to be a vessel, since she was moved about much more often than this structure would normally be moved about.

182 For example, in *The Blow Boat* [1912] P 217, a dredger; in *Merchant's Marine Insurance Co Ltd v North of England P&I Club* (1926) 25 LlL Rep 446, a pontoon carrying a crane was held not to be a ship by English courts.

voyage? Although this issue was not considered in *Lane v Nixon*, applying the same logic, the solution must be the same. Section 39(1) requires the ship to be seaworthy at the commencement of the voyage. Conveyance of the cargo to the carrying vessel is a stage which occurs before the commencement of the voyage, so no implied warranty of seaworthiness is imposed on these crafts by the MIA 1906, even though they can be regarded as ships. If, however, these crafts, which are used for the conveyance of the cargo to the ship, are unfit, the underwriter can exclude his liability. Accordingly, cl 5.1 of the Institute Cargo Clauses (ICC) (1982) (type A, B, C) excludes liability caused by the unfitness of these crafts. This clause is worded as follows:

> In no case shall this insurance cover loss damage or expenses arising from unseaworthiness of vessel or craft, unfitness of vessel, craft, conveyance, container or liftvan for the safe carriage of the subject matter insured, where the assured or their servants are privy to such unseaworthiness ... at the time the subject matter insured is loaded therein.

This wording of the section suggests that the underwriter, when defending the claim, is under an obligation to prove that unfitness of the conveyance *proximately* caused the loss. Accordingly, the underwriter will be provided with a defence in cases where unfitness is one of the *proximate causes* of the loss and he can show the existence of a causal link between the unfitness and loss. For his defence to succeed under cl 5.1, the underwriter has also to show that the assured or their servants were privy to the unfitness at the time the goods were loaded onto the craft. In modern shipping practice, few cargo assured are in a position to know whether or not the craft used for carrying the cargo to the ship is fit or not, and, in effect, cl 5.1 is of little practical value to cargo underwriters where most cargo insurances are concerned.

3.56   There is only one extraordinary case in which s 39(1) can play an important role for the lighters or other crafts employed for the conveyance of the cargo. Since these crafts can be considered as ships in the light of case law discussed above,[183] if the stage which the goods are conveyanced to or from the carrying vessel is insured separately from the main voyage, then s 39(1) imposes a warranty of seaworthiness for these crafts as well. This is a hypothetical scenario, considering that in all cargo policies, the risk attaches when the goods leave the warehouse and terminates when the goods are put into the warehouse at the port of discharge.[184]

(b)   Doctrine of stages

3.57   The voyage undertaken may be so long that it is impossible to take in a sufficient amount of bunkers for the entire journey. Similarly, different preparations or equipment may be required for different stages of the journey and it is impractical to have this equipment at the commencement of the voyage when there is an opportunity of taking it on board from an intermediate port. If, however, the implied warranty of seaworthiness in voyage policies is applied in a strict sense, the assured may lose his insurance cover in cases explained above. For this reason, s 39(3) states:

---

183 It must be noted that there is no case law in respect of lighters or other crafts employed for the conveyance of the cargo.
184 See cl 8 of the ICC (1982) (type A, B, C).

Where the policy relates to a voyage which is performed in different stages, during which the ship requires different kinds of or further preparation or equipment, there is an implied warranty that at the commencement of each voyage the ship is seaworthy in respect of such preparation or equipment for the purposes of that stage.

3.58   The origin of this rule is *Bouillon v Lupton*,[185] which will later be evaluated in detail. The doctrine of stages has been developed mainly to reconcile the interests of the assured, on the one hand, and those of the insurers, on the other, in voyage policies. As discussed above, there have been attempts to extent the boundaries of the doctrine since its enactment. First, it was argued that the part of the voyage for which pilotage was compulsory formed a different stage.[186] Then, the conveyance of cargo from a ship to a discharge port by means of a lighter was claimed to be a separate stage.[187] The courts, however, always refused to extend the limits of the doctrine. From the wording of s 39(3), it is obvious that there has to be a physical or commercial need to warrant a division of the voyage into stages. Merely because a vessel may legitimately call at an intervening port does not produce a voyage in stages.[188] Case law suggests that the doctrine applies in two instances.

(i)   Physical factors

3.59   Due to physical factors, different equipment, preparation or crew may be required for different parts of the voyage. The presence of such circumstances justifies the division of the voyage into stages. This situation is well illustrated, as regards a river and sea voyage, by the case of *Bouillon v Lupton*.[189] In this case, the vessel was insured from Lyons to Marseilles (on the River Rhone), thence to Galatz (by sea). For the voyage on the river, only the crew was carried and she was without her masts and heavy tackle, as they would have rendered this section of the journey impossible. These were customarily left at Marseilles. At Marseilles, the sea crew took the vessel to sea properly equipped; however, she was lost in the Black Sea during a storm. The underwriters maintained that the vessel was not seaworthy for the whole voyage, while the court decided that she was reasonably fit to encounter the perils on the river and at sea and was, therefore, 'seaworthy' for both stages. Similarly, the division of a voyage into stages, in relation to the warranty of seaworthiness, may take place in different parts of a sea voyage as a result of physical factors. For example, a ship insured for a voyage from a port in the Mediterranean to a port in the North Atlantic may require some extra equipment or preparation for the Atlantic part of the voyage and the voyage may be divided into stages in this respect.

(ii)   Stages for coaling and bunkering

3.60   The doctrine has also been applied where a ship cannot and does not, at the commencement of the voyage, carry enough fuel for the whole of the insured voyage, and is, therefore, obliged to take in fuel at some further port or ports. That it should be possible to apply the doctrine of stages for bunkering and coaling, was first

---

185 (1863) 33 LJ PC 37.
186 *Hollingworth v Brodrick* (1837) 7 A & E 40.
187 *Lane v Nixon* (1866) LR 1 CP 412.
188 *Thin v Richards & Co* [1892] 2 QB 141.
189 (1863) 33 LJ PC 37.

highlighted in *Thin v Richards & Co.*[190] The doctrine, however, was applied for bunkering and coaling for the first time in *The Vortigern*,[191] at the end of the 19th century. In that case it was held that the unseaworthiness of the vessel due to insufficiency of coal or other fuel would be decided according to the capability of dividing the voyage. Whether a voyage was divisible depended upon necessity and, the insurers having established that the vessel was unseaworthy from the outset of the voyage, the assured was allowed to show the necessity for dividing the voyage. This ruling was later upheld in *Greenock SS Co v Maritime Insurance Co Ltd*,[192] which involved a vessel coaling in stages, one of which was between Montevideo and St Vincent. Due to the negligence of the engineer, supplies of coal were insufficient for that stage and, in order to reach port without assistance, some of the ship's fittings and spars and also part of the cargo were burnt as fuel. In the Court of Appeal, upholding the principle established by *The Vortigern*, Romer LJ stated that the voyage could have been divided into stages for coaling if there was a necessity, but it was the duty of the assured to make sure that there was sufficient coal for that stage of the voyage. In this sense, the vessel was found unseaworthy on leaving Montevideo and, therefore, the insurers were not liable. The application of the doctrine laid down by *The Vortigern* was made clearer in *Timm & Son v Northumbrian Shipping Co.*[193] After passing through the Panama Canal, *en route* for St Thomas in the Virgin Islands, the captain realised that he had insufficient bunker coal to reach the destination and altered the course for Jamaica. However, whilst proceeding to Jamaica, the vessel struck a reef and with her cargo became a total loss. It was held by the House of Lords that the intention on sailing definitely fixed the stage of the voyage and that the quantity of the bunkers sufficient to make a vessel seaworthy for that stage must be determined in view of all contingencies that a prudent shipowner ought to contemplate; that, in fixing that quantity, a shipowner was not entitled to take into account the existence of optional bunkering facilities *en route*. Therefore, the vessel could not be held to have been sufficiently supplied with bunkers for that stage, from Vancouver to St Thomas, which was the next bunkering port fixed by the owners and she was unseaworthy on leaving Vancouver.

3.61   One might consider whether it is possible to divide the voyage into stages even if the vessel could carry enough fuel for the whole voyage. In shipping practice, commercial necessities may require such a division in the voyage. Although this issue was not discussed in *Timm & Son v Northumbrian Shipping Co*, a positive answer can be given to this inquiry by evaluating the reasoning of the judges in the House of Lords. As the shipowner has a freedom to divide the voyage into stages for bunkering purposes provided that they are reasonable, there is nothing preventing him from doing so, even if the vessel could carry enough fuel for the entire voyage. Support for this argument is found in the judgment of Tucker LJ, in *Neomijulia SS Co v Minister of Food*.[194] In this case, it was expressly stated that the shipowner was under no obligation to use bunkering stages and was entitled, at his election, to carry fuel for the

---

190 [1892] 2 QB 141.
191 [1899] P 140.
192 [1903] 1 KB 367.
193 [1939] AC 397.
194 [1951] 1 KB 223, p 234.

whole voyage. This point implies the converse proposition that the shipowner may elect to bunker in stages even if he could carry fuel for the whole voyage.

(c)   No continuing warranty of seaworthiness

3.62   There is no warranty that a ship, originally seaworthy for the voyage insured, shall continue to be seaworthy, or that the master and crew shall do their duty during the voyage. The negligence and misconduct of master or crew after the voyage has commenced, therefore, is no defence to an action on the policy where the loss has been immediately occasioned by the perils insured against. In other words, the assured makes no warranty that the ship shall continue to be seaworthy throughout the voyage.[195] This principle, laid down by Lord Mansfield in the late 18th century, is full of good sense and in accordance with shipping realities. Neither the assured nor his managers has any means of ascertaining the condition of the vessel after the voyage has commenced. To make them liable for something which is completely out of their control would be harsh. In this sense, it is logical that they are not responsible for the unseaworthiness caused by the negligence or misconduct of their servants.

3.63   Even though the policy is on a voyage out and home, the risk being entire and indivisible, it is sufficient if the ship is seaworthy for the entire voyage when she first sails from the homeport of loading. Thus, in *Holdsworth v Wise*,[196] where a ship was insured 'at and from Belfast to her port or ports of loading in British America, during her stay there, and back to the port of discharge in the UK' and the evidence showed that she was seaworthy for the entire voyage when she sailed from Belfast, but unseaworthy when she left St Andrew's on the homeward passage, it was held that the implied warranty of seaworthiness was satisfied.

3.64   In fact, there is no express provision in the MIA 1906 that the ship must be seaworthy only at the commencement of the voyage. However, s 39(5) provides that there is no implied warranty that the ship shall be seaworthy at any stage of the adventure in respect of time policies. This wording makes it clear that the law on the voyage policies established by Lord Mansfield remains unamended under the MIA 1906 and there is no continuing warranty status.

(C)   Time policies

3.65   In time policies,[197] there is no implied warranty of seaworthiness. This does not, however, mean that the question of seaworthiness is irrelevant in time policies. There is a somewhat lesser provision, in respect of seaworthiness, for time policies now embodied in s 39(5). This sub-section will be the main focus of this part of the chapter and its legal implications on time policies will be analysed. Before embarking on a legal examination of this nature, reasons for the distinction between voyage and time policies, in respect of the application of the implied warranty of seaworthiness, will be considered.

---

195 *Berman v Woodbridge* [1781] 2 Dougl 781, p 788; *Eden v Parkinson* (1781) 2 Dougl KB 732, p 735; *Watson v Clark* (1813) 1 Dow 336, p 344; *Busk v Royal Exchange Assurance Co* (1818) 2 B & Ald 73 and *Biccard v Shepherd* (1861) 14 Moo PC 471.
196 (1822) 7 B & C 794. See, also, *Redman (SP) v Wilson* (1845) 14 M & W 476.
197 See s 25(1) for the definition of time policies.

*(a)   Rationale for the distinction between voyage and time policies in respect
        of seaworthiness and its justification*

3.66   It is not just a coincidence that a warranty of seaworthiness is implied for
voyage policies and not for time policies. The rationale for the difference in the law
between time and voyage policies, in respect of seaworthiness, can be found in the
celebrated case of *Gibson v Small*.[198] First, there was seen to be a problem in identifying
the moment at which the warranty would bite if seaworthiness was an implied
warranty in time policies. Should this be the time when the contract of insurance is
made, or at the time fixed for the inception of the risk, or at the moment when the ship
breaks ground on the first voyage after the inception of the risk? Or, alternatively,
should the warranty relate to the moment when the ship has commenced the intended
enterprise? Whichever of these alternatives is chosen, some consequences, which
might not be consistent with basic principles of insurance law, may arise. If the time
when the contract is made, or the time fixed for the inception of the risk is regarded as
the moment at which the warranty will bite, some difficulties may arise particularly if
the insured vessel is at sea at this period in time. In that case, the assured has no means
of ascertaining the condition of the vessel at the time she comes on risk. The insurance
cover may, however, be lost if the vessel becomes unseaworthy at sea at the moment
when the warranty starts to bite.

    Similarly, if the moment when the ship breaks ground on the first voyage after the
inception of the risk is taken into account, this may have some harsh consequences for
the insurer. If, at the time the policy is effected the insured vessel is at sea and is lost
before reaching her next port of call due to the unseaworthiness, which existed at the
commencement of this voyage, the insurers will still be liable. Choosing the moment
when the ship has commenced the intended enterprise as the time to which the
warranty relates seems more appropriate than the other alternatives as the assured has
control of the vessel at this time. However, in this way, a retrospective effect is given to
the new insurance contract as the assured is made liable for something which might
have occurred before the insurance contract is concluded and this is definitely beyond
the mainstream of insurance contracts.[199]

3.67   The second reason given, in *Gibson v Small*, for the distinction in law between
voyage and time policies is less convincing than the first one discussed above.
Whereas under a voyage policy the standard of seaworthiness could be pitched by
reference to the contemplated voyage, this will not work where the cover may
encompass only the later part of a voyage that is already in progress, or the part of the
voyage, plus one or more wholly different voyages, with or without the addition of the
first part of yet another voyage. In respect of these voyages, the standard required
might be quite different and quite unpredictable at the moment of inception. Lord
Mustill, criticising this argument, supports the view that the increased homogeneity of
sea transport has greatly diminished the former importance of this problem.[200]

---

198 (1853) 4 HL Cas 353.
199 It should also be borne in mind that almost all time policies keep the insured vessel insured
     if, at the time the policy expires, she is at sea, provided that notice is given and additional
     premium is agreed. See cl 2 of the ITCH 1983 and 1995 versions. See, also cl 12 of the IHC
     2003.
200 Mustill 'Fault and marine losses' (1988) *LMCLQ* 310, p 347.

According to Lord Mustill, most of marine insurance is concerned with non-specialised ocean-going vessels. These vessels are expected to be fit for the carriage of all but abnormal cargoes on all but abnormal voyages. Whether engaged on a short coastal hop in mid-summer or a North Atlantic passage in mid-winter, the ship ought to be able to deal with any weather conditions which are reasonably to be contemplated.

3.68   Admittedly, there are some sound reasons for not imposing an implied warranty of seaworthiness in respect of time policies. The insured vessel may be at sea when a time policy commences and, in this respect, the assured may have no opportunity to verify the condition of his vessel on inception. At the same time, there may be some difficulties in determining the moment when the warranty will bite. It, however, appears almost equally inequitable that, after a vessel has returned to the control of her owner or manager, or of those who are, in other respects, acting as his agents in her management, the underwriter should still remain deprived of the protection which he would enjoy if the vessel were insured voyage by voyage. Even in time policies, the assured, through his agents, is in a position to access the requirements in order to render the vessel seaworthy for the voyages after the attachment of the risk.

3.69   The current state of the law will be examined later in the following part of the chapter and the possibility of a reform in this area will be considered in the final chapter of this book. Suffice to say at this stage that the justification for creating a different status for time policies in relation to the application of the implied warranty of seaworthiness is far from being convincing.

(b)   Legal situation in respect of seaworthiness in time policies

3.70   As mentioned on several occasions in this chapter, the legal situation is different in time policies than in voyage policies, in respect of seaworthiness. A line of 19th century case law refused to imply any seaworthiness warranty into time policies, but recognised a defence based upon knowledge of the assured.[201] The case law on this point has been codified by s 39(5), which provides as follows:

> In a time policy, there is no implied warranty that the ship shall be seaworthy at any stage of the adventure, but where, with the privity of the assured, the ship is sent to sea in an unseaworthy state, the insurer is not liable for any loss attributable to unseaworthiness.

The meaning of this provision and the cases when a s 39(5) defence can be raised by the underwriter will be examined now.

(i)   Unseaworthiness when the ship is sent to sea

3.71   Under the wording of s 39(5), the assured is prevented from recovery only where the vessel was unseaworthy when she was sent to sea. It is crystal clear from this wording that this sub-section is not operated by subsequent unseaworthiness. In

---

201 *Gibson v Small* (1853) 4 HL Cas 353; *Michael v Hooper* (1856) 17 CB 551; *Thompson v Hopper* (1856) 6 E & B 172; *Fawcus v Sarsfield* (1856) 6 E & B 192; *Dudgeon v Pembroke* (1877) 2 App Cas 284.

other words, if a ship, which has commenced her voyage in a seaworthy state, becomes unseaworthy at a later stage of the voyage and a loss occurs due to this unseaworthiness, the underwriter cannot rely on s 39(5) to deny liability.[202]

3.72   Section 39(5) also refers to the ship being sent to sea. Therefore, this section can only protect underwriters in respect of unseaworthiness on sending to sea, not merely for a transit within a port, canal lake or river, nor where a vessel is lost or damaged in port, or at her moorings. It must, on the other hand, protect the underwriters when the ship is sent on a sea voyage in an unseaworthy stage and the first part of this voyage is in a canal, river or lake. There is no case law regarding these matters, but the above principles can be concluded by evaluation of the section and taking the logic behind it into account.

(ii)   Privity of the assured

3.73   The assured's state of mind is a relevant factor in the application of s 39(5), for the vessel must have been sent to sea in a unseaworthy state with the privity of the assured. The phrase, 'privity of the assured', has given rise to a series of problems over the years due to its vague wording.

3.74   The first question arising in this context is the meaning of the phrase 'privity of the assured'. Until Compania Maritime San Basilio SA v Oceanus Mutual Undertaking Association (Bermuda) Ltd (The Eurysthenes),[203] the meaning of the word 'privity' in s 39(5) had not been considered at length.[204] In this case the meaning of the word 'privity' was examined and clarified by the Court of Appeal when a member of a P&I club claimed indemnity for a cargo claim arising from the unseaworthiness of the vessel. The P&I club refused to indemnify the member on the ground that the member was privy to the alleged unseaworthiness.[205] The question in this case was whether, in order to prove 'privity' within s 39(5), it was necessary for the club to prove (a) negligence, and/or (b) knowledge of the fact constituting unseaworthiness, and/or (c) some deliberate or reckless conduct in sending the ship in an unseaworthy state. It was contended by the shipowners that the word 'privity' in s 39(5) meant 'wilful misconduct' and, accordingly, the assured was deprived of the indemnity if he deliberately or recklessly sent the ship to sea knowing that she was unfit. When constructing this argument, much reliance was placed upon certain 19th century

---

202 In general, a subsequent unseaworthiness occurring as a result of a latent defect or negligence of the crew is covered by the policy. See cl 6.2 of the ITCH 1983 and 1995 and cl 2.2 of the IHC 2003.

203 [1977] 1 QB 49, hereafter referred to as The Eurysthenes.

204 In Compania Naviera Vasconqada v British & Foreign Marine Insurance Co Ltd (The Gloria) (1935) 54 LlL Rep 34 (hereafter referred to as The Gloria), Barson LJ, at p 58, although rejecting an argument that privity was confined to actual knowledge of seaworthiness, stated his opinion as follows:

> I think if it were shown that an owner had reason to believe that his ship was, in fact, unseaworthy, and deliberately refrained from an examination which would have turned his belief into knowledge, he might properly be held privy to the unseaworthiness of his ship. But the mere omission to take precautions against the possibility of the ship being unseaworthy cannot, I think, make the owner privy to any unseaworthiness which such precaution might have disclosed.

205 The application of s 39(5) in cases between a P&I club and its member will later be examined at [3.94].

cases[206] upon which it was argued that Sir Mackenzie Chalmers had based s 39(5). In effect, it was urged that 'privity' in s 39(5) had to be equated with 'wilful misconduct' in s 55(2)(a). The P&I club, on the other hand, argued that the word 'privity' in s 39(5) was indistinguishable from the phrase 'actual fault or privity' which appears in some limitation conventions and that any personal act of commission or omission by the shipowner, in relation to sending the ship to sea in an unseaworthy state, would amount to 'privity' within s 39(5).[207]

3.75   One of the arguments about the meaning of 'privity' in s 39(5) traced the origins of the section to the antecedent case law, while the other attracted attention to the long line of limitation statutes. All three judges in the Court of Appeal rejected these arguments. If the intention of the draftsman was to equate 'privity' with 'wilful misconduct', this could easily have been achieved by using the same language both in ss 39(5) and 55(2)(a). Moreover, the attempt to equate the word 'privity' to the words 'wilful misconduct' is open to a fatal objection. As was stated by Lord Roskill,[208] circumstances can be envisaged in which sending a ship to sea in an unseaworthy state to which the assured was privy could be said to amount to wilful misconduct and, if a loss followed, the underwriter might successfully plead both ss 39(5) and 55(2)(a) by way of defence. However, whilst there could not be wilful misconduct by an assured without privity, in the sense of conscious knowledge, an assured might be privy in the sense of sending a ship to sea in an unseaworthy state without, at the same time, being guilty of wilful misconduct. In other words, the fact that the assured is aware of the unseaworthy condition of the ship when she is sent to sea does not necessarily mean that he is guilty of wilful misconduct. Arnould, sharing the same view, has provided an illustration.

> It is possible to conceive cases where, with the privity of the assured, an unseaworthy ship may be sent to sea without any real misconduct on his part. For instance, in time of war, a shipowner fearing an attack upon a naval port may very properly order his vessel to sail at once, although he knows that she is not perfectly seaworthy in all respects.[209]

This basic analysis shows that the privity in s 39(5) means something other than the term 'wilful misconduct'. It was also held that there was nothing in the antecedent cases, cited as the origin of s 39(5), which justified a different view of the construction of the sub-section from the construction of the language of the Act.[210]

Similarly, if the word 'privity' means the same as the phrase 'actual fault or privity', why was the latter not used in s 39(5)? Moreover, that the word 'privity' and the phrase 'actual fault or privity' do not mean the same thing, can easily be shown by reference to the previous case law. The definition of the phrase 'actual fault or privity' is to be found in *Asiatic Petroleum Co v Lennard's Carrying Co*, in the judgment of Buckley LJ:[211]

---

206 *Thompson v Hopper* (1856) 6 E & B 937; *Dudgeon v Pembroke* (1877) 2 App Cas 284; *Trinder Anderson & Co v Thames & Mersey Marine Insurance Co* [1898] 2 QB 114.
207 The 1924 and 1957 Limitation Conventions take the 'actual fault or privity' test into account in determining whether the shipowner loses his right to limit or not.
208 [1977] 1 QB 49, p 78.
209 Arnould, 1981, para 720, fn 62.
210 [1977] 1 QB 49, *per* Lord Roskill, p 79.
211 [1914] AC 419, p 432. Hamilton LJ also made a very similar definition in the same case, p 436.

The words 'actual fault or privity' infer something personal to the owner, something blameworthy in him ... If the owner be guilty of an act of omission to do something which he ought to have done, he is no less guilty of an 'actual fault' than if the act had been done one of omission.

This judgment, which was later affirmed in the House of Lords,[212] clearly states that the personal act or privity is the acts or matters which the shipowner did or omitted to do. It includes positive and negative forms of personal wrongful act. 'Privity', on the other hand, is directed to a different subject matter, namely, to acts or matters which were done with the assured's knowledge and consent.

It was, therefore, the intention of the draftsman when using the word 'privity' in s 39(5) to give a different meaning to the concept rather than 'wilful misconduct' or 'actual fault or privity'. That the meaning of the word 'privity' in s 39(5) must be ascertained by looking at, and only at, the MIA 1906, was stated by Lord Roskill in his judgment.[213] Similarly, Lord Geoffrey Lane considered the word 'privity' as a neutral word deriving colour from its surroundings.[214]

3.76   After specifying the position of the word 'privity', the judges in the Court of Appeal tried to define and draw the lines of the concept. Eventually, they were in agreement that the word 'privity' meant with 'knowledge and consent'. Their Lordships indicated that 'knowledge' did not only mean positive knowledge, but also the sort of knowledge expressed in the phrase 'turning a blind eye'. Thus, if a man, suspicious of the truth, turns a blind eye to it and refrains from inquiry – so that he should not know it for certain – then he is to be regarded as knowing the truth. On the other hand, negligence in not knowing the truth is not equivalent to knowledge of it.[215] If the owner of a ship says to himself: 'I think a reasonable prudent owner would send this vessel to sea with a crew of 12, so, I will send her with 12,' he is not privy to unseaworthiness, even though a judge may afterwards say that she ought to have had 14. He may have been negligent in thinking so, but he would not be privy to unseaworthiness. However, if he says to himself: 'I think that a reasonably prudent owner would send her to sea with a crew of 12, but I have only 10 available, so I will send her to sea with a crew of 10,' then he is privy to the unseaworthiness if a judge afterwards says he ought to have had 12. The reason being that he knew that she ought

---

212 *Sub nom, Lennard's Carrying Co v Asiatic Petroleum* [1915] AC 705.

213 [1977] 1 QB 49, p 75. When holding this, Lord Roskill cited the speech of the Lord Hershell in *Bank of England v Vagliano Bros* [1891] AC 107, pp 144–45 (the code in question was the Bills of Exchange Act 1882):

> I think the proper course is in first instance to examine the language of the statute and ask what is its natural meaning, uninfluenced by any considerations derived from the previous state of the law, and not to start with inquiring how the law previously stood, and then, assuming that it was probably intended to leave it unaltered, to see if the words of the enactment will bear an interpretation in conformity with this view ... I am, of course, far from asserting that resort may never be had to the previous state of the law for the purpose of aiding in the construction of the provisions of the code. If, for example, a provision be of doubtful import, such resort would be perfectly legitimate ... What, however, I am venturing to insist upon is, that the first step taken should be to interpret the language of the statute, and that an appeal to earlier decisions can only be justified on some special ground.

214 [1977] 1 QB 49, p 81.

215 *Ibid*, p 68, *per* Lord Denning MR.

to have had 12 and consciously sent her to sea with 10. Geoffrey Lane LJ agreeing with Lord Denning MR added that:[216]

> Knowledge of what? Again the sub-section is clear. It says 'unseaworthiness', not 'facts which in the upshot prove to amount to unseaworthiness'. Accordingly, it seems clear to me that if this matter were *res integra*, the section would mean that the assured only loses his cover if he has consented to or concurred in the ship going to sea when he knew, or believed, that it was in an unseaworthy condition. I add the word 'believed' to cover the man who deliberately turns a blind eye to what he believes to be true in order to avoid obtaining certain knowledge of the truth.

Accordingly, the assured ought not to be held privy to something if the court is satisfied that he did not know the facts, or did not realise that they rendered the ship unseaworthy, even though he was negligent in not knowing. In this respect, it was held, in *The Gloria*,[217] that the omission of a regular survey, which if held would presumably have discovered a state of unseaworthiness, did not mean the assured turned a blind eye to the knowledge.

3.77   Recently, the House of Lords in *The Star Sea*[218] was presented the opportunity to clarify the scope of the test laid down by the Court of Appeal in *The Eurysthenes*. *The Star Sea* was insured under a time policy. She and two other ships, *Kastora* and *Centaurus*, which had been lost in the previous couple of years as a result of fire, were beneficially owned by the Kollakis family and they were all managed by the same ship-managers, Kappa Maritime Ltd, of which the directors were Captain Kollakis, his two sons, and Mr Nicholaidis. After having sailed from Nicaragua bound for Zeebrugge with a full cargo of bananas, mangoes and coffee, a fire started in *The Star Sea*'s engine room. It later spread to other parts of the ship and was not put out for several days, by which time the ship had become a constructive total loss.

The Star Sea was unseaworthy in several aspects, but only two of them, the ineffective sealing of the engine room and the 'massive ignorance' of the recently appointed master to activate the CO_2 system as soon as it was realised that the fire could not be fought in any other way, were causative of the loss. The additional damage was brought about by a combination of both aspects of unseaworthiness. In other words, *The Star Sea* was rendered a constructive loss when she was wholly consumed by a fire, the extent of which could have been easily contained had the dampers been effective and the master competent. When the shipowners brought a claim for the additional damage caused by fire, the insurers relied on a s 39(5) defence, alleging that the assured was 'privy' to the unseaworthiness of the vessel which caused the additional damage, so they were to be denied of the right of recovery.[219]

The underwriters argued that the two earlier fires, on *Kastora* and *Centarus*, must have aroused the assured's suspicion that there might be something faulty or defective in the fire-fighting armoury of their fleet and they were privy to the unseaworthiness simply because they refrained from carrying out further inspections fearing that they

---

216 [1977] 1 QB 49, p 81.
217 (1935) 54 LlL Rep 34.
218 [2001] 1 UKHL 1; [2003] 1 AC 469; [2001] 1 Lloyd's Rep 389.
219 The insurers also alleged that the assured was in breach of the utmost good faith duty, emphasised in s 17 of the MIA 1906; however, this was rejected. The findings of the House of Lords on this point will be evaluated in detail in Chapter 7.

would discover the unseaworthy state of the vessel. Tuckey J, at first instance, held that the assured was privy to unseaworthiness which caused the loss. He said as follows:[220]

> However, I do find that there was blind eye knowledge on the part of the assured. The inadequate response to earlier fires and the state of *The Star Sea* on 27 May [1990], demonstrate in my judgment that the assured did not want to know about her unseaworthiness in relevant respects. What it comes down to specifically is this. With the message staring them in the face, that the CO2 systems on *Centaurus* and *Kostara* had not been used so as to prevent those ships from becoming constructive total losses, the assured took no effective steps to ensure that this would not happen again. The incompetence of the master and the state of the safety equipment for sealing the engine room, essential to the effectiveness of the CO_2 system on *Star Sea*, show only too clearly how ineffective those steps were and how inadequately equipped she was to fight a fire effectively. The assured did not want to know about the competence of the master to use the CO_2 system effectively. It is not easy to find a reason for this, since it would not have involved much time or money to ensure that the master was competent. The assured did not want to know about the state of the safety equipment. One reason for this is not difficult to find: money. This was an elderly vessel for which, as I find, there was a tight budget for repairs. A good deal of time and money had been spent on repairing in lay-up and maintaining at sea the reefer machinery which was, of course, essential to its revenue earning ability.

The Court of Appeal rejected Tuckey J's factual findings on 'blind eye' knowledge, on the basis that the wrong test had been applied. In the Court of Appeal's view, the crux of the matter was whether the assured had suspected that the master of the vessel had been incompetent and had then turned a blind eye to that possibility. On the facts, while it might have been negligent for the assured not to learn lessons from the fires on the *Centarus* or *Kastora* and not to give instructions to the crew of *The Star Sea* in fire-fighting, there was no blind eye knowledge as the insurer had not established that the assured had suspected that there was a problem on *The Star Sea* and failed to give proper instructions in fire-fighting.

The House of Lords upheld the Court of Appeal's view on this point. According to their Lordships, when deciding whether the assured turned a blind eye or not, the question which needs to be asked is: 'Why did the assured not inquire?' It was not enough to establish privity to show that, objectively, the assured did not make necessary inquiries as to seaworthiness due to laziness or gross negligence; it had to be shown that, subjectively, the assured had at least a suspicion of the relevant unseaworthiness, coupled with a decision not to check. In so deciding, their Lordships noted that Tuckey J may have been misled by certain comments of Roskill LJ in *The Eurysthenes*, where he said that:[221]

> If the facts amounting to unseaworthiness are there staring the assured in the face so that he must, had he thought of it, have realised their implication upon the unseaworthiness of the ship, he cannot escape from being held privy to that unseaworthiness by blindly or blandly ignoring those facts or by refraining from asking relevant questions regarding them in the hope that by this lack of inquiry he

---

220 [1995] 1 Lloyd's Rep 651, p 664.
221 [1977] 1 QB 49, p 76.

will not know for certain that which any inquiry must have made plain beyond possibility of doubt.

The phrase 'had he thought of it', was held by the House of Lords to be ambiguous, and was not to be taken as meaning that the test was objective. Actual knowledge that there might be a problem was required. Lord Scott makes this point clear in his judgment.[222]

> I have some difficulty with Roskill LJ's inclusion in the cited passage of the qualification 'had he thought of it'. If the assured had not 'thought of it' he would, presumably, not have realised the implications of the facts. His refraining from inquiry would not then have been attributable to the hope that he would not know for certain. I do not, myself, see how a failure to think about the facts, and hence a failure to realise their implications, can afford the basis for a finding of blind eye knowledge.

Towards the end of his judgment, Lord Scott states the present state of law in this area with the following speech:[223]

> In summary, blind eye knowledge requires, in my opinion, a suspicion that the relevant facts do exist and a deliberate decision to avoid confirming that they exist. But a warning should be sounded. Suspicion is a word that can be used to describe a state of mind that may, at one extreme, be no more than a vague feeling of unease and, at the other extreme, reflect a firm belief in the existence of the relevant facts. In my opinion, in order for there to be blind eye knowledge, the suspicion must be firmly grounded and targeted on specific facts. The deliberate decision must be a decision to avoid obtaining confirmation of facts in whose existence the individual has good reason to believe. To allow blind eye knowledge to be constituted by a decision not to enquire into an untargeted or speculative suspicion would be to allow negligence, albeit gross, to be the basis of finding of privity. That, in my opinion, is not warranted by s 39(5).

Even though the employment of an subjective test can be criticised on the basis that it might encourage slovenly and unprofessional behaviour on the part of the assured,[224] it is submitted that the wording of s 39(5) seems to favour a subjective test rather than an objective one.[225]

3.78   The second issue concerning privity is the identification of the person to whom the 'privity' requirement applies. If the assured is an individual who runs his own affairs, it is the knowledge of that individual that is relevant.[226] If the assured, on the other hand, is a company, it cannot attain knowledge simply because it is an artificial entity. In such a case, the task is to determine the extent to which knowledge of the servants of a company can be regarded as the knowledge of the company itself. A line of English case law appears to establish that the principles governing the attribution of knowledge to companies in these circumstances requires the search for the company's 'directing mind and will'. The accepted source of the abstract 'directing mind and will' test for attributing knowledge to a company is the opinion of Viscount Haldane LC in

---

222 [2001] 1 UKHL 1; [2003] 1 AC 469; [2001] 1 Lloyd's Rep 389, [114].
223 *Ibid*, [116].
224 Thomas, 2002, p 216.
225 See the difference in terms of wording between s 18(2), which employs an objective test, and s 39(5). In the latter case, the attention is focused upon the privity of the person in question.
226 Here, the word 'knowledge' has been used as including both the actual knowledge and the knowledge that could be expressed in the form of 'turning a blind eye'.

Lennard's Carrying Co Ltd v Asiatic Petroleum Co Ltd.[227] This test has been interpreted as requiring the court to search for the 'brain and nerve centre',[228] or the 'soul',[229] of the company. Accordingly, the 'directing mind and will' of a company is, generally, a person or persons in control of corporate policy. As such, a company's board of directors, or individual directors possessed of executive powers of management, may normally be regarded as the company's 'directing mind and will'.

3.79   In *Meridian Global Funds Management Asia Ltd v The Securities Commission,*[230] the Privy Council redirected attention away from the widely applied concept of the 'directing mind and will' of a company and offered a much more flexible 'functional' approach, focusing on the true construction of the particular substantive rule of law concerned. Lord Hoffmann suggested that the 'directing mind and will' test was not applicable on all occasions to all statutory provisions and, accordingly, whether the company has knowledge of a certain fact must be determined by the rules of attribution. His Lordship drew a distinction between primary, general and special (particular) rules of attribution. The primary rules of attribution, that is to say the acts specifically authorised by a resolution of the board of directors, or an unanimous agreement of shareholders, are generally to be found in the company's constitution, most typically in its articles of association. Some, on the other hand, are implied by company law. These primary rules, however, are supplemented by more general rules, rules that apply equally to individuals, such as agency and estoppel. However, there are cases where these rules may be inapplicable. The particular (specific) rule of law under consideration may, expressly or impliedly, rule out reliance on both the primary and the more general rules of attribution. 'For example, a rule may be stated in a language primarily applicable to a natural person and require some act or state of mind on the part of that person "himself" as opposed to its servants or agents.'[231] This is exactly the case in s 39(5) which reads as follows: '... but where, with the privity of the assured, the ship is sent to sea in an unseaworthy state ...'

In such cases, according to Lord Hoffmann, if it is decided that the substantive rule is, nevertheless, to be applied to companies, the court must fashion a special (particular) rule of attribution to determine whose knowledge was for this purpose intended to count as the act of the company.

3.80   Thus, such a special rule of attribution in respect of s 39(5) can be fashioned by applying the usual canons of interpretation and taking into account the language of the sub-section and its content and policy. Section 39(5) is available for the insurers in cases where the ship is sent to sea in an unseaworthy state with the knowledge of the assured. Therefore, after a careful literal construction of the sub-section, it is clear that

---

227 [1915] AC 705, p 714.
228 *HL Bolton (Engineering) Co Ltd v TJ Graham & Sons Ltd* [1957] 1 QB 159, p 171, *per* Denning LJ.
229 *Deutsche Genssenschaftsbank v Burnhope* [1995] BCC 488, p 492, *per* Staughtot LJ.
230 [1995] 2 AC 500.
231 *Ibid*, p 507.

the task is to find the interrelation between the process of sending the ship to sea and the persons in the company who have authority to do this.[232]

Accordingly, in cases where the assured is a company, it is necessary to identify the person or persons within the company, who are involved in the decision-making process required for sending the ship to sea. It is only the knowledge of these people regarding unseaworthy state of the vessel that can be attributable to the knowledge of the company. The test in this context is not to identify the person or persons within the company who have full discretion or autonomy in relation to acts or omissions in question. The knowledge of a junior manager, who has no authority in deciding to send the ship to sea, cannot be attributed to the assured company for the purposes of s 39(5). It is a question of fact in each case to determine whose knowledge within the company as to unseaworthiness of the vessel is attributable to the company.

3.81   The same test also applies in cases where the assured is a company that has appointed a ship management company to manage its ships. Such an appointment is usually carried out under the standard ship management contracts, such as the Baltic and International Maritime Council (BIMCO) Ship Management Form (Shipman).[233] The person or persons in the ship management company, which is involved in the decision-making process required for sending the ship to sea, must be identified. The knowledge of that person or persons within the ship management company as to the unseaworthy state of the vessel will be attributable to the knowledge of the assured company.[234]

3.82   The position is obviously more complicated where one corporation owns the ship and is, technically, 'the assured', but where the management and responsibility of

---

232 Whether the principles stated in *Meridian Global* could also apply to cases where the commission of a criminal offence is sought to be attributed to the company has recently been evaluated by the Court of Appeal in *Odyssey Re (London) Ltd and Another v OIC Run-Off Ltd (formerly Orion Insurance plc)* [2001] Lloyd's Rep IR 1. In that case, the claimant sought to have the judgment of Hirst, J, delivered in a related case, *Orion Insurance plc v Sphere Drake Insurance plc* [1990] 1 Lloyd's Rep 465, set aside on the ground that it was procured by fraud. It was alleged that the witness, who was the director of the defendant at the time the relevant agreement was made (in 1975), but not at the time of the trial (in 1989), committed perjury when giving evidence to Hirst J. Despite the findings of the first instance judge to the contrary, the Court of Appeal came to the conclusion that the witness had been guilty of perjury. Accordingly, the judgment of Hirst J could be set aside only if the claimant could show, as a matter of law, that the witness's evidence could, by reason of attribution, be treated as having been the evidence of the defendant company. Nourse and Brooke LJJ held that the witness's evidence was attributable to the defendant company. When reaching this decision, apart from other tests, Lord Hoffmann's functional approach was also held to be applicable, though the rule in question was a substantive rule of judge-made law, namely, the fraud of a party rule. Nourse LJ stated the test in this context in Lord Hoffmann's words, at p 11: 'Whose act [ie, giving of perjured evidence] was *for this purpose* intended to count as the act of the company.' Note that Buxton LJ dissented and stated that the rule in *Meridian Global* had no application when the criminal liability of corporations were concerned, at pp 91–97.

233 This standard contract was drafted in 1987 by a subcommittee of BIMCO and, now, is widely used. In particular, the 1998 version of the contract has been almost universally adopted in the Japanese market – the strongest 'new' ship management market of the past decade.

234 If the vessel is sent to sea in an unseaworthy state, with the knowledge of the ship management company, and this enables the insurers to bring a s 39(5) defence successfully, the managers might be liable to the assured company for breach of the management contract. The BIMCO Shipman, cl 18, eg, provides that the managers shall be under liability to the owners in cases where a loss has arisen from the negligence, gross negligence or wilful misconduct of the manager or his agents or subcontractors. In which case, the manager's liability for each incident shall be limited to a total 10 times the annual management fee. This limitation of the manager's liability will, however, not apply where the loss resulted from the manager's personal act or omission, committed with the intent to cause such loss, or recklessly and with knowledge that such loss, damage, delay or expense would probably result.

the ship has been placed in the hands of another corporation. This is usually the case in one-ship companies.[235] This situation was considered by the Court of Appeal in *The Star Sea*, where the assured was a one-ship company managed by Kappa, an English company based in London. The registered managers were Charterwell, a Greek company registered in Greece. Mr Faraklas was the sole director of the one-ship company. Captain Kollakis, Lou Kollakis, George Kollakis and Mr Nicholaidis were the directors of Kappa. Captain Kollakis and Mr Faraklas were the directors of Charterwell. The Court of Appeal had to determine whose knowledge, as to unseaworthiness, would be considered as the knowledge of the one-ship company for the purposes of s 39(5).

Although the court's task is more complicated when a one-ship company is involved, there is no difference in the test that will be applied. Again, the ultimate question is the identification of the persons who participated in the decision making process that resulted in the vessel being put to sea. The Court of Appeal suggested that, in each case, a circle must be drawn and the persons who have *de facto* management and control of the relevant aspect of the company's business (putting the vessel to sea) must be placed in that circle. The knowledge of persons in that circle about the unseaworthiness of the vessel will amount to knowledge of the company. Accordingly, it was held that the knowledge of directors of the management company, namely Captain Kollakis, Lou Kollakis, George Kollakis and Mr Nicholiadis and the sole director of the one-ship company, Mr Faraklas, could have been attributable to the knowledge of the one-ship company.[236]

3.83   The final unclear point in this context was whether the insurer would be exempted from liability for loss attributable to any kind of seaworthiness, or to the particular unseaworthiness to which the assured was privy when he sent the ship to sea. The answer to this question is crucial, especially if the ship is sent to sea in an unseaworthy state in two respects, the assured being privy to the one and not privy to the other, and the ship is lost due to the unseaworthiness which he is not privy. Here, it could be said that the assured should recover as he was not aware of the unseaworthiness that caused the loss; but it is equally possible to argue that, as the vessel was sent to sea in an unseaworthy condition with the privity of the assured and the loss was attributable to unseaworthiness, the plain wording of s 39(5) precludes recovery.[237]

This question arose in *Thomas v Tyne & Wear SS Freight Insurance Association*.[238] In this case, the vessel was put to sea in an unseaworthy condition by reason of the state

---

235 The one-ship company is a way of organising the maritime enterprise, which presents great advantages for maritime entrepreneurs. The essential feature of a one-ship company is that it has a distinct personality from the persons which formed it and, as a result of this, the company has the capacity to conduct business and to sue and be sued in its own name. Furthermore, a one-ship company's property is owned by the company as a separate entity and not by the members that formed it. Accordingly, the members of the company are not personally liable for the latter's debts and, if the company becomes insolvent, its members stand to lose only the amount of their investment in the company.

236 The House of Lords did not disturb the findings of the Court of Appeal on this point.

237 Interestingly, s 39(5) adopts the word 'unseaworthy' and not 'unseaworthiness'. This might be interpreted as allowing the insurer to rely on this provision in cases where the ship is sent to sea in an unseaworthy state, despite the fact the assured is not privy to this particular situation.

238 [1917] KB 938.

of the hull and, also, an inadequate crew. The assured was privy to inadequacy of the crew, but not to the state of the hull; the vessel was lost due to the state of the hull. Atkin J adopted the former approach and held the insurers liable. Consequently, the assured must be privy to the particular, or actual, unseaworthiness that results in loss before he will be debarred from recovery. It is submitted that Atkin J construed the sub-section accurately and reached the right decision. The intention behind s 39(5) was that the assured should be unable to recover in respect of a loss occasioned by his own fault. If, therefore, a loss occurs as a result of a factor to which the assured was not privy, he should be able to recover even though he was privy to another factor, which could cause the loss, but did not.

3.84   Similarly, if the vessel is unseaworthy in more than one aspect and the loss is caused by operation of both of them, 'privity to both aspects of unseaworthiness' is necessary for the application of s 39(5). This was highlighted, in *The Star Sea*, by Leggatt LJ,[239] who held that the assured was not privy to one aspect of the unseaworthiness that caused the loss, namely, the incompetence of the master and, for this reason, it was unnecessary for the court to go further to attend to the second aspect of unseaworthiness suffered by the vessel.[240]

(iii)   Loss attributable to unseaworthiness and causation problem

3.85   If a vessel suffers a loss as a result of her being sent to sea in an unseaworthy state, s 39(5) can only operate where that loss is attributable to the unseaworthiness. Seaworthiness and causation is, therefore, directly relevant in time policies. In marine insurance, the causation problem was solved by the *proximate cause* doctrine. Accordingly, s 55(1) stipulates as follows:

> Subject to the provisions of this Act, and unless the policy otherwise provides, the insurer is liable for any loss *proximately* caused by a peril insured against.

In the light of this provision, in cases where there are two or more possible causes of loss, an insurer is liable for a loss if it is *proximately* caused by a peril insured against. For a considerable period of time the principle of *causa proxima* was applied in different ways in marine insurance. According to one point of view, which applied in *Pink v Fleming*,[241] only the last cause must be looked to and the others rejected in determining the *proximate cause*. Another school of thought had looked for what was 'efficient' and 'predominant' as the *proximate cause*. This was applied by the Court of Appeal in *Reischer v Borwick*.[242] The school of thought that uses time as the criterion in determining the *proximate cause* is open to a fatal objection. The last event that occurred in the chain is not necessarily the main cause of the loss. Besides, in many cases, the last event would not have occurred if the previous event or events had been avoided. The law in this area was uncertain and contradictory until the celebrated case of *Leyland Shipping Co Ltd v Norwich Union Fire Insurance Society Ltd*.[243] In this case, the House of Lords conclusively settled the law of *proximate cause* under s 55(1). The decision in *Reischer v Borwick* was approved and the *proximate cause* was held to be the

---

239 [1997] 1 Lloyd's Rep 360, p 378.
240 The findings of the Court of Appeal on this point were not challenged on appeal.
241 (1890) 25 QBD 396, p 397, *per* Lord Esher MR.
242 [1894] 2 QB 548.
243 [1918] AC 350, hereafter referred to as *The Leyland* case.

cause which was *proximate* in efficiency.[244] By equating the *proximate cause* with that which is efficient, real and dominant, the law has, in effect, invited judges to weight the causes of loss to determine their strength, influence and predominance. Under this rule, it is possible for there to be more than one *proximate cause*, while there would be only one under the last in time approach.[245]

3.86   However, in s 39(5), the causation problem has been addressed with the phrase 'attributable to'.[246] What is meant by this phrase and why did Sir Mackenzie Chalmers abandon the phrase '*proximately* caused by' when drafting s 39(5)? The adoption of the phrase 'attributable to', in the context of seaworthiness, can be readily comprehended given that the Act was drafted toward the end of the 19th century, when the last in time approach to causal proximity was in fashion.[247] If, therefore, the phrase '*proximately caused* by' was used in s 39(5), as a result of the dominant causation theory of that time, the last in time theory, the insurer would not be able to rely on a s 39(5) defence in many cases. For example, if a loss was caused by entry of sea water due to the unseaworthy state of the hull, the *proximate cause* of the loss would have been held to be 'perils of the seas' and, accordingly, the insurer would have been deprived of the s 39(5) defence. In addition to this, in the 19th century, a linear view of causation was dominating the law of causation. On this approach, the peril of the sea used to rank as the *proximate cause*, as that which was last in time, and the unseaworthiness was regarded as causally remote. Even though the unseaworthiness was accepted as continuing to operate through the occurrence of the loss, the peril of the sea was viewed as a separate operative loss.[248] For instance, in *Redman v Wilson*,[249] negligent loading of cargo rendered a vessel unseaworthy, leading the master to run the vessel ashore in order to save both vessel and cargo. The insurers were held liable for a loss immediately caused by a peril of the sea (viz stranding), with negligence being regarded as remote and the unseaworthiness receiving no causation mention. For these reasons, a different causal formula was required to permit the courts to look behind the cause most immediate in point of time.

3.87   After *The Leyland* case, as illustrated above, there had been dramatic changes in the law of causation. The courts began to look for the dominant or efficient cause or causes, when determining the *proximate cause* of a loss. Thus, more than one cause can

---

244 *Ibid*, p 369, Lord Shaw illustrated his understanding of the law of *proximate cause* in the following words: 'To treat *proxima causa* as the cause which is nearest in time is out of the question. Causes are spoken of as if they were distinct from one another as beads in a row or links in a chain, but – if this metaphysical topic has to be referred to – it is not wholly so. The chain of causation is a handy expression, but the figure is inadequate. Causation is not a chain, but a net. At each point influences, forces, events, precedent and simultaneous, meet; and the radiation from each point extends infinitely. At the point where these various influences meet, it is for the judgment as upon a matter of fact to declare which of the causes, thus, joint at the point of effect was the *proximate* and which was the remote cause ... What does *"proximate"* here mean? To treat *proximate* cause as if it was the cause which is *proximate* in time is, as I have said, out of the question. The cause which is truly *proximate* is that which is *proximate* in efficiency.'

245 The principle of *The Leyland* case [1918] AC 350 was subsequently applied in two House of Lords decisions, namely, *Board of Trade v Hain SS Co Ltd* [1929] AC 534 and *Yorkshire Dale SS Co Ltd v Minister of War Transport (The Coxwold)* [1942] AC 691.

246 The situation is the same in the context of the defence of wilful misconduct in s 55(2)(a).

247 *Pink v Fleming* (1890) 25 QBD 396.

248 See, Thomas, Volume 1, 1996, p 192.

249 (1845) 14 M & W 482.

be held to be the *proximate cause* and, in this sense, there is nothing preventing the courts from regarding unseaworthiness as the sole *proximate cause*, or one of the *proximate causes* of the loss.[250] This change in the legal approach does not affect the situation in respect of s 39(5). The phrase 'attributable to' must be viewed as having always been held to be synonymous with the *proximate* in efficiency test. The application of s 39(5) when seaworthiness is a *proximate* cause, or the *proximate cause* of the loss, together with the possible causation problems and how they are addressed, will be discussed next with reference to the case law.

3.88   If unseaworthiness is found to be a *proximate cause* (one of the *proximate causes*) of the loss, the assured will be precluded from recovery if he is privy to this specific unseaworthiness when the vessel is sent to sea. If, however, the assured is not privy to the specific unseaworthiness that was a *proximate cause* of the loss, the insurer will be precluded from bringing a s 39(5) defence and the general principles of causation determine whether the assured will be indemnified for the loss or not. In such a case, if unseaworthiness is a *proximate cause* of the loss with another *proximate cause* of equal or nearly equal efficiency, then the insurer must indemnify the assured in cases where the other *proximate* cause comes within the terms of the policy. The reason for this is that unseaworthiness is not expressly excluded by the policy and other *proximate causes* of the loss are expressly covered by the policy. This principle is derived from one of the most famous marine insurance cases of the 1980s, *The Miss Jay Jay*.[251] In that case, the subject matter of the insurance was a fast and luxurious motor yacht. In the event, it proved that the class of boats of which *The Miss Jay Jay* formed part was, by design and construction, quite unfitted for this purpose and, when this particular example met some nasty weather on the way back from Le Havre, large sections of the hull peeled off, happily without fatal results. It was held that the owner was entitled to recover under the policy insuring against losses caused by 'external accidental means', notwithstanding that the boat was obviously unseaworthy on sailing.[252]

On the other hand, underwriters can deny liability when unseaworthiness is a *proximate* cause of the loss with another *proximate* cause of equal, or nearly equal efficiency and the other *proximate* cause of the loss is expressly excluded by the policy. This principle was well settled in insurance law long before the judgment in *The Miss Jay Jay*. In the case of *Board of Trade v Hain SS Co Ltd*,[253] the House of Lords, in relation to a dispute under a charterparty, expressed the view that, if a loss is 'the product of two causes, joint and simultaneous', and one of the causes is expressly excluded by an exclusion clause, the insurers are not liable. Similarly, in a case concerned directly with insurance, albeit not marine, *Wayne Tank & Pump Co Ltd v Employer's Liability Insurance*

250 Accordingly, in *Frangos v Sun Insurance Office Ltd* (1934) 49 LlL Rep 354; *Monarch SS Co Ltd v Karlshamns Olie Fabriker* [1947] AC 196; and, more recently, in *The Miss Jay Jay* [1987] 1 Lloyd's Rep 32 (CA), seaworthiness was held to be one of the *proximate* causes of the loss.
251 [1987] 1 Lloyd's Rep 32 (CA).
252 *Ibid*. This principle was laid down in *The Miss Jay Jay*, by Lord Justice Lawton, as follows: 'It now seems settled law, at least as far as this court is concerned, that, if there are two concurrent and effective causes of a marine loss, and one comes within the terms of the policy and the other does not, the insurers must pay.'
253 [1929] AC 554.

Corp Ltd,[254] an exception was held to take priority over the general words of a policy.[255] Such a situation may arise when a ship is lost due to the unseaworthiness resulting from ordinary wear and tear. Ordinary wear and tear is excluded in policies by virtue of s 55(2)(c), provided that the policy does not state otherwise. None of the modern time policies on hulls provide otherwise, so, in a case like this, the underwriter can deny liability.

3.89   There may be some cases in which unseaworthiness is the sole *proximate cause* of the loss. For example, if a vessel with an unseaworthy hull takes on water or sustains damage on encountering only ordinary risks simply because of the defective character of the hull, the only *proximate cause* of the loss is unseaworthiness. In cases like this, even if the assured is privy to the unseaworthiness when she was sent to sea, the insurer does not need to bring s 39(5) defence to avoid liability simply because unseaworthiness is not a peril insured against in time policies. To invoke s 39(5), the loss has to be covered by the policy. This principle was laid down in *Fawcus v Sarsfield*.[256] In this case, the vessel, without encountering any more than ordinary risks, was obliged because of her defective state when she set sail to put into port for repair. The court ruled that, as the sole *proximate cause* of loss was unseaworthiness, which was not a peril insured against, the assured failed in their claim.[257]

3.90   One might be tempted to argue along the lines that the common law situation existing before the enactment of the MIA 1906 has been altered by s 39(5). This argument can be supported on the strict literal construction of the sub-section. Section 39(5) provides that the insurer is not liable for losses *proximately* caused by the unseaworthiness of the vessel with the privity of the assured. This wording does not make a distinction between unseaworthiness being the only *proximate cause* or one of the *proximate causes*. This must mean that s 39(5) can also operate in cases where the unseaworthiness is the sole *proximate cause* of the loss. The result of the construction of s 39(5), in the way stated above, is that the insurers will be liable for any loss solely caused by unseaworthiness of the vessel in time policies, provided that the assured is not privy to such unseaworthiness.[258] This argument was brought into discussion by an Irish case, *Ashworth v General Accident & Fire & Life Assurance Corp*.[259] In this case, the Supreme Court of Ireland held that the sole *proximate cause* of the loss was unseaworthiness, but differed in their findings as regards the question of privity. The

---

254 [1974] QB 57. *Board of Trade v Hain SS Co Ltd* [1929] AC 534, was cited with approval by Lord Denning MR.
255 The same approach can be observed in the pre-statute case *Cory v Burr* (1883) 8 App Cas 393, decided by the House of Lords, in respect of marine insurance. Lord Sumner said much of the same thing in his dissenting speech in *Samuel & Co Ltd v Dumas* [1924] AC 431, p 467. 'Where a loss is caused by two perils operating simultaneously at the time of loss, and one is wholly excluded because the policy is warranted free of it, the question is whether it can be derived that the loss was so caused, for, if not, warranty operates.' This passage was approved by Morris LJ, in *Atlantic Maritime Co Inc v Gibbon* [1954] 1 QB 88, p 138.
256 (1856) 6 E & B 192, p 204.
257 See, also, *Ballantyne v Mackinnon* [1896] 2 QB 455, where the Court of Appeal held that: '... the loss complained of arose solely by reason of the inherent vice of the subject matter insured which was not a risk insured against. Accordingly, the insurers cannot recover under the policy.'
258 Arnould has construed s 39(5) in a similar way; Arnould, 1981, para 718.
259 [1955] IR 268, hereafter referred to as *The Ashworth* case.

majority, which found that the assured was aware of the condition of the ship in all aspects that made her unseaworthy, held that the loss was not recoverable. The judges did not expressly pronounce that s 39(5) was applicable in cases where unseaworthiness was the only *proximate cause* of the loss, but they rejected the claim on the ground that the assured was privy to the unseaworthiness that caused the loss. This shows that they were of the opinion that this sub-section could afford indemnity to the assured in cases where unseaworthiness is the sole *proximate cause* of the loss and the assured is not privy to this unseaworthiness.

3.91   Such a finding seems to contradict basic principles of marine insurance. Section 55(1) clearly provides that, subject to the provisions of this Act and unless the policy otherwise provides, an insurer is liable for any loss which is *proximately* caused by a peril insured against. This means that, unless there is a specific provision in the Act or in the policy, the insurer is not liable for any loss which is *proximately caused* by a peril uninsured against. There is no specific provision in the modern standard time policies suggesting that the insurer is liable for the loss caused by unseaworthiness.[260] Then, *The Ashworth* case suggests that s 39(5) is one of the exceptions to the general rule of causation stated in s 55(1). When the comments of Mackenzie Chalmers, the drafter of the Act, and the Parliament discussions are examined, it can be clearly seen that it was not the intention of the drafter to make s 39(5) one of the exception provisions of the Act stated in s 55(1). Furthermore, an outcome of this nature could be challenged by considering the logic behind s 39(5). The intention was that this sub-section would preclude the assured from recovery in respect of a loss occasioned by his own fault. If, however, s 39(5) is construed in the way the judges in *The Ashworth* case and Arnould suggested, the assured is somewhat rewarded as he is entitled to be indemnified for losses caused by a peril that is not insured against in the policy. Such a result is, obviously, beyond the intended ambit of this sub-section.[261]

3.92   Considering all the arguments advanced above, it can be concluded that s 39(5), as worded, should not be read as capable of imposing liability upon an insurer

---

260 The position is, however, different when a vessel is rendered unseaworthy, due to a latent defect in her hull or machinery or negligence of the crew, and such unseaworthiness is found to be the only *proximate cause* of the loss. In such cases, modern marine policies (cl 6.2.2 of the ITCH (1995)) provide cover unless such loss or damage has resulted from want of due diligence by the assured, owner or manager. Therefore, if the assured is not privy to such a situation, he should be indemnified under the policy. See *Coast Ferries Ltd v Century Insurance Co of Canada & Others (The Brentwood)* [1973] 2 Lloyd's Rep 232, where unseaworthiness caused by wrong loading, for which the master was to blame, was found to be the *proximate cause* of the loss. In that case, the Court of Appeal of British Columbia was prepared to hold the underwriters liable under the policies, unless the owner was privy to the master's negligence within the meaning of s 41(5) (same as s 39(5) of the MIA 1906), since such unseaworthiness was covered by cl 2 of the policy, which was worded as follows: '(2) This insurance specially to cover (subject to the average warranty) loss of or damage to the subject matter insured directly caused by the following – ... negligence of masters, charterers other than an assured, mariners, engineers or pilots; provided such loss or damage has not resulted from want of due diligence by the assured, the owners or managers of the vessel ...' The assured was not privy to the master's negligence, but the Court of Appeal held that on evidence the loss had resulted from want of due diligence on their part within the meaning of cl 2, so they were refused indemnity.

261 This kind of construction of s 39(5) was also criticised by Black J, in his dissenting judgment in *The Ashworth* case [1955] IR 268, p 293, in which he said that: '... whether the action of the sea upon the ship in question at any material time constituted a peril of the sea at all; for if it did not, no time need be wasted on the other question, since the loss would not be covered by the policy.'

for a risk that he has not, under the contract of insurance, specially agreed to insure. Its use has to be limited to the particular case where the loss is, *prima facie*, recoverable under the policy in question. Therefore, it is not wrong to say that the law in this area has not been altered by the enactment of s 39(5) and, if unseaworthiness is the sole *proximate cause* of the loss, then the insurer is deprived of liability, since unseaworthiness is not a peril insured against.

(D)   Mixed policies

3.93   The concluding sentence of s 25(1) states that a contract for both voyage and time may be included in the same policy. Such a policy is called a mixed policy and is generally effected in respect of vessels. A mixed policy usually insures the hull, etc, of a vessel for a voyage and, by agreement, for a certain period after her arrival at the port of destination.[262] There was no authority deciding whether a warranty of seaworthiness had been implied into a mixed policy until *Almojil (M) Establishment v Malayan Motor & General Underwriters (Private) Ltd (The Al-Jubail IV)*.[263] In this case, a vessel was insured for a voyage from Singapore to the Persian Gulf and 12 months from her arrival, while trading within the Persian Gulf. On her voyage from Singapore to the Persian Gulf, she was capsized. The underwriters denied liability on the ground that the vessel was not seaworthy at the commencement of the voyage. The Singapore Court of Appeal considered the logic behind the implied warranty of seaworthiness in voyage policies, when reaching a decision on this point. The reason why the warranty of seaworthiness is implied in the case of voyage policies is that an assured is usually in control and possession of a vessel before she embarks on a voyage and, in this respect, is capable of rendering her seaworthy. In a mixed policy, as far as the voyage stage is concerned, the assured is in possession and control of the vessel and this part of the cover has all the attributes of a voyage policy. The Court of Appeal, accordingly, held that the warranty of seaworthiness was implied in mixed policies in respect of the voyage part of the cover, even though this was not expressly stated by the MIA 1906.[264] The solution adopted by the Singapore Court of Appeal is full of sense and should, also, have application in English marine insurance law.

(E)   P&I club cover

3.94   It has always been the intention of the P&I clubs to cover the liabilities of the shipowners that are not covered by hull and machinery policies. The principal cover provided by the P&I clubs falls generally into the following categories: cargo claims, collision claims (not covered under the three-fourths collision liability clause in the hull and machinery policy), contact with fixed and floating objects, personal injury

---

262 A policy covering a vessel for a period of time within certain specified geographical limits is, however, a time policy and not a mixed policy. See the Australian case of *Wilson v Boag Sup Ct NSW* [1956] 2 Lloyd's Rep 564.

263 [1982] 2 Lloyd's Rep 637.

264 The MIA 1906 has been enacted into the domestic legislation in Singapore.

claims, wreck raising, pollution and clean up costs, crew claims, passenger claims, port charges, life salvage, some towage costs, and general average contributions that are irrecoverable under the hull policy.[265] The provisions regarding seaworthiness have a role to play in the cover offered by the P&I clubs. In *The Eurysthenes*, the Court of Appeal held that the contract between the club and the owners was a time policy within the meaning of s 25. Since entry into a P&I club is regarded as a time policy, then the member of the club is subject to s 39(5) and might lose his P&I cover if he sends the vessel to sea in an unseaworthy condition knowing the state of the vessel.[266] The parties to a contract of insurance can expressly, or impliedly, contract out of the operation of s 39(5). Therefore, the rules of a club may exclude the application of s 39(5).[267] However, this would only occur if the rules of the club are such that they exclude or contradict the sub-section, or render its implied inclusion nonsensical. It was held, in *The Eurysthenes*, that a club rule, which contains a promise by the association to indemnify a member against liability for damage to cargo arising out of unseaworthiness and unfitness of the entered vessel, was not sufficient to suppose that the application of s 39(5) was excluded. A more express, pertinent and apposite language is required to contract out of the operation of s 39(5).

(F)   Burden of proof in unseaworthiness allegations

3.95   As a general rule, the insurer carries the burden of proving a vessel unseaworthy at the relevant time.[268] Therefore, if the insurers claim that the seaworthiness warranty was breached, they are under an obligation to show that the vessel was unseaworthy at the relevant time. Similarly, in time policies, in order to be able to successfully bring a s 39(5) defence, the insurer must prove that the ship was unseaworthy when she was sent to sea and the assured were privy to this unseaworthiness.

3.96   Where, however, a ship soon after sailing starts leaking, becomes disabled, or sinks without apparent cause and this cannot be ascribed to any violent storm or other adequate cause, there is a presumption of fact that it arose from unseaworthiness at the commencement of the voyage and the burden of proof is then shifted to the assured. The reluctance of the Court of Appeal to raise the presumption of unseaworthiness can clearly be seen in *Pickup v Thames & Mersey Marine Insurance Co*,[269] where the vessel had to put back to port 11 days after sailing. The court held that the facts of the case did not raise the 'irresistible inference' that the ship was unseaworthy when she sailed. The trial judge was held to have misdirected the jury when he instructed them that the mere fact that the ship had returned to port so soon after sailing was, in itself, sufficient to raise the presumption that she was unseaworthy at the time of sailing. All the

---

265 Legal expenses in defending claims are often separately covered by clubs, under Freight Demurrage and Defence Rules.
266 Club rules, generally, provide with express terms that the club may avoid liability in respect of claims that have arisen by virtue of the unseaworthiness of the vessel where the member was privy to such unseaworthiness.
267 None of the the modern P&I clubs, however, contract out of s 39(5) in their rules.
268 *Davidson v Burnard* (1868) LR 4 CP 117 and *Hoffmann (C) & Co v British Insurance Co* (1922) 10 LlL Rep 434.
269 (1878) 3 QBD 594.

judges in the Court of Appeal agreed on the fact that time cannot, of itself, without more, give rise to the presumption that shifts the onus of proof. Time is only one of the factors and of 'secondary consideration'. They also emphasised the fact that, if the circumstances of the case are such that, '... it is possible to ascribe the result to any other cause than the condition of the vessel on starting on the voyage' the presumption cannot be invoked. As a final point, the Court warned that it is in each case a question of fact, not of law, for the jury to draw the necessary inference.[270] Again, in *Lindsay v Klein (The Tatjana)*,[271] Lord Shaw fully acknowledged that the burden of proving unseaworthiness lay on the party so alleging, but affirmed that this principle of law in no way impaired 'certain presumptions of fact' arising from, for example, the age, admitted defects and classification, or absence of classification or survey of the ship, generally poor and deteriorating record of the vessel and breakdown of machinery immediately, or almost immediately, after sailing.[272]

3.97   In the United States, however, the sinking of a vessel in calm water gives rise to a presumption of unseaworthiness (a presumption of law) that denies recovery, unless either the assured can adduce rebuttal evidence of seaworthiness that will, in turn, arise a counterpresumption of loss by perils of the sea, or the unseaworthiness caused by a latent defect or act covered by the Inchmaree Clause.[273]

IV – POTENTIAL LEGAL IMPLICATIONS OF RECENT DEVELOPMENTS ON PROVISIONS RELATING TO SEAWORTHINESS

3.98   Enhancing safety at sea has always been a priority for the maritime industry. This was the underlying theme behind the development of the SOLAS Convention 1974, which has been adopted and ratified by the vast majority of the world's flag states, covering about 96% of the world's merchant tonnage. The tacit amendment procedure of the SOLAS 1974 makes it a very suitable regulatory framework that is equipped to deal with contemporary problems maritime industry might face.

---

270 The Court of Appeal took the opportunity to clarify the decision of *Watson v Clark* (1813) 1 Dow 336, which has sometimes been cited as having laid down the rule that the presumption was one of law and that the mere fact that a ship had to return to port shortly after leaving it was in itself sufficient to raise a presumption of unseaworthiness. What Lord Eldon did, in fact, say in that case was that: '... if a ship was seaworthy at the commencement of the voyage, though she became otherwise only one hour after, still the warranty was complied with and the underwriter was liable.'

271 [1911] AC 194.

272 See, also, *Ajum Goolam Hossen & Co v Union Marine Insurance Co* [1901] AC 362, where a ship inexplicably capsized and sank just 24 hours after leaving the Port Louis, but again insufficient evidence was presented to make an 'irresistible inference' of unseaworthiness.

273 See *Capital Coastal Shipping Corp v Hartford Fire Insurance Co (The Cristie)* [1975] 2 Lloyd's Rep 199; *The Ettore* [1933] AMC 323; *The Doyle* [1939] AMC 852; *The Ionian Pioneer* [1956] AMC 1780; *The Southern Sword* [1956] AMC 1518. The situation is exactly the same in Norwegian law. The Norwegian Marine Insurance Plan 1996, s 3–22 provides that, in cases where the ship springs a leak whilst afloat, the burden of proof of seaworthiness shifts to the assured. This formulation of American and Norwegian laws, however, goes beyond English law.

Over the last two decades the maritime industry has faced two challenges. In the 1990s, there was a general concern about the impact of human fault on maritime casualties. Official figures for shipping casualties[274] and insurance reports[275] confirmed that human error was the principal cause of almost 80% of all shipping accidents. In similar vein, human error was at the heart of several maritime tragedies, which had destructive effects on the marine environment, such as *The Exxon Valdez*.[276] It, therefore, became clear to the interested parties that drastic measures had to be taken to allow the industry to address the problem of the human element. The response of the industry was the introduction of the ISM Code by the IMO. This Code focuses on the management of shipping companies and requires them to make use of and develop a standard management system.

At the turn of the millennium, terrorist attacks on the World Trade Center have changed the way states deal with security matters. It was felt that the maritime sector was vulnerable to terrorist attacks and that there was a danger that ships could be used by terrorists in their fight against the civilized world. Again, the IMO was entrusted with the task of preparing a framework that would enhance maritime safety and security, particularly against terrorism. The outcome was the ISPS Code.

Both of these Codes have been made part of the SOLAS Convention 1974 via the tacit amendment procedure of the Convention. It is the feeling of the author that a detailed analysis on seaworthiness could not be completed without considering the potential legal implications of these international developments on provisions relating to seaworthiness. Therefore, the object of the final part of this chapter is to conduct a through analysis of this point.

(A) Potential legal implications of the ISMC on the provisions relating to seaworthiness

(a) Introduction

3.99   In order to minimise the human error in shipping operations, there was a need to create a culture of self-regulation of safety. In other words, it was essential to concentrate on internal management and organisation for safety and encourage individual industries and companies to establish targets for safety performance. By

---

274 In 1980 the British Department of Transport entrusted the first research into the influence of human factors in shipping casualties to the Tavistock Institute of Human Relations. The report prepared for this Institute, by Bryant, De Bievre and Dyer-Smith (1988), revealed that 90% of collisions and 75% of fires and explosions occurring in the British merchant fleet from 1970–79 were caused by human error. A similar study was carried out in Germany by the Institute of Shipping Economics and Logistics in 1994. As a result of an analysis of 380 accidents occurring between 1987 and 1991, concerning 481 merchant ships, it emerged from the report that 75% of these accidents were caused by either heavy workloads for the crew, particularly in port, and inadequate specialised training. See, also, Donaldson, 1994.

275 A survey published in West of England P&I Club Annual Revision 1992, pp 34–35, illustrates that 65% of all compensation claims submitted to this club between 1987 and 1992 were due to human error. Dangerous practices, mainly by the crew alone, were responsible for nearly a quarter of insurance claims.

276 Following a navigational error, *The Exxon Valdez* ran aground on Bligh Reef, tearing its hull and spilling 40,000 tonnes of crude oil into the sea. Nine hours after the accident, the National Transport Safety Board carried out alcohol tests on the ship personnel and the captain was found to be over the limit.

looking at the practices of the industry for a solution, IMO came to the conclusion that a quality assurance system, similar to that of ISO 9000, could help in minimising human error. ISO 9000 was developed by the International Organisation for Standardisation and was originally designed for the needs of production originated companies.[277] Its object is to improve safety standards in the companies and, thus, limit eventual damages to employees and other people. By taking ISO 9000 as a model, the Marine Safety Committee of the IMO designed the ISM Code for shipping companies in 1993.[278]

(b) Implementation and scope of the ISMC

3.100   The ISM Code was drafted as a self-contained document. Its provisions were, in effect, brought into force internationally when, at the SOLAS Conference in 1994, compliance with the Code became mandatory under a new Chapter IX to the SOLAS Convention. The Code became mandatory for passenger ships, high speed vessels, tankers, bulk carriers and gas carriers of more than 500 gross tons from 1 July 1998,[279] and for all cargo ships of more than 500 gross tons from 1 July 2002.[280]

3.101   The ISM Code is mainly concerned with the procedures whereby a ship is managed, both on board and ashore. The shipping company must define and document the levels of authority and lines of communication between the ship and shore and the roles of all personnel involved in safety issues and, in this way, establish a safety management system (SMS) in respect of each vessel.[281] There must be adequate shore-based personnel and, perhaps most importantly, there must be a 'designated person' onshore, to provide a link with the vessel, who has direct access to the highest levels of management within the company.[282] The company must also define and document numerous issues relating to the responsibilities and authority of the master for safety and environmental matters and training of the master and others on board.[283] There are key provisions of the Code dealing with the development, verification, reporting and auditing plans for the shipboard operations, emergency preparedness, reporting hazardous or emergency situations and accidents.[284] Finally, the Code contains provisions dealing with the systems required for ensuring the maintenance of the ship and her equipment generally.[285]

---

277 Some shipping companies had implemented the requirements of the ISO 9000 voluntarily before the implementation of the ISMC was made mandatory.

278 Discussions on this issue started as early as April 1988, one year after *The Herald of Free Enterprise* disaster. The Maritime Safety Committee, during its 55th session, called for the development of guidelines on safe ship management.

279 The provisions of the ISMC has been implemented into English law by the Merchant Shipping (International Safety Management (ISM) Code) Regulations 1998 SI 1998/1561.

280 However, the Council of the European Union adopted the ISMC on 8 December 1995 and declared that it should be mandatory for the owners of ro-ro ferries operating a regular service to or from a part of a Member State of the European Community with effect from 1 July 1996: Council Regulation (EC) 3051/95.

281 See Arts 1.3, 1.4, 2 and 3.

282 See Arts 3.3 and 4.

283 See Arts 5 and 6.

284 See Arts 7, 8, 9 and 12.

285 See Art 10.

(c)   Implications of the ISM Code on provisions relating to seaworthiness

(i)   Implications of the ISMC on the implied warranty of seaworthiness

3.102   As examined above,[286] s 39(1) imposes an implied warranty of seaworthiness in respect of voyage policies. Accordingly, at the commencement of the voyage, the vessel must be seaworthy for the purpose of the particular adventure insured. Seaworthiness is a relative term which extends, not only to the physical condition of the vessel, but also to other aspects of the ship, such as adequacy of fuel, sufficiency of the crew and even stability. Compliance with the ISM Code does not establish that a particular vessel is seaworthy in all aspects. A ship which has a satisfactory SMS and complies with the requirements of the ISM Code may still be unseaworthy due to a latent defect in her hull. Compliance with the ISM Code, therefore, is not conclusive evidence of seaworthiness.

3.103   On the other hand, as the ISM Code has been made mandatory by the SOLAS Convention, the standard of seaworthiness with which the vessel must comply is now to be tested against the requirements of the Code. Thus, there is a strong possibility that an English court will find a ship unseaworthy if she fails to comply with the requirements of the ISM Code. If, for example, the vessel does not have a satisfactory SMS (for example, she lacks a safety management certificate or safety and environmental protection policy), she might be considered unseaworthy. Similarly, in cases where a satisfactory SMS is in place, but the owner or operator has failed to comply with it on the occasion in question, it may be argued that the ship is unseaworthy. Consequently, in voyage policies, non-compliance with the requirements of the ISM Code at the commencement of the voyage may render a ship unseaworthy and the insurers are discharged from liability unless the implied warranty of seaworthiness has expressly been waived.

3.104   It has to be noted that no judicial view has yet been given on the potential impact of the ISM Code on seaworthiness by British courts. There is, however, clear indications that the Code will be relevant to any inquiry into matters of seaworthiness in years to come. Cresswell J, for instance, commented on the ISM Code in *The Eurasian Dream* in the following manner:[287]

> ... the ISM Code ... is a framework upon which good practices should be hung. Even for companies – or for that matter vessels – who waited until the last minute to apply for certification the principles are so general and so good that a prudent manager/master could very well organise their companies/vessels work following those [at present] guidelines – unless hindered to do so by other instructions that have yet been withdrawn.[288]

(ii)   Burden of proof in unseaworthiness allegations

3.105   When underwriters intend to bring an unseaworthiness defence, as a general principle, they carry the burden of proof that the vessel was unseaworthy at the

---

286 See [3.51] to [3.64].
287 [2002] EWCH 118 (Comm); [2002] 1 Lloyd's Rep 719, [143].
288 The ISM Code was not determinative on the outcome of the case as the vessel in question, a car-carrier, was not at the time of the casualty required to be certificated.

relevant time.[289] This has caused difficulties for insurers on many occasions in the past, but it might become easier with the ISM Code. The Code imposes substantial requirements on shipowners to produce and maintain documents and data relevant to the SMS. The requirements invoke systems for dealing with reporting, filing, correcting and verifying deficiencies.[290]

The documentary and filing procedures will, undoubtedly, make it easier for underwriters to prove unseaworthiness by obtaining information and documentation regarding shipboard operations, including instances in which the vessel failed to comply with the SMS. Such documentation and information will, almost certainly, be discoverable in litigation, as r 31(6) of the Civil Procedure Rules (CPR) 1998 makes obligatory the disclosure of such documents by the assured.[291]

(iii) Section 39(5) of the MIA 1906

3.106   As examined in detail above,[292] s 39(5) clearly states that there is no implied warranty of seaworthiness in time policies. However, if the vessel is sent to sea in an unseaworthy state with the privity of the assured, the underwriter is not liable for any loss attributable to unseaworthiness. The ISM Code might have a considerable impact on this provision as it obliges every ship operating or managing company to designate a person or persons ashore who have direct access to the highest level of management. The designated person must monitor the safety and pollution prevention aspects of the operation of each ship. Under a satisfactory SMS, therefore, the designated person must have all relevant information about the recent condition of the vessel.

3.107   The interesting question that has been raised in this context is whether the privity of the designated person about the unseaworthy state of the vessel when she is sent to sea would constitute privity of the assured for the purpose of s 39(5). In other words, can the designated person be considered to be the 'directing mind and will' of the assured company for the purposes of this sub-section?

As examined earlier, the Privy Council, in *Meridian Global Funds Management Asia Ltd v Securities Commission*,[293] brought a new dimension to the discussion by attracting attention to the rules of attribution of a company. In this respect, a special rule of attribution must be fashioned to determine 'whose knowledge' is, for the purpose of s 39(5), intended to count as the knowledge of the company. The knowledge, for the purpose of s 39(5), is the knowledge of the person who is involved in the process of sending the ship to sea. A careful analysis of the Code reveals the fact that the designated person can under no circumstances be regarded as a person who is

---

289 See, above [3.95] to [3.97].
290 Section 9.1, eg, establishes requirements for reporting, investigating and analysing non-conformities, accidents and hazardous situations. See, also, ss 9.2, 9.3, 10.2, 11 and 12.
291 Rule 31(6) of the CPR 1998 provides that: 'Standard disclosure requires a party to disclose only: a) the documents on which he relies; and b) the documents which – i) adversely affect his own case, ii) adversely affect another party's case, or iii) support another party's case; and c) the documents which he is required to disclose by a practice direction.'
292 See [3.65] to [3.92].
293 [1995] 2 AC 500.

involved in such a process.[294] The Code specifically contemplates that the designated person should have direct access to the highest level of management. This must, presumably, indicate that he is not a 'directing mind and will' for the purposes of the sub-section. In this sense, he would be regarded as an employee, akin to the master, and it was expressly stated in *The Star Sea*, both by Tuckey J and the Court of Appeal, that the knowledge of an employee of that type could not have been attributed to the assured company for the purpose of s 39(5).[295]

3.108   Having said this, it must be borne in mind that the ISM Code can still play a crucial role in the application of s 39(5). The Code obliges the designated person to pass on what he knows about the condition of the vessel to 'the directing mind and will' of the company. So if the designated person informs the directing mind and will of the company about a defect in the vessel that constitutes unseaworthiness, but the latter person takes no action and the ship is sent to sea in an unseaworthy state, the underwriter could possibly bring a s 39(5) defence for losses attributable to this unseaworthiness. The assured, in this specific example, has turned a 'blind eye' to the unseaworthiness.[296]

Generally speaking, the privity of the designated person about unseaworthiness is, *prima facie*, the privity of the insured company. The insured company might claim that it did not have information about the unseaworthy state of the vessel because the designated person did not pass that information to it. In such a case, the burden of proof is on the assured to show that the information was not passed on by the designated person. This is a very heavy burden and the assured must not only prove that the information was not passed on, but also that adequate resources and shore-based support were provided to enable the designated person to carry out his functions.[297]

3.109   Even if the assured proves that the information was not passed on, this may create some harsh consequences for him in other respects. This proof simply means that the SMS, in respect of that vessel, is defective or inefficient. The cargo claimants, for example, may use this, as the thrust of their case would probably be to show that just such a problem existed. As can be observed, the provisions of the ISM Code make life easier for underwriters. Following the introduction of the ISM Code, it seems likely that the s 39(5) defence, which has not yet been used widely by insurers due to evidential reasons, may be used more frequently in future.

(iv)   Legal implications of the ISM Code for particular forms of policy

3.110   The standard Institute voyage policies on hull and freight do not expressly waive the breach of the implied warranty of seaworthiness. The vessel, therefore,

---

294 In smaller companies, the senior manager may be appointed as the designated person. However, this is an exceptional situation and will not be taken into account when considering the legal effects of the Code on the sub-section.

295 The House of Lords did not disturb the findings of the lower courts on this point.

296 Knowledge, for the purpose of s 39(5), includes both positive knowledge and knowledge that can be expressed in the form of 'turning a blind eye'. See *The Eurysthenes* [1977] 1 QB 49 and *The Star Sea* [1995] 1 Lloyd's Rep 651; [1997] 1 Lloyd's Rep 360 (CA); [2001] 1 UKHL; [2003] 1 AC 469; [2001] 1 Lloyd's Rep 389 (HL).

297 Section 3.3 of the ISMC.

must be seaworthy at the commencement of the relevant voyage as required by these policies. The ISM Code is not expected to have a direct impact on these policies. The only possible effect may be that the underwriters may prove the unseaworthiness at the commencement of the voyage by means of the documentation under the SMS, as discussed above under the effect of ISM Code on burden of proof in unseaworthiness allegations. It also has to be noted that the assured might lose his insurance cover under the IHC 2003, if the assured or the insured vessel is not ISM Code compliant. Clause 13 of the IHC 2003 reads as follows:

> At the inception of and throughout the period of this insurance and any extension thereof ... the Owners or the party assuming responsibility for operation of the vessel from the Owners shall hold a valid Document of Compliance in respect of the vessel as required by chapter IX of the International Convention for the Safety of Life at Sea (SOLAS) 1974 as amended and any modification thereof; the vessel shall have in force a valid Safety Management Certificate as required by chapter IX of the International Convention for the Safety of Life at Sea (SOLAS) 1974 as amended and any modification thereof. Unless the Underwriters agree to the contrary in writing, in the event of any breach of 'this provision', this insurance shall terminate automatically at the time of such breach ...

3.111 In the standard Institute cargo policies, on the other hand, the breach of the implied warranty of seaworthiness has been expressly waived, provided that the assured, or his servants, are not privy to such unseaworthiness.[298] As the assured in cargo policies is either the cargo-owner or freight forwarder, the ISMC will not have any direct or indirect impact on the current provisions of these policies.[299] The filing

---

298 See cl 5.2 of the ICC 1982 (type A, B, C).

299 On the other hand, two new cargo clauses have been introduced and recommended by the Joint Cargo Committee of Lloyd's and Institute of London Underwriters to deal with ISM compliance and consequences of non-compliance. These clauses could be introduced into cargo policies, if the parties wish to do so. The first clause, ISM Endorsement Clause (JC 98/019), which intends to give full support to the ISMC's introduction, reads as follows:

> In no case shall this insurance cover loss, damage or expense where the matter insured is carried by a vessel that is not ISMC certified or whose owners or operators do not hold an ISMC Document of Compliance when, at the time of loading of the subject matter on board the vessel, the assured were aware or in the ordinary course of business should have been aware: either that such vessel was not certified in accordance with the ISMC or that a current Document of Compliance was not held by her owners or operators as required under the SOLAS Convention as amended. This exclusion shall not apply where the insurance has been assigned to the party claiming hereunder who has brought or agreed to buy the subject matter insured in good faith under a binding contract.'

The other clause, ISM Forwarding Charges Clause (JC 98/019), deals with issues that might arise when the vessel that carries the insured cargo is detained by authorities because of failure to comply with the ISMC. This clause, which can be used only with the ISM Endorsement Clause, reads as follows:

> In consideration of an additional premium to be agreed, this insurance is extended to reimburse the assured, up to the limit of the sum insured for the voyage, for any extra charges properly and reasonably incurred in unloading, storing and forwarding the subject matter to the destination to which it is insured hereunder following release of cargo from a vessel arrested or detained at or diverted to any other port or place (other than the intended port of destination) where the voyage is terminated due either (a) to such vessel not being certified in accordance with the ISMC or (b) to a current Document of Compliance not being held by her owners or operators as required under the SOLAS Convention 1974 as amended. This clause, which does not apply to General Average or salvage or salvage Charges, is subject to all other terms or conditions and exclusions contained in the policy and to JCC Cargo ISM Endorsement JC 98/019.

and documentation procedures carried out under the SMS of the vessel, therefore, cannot help the underwriters in proving that the cargo-owner or his servants are privy to unseaworthiness.

(B)   Potential legal implications of the ISPS Code on provisions relating to seaworthiness

(a)   Background, implementation and nature of the ISPS Code

3.112   In the wake of the events of 11 September 2001, enhancing maritime safety has been a priority for the international community. Undoubtedly, the most significant step taken to this end has been the introduction of the ISPS Code.[300] This has been achieved by adding a new Chapter XI-2 in the SOLAS 1974. The purpose of this new Chapter is to agree specific regulations which are to form the background to the adaptation and implementation of the ISPS Code.[301] The Chapter and, accordingly, the ISPS Code apply to: passenger ships, including high-speed passenger craft; cargo ships, including high-speed craft, of 500 gross tonnage and upwards; mobile offshore drilling units; and port facilities serving such ships engaged on international voyages.[302]

3.113   What makes the ISPS Code distinct is the fact that it is designed to apply not only to vessels, but also to shore-side operations and port facilities.[303] Therefore, the Code comprises a series of legally binding obligations on the part of the vessel, her owners and operators on the one hand and on the other hand imports a series of interlocking legal obligations on contracting or member governments of the IMO, flag state administrations and port facilities and their administration. The Code takes the approach that ensuring the security of ships and port facilities is a risk management activity and that, to determine what security measures are appropriate, an assessment of the risks must be made in each particular case.

3.114   The ISPS Code is comprised of two parts. The duties and obligations of relevant parties, that is the ship owning company, contracting states and port facility administration, and mechanisms of discharging these duties are set out in Part A of the Code. Part B is voluntary and contains guidance notes that provide an explanatory

---

300 It should be borne in mind that the ISPS Code is not the only measure taken with a view to enhance maritime security. A new Chapter XI-1 to the SOLAS Convention 1974 requires: (i) the installation of Automatic Information System (AIS) in most vessels (Regulation 19 of Chapter XI-1); (ii) vessels to be marked with their IMO identification number in a permanent way (Regulation 3), and (iii) the owners and of operators of every vessel, to which the provisions of the SOLAS 1974 apply, to issue and maintain a document called Continuous Synopsis Record (CSR) (Regulation 5). It is intended that the AIS, together with CSR and the requirement as to the marking of the vessel with an identification number in a permanent way, may prove of assistance in identifying, tracking and apprehending vessels that have been the subject of hijacking or acts of piracy.

301 See Regs 4 and 10 of Chapter XI-2 of the SOLAS 1974.

302 See Reg 2 of Chapter XI-2 of the SOLAS 1974 and also s 3.1 of Part A of the ISPS Code.

303 By virtue of s 3.1.2 of Part A of the ISPS Code, the Code applies to port facilities serving ships engaged on international voyages. It is in the discretion of any Contracting State to extend the application of the Code to those port facilities within their territory which, although used primarily by ships not engaged on international voyages, are required, occasionally, to serve ships arriving or departing on an international voyage; see s 3.2 of the ISPS Code Part A.

basis upon which the mandatory provisions of Part B of the Code should be implemented and operated.[304]

(b) Scope of the Code

3.115 The main objective of the Code is to provide a standardised, consistent framework for evaluating risk and detecting security threats affecting ships or port facilities used in international trade. To this end, ship-owning companies, contracting states, port facilities and their administration and flag states have been placed under various obligations by the ISPS Code. It is intended to sum up main obligations of relevant parties in this part of the chapter.

3.116 Under the ISPS Code, each ship-owning company operating in a contracting state must satisfy the following requirements. First, a ship-owning company must make sure that each of its vessels carries on board a ship security plan (SSP) approved by the relevant administration.[305] The SSP is a plan developed to ensure the application of measures on board the ship designed to protect persons on board, cargo, cargo transport units, ship's stores or the ship from the risk of a security incident.[306] The ship-owning company must make sure that the SSP contains a clear statement to the effect that the master has the overriding authority and responsibility to make decisions with respect to the safety and security of the ship.[307]

Secondly, the ship-owning company is under an obligation to appoint a ship security officer (SSO) for each of its vessels.[308] The responsibilities of the SSO are listed in s 12.2 of Part A of the ISPS Code and include implementation and maintenance of the ship security plan and liaison with the management of the vessel and other on-shore authorities. The job of the SSO can be summarised as building a culture of security on board the ship through training and exercises and by reviewing the SSP to ensure that it is workable.[309]

Thirdly, each ship-owning company is required to designate a company security officer (CSO) for every vessel it owns.[310] The CSO is a member of the shore-side management who is to undertake responsibilities with regard to the monitoring of security for the vessel for which he is responsible within the organisation. The main

---

304 In the United States, the Maritime Transport and Security Act 2002, which incorporates the ISPS Code into the national law, has made both parts of the Code mandatory. Similarly, the European Parliament and Council have passed an EU Regulation that envisages the adoption by Member States of the EU of the whole of Part A of the ISPS Code and the mandatory adoption of certain provisions in Part B by July 2004 (EC Regulation No. 725/2004).
305 See s 9.1 of Part A of the ISPS Code.
306 See s 2.4 of Part A of the ISPS Code. Section 9.4 of Part A and s 9 of Part B contain detailed requirements as to contents, preparation and maintenance of the SSP.
307 See s 6 of Part A of the ISPS Code. See, also, Reg 8 of Chapter XI-2 of the SOLAS 1974.
308 See s 12 of Part A of the ISPS Code.
309 It has not been expressly stated whether the master of the ship can be designated as the SSO. By virtue of s 2.6 of Part A of the ISPS Code, the SSO shall be accountable to the master, which in turn does not prohibit designation of the master himself as the SSO. It is submitted that involving a person other than the master in the decision-making process on matters relating to security of the vessel might be a more efficient way of ensuring the required degree of security.
310 See s 11 of part A of the ISPS Code.

duties and responsibilities of the CSO are set out in s 11.2 of Part A of the ISPS Code. One of the main duties of the CSO is to ensure that the ship security assessment is carried out.[311] Furthermore, the CSO is responsible for ensuring adequate training for personnel responsible for the security of the ship and also for ensuring effective communication between the SSO and relevant administrative bodies.

Last but not least, the Code requires each ship-owning company to retain a vast amount of records relating to: training; drills and exercises; security threats and incidents; breaches of security; changes in security level; communications relating to the direct security of the ship, such as specific threats to the ship or to port facilities the ship is, or has been, in; internal audits and reviews of security activities; periodic review of the ship security assessment; periodic review of the ship security plan; implementation of any amendments to the plan; and, maintenance, calibration and testing of security equipment, if any, including testing of the ship security alert system.[312]

3.117   The responsibilities of Contracting States under the Code are several and rigorous. First and foremost, each Contracting State has to complete a port facility security assessment (PFSA) for each port facility within its territory that serves ships on international voyages.[313] This assessment is based on a risk analysis of all aspects of a port facility's operation in order to find out which parts of that port are more likely to be the subject of an attack.[314] It is possible that a Contracting State may authorise a recognised security organisation to carry out the PFSA in relation to ports in its territory.[315] On the basis of the PFSA, it is the duty of the Contracting State to develop and maintain a port facility security plan (PFSP).[316] The PFSP must identify the physical and operational security measures that must be taken to ensure that it always operates at security level 1. The Plan should also indicate the additional measures that are necessary to operate at security levels 2 and 3 if and when required to do so.[317] The Contracting State is also responsible for appointing a port facility security officer (PFSO) for each port facility.[318] The PFSO has a detailed list of responsibilities, which

---

311 The elements, which a ship safety assessment should include, are stated in s 8.4 of Part A of the ISPS Code.

312 See s 10 of Part A of the ISPS Code.

313 See s 15 of Part A of the ISPS Code.

314 By virtue of s 15.5 of Part A of the ISPS Code, the port facility security assessment should include, at least, the following elements:
   (i)   identification and evaluation of important assets and infrastructure that it is important to protect;
   (ii) identification of possible threats to the assets and infrastructure and the likelihood of their occurrence, in order to establish and prioritise security measures;
   (iii) identification, selection and prioritisation of counter measures and procedural changes and their level of effectiveness in reducing vulnerability; and
   (iv) identification of weaknesses, including human factors, in the infrastructure, policies and procedures.

315 See s 15.2 of Part A of the ISPS Code.

316 See s 16 of Part A of the ISPS Code.

317 The issues, which are expected to be addressed by the Plan, are set out in s 16.3 of Part A of the ISPS Code.

318 See s 17 of Part A of the ISPS Code. A person may be designated as the port facility officer for one or more port facilities.

can be summarised as building a culture of security within the port facility through training and exercises.[319]

Setting security levels for the ships flying its flag, ships within its jurisdiction and port facilities within its territory is another responsibility of each Contracting State.[320] Security levels range from 1 to 3. At security level 1 minimum appropriate protective security measures should be maintained at all times. Security level 2 means the level at which appropriate additional protective security measures should be maintained for a period of time as a result of heightened risk of a security incident. Security level 3 means the level at which further specific protective measures should be maintained for a limited period of time when a security incident is probable or imminent, although it may not be possible to identify the specific target.[321]

Finally, each Contracting State is under an obligation to determine in which instances a Declaration of Security (DOS) should be completed by vessels visiting their ports.[322] The main purpose of a DOS is to ensure agreement is reached between the ship and the port facility as to the respective security measures each will undertake in accordance with the provisions of their approved security plans.[323]

3.118   Furthermore, the ISPS Code has assigned specific duties to each Contracting State in which vessels coming under the scope of the ISPS Code are registered.[324] The most significant function of a flag state is to appoint officers who will verify compliance of the SSP with the requirements of the ISPS Code.[325] Following verification, the same officers shall issue an International Ship Security Certificate. The certificate shall normally valid for a period of five years.[326] A flag state is also entrusted with the task of reviewing and approving the SSP of each ship flying its flag.[327]

---

319 For a list of the duties and responsibilities of the PFSO, see s 17.2 of Part A of the ISPS Code.

320 See s 4 of Part A of the ISPS Code. Security procedures that need to be followed by each ship at each security level have been listed in s 7 of Part A of the ISPS Code. Section 14 of Part A of the ISPS Code does the same for port facilities.

321 See ss 2.9, 2.10 and 2.11 of Part A of the ISPS Code. See, also, ss 4.8 and 4.9 of Part B of the ISPS Code.

322 See s 5 of Part A of the ISPS Code.

323 See s 5.4 of Part B of the ISPS Code. A sample form of a DOS is annexed as Appendix 1 to Part B of the ISPS Code. Note that a ship can request completion of a DOS in instances listed in s 5.2 of Part A of the ISPS Code.

324 States of this kind are commonly referred to as flag states.

325 See s 19.1.1 of Part A of the ISPS Code. The verification process can be entrusted to a recognised security organisation.

326 See s 19.3.1 of Part A of the ISPS Code. By virtue of s 19.4 of Part A of the ISPS Code, an interim ship security certificate may be issued for a vessel which:
   – does not have a certificate, on delivery or prior to its entry or re-entry into service;
   – is transferred from the flag of a Contracting Government to the flag of another Contracting Government;
   – is transferred to the flag of a Contracting Government from a State which is not a Contracting Government: and
   – is operated by a new company.

327 See ss 9.1, 9.2 and 9.3 of Part A of the ISPS Code.

(c)   Implications of the ISPS Code on provisions relating to seaworthiness

(i)   Implied warranty of seaworthiness

3.119   Having been attached to the SOLAS 1974, an international convention which, amongst other objectives, intends to achieve a reasonable degree of safety during the operation of ships, it is beyond doubt that the provisions of the ISPS Code will determine the minimum standards that need to be complied with by vessels flying the flag of a Contracting State. The first step in demonstrating compliance with the Code is the existence of the International Ship Security Certificate for such certificate can only be issued following the verification of flag state authorities to the effect that the safety plan of the ship is ISPS Code compliant. It is well established that seaworthiness extends to factors such as existence of certificates and documents necessary for the safety and protection of the vessel,[328] in addition to other factors, such as her structure and technical equipment. Therefore, a vessel navigating without a valid Security Certificate would in all probability be regarded as unseaworthy for the purposes of the implied warranty of seaworthiness.

3.120   One should not, however, lose sight of the fact that a vessel with a valid Security Certificate might still be regarded as unseaworthy. It is, for instance, possible that a vessel which is ISPS Code compliant has a latent defect in her hull plating. There is also a chance that failure of the key players identified, that is the ship security officer or company security officer, to perform their duties under the Code might render the vessel unseaworthy. One of the duties of the ship security officer and company security officer is ensure that adequate training for personnel responsible for the security of the ship is provided.[329] Lack of such training is likely to make the vessel unseaworthy as this would amount to breach of a statutory duty in relation to security of ships.

(ii)   Section 39(5) of the MIA

3.121   It is apparent in the light of the above analysis that there is a correlation between compliance with the ISPS Code and seaworthiness of the insured vessel. In time policies, unseaworthiness might act as defence only if conditions expressed in s 39(5) are satisfied; that is to say, there has to be a causal link between the unseaworthiness and the resulting loss and also the assured must be privy to such unseaworthiness. Whether unseaworthiness arising out of non-compliance with the ISPS code might assist underwriters in advancing a defence based upon s 39(5) of the MIA 1906 is an interesting question that calls for further analysis.

3.122   It should be borne in mind that the philosophy behind the ISPS Code is to ensure that adequate maritime security measures are in place to protect vessels against threats and acts of violence. Non-compliance with the code, therefore, is an indication that the mechanisms to protect the vessel in question against such eventualities are either not in place or are in a defective state. It is hard to envisage a case where

---

328 *The Madeleine* [1967] 2 Lloyd's Rep. 224. See, also, *Alfred C Toepfer v Tossa Marine Co Ltd (The Derby)* [1985] 2 Lloyd's Rep 325, p 351, *per* Kerr LJ.
329 See ss 11.2.9 and 12.2.7 of Part A of the ISPS Code.

defective security measures can cause loss on their own without intervention of other external factors. If the personnel on board, for instance, have not been given sufficient training to deal with unauthorised access to the vessel, an issue which should have been addressed in the ship security plan,[330] and terrorists manage to board the vessel and detonate the explosives they brought with them, the first task facing the court would be to identify the *proximate* cause of the loss. It is likely that unseaworthiness of the vessel is going to be at least a *proximate* cause of the loss in that event.[331] Provided that other *proximate* cause or causes are covered by the policy in question,[332] then the only way to resist the claim, from the insurer's point of view, is to demonstrate that the assured was privy to the unseaworthiness in question.

3.123 Being an employee, akin to the master, on the vessel in question, it is highly unlikely that knowledge of the SSO can be attributed to the assured for the purposes of s 39(5). However, it is vital in this context to analyse the position of the CSO. Can the CSO be regarded as the head man representing the ship-owning company for the purposes of s 39(5) so that his knowledge on safety and security matters in itself amounts to privity on the part of the assured? Put another way, is there a difference between the designated person under the ISM Code and the CSO under the ISPS Code?

3.124 The designated person under the ISM Code has a supervisory role. He is expected to monitor the operation of the safety management system and ensure that superintendents, safety managers or other designated line managers have taken steps to implement the safety management system. However, it is clear that he has no authority to maintain or implement the safety management system himself; that is the responsibility of the line management. He is the independent person who has a duty to report deficiencies in the system to the highest level of management. It is noteworthy that the designated person has been described as a 'person ashore having direct access to the highest level of management.'[333]

3.125 The ISPS Code has, on the other hand, assigned a rather different role to the CSO. He is personally responsible that the SSA is carried out[334] and he is also involved in implementation of the SSP.[335] The impression one gets when considering the relevant provisions of the Code is that the CSO has been entrusted with the task of ensuring that the vessel operates in a safe manner. This view is supported by the fact that the SSO is obliged to report any deficiencies and non-conformities identified during internal audits, periodic reviews, security inspections and verifications of compliance and implementing any corrective actions to the CSO.[336] It is, therefore, fair

---

330 See s 9.4.4 of Part A of the ISPS Code.
331 *The Miss Jay Jay* [1987] 1 Lloyd's Rep 32.
332 Institute War and Strikes Clauses Hulls (Time) (1/11/95) offers protection against loss of or damage to the insured vessel caused by any terrorist or any person acting maliciously or from a political motive.
333 See Art 4 of the ISM Code.
334 See s 8.1 of Part B of the ISPS Code.
335 Section 12.2.9 of Part A of the ISPS Code requires the SSO to co-ordinate implementation of the SSP with the CSO and the relevant PFSO.
336 See s 12.2.5 of Part B of the ISPS Code.

to conclude that the CSO has been delegated a degree of managerial responsibilities on safety and security matters.[337]

Does this, however, mean that the knowledge of the CSO amounts to the knowledge of the company for the purposes of s 39(5)? As long as the CSO is not the director of the ship-owning or managing company, the answer to this question should be in the negative. The directors of the company cannot be expected to be aware of everything that the person they have designated authority on security matters knows. At the end of the day, it is merely the CSO's responsibility to ensure that requirements under the ISPS Code are complied with. He has no involvement in the decision-making process of sending the ship to sea and, therefore, is too junior in the chain of management to be regarded as the company itself for the purposes of s 39(5).

Of course, the position would be different if there was evidence to the effect that the CSO had informed the highest levels of management regarding security defects in a particular vessel and sought their assistance. The director of a ship managing company, who chooses to ignore a warning of that nature, is likely to be turning a blind eye to unseaworthiness, for a warning coming from the person in charge of security should be sufficient to create sufficient suspicion.

(iii)   Various market clauses

3.126   The IHC 2003 has introduced a new management clause which is intended to assist the process of eliminating sub-standard shipping practices. Clause 14.4 of the IHC provides that:

It is the duty of the Assured, Owners and Managers at the inception of and throughout the period of this insurance and any extension thereof to comply with all statutory requirements of the vessel's flag state relating to construction, adaptation, condition, fitment, equipment, operation and manning of the vessel ...

In the event of any breach of any of the duties in this Clause 14.4, the Underwriters shall not be liable for any loss, damage, liability or expense attributable to such breach.

This clause creates a continuing contractual duty on the part of the individuals in charge of the insured vessel to make sure that all statutory requirements relating to construction, adaptation, condition, fitment, equipment, operation and manning of the vessel are complied with. If not, the insurer is not liable for any loss that is causally linked to the breach of the relevant statutory duty. The relationship between cl 14.4 of the IHC 2003 and s 39(5) of the MIA 1906 is far from clear,[338] but this new clause seems to have strengthened the hands of the insurer, at least in two respects. First, the clause is applicable even though the statutory breach does not render the vessel unseaworthy. More significantly, there is no requirement that the insurer demonstrates that the assured was privy to the breach of the statutory obligations. It is sufficient if it can be proved that the manager in charge of the ship's operations failed to comply with statutory requirements.

---

337 This is probably why the CSO is not required under the ISPS Code to be in continuous contact with the highest level of management.

338 See Soyer, 'A survey of the new International Hull Clauses 2002' (2003) 9 *JIML* 256, pp 277–78.

As one of the objectives of the ISPS Code is to ensure that adequate and proportionate maritime security measures are in place on board of each ship,[339] most would agree that the Code contains provisions dealing with operation of vessels. There is also no doubt that the requirements of the ISPS Code are statutory as the Code has been implemented into English law.[340] The question is whether the CSO can be regarded as a manager for the purposes of this clause so that his inability to deal with security failures on board the ship could potentially trigger cl 14.4 of the IHC 2003, provided of course there is a causal link between breach and the loss.[341] No doubt a special rule of attribution would be required to assess the position of the CSO under this clause. It is submitted that it is possible to consider the CSO as manager for the purposes of this clause as he has been delegated managerial responsibilities on operational matters, that is the security of the ship.

3.127   Similarly, most P&I club rules would require their vessels to comply with such statutory requirements in addition to holding a valid International Ship Security Certificate. Unlike cl 14.4 of the IHC 2003, the rules of most P&I clubs are not very explicit on the consequence of breach of this obligation. For instance, r 10, s1(3) of the Swedish Club (2005/06 version) reads as follows:

> The Member must comply with the flag State's or other competent authorities' requirements relating to the entered ship's design, construction, adaptation, fitment, condition, equipment, manning, safe operation, management and maritime security. Valid certificates covering such requirements, including ISM Code certificates and ISPS Code certificates, must at all times be maintained. If the Member fails to fulfil his obligations under this point the Association may reject to compensate liabilities, costs or expenses caused by such failure.

---

339 See s 1.2.5 of Part A of the ISPS Code.
340 See The Ship and Port Facility (Security) Regulations 2004 (SI 2004/1495).
341 Bearing in mind that IHC 2003 intends to provide cover for marine risks, it is highly unlikely that breach of the ISPS Code will cause a loss covered by the clauses.

CHAPTER 4

OTHER IMPLIED WARRANTIES

I – IMPLIED WARRANTY OF PORTWORTHINESS

4.1   Where a voyage policy attaches 'at and from' the place named in the policy, s 39(2) requires that the vessel, while in port, must be reasonably fit to encounter the ordinary perils of the port. The term 'portworthiness' does not appear either in s 39(2) or anywhere else in the Act. It is quite a new term, which was first employed by Hodges.[1] Other authors, such as Arnould, Ivamy and Bennett, treat this warranty simply as an aspect of the seaworthiness warranty and examine it under that heading. Although the warranty of portworthiness seems like an aspect of the seaworthiness warranty due to the similarity in their nature, at least for pragmatic reasons it has to be dealt with as a separate type of implied warranty.

4.2   Unlike the implied warranty of seaworthiness, there is almost no litigation concerning the implied warranty of portworthiness.[2] The reason for this is partly technical. As a result of regular surveys and controls carried out by classification societies, the vessels are usually fit enough to encounter the ordinary perils of the ports when the risk attaches and for this reason very few disputes have arisen on the breach of this warranty.

(A)   Nature of the implied warranty of portworthiness

4.3   The words used in s 39(2), '... reasonably fit to encounter the ordinary perils of the port', indicate the relative nature of the implied warranty of portworthiness. The degree of fitness required to encounter the ordinary perils of the port may vary according to different factors.[3] First, the class of the vessel in question can be quite crucial in determining the degree of fitness required. In this sense, while a cargo ship can be considered as portworthy for a specific port, a pleasure boat may not. Similarly, the degree of fitness may vary from port to port. A lower degree of fitness is required in a port that is located in a bay than in a port that is open to waves and tides of an ocean. The time of the year is another factor that plays an important role in determining the degree of fitness required. A vessel that is portworthy for a certain port in the summer season may not be so in the winter season. As a result of this relative nature of the term, whether a vessel is portworthy or not is a question of fact.

---

1   *Law of Marine Insurance*, (by S Hodges) London, 1996, pp 122–23 and *Cases and Materials on Marine Insurance Law*, (by S Hodges) London, 1999, pp 302–03.

2   The implied warranty of portworthiness has been judicially explored in *Parmeter v Cousins* (1809) 2 Camp 235; *Gibson v Small* (1853) 4 HL Cas 353; and *Buchanan & Co v Faber* (1899) 4 Com Cas 223.

3   The degree of fitness required for portworthiness is definitely less than the degree required for seaworthiness, ie, a full crew is not required and the vessel need not be fully provisioned or fuelled.

(B)   Scope of the implied warranty of portworthiness

4.4   In a policy that attaches while the vessel is in port, namely an 'at and from' policy, there is an implied warranty of portworthiness according to s 39(2). This section is obviously not applicable when the subject matter is insured 'from' a particular place, as the risk under such a policy does not attach while she is at that port. Section 39(2) is worded to apply to all voyage policies, whether on ship, cargo or freight unless expressly excluded by the policy. The extent of this warranty has been dramatically narrowed by standard insurance clauses. In Institute Cargo Clauses (ICC), for example, there is no implied warranty of portworthiness simply because the policy attaches from the time the goods leave the warehouse or place of storage and not while the ship is in port.[4]

4.5   The warranty of portworthiness, on the other hand, is implied in an 'at and from' policy on the ship effected under IVCH. According to r 3(a) of Sched 1 of the Rules for Construction of the Policy, the risk attaches immediately on such a policy if the vessel is at that place in 'good safety' when the contract is concluded. Rule 3(b) of Sched 1 states that if the vessel is not at that place when the contract is concluded, the risk attaches as soon as she arrives there in 'good safety'.

4.6   Whether a ship has to be fit to endure the ordinary perils of the port throughout the period of her stay while 'at' that port is an issue that has never been raised. Section 32(2) is worded in exactly the same way as s 39(1), which regulates the implied warranty of seaworthiness in voyage policies. As the implied warranty of seaworthiness is applicable only at the commencement of the voyage, it could be said that the implied warranty of portworthiness should, likewise, apply on the commencement of the risk. The wording of s 39(2) is sufficiently clear to support the assumption that the vessel need only be portworthy at a specific point in time. Therefore, it can be concluded that there is no continuing warranty status. If the vessel becomes unportworthy due to, for example, negligence of the crew after the attachment of the risk and is lost, the insurer is still liable for that loss.

II – IMPLIED WARRANTY OF CARGOWORTHINESS

4.7   The main purpose of each transportation facility is to transfer the goods from one place to another safely and in the same state as they were loaded into the transportation vehicle. The aim is not different in marine transport. To this end, the vessel on which the goods are shipped must not only be strong enough to encounter the ordinary perils of the voyage, but also fit enough to carry the goods without causing any deterioration in their original nature.

The cargoworthiness warranty has been employed to make sure that the goods shipped are carried safely to their destination and it requires the ship and her equipment to be fit for this purpose. In carriage of goods by sea, the scope of the implied warranty of seaworthiness is wide enough to cover 'cargoworthiness' as well.[5]

---

4   See cl 8 of ICC 1982 (type A, B, C).
5   *Reed v Page* [1927] 1 KB 743, p 755, *per* Scrutton J.

Therefore, the term 'seaworthiness' in a bill of lading, *prima facie*, includes both fitness of the ship to encounter the perils of navigation and her fitness to carry cargo.[6] In marine insurance, on the other hand, cargoworthiness has been regulated as a separate implied warranty, other than the implied warranty of seaworthiness, by s 40(2) which is worded as follows:

> In every voyage policy on goods or other moveables there is an implied warranty that at the commencement of the voyage the ship is not only seaworthy as a ship, but also that she is reasonably fit to carry the goods or other moveables to the destination contemplated by the policy.

4.8   The implied warranty of cargoworthiness has been severely criticised on the ground that it might create freakish results for the assured in cargo insurance. A claim under the policy will fail if the carrying vessel was uncargoworthy at the start of the voyage, even though the assured has no means of ensuring whether the ship was cargoworthy or not. For this reason, in almost all cargo policies, the implied warranty of cargoworthiness has been waived provided that the assured or their servants are not privy to such unfitness.[7] In this way, the significance of this warranty has been reduced dramatically in practice.

(A)   Meaning and nature of the implied warranty of cargoworthiness

4.9   Section 40(2) defines 'cargoworthiness' as being reasonably fit to carry the goods or other moveables to their destination. According to this definition, the main factor that has to be taken into account when determining whether a ship is cargoworthy or not is her capability to carry the particular cargo in question. Cargoworthiness means, in the first place, that the vessel is in a fit state to receive the contractual cargo. Therefore, the warranty would not be satisfied where the vessel's holds needed fumigating or cleaning before being in a fit state to receive cargo. In *Tattersall v National SS Co*,[8] for example, a vessel that had carried cattle with foot and mouth disease was not properly cleansed and disinfected before a new herd of cattle were received on board and these consequently caught the disease; it was held that the cargoworthiness warranty was breached.[9]

4.10   In order to be considered cargoworthy, a ship must also be equipped to carry the particular kind of cargo that she has contracted to carry.[10] If, for example, the cargo is frozen meat, then the refrigerating machinery, holds, etc, must be in proper order,

---

6   *Rathbone Bros & Co v Maciver Sons & Co* [1903] 2 KB 378. Rule 1 of Art III of the Hague-Visby Rules stipulates as follows: The carrier shall be bound before and at the beginning of the voyage to exercise due diligence to: (a) make the ship seaworthy; (b) properly man, equip and supply the ship; (c) make the holds, refrigerating and cool chambers, and all other parts of the ship in which goods are carried, fit and safe for their reception, carriage and preservation.

7   See cl 5.2 of ICC 1982 (type A, B, C).

8   (1884) 12 QBD 297.

9   See, also, *Ciampa v British India SN Co* [1915] 2 KB 774 and *Compañia de Naveira Nedelka v Tradex Internacional SA (The Tres Flores)* [1973] 2 Lloyd's Rep 247.

10   *Stanton v Richardson* (1874) LR 7 CP 421.

efficient and fit to receive and carry that particular cargo.[11] Similarly, a vessel intended for the carriage of grain in bulk must be supplied with sufficient separation cloths and adequate shifting boards.

4.11   Section 40(2) requires the vessel to be reasonably cargoworthy. It appears from this wording, that the implied warranty of cargoworthiness will be construed in the light of the technical efficiency of the ship, both in design and equipment. A vessel may, therefore, be cargoworthy for the carriage of lumber and not for a load of steel rails.[12] Similarly, a vessel built for the carriage of fruit cargoes would probably be quite unsuitable for the transport of heavy mineral ores. The voyage undertaken is another factor that is extremely important in determining whether a vessel is cargoworthy or not. While a vessel is perfectly cargoworthy for carrying one type of cargo around the harbour, it may not be for carrying the same cargo on an ocean voyage. To sum up, the implied warranty of cargoworthiness is relative in nature, just like the implied warranty of seaworthiness, and it is a question of fact in each case to determine whether a vessel is cargoworthy or not.

(B)   Scope of the implied warranty of cargoworthiness

4.12   The extent of the implied warranty of cargoworthiness is much narrower than the implied warranty of seaworthiness. Section 40(2) makes it clear that it only applies to a voyage policy on goods or other moveables.[13] This distinction can be justified when the logic behind the warranty of cargoworthiness, to enable the transport of the goods shipped to their destination without changing their nature or damaging them, is taken into account.

4.13   Section 40(2) requires the ship to be cargoworthy at the commencement of the voyage. A maritime voyage is usually considered as commenced when she breaks ground. In carriage of goods, however, in each case the implied undertaking as to cargoworthiness is operative as from the commencement of loading. So, in *McFadden v Blue Star Line*,[14] after cargo had been safely loaded, the ship's engineer opened a sluice door on a watertight bulkhead and in closing it failed to secure it properly, with the result that water percolated through and damaged the plaintiff's cargo. It was held that, since the defective closure of the sluice door occurred after the cargo had been loaded, it did not constitute a breach of the cargoworthiness undertaking.

4.14   *McFadden v Blue Star Line* not only emphasises the difference between carriage of goods and marine insurance in respect of the commencement of the implied warranty of cargoworthiness, but it also makes clear that there is no continuing duty to keep the vessel cargoworthy throughout the voyage in carriage of goods by sea. Lord Mansfield had, in fact, stated the same principle in respect of the seaworthiness warranty in marine insurance in *Berman v Woodbridge*.[15] As the wording of the

11 See, also, *Maori King (Cargo-owners) v Hughes* [1895] 2 QB 550 and *The Waikato* [1899] 1 QB 56.
12 *The Briton* [1934] AMC 667.
13 Rule 17 of the Rules for Construction of the Policy provides that: 'The term goods means goods in the nature of merchandise, and does not include personal effects or provisions and stores for use on board.'
14 [1905] 1 KB 697.
15 [1781] 2 Dougl 781, p 788.

provisions that regulate these warranties in marine insurance, ss 39(1) and 40(2), is the same, there is nothing preventing us from evaluating them in the same way. Thus, it can be concluded that uncargoworthiness that occurs after the commencement of the voyage does not amount to breach of the implied warranty of cargoworthiness in marine insurance. This situation can be made clearer with an example. If the refrigerator in a vessel, which was in good order and condition at the beginning of the voyage, breaks down at one point after the commencement of the voyage, this would not amount to breach of the implied warranty of cargoworthiness.

III – IMPLIED WARRANTY OF LEGALITY

4.15   The intention of every insurance contract, whether marine or non-marine, is to provide indemnity to the assured within the limits of the law. Therefore, in non-marine insurance if the subject matter insured, for example a car in motor insurance and property in home insurance, has been put to some unlawful use, the assured is precluded from indemnity by public policy. The situation is much more complicated in marine insurance. The reason for this is the presence of an extra element in marine insurance that has no equivalent in non-marine insurance, namely, marine adventure.[16] In marine insurance, therefore, not only must the subject matter insured (for example, ship, freight, cargo) not be tainted with illegality, but the adventure insured must be lawful and must be performed lawfully.

To this end, s 3(1) provides that: '... every lawful marine adventure may be the subject of a contract of marine insurance', and s 41 imposes the implied warranty of legality in the following way:

> There is an implied warranty that the adventure insured is a lawful one, and that, so far as the assured can control the matter, the adventure shall be carried out in a lawful manner.

As can be observed, the warranty regulated by s 41 is a continuing one and, therefore, subsequent illegality due to events within the assured's control will infringe the warranty. The scope of the warranty will be examined in detail in the rest of this chapter. However, before such an examination is carried out, the reasons that made the draftsman of the Act regulate 'legality of the adventure' as a warranty will be discussed.[17]

---

16   That the implied warranty of illegality does not exist in non-marine insurance has been stated by the Court of Appeal in *Euro-Diam Ltd v Bathurst* [1990] 1 QB 1.

17   It must be borne in mind that, in some cases, a marine insurance contract can be regarded as 'unenforceable' due to illegality even though the adventure insured is legal and, accordingly, there is no breach of the implied warranty of legality. This is the case when a marine insurance contract is effected by, or on behalf of, an enemy alien (for the definition of an enemy alien see s 2(1) of the Trading with Enemy Act 1939, as amended by s 2 of the Emergency Laws (Miscellaneous Provisions) Act 1953) or a marine insurance contract is effected with a person lacking insurable interest (see s 1 of the Marine Insurance (Gambling Policies) Act 1909, where such contracts are expressly prohibited). Furthermore, it must be noted that the fact that certain marine insurance contracts are void, does not necessarily mean that they are illegal. If a marine insurance contract is void, the law refuses legal enforcement to the contract, but the parties remain at complete liberty to make and perform it if they want to do so. It is the illegal contracts that cannot be made and performed even though the parties want to do so. In this respect, wagering policies (policies where the parties, by express terms, disclaim the intention of making a contract of indemnity) are merely void and not illegal, since issuing such policies has not been expressly prohibited by law (s 1(b) of the 1909 Act).

(A)   Why has 'legality of adventure' been regulated as a warranty?

4.16   Section 41 regulates the legality of the adventure as an implied warranty. There is no doubt that marine insurance contracts that insure unlawful adventures or are performed illegally would still be regarded as void on the grounds of public policy in the absence of s 41. In fact, before the enactment of the MIA 1906, marine insurance contracts insuring unlawful adventures or performed unlawfully were held to be void and unenforceable, even though the MIA 1906 was not in force at that time.[18] At this juncture, a very interesting question arises. Why did the draftsman prefer to give a warranty status to the 'legality of the adventure'? The reasons for this have not been discussed anywhere before and even the drafter of the Act, Sir McKenzie Chalmers, made no reference to this point. It is possible to find some sensible justifications for such a regulation simply by evaluating the general principles of insurance law and taking the case law into account. This issue must be discussed from two different and opposite angles. Namely, both the insurer's and the assured's position must be taken into account in order to comprehend the logic behind s 41.

(a)   Insurer's position

4.17   The warranty status employed by s 41 provides some sort of protection for the insurer and makes life much easier for him. If s 41 had not created a continuing warranty status, illegality, which arises during the performance of the adventure insured, would not have affected the validity of the policy at the date of its formation. The position of English law on this point has been summarised by Tenterden CJ, in *Wetherell v Jones*:[19]

> Where the consideration and the matter to be performed are both legal, we are not aware that a plaintiff has ever been precluded from recovering by an infringement of the law, not contemplated by the contract, and in the performance of something to be done on his part.

4.18   Accordingly, English law does not recognise the possibility that a contract, which is lawful in its inception and which is capable of lawful performance, can become illegal simply because one of the parties to it breaks the law in the course of his performance of his side of the contract. Therefore, in the absence of s 41, the insurer would not be able to claim that an insurance contract, lawful at the inception, has become illegal later due to the unlawful act of the assured. The most that could happen in such circumstances was that the assured would be precluded from enforcing the agreement, simply because recovery would be against the notions of public policy.

Public policy would certainly prevent the assured from recovery in cases where the unlawful act is directly connected to the circumstances of loss.[20] In cases where the

---

18   See *Farmer v Legg* (1797) 7 TR 186; *Camden v Anderson* (1798) 6 TR 723; *Johnston v Sutton* (1799) 1 Doug 254; *Marryat v Wilson* (1799) 1 Bos & P 430; *Cunard v Hyde (No 2)* (1859) 29 LJ QB 6; *Pipon v Cope* (1808) 1 Camp 434; *Wilson v Rankin* (1865) LR 1 QB 162.

19   (1832) 3 B & Ad 221, p 225.

20   *Baresford v Royal Insurance Co Ltd* [1938] AC 586. Similarly, in cases where the claimant pleads his illegality in order to support his claim, public policy would prevent him from recovery. See *Tinsley v Milligan* [1992] 2 All ER 391, a non-insurance case.

unlawful act is not directly connected to the circumstances of loss,[21] or where the unlawful act that causes the loss was not intended to cause the loss,[22] it is left to the courts to decide whether public policy prevents recovery or not. When deciding whether public policy should preclude recovery in such a case, the courts analyse the nature of illegality and the consequences of a finding for or against the guilty party. The leading statement of principle in the insurance context is to be found in the judgment of Diplock LJ in *Hardy v Motor Insurers Bureau*.[23]

> The court's refusal to assert a right even against the person who has committed the anti-social act, will depend not only on the nature of the anti-social act, but also on the nature of the right asserted. The court has to weigh the gravity of the anti-social act and the extent to which it will be encouraged by enforcing the right sought to be asserted against the social harm which will be caused if the right is not enforced.

Following the analysis of Diplock LJ, the Court of Appeal, in *Gray v Barr*,[24] held that public policy prevented the assured from recovery in a case where the unlawful act was directly connected to the loss, but was not intended to cause it. In that case, the assured, under a domestic householder's policy, suspected his wife of having an affair with Gray and entered Gray's house carrying a loaded shotgun with the intention of catching them together. Gray attempted to stop the assured from searching an upstairs room of the house and, during this process, the shotgun went off and Gray was killed. The assured was tried for manslaughter, but was acquitted and in the proceedings Gray's estate sued the assured in negligence, the assured joining his insurers as third parties. The Court of Appeal ruled that the assured was unable to recover an indemnity from his insurers for the damages awarded against him because public policy militated against recovery. Their Lordships denied recovery mainly on the ground that a man who carries a loaded shotgun is not to be protected by insurance, even if the gun goes off accidentally. Causing death by the use of shotgun was found to be shocking to public morality.[25]

(b)   Assured's position

4.19   If illegality that arises during the performance of the contract had not been regulated as a warranty by s 41, public policy, as illustrated above, would have in some cases prevented such insurances from being enforced. In such a case, the assured would lose his insurance cover even if the illegal conduct has been committed by one of his employees beyond his control. In other words, it would not be a defence to the assured to allege that illegality has arisen due to factors beyond his control.

Section 41 provides that the assured under a marine policy impliedly warrants that, so far as he can control the matter, the adventure upon which insured property is bound shall be carried out in a lawful manner. Therefore, under s 41, the assured is not

---

21   *Euro-Diam Ltd v Bathurst* [1990] 1 QB 1.
22   *Tinline v White Cross Insurance Association Ltd* [1921] 3 KB 327; *James v British General Insurance Co Ltd* [1927] 2 KB 311; *Gray v Barr* [1971] 2 QB 554.
23   [1964] 2 QB 745, pp 767–68.
24   [1971] 2 QB 554.
25   Cf *Tinline v White Cross Insurance Association Ltd* [1921] 3 KB 327; *James v British General Insurance Co* [1927] 2 KB 311.

responsible for any unlawful act committed by his master or employees during the performance of the voyage unless he has control over the issue. It is apparent that such a regulation is designed to protect the interest of the assured.

(B)   Scope of the implied warranty of legality

4.20   The implied warranty of legality is laid down in s 41 as follows:

> There is an implied warranty that the adventure insured is a lawful one, and that, so far as the assured can control the matter, the adventure shall be carried out in a lawful manner.

In this provision no distinction has been made between voyage and time policies in respect of the application of the implied warranty of legality. The common feature of time and voyage policies is the fact that, in both, an asset with an economic value is exposed to a marine adventure. As the word 'adventure' is used in s 41, this shows that the warranty is imposed by law, both for time and voyage policies. Therefore, where the policy covers a ship for a period of time, the implied warranty is imposed for each voyage on which the ship embarks. Similarly, the implied warranty of legality is incorporated, by law, in the marine insurance policy, covering each separate interest in a common maritime adventure. Therefore, s 41 has applicability whether the subject matter of the insurance is ship, cargo, freight or anything else.[26]

4.21   Section 41 regulates not only the legality of the adventure, but also the legality of the performance of the adventure. Accordingly, a marine adventure must not only be legal at the inception of the policy, but it must be performed legally, so far as the assured can control the matter. This distinction, which is basic to any discussion of the effects of illegality, originated in the 18th century. For pragmatic reasons, s 41 will be divided into two parts and examined under two different headings.

(a)   Illegality of the adventure insured

4.22   If the adventure insured is illegal from the outset, the implied warranty of illegality is broken and this is so irrespective of the ignorance, or otherwise, of the parties. In fact, the remedy for the breach of warranty is the discharging of the insurer from further liability.[27] Since breach occurs before the attachment of risk and accordingly no rights or liabilities can accrue, one might consider that the discharging remedy operates in the same way as holding the contract void *ab initio*. Such a statement is, in a general sense, accurate. The only thing that needs to be kept in mind is that, when the implied warranty of legality is breached due to illegality of the adventure insured, the assured can, under no circumstances, recover the premium paid in advance.[28]

---

26   Moveables, passage money, commission, profit, loan, disbursements or any liability to a third party may also be the subject matter of a marine insurance contract under s 3(2)(a), (b), (c).

27   See s 33(3).

28   Section 84(1) reads as follows: 'Where the consideration for the payment of the premium totally fails, and there has been no fraud or illegality on the part of the assured or his agents, the premium is thereupon returnable to the assured.'

4.23 At this point, it is necessary to examine under which circumstances a marine adventure can be regarded as illegal. A marine adventure may be illegal by statute, or because it is in violation of common law or the prize law as administered in England, or of proclamations or orders made by the Queen in Council, or of EC legislation and other international instruments. These circumstances will now be examined in detail.

(i) By statute

4.24 It has to be said that it is not always easy to answer the question of whether a contravention of a particular statute or regulation would render an adventure illegal. The literal meaning and the object of the statute in question must be interpreted carefully to reach a conclusion on this point.[29]

In cases where a statute specifically prohibits insurances in respect of a particular class of adventure, it seems that the court has no discretion in the matter and a policy insuring such an adventure will be rendered illegal by that statute. If, for example, a statute prohibits the exportation of goods without a licence, it generally follows that an insurance in respect of a voyage which contravenes this requirement is illegal.[30]

4.25 The statutes, however, are usually silent as to the effects of illegality and in such cases it is necessary to determine, by means of interpretation, whether violation of that statute renders the adventure insured illegal or not. In the earlier editions of Arnould, it was argued that where Acts of Parliament form part of the general commercial policy of the state, a violation of their provisions generally rendered the adventure illegal.[31] It is submitted that such a statement is too general and exceeds the boundaries set by courts. For example, even though they form part of the general commercial policy of the state, shipping safety legislation has, in general, been treated as collateral and breach of its provisions has been held not to render an adventure illegal.[32]

4.26 The courts have developed some tests to determine whether violation of a particular statute renders the adventure insured illegal. Accordingly, when determining the legal effect of a statute, a court has to apply these tests and must not reach a decision simply by a single consideration.[33] The most important factor to be considered is whether the policy of the statute is aimed at prohibiting dealings in the course of which its provisions are infringed, or whether its scope is limited to the mere infliction of a penalty. In other words, in every case it is a matter of construing the statute to determine whether the intention of parliament was to ban such contracts or merely to impose fines upon those transgressing its terms, a process which will be straightforward.[34] Another important consideration is whether the act prohibited by the statute affects the core of the contract. If the contract has as its whole object the

---

29 See the speech made by Lord Ellenborough CJ on this point, in *Atkinson v Abbott* (1909) 11 East 135, p 141.
30 *Lubbock v Potts* (1806) 7 East 449; *Gray v Lloyd* (1812) 4 Taunt 136; *Gibson v Service* (1816) 5 Taunt 433; *Re Mahmoud and Ispahani* [1921] KB 717; *Strongman Ltd v Sincock* [1955] 2 QB 525.
31 Arnould, 1954, para 745.
32 *Redmond v Smith* (1844) 7 Man & Gr 457.
33 *St John Shipping Corp v Joseph Rank Ltd* [1957] 1 QB 267.
34 *Ibid*. The leading analysis remains that of Devlin J, in *St John Shipping Corp v Joseph Rank Ltd*, p 287.

doing of the very act which the statute prohibits, there is generally a clear implication that the contract is also prohibited, but this is not the case if the prohibited act is merely incidental to the contract.[35]

(ii)   By common law

4.27   A marine adventure can usually be rendered illegal by common law if it is in contravention of war policy of the UK. The sovereign power of every state has, in time of war, a clear right to establish an embargo on all ships in any port of its dominion. Thus, if an insurance contract insures an adventure that will be carried out in contravention of such embargo, it will be deemed to be illegal. In *Delmada v Motteux*,[36] where the British government, in time of war, had laid an embargo on all ships with provisions from any port in Ireland, an insurance effected on a neutral (Venetran) ship in contravention of such an embargo was held to be void on the ground that the adventure insured was illegal.

(iii)   By prize law

4.28   As a general rule, whenever any property, according to prize law as administered by the courts of UK ,is liable to British capture, the insurance in England on that property is illegal and void. A property may be subject to British capture on many various grounds, for example, because it is enemy property or contraband carried to a hostile country; or because it is employed in violation of a blockade by the UK government or its allies; or because it is engaged in carrying the enemy's troops; or because it is engaged in any other manner that is considered by the English prize law to be illicit or illegal.[37]

(iv)   By orders made by the Queen/King

4.29   An adventure may also be rendered illegal by the orders made by the Queen/King. Thus, during the Napoleonic war an Act had been passed empowering His Majesty to prohibit exportation of all naval stores without a licence[38] and an Order in Council was accordingly made in which such exportation was prohibited. In *Parkin v Dick*,[39] a marine insurance contract, which insured a voyage that would have been made without such a licence, was held to be void on the ground of illegality of the adventure insured.[40]

(v)   By EC legislation and other international instruments

4.30   Certain adventures could be rendered illegal through European Community (EC) legislation. While provisions of the EC Treaty have direct effect in the Member States and there is no general and invariable duty to adopt national rules to implement

---

35   *Ibid*, p 288, *per* Devlin J. See, also, *Archbolds (Freightage) Ltd v Sparglett (S) Ltd, Rendall Third Party* [1961] 1 QB 374; *Crouch & Lees v Haridas* [1972] 1 QB 158; *Curragh Investments Ltd v Cook* [1974] 1 WLR 1559.

36   (1785) ITR 85n.

37   *Janson v Driefontein Consolidated Mines Ltd* [1902] AC 484, p 499, *per* Lord Davey.

38   The Act was 16 Geo 3 c 5 (1775–6).

39   (1809) 2 Camp 221.

40   See, also, *Johnston v Sutton* (1799) 1 Doug 254.

Treaty provisions, it is highly unlikely that a marine adventure is going to be banned by these provisions. However, secondary Community legislation, particularly regulations, might have such an effect. A regulation is binding in its entirety and directly applicable in all Member States.[41] One regulation that might affect the legality of marine adventures is the Council Regulation (EC) 97/338 on the Protection of Species of Wild Fauna and Flora by Regulating Trade Therein.[42] This regulation enables the application of the Convention on International Trade in Endangered Species of Wild Fauna and Flora, signed on 3 March 1973, throughout the EC. According to this regulation, the introduction into the EC and the export outside the EC of species covered by the Convention is subject to the presentation of a permit or certificate at the customs office at which the custom facilities are completed. An import permit will only be issued if certain conditions are satisfied. Accordingly, a voyage that is carried out without such a permit is an illegal one.[43]

4.31   Similarly, certain voyages may be rendered illegal by international law. For instance, in cases where United Nations (UN) sanctions are introduced against a country, say an embargo is imposed and accordingly trading with that country is prohibited, all members of the UN are required to enact legislation that prohibits trading with that country in order to comply with these sanctions.[44] After the enactment of national legislation that prohibits trade with the country in question, if an insurance policy insuring a voyage to that country is effected it will lead to the breach of the implied warranty of legality.

(b)   *Illegality during the performance of the adventure insured*

4.32   The implied warranty imposed by s 41 requires an insurance contract, which is concluded to provide indemnity for a legal adventure, to be performed in a lawful manner.[45] That means the implied warranty of illegality is again going to be broken in cases where the adventure is lawful, but during its performance the assured violates a statute or regulation.[46] As discussed in the previous part of this chapter, the statute or regulation that is violated must be one prohibiting an act and illegality must also go to the core of the adventure. It was held, in *Ingham v Agnew*,[47] that although the adventure insured was lawful at its outset, it was not performed legally as the assured

---

41 Article 249 (ex 189) of the EC Treaty.

42 This Regulation replaces Regulation (EEC) 82/3626.

43 Directives, also, could restrict or prohibit the performance of certain voyages. However, it should be remembered that directives shall be binding on the Member States only when they are implemented into the national law of that state (Art 249 (ex 189) of the EC Treaty).

44 For instance, during the Gulf War the UN placed an embargo on trade with Iraq and all the members of the UN were required to take the necessary steps to prohibit trading with Iraq: UN Resolution 1990/661.

45 The origins of this rule, in s 41, can be traced to *Farmer v Legg* (1797) 7 TR 186; *Carstairs v Allnutt* (1813) 3 Camp 497; *Metcalfe v Parry* (1814) 4 Camp 123; *Cunard v Hyde (No 1)* (1858) EB & E 670; *Cunard v Hyde (No 2)* (1859) 20 LJ QB; *Wilson v Rankin* (1865) LR 1 QB 162.

46 It must be borne in mind that, where goods are insured on a 'warehouse to warehouse' basis, the implied warranty of legality applies through the period covered by the policy and, therefore, the warranty may be broken even after the goods are discharged at the port of discharge and while they are transported to the warehouse. See cl 8 of standard ICC 1982 (type A, B, C).

47 (1812) 15 East 517.

sailed without a convoy in violation of a statute that prohibited sailing without a convoy. In *James Yachts Ltd v Thames & Mersey Marine Insurance Co Ltd and Others*,[48] the Supreme Court of British Columbia had to decide whether the violation by the assured of the bylaws and regulations of the local authority rendered the performance of the adventure insured (shipbuilding business) illegal. After a careful consideration, the court held that the performance of the adventure insured was illegal as the object of those regulations was to forbid the performance of such a business in that specific place. Similarly, if a certificate required by a statute to carry passengers is not obtained, the performance of the adventure will be illegal, despite the fact that the adventure insured is lawful.[49] The warranty is again broken in cases where the adventure insured is legal, but the vessel is used for smuggling.[50]

4.33   However, if the object of the statute or regulation that is violated is merely to impose a fine in case of its violation, then its violation does not render the performance of the adventure illegal. Accordingly, violation of shipping safety legislation has not been considered as a factor that makes the performance of the adventure illegal. In *St John Shipping Corp v Joseph Rank Ltd*,[51] a shipowner committed a statutory offence by overloading his ship while performing a number of contracts for carriage of goods. Devlin J held that he was, nonetheless, entitled to freight because the object of the statute was to prevent overloading and not to prohibit contracts. This object was to be achieved by imposing a fine and not by subjecting the owner to the additional loss that would result from invalidating the contract of carriage because of illegality. Similarly, the want of a written agreement with the crew, in the form and of the content required by the Merchant Seamen's Act,[52] was held not to render the performance of the adventure illegal.[53]

4.34   The law, however, has developed in a different way in Australia and violation of shipping safety legislation has been regarded as a factor that renders the performance of the adventure illegal. In *Doak v Weekes & Commercial Union Assurance Co plc*,[54] Ryan J held that leaving a port without persons holding the required certificates, as required by a regulation made with the power given by s 196(4)(vi) of the Marine Act (MA) 1958, rendered the voyage illegal. The assured, in that case, argued that the relevant provision only provided a monetary penalty so the intention of the Act was not to prohibit such voyages, but assure safety at sea. Ryan J, however, had a different view and held that:[55]

> I consider that a regulation, which requires a ship which goes to sea to be provided with a duly certificated crew and imposes a penalty on the owner and master if this requirement is not complied with, must be treated as one which is in effect a prohibition of the voyage unless performed with the crew or master that the law required.

---

48 [1977] 1 Lloyd's Rep 206.
49 *Dudgeon v Pembroke* (1877) 2 App Cas 284. See, also, the judgment of the Privy Council in *Australasian Insurance Co v Jackson* (1875) 33 LT 286 (breach of the Pacific Islanders Protection Act 1872 (repealed)).
50 *Pipon v Cope* (1808) 1 Camp 434.
51 [1957] 1 QB 267.
52 5 & 6 Will 4, c 19. Now regulated by s 25 of the Merchant Shipping Act 1995.
53 *Redmond v Smith* (1844) 7 Man & Gr 457.
54 [1986] 82 FLR 334.
55 [1986] 82 FLR 334, p 339.

This decision was later, impliedly, affirmed by the Federal Court of Australia in *Switzerland Insurance Australia Ltd v Mowie Fisheries Pty Ltd*.[56] In this case, the underwriters argued, *inter alia*, that the insured vessel (a fishing boat) sailed from a port without the prescribed complement of officers, as required by s 119 of the MA 1976 (Tasmania) and this rendered the insured voyage illegal. The court was prepared to hold that violation of s 119 of the relevant Act was sufficient to render the voyage illegal; however, s 119 had no application in the case since the port of refugee where the vessel had sailed from was not regarded as a port under the MA 1976 (Tasmania). Accordingly, s 119 of the said Act was not violated by the assured and, in this respect, he was not in breach of the implied warranty of legality.

4.35   As can be observed, the Australian courts have adopted a different interpretation as to the effect of breach of safety regulations. The position in English law, stated in *St John Shipping Corp v Joseph Rank Ltd*, however, remains unaffected from the decisions of the Australian courts, at least until it is overruled by a competent English court. It could be argued that the solution developed by English law serves the realities of marine insurance more than does the Australian one. If violation of each safety regulation constitutes illegality, a great number of marine insurance contracts are going to be affected and this will, without a doubt, harm the balance between the assured and insurer. Furthermore, parliament focuses on a different subject matter when it passes a specific safety regulation. The main object of a safety regulation is to protect the seafarers and other interests from the possible hazards of sub-standard vessels, rather than prohibiting insurance contracts where at one point after their formation a safety regulation is breached.

4.36   The continuing warranty status imposed by s 41 is qualified by the term 'so far as the assured can control the matter'. It is crystal clear from this wording that the assured will be in breach of the warranty when he is a party to the illegality.[57] However, mere knowledge on the part of the assured that there is some illegality in the performance of the voyage does not make him a party to the illegality when he has no control over the navigation of the ship.[58] Usually, the assured, by way of an agency agreement, gives full authority to his managers on the question of the navigation of the vessel. In such a case, it can be concluded that the assured has control over the matter through his managers, and if the managers are negligent in taking the necessary steps to prevent an illegality during the performance of the adventure, the assured will be in breach of the implied warranty of legality.[59]

---

56 [1997] FCA 231.
57 In cases where the assured is a company, the company will be a party to the illegality when its 'directing mind and will', or the person (senior or junior manager) within the company who is authorised to carry out transactions in respect of that specific business, is committed to the illegal act. See the judgment of the Privy Council in *Meridian Global Funds Management Asia Ltd v The Securities Commission* [1995] 2 AC 500.
58 *Cunard v Hyde (No 1)* (1858) EB & E 670.
59 Of course, in such a case, the manager will be in breach of his management contract and be held liable to the shipowner for damages.

4.37   To sum up, if an act of illegality is committed contrary to the assured's instruction or wishes, or if the assured is not in a position to have control over the illegal performance, then there is no breach of continuing warranty of illegality. In *Wilson v Rankin*,[60] the master of a ship bound on a voyage from British North America to England loaded part of a timber cargo on deck, contrary to the provisions of the Consolidation Act 1853,[61] and sailed without the certificate required by that statute. The Exchequer Chamber held that the owner could recover on a policy on the freight of the voyage as he had no information about illegality committed by his master and crew during the performance of the voyage.

In cases where the assured has no control over the illegality and, accordingly, the implied warranty is not broken, he will be entitled to recover loss caused by illegality of the performance of the adventure as long as the loss is caused by an insured peril.[62] For example, if the illegality is on the part of the master or crew, the assured is entitled to recover on the basis of the insured peril of barratry.[63]

4.38   Illegality occurring during the performance of an adventure, which is legal at the outset, might have different effects on different types of policies. In some cases, for example, illegality that occurs on one leg, might render the insurance on the entire voyage illegal. In case of a policy on a ship 'at and from', if there is any illegality in the risk while the ship is at port, this will render the whole voyage illegal though the illegality may cease before the ship sails. Thus, in *Bird v Appleton*,[64] where a policy was effected on an American ship 'at and from Canton to Hamburg', and it appeared that the ship, on arriving at Canton, and for a short time while she lay in harbour there (consequently after the inception of the risk on ship under this policy), had on board an illegal cargo that she had taken in Bombay for sale at Canton in the course of a separate and distinct voyage, this was held to vitiate the policy on the ship, though she disposed of all of her illegal cargo at Canton and sailed for Hamburg with another cargo.

4.39   If the voyage is an integral and entire voyage, under charterparty or otherwise, any illegality at the commencement, or in the course of it, which will make the whole illegal, will prevent the assured from recovering on a policy effected to protect any part of it, although there may have been no illegality in the part of the voyage so insured.[65] Thus, in *Wilson v Marryatt*,[66] where a ship was chartered for one entire voyage, 'from London to Madeira and thence to the East Indies', and a policy was effected on the ship only 'from Madeira to the East Indies', the assured was prevented from recovering on the policy 'from Madeira to East Indies' (although there had been no illegality in this latter stage of the voyage) as the ship had been engaged in smuggling between London and Madeira with the privity of the assured. This judgment, although at first glance, it seems to extend the effect of the warranty, is sound and can be justified. If the whole voyage (voyage from London to East Indies) was insured under

---

60   (1865) LR 1 QB 162.
61   16 & 17 Vict c 107.
62   *Carstairs v Allnutt* (1813) 3 Camp 497 and *Wilson v Rankin* (1865) LR 1 QB 162.
63   For the definition of barratry see r 11 of Sched 1 to the MIA 1906.
64   (1800) 8 TR 562, pp 566, 569.
65   This possibility was raised by Lord Kenyon in *Wilson v Marryatt* (1798) 8 TR 31, p 46, and later expressly ruled by him in *Bird v Pigon* (1800) 2 Selw NP (13th edn) 932.
66   (1798) 8 TR 31.

the policy, the breach of the warranty at an earlier stage would discharge the insurer from further liability and the assured would be uncovered for the rest of the voyage. The same result, therefore, must be achieved even if the part of the voyage is insured under the policy. In the absence of such a ruling, a chance would be given to the assured to disregard the effect of the breach of the warranty of illegality simply by instating an insurance cover for the later stage of a voyage that was performed illegally at the commencement or earlier stage. The same principle must be applied if a time policy attaches when the voyage is in the course of being performed. Accordingly, if the vessel is at sea when the policy attaches, the implied warranty of illegality will be broken if at a prior stage the voyage is performed illegally.

4.40   Lord Kenyon, in the *Wilson* case, did not mention the effect of illegality of a wholly distinct and separate voyage on the voyage described in the policy. Considering basic principles of insurance law, one can reach a conclusion that an illegality occurring in a distinct and separate voyage should have no effect on the voyage described in the policy, simply because the adventures insured are separate. A couple of years after the *Wilson* case, the law on this point was clarified in *Bird v Appleton*,[67] where it was held that the illegality of a wholly distinct and separate voyage had no effect on the voyage insured by the policy. Thus, where it appeared that an American ship had sailed from London to Canton and thence back to Europe, but it was found that the voyage from London to Canton and that from Canton to Europe were two distinct voyages, it was stated that an illegality committed in the course of the ship's voyage between London and Canton would not possibly affect a policy intended to protect the ship on the voyage from Canton to Europe.

4.41   The final point that has to be considered in this context is supervening illegality. The further performance of an adventure, which is lawful at outset and starts off as lawful, might become unlawful later as a result of change of events, such as outbreak of war.[68] In such a case, the assured must abandon the voyage. If he persists in the adventure, this will lead to an illegality in the performance of the adventure and he will be in breach of the implied warranty of legality.[69]

(C)   Miscellaneous issues

(a)   Illegality must form part of the insured adventure

4.42   The scope of the warranty of legality has been qualified with the term 'adventure insured' in s 41. In this respect, illegality which occurs at the outset of the insured adventure, or during its performance, can violate the implied warranty of legality. What happens if an illegal act, which is not related to the adventure insured, occurs either before the commencement of the adventure insured or even during its performance? For instance, what if the assured, who has effected a hull policy (voyage) for his vessel, is involved in an illegal transaction, that is, bribing the port authorities to secure a berth for the vessel on her return. Taking the literal meaning of s 41 into

---

67   (1800) 8 TR 562.
68   *Sanday & Co v British & Foreign Marine Insurance Co Ltd* [1915] 2 KB 781.
69   *Ibid*, p 788, *per* Bailhache J.

consideration, it can be suggested that, in such a case, illegality is not a part of the insured adventure so the insurer cannot rely on the breach of warranty of legality defence to discharge himself from liability.

This is a sensible solution, but there was no case law supporting this argument until *Royal Boskalis Westminster and Others v Trevor Rex Mountain and Others*[70] was decided in the Court of Appeal. The facts of this case can be summarised as follows: the plaintiffs were five Dutch companies who owned and operated a dredging fleet. Two of them formed a joint venture and, on 28 October 1989, contracted with the General Establishment of Iraqi Ports (GEIP) to carry out dredging work at the port of Umm Quasr, close to the Iraq-Kuwait border. The contract was subject to Iraqi law and Paris arbitration. The fleet was insured, under policies subject to English law, against war risks with the defendant insurers. While the work was being performed Iraq invaded Kuwait on 2 August 1990. A short while after the invasion, UN sanctions were introduced against Iraq. On 16 September 1990, Iraq passed Law No 57, which purported, with effect from 6 August 1990, to seize all the assets of companies whose countries had enacted sanctions legislation against Iraq. The plaintiff's fleet and ancillary equipment were under threat of seizure pursuant to these laws. Further, the Iraqis threatened to use persons employed by the joint venture as human shields in the impending conflict with the USA and its allies. In order to permit demobilisation of the fleet and personnel, the joint venture entered a Finalisation Agreement with GEIP, under which it renounced all contractual claims against GEIP and released a substantial part of a deposit held by AMRO bank in Holland under a letter of credit opened by GEIP as security for payment under the dredging contract. The Court of Appeal held that such an agreement would have constituted a sue and labour expense if the plaintiff (joint venture) had been able to show that it was an enforceable agreement. They failed to do so. The court concluded that any civilised tribunal would have refused to give effect to such a waiver. Furthermore, GEIP had intended throughout to perform the Finalisation Agreement in an unlawful way, namely, in breach of Dutch sanctions legislation. Therefore, for that reason, too, the waiver could not be enforced by GEIP in a Paris arbitration unless the illegal part of the contract (release of deposit) could be severed. It could not, either because it would be contrary to English public policy to circumvent the effect of UN sanctions or because the relevant terms were inextricably linked with the waiver.

After reaching the decision on this ground, the Court of Appeal, *obiter dictum*, briefly considered the argument made by the underwriters that the assured's claim under the sue and labour clause was illegal since the adventure was unlawful or performed in an unlawful manner and accordingly the implied warranty of legality was breached. It was held that making an unlawful payment to secure the release of the insured subject matter from detention had not been a part of the marine adventure insured. Accordingly, this argument was rejected. It is, therefore, clear after the *dictum* of the Court of Appeal in *Royal Boskalis Westminster and Others v Trevor Rex Mountain and Others*, that illegality which does not form part of the adventure insured does not violate the implied warranty of legality.

---

70 [1999] QB 674; [1997] LRLR 523.

(b) Illegality must arise under English law

4.43 It is not expressly stated in s 41 whether the word 'lawful' means that the adventure must be legal merely in accordance with English law, or whether foreign law must also be taken into account when determining the legality of the adventure. There is no doubt that the legality of the adventure must, first of all, be determined in accordance with English law. Until the 1950s, illegality of the adventure under the laws of a foreign state was not taken into account in determining whether the implied warranty of legality was breached. The reason for this was explained by some judges, notably Lord Hardwicke and Lord Mansfield, as the paramount importance in the UK of the fullest freedom of trade.[71] More recently, in accordance with changing notions of international comity, there has been a change in this rule which was adopted by English judges at the end of the 18th century. The House of Lords held, in *Regazzoni v KC Setnia (1944) Ltd*,[72] that the privilege of not having taken notice of any foreign laws cannot, nowadays, be carried too far, especially when a 'friendly' state is involved.[73] In this case, the contract was for the sale of jute bags of Indian origin, to be shipped from India to Italy for resale in South Africa. The export of jute from India to South Africa was prohibited by Indian law. The respondents repudiated the contract and relied on the illegality by Indian law; it was held that they were entitled to do so. Tt is submitted that, after this decision, any contract coming within the rule in the *Regazzoni* case will be 'unlawful' within the meaning of s 3. Therefore, the implied warranty expressed in s 41 of the Act will be broken if the adventure is illegal under the laws of a 'friendly' foreign state.[74]

(c) Potential effect of recent international developments on the implied warranty of legality

4.44 It must be borne in mind that the ISM and ISPS Codes, which were evaluated in detail in the previous chapter, might have a certain impact, or at least might be alleged by the underwriters to have an impact, on the implied warranty of legality. Inspections carried out by port authorities, to a certain degree guarantee that the vessels that do not have a valid ISM or ISPS certificate will not be able to operate between ports. If, however, a vessel without a valid ISM or ISPS certificate is involved in a marine adventure and this adventure is insured, would that be sufficient to warrant the adventure an unlawful one as far as s 41 is concerned? If it would, then the shipowner's insurances during the period of that adventure may well prove to be void due to breach of the implied warranty of legality.

---

71 Arnould, 1954, para 744.

72 [1958] AC 301; [1957] 2 Lloyd's Rep 289.

73 *Ibid*, p 319, Viscount Simonds who said that: 'Just as public policy avoids contracts which offend against our own law, so it will avoid at least some contracts which violate the laws of a foreign State and it will do so because public policy demands that defence to international comity.'

74 Note that any adventure contravening a foreign law that had not been acted upon or enforced by its own country would not constitute a breach of the implied warranty. See *Francis v Sea Insurance Co* (1898) 3 Com Cas 229.

4.45   Both of these codes have been developed to enhance maritime safety and security. They do, therefore, act as safety regulations and they are not intended to prohibit insurance policies in contravention of their provisions. There is established case law that states that breach of safety regulations does not render a voyage illegal.[75] Accordingly, it can be concluded that, even if the assured manages to engage in a marine adventure without having a valid ISM or ISPS certificate and obtain an insurance cover for that adventure, such an adventure will not be regarded as illegal under the principles of English law.[76] The vessel, which commences such a voyage, however, might be regarded as unseaworthy due to breach of a safety regulation.[77]

(d)   Implied warranty of legality: a sui generis warranty

4.46   There are two factors that give the implied warranty of legality a *sui generis* character. First, although s 34(3) states that a breach of warranty may be waived, a breach of the implied warranty is an exception to this rule.[78] Legality of the adventure insured and legality in its performance, as stated before, determines the limits of a marine insurance contract. For this reason, the parties may not be given an opportunity to disregard these limits by waiving the implied warranty of legality.

4.47   Second, there is no implied warranty of legality in non-marine insurance. The reason for this is that the policy in non-marine insurance is one on property and nothing more. This was explained by Staughton J, in the first instance in *Euro-Diam Ltd v Bathurst*,[79] in the following speech:

> Suppose that a motor car is insured for a calendar year, and is driven in January in excess of the speed limit. Would that be an answer to a claim for loss by theft or fire or a road accident in June? If a publican insured his stock of glasses and they were stolen in June, would it matter that they had been used for drinking after permitted hours in January? Those examples demonstrate the point that the insurance here was upon goods, and not upon any adventure. I therefore reject the argument of the implied term.

The Court of Appeal[80] affirmed this approach; in its view, implying a term that potentially had these consequences was not necessary to give business efficacy to the agreement.

---

75   *St John Shipping Corp v Joseph Rank Ltd* [1957] 1 QB 267.
76   As indicated above, there is always the possibility that the law of another friendly state, ie the law of the flag state, might render such an adventure unlawful. In that case, English courts are likely to take into account the findings of the flag state.
77   See above [4.24] to [4.26].
78   *Gedge & Others v Royal Exchange Assurance Corp* [1900] 2 QB 214.
79   [1987] 1 Lloyd's Rep 178, p 186.
80   [1990] 1 QB 1.

CHAPTER 5

NATURE OF MARINE WARRANTIES

5.1   Despite their structural differences, express and implied warranties have one thing in common. They are both terms of a marine insurance contract. This explains why certain legal features are common to both express and implied warranties. The object of this chapter, by way of scrutinising these common grounds, is to clarify the nature of this contractual term. These features, which have been laid down by the case law and the Marine Insurance Act (MIA) 1906, distinguish marine warranties from other terms of a marine insurance contract. After clarifying the exact nature of marine warranties, the examination of the current status of marine warranties will be completed with an intensive analysis on the waiver of breach of warranties in Chapter 6.

I – EXACT (STRICT) COMPLIANCE IS REQUIRED

5.2   It has always been the case, since Lord Mansfield's day, that the obligation undertaken by a marine warranty must be exactly complied with, so that, as he himself said, *obiter dictum* in *Pawson v Watson*,[1] '... nothing tantamount will do or answer the purpose'. Accordingly, in *De Hahn v Hartley*,[2] a warranty that required the insured vessel to sail with at least 50 hands was held to be breached when the insured vessel sailed with 46 crew members on board, although six more did join soon after departure.[3] The exact compliance doctrine as set out by Lord Mansfield was later adopted in s 33(3) by Sir Mackenzie Chalmers.

5.3   The exact compliance doctrine, one of the features of warranties, is certainly not the one which distinguishes warranties from other terms of an insurance contract. For example, conditions, which deal with particular matters, in insurance contracts also need to be exactly complied with, substantial performance being insufficient. In other words, if the condition goes to details, those details must be literally fulfilled and it is no defence for the assured to assert that such details are immaterial. Accordingly, in *Jacobson v Yorkshire Insurance Co Ltd*,[4] where a condition in a burglary insurance that required the insured to keep proper books of account with a complete record of all purchases or sales, was held not to be fulfilled by keeping records of purchases only.

5.4   It has been observed, on numerous occasions, that the courts are ready to interpret the obligations imposed by warranties narrowly in order to overcome the strictness of the exact compliance doctrine. For instance, in *Hide v Bruce*,[5] an express

---

1   (1778) 2 Cowp 785, p 787.
2   (1786) 1 TR 343.
3   See, also, *Hore v Whitmore* (1778) 2 Cowp 784; *Earle v Harris* (1780) 1 Dougl 357; *Sanderson v Busher* (1814) 4 Camp 54n.
4   (1933) LlL Rep 281.
5   (1773) 3 Doug KB 213.

warranty, which required the insured vessel to commence the intended adventure with 20 guns, was held to be satisfied even though there were 20 guns on board, but not the men necessary to work them. Similarly, it was held, in *Muller v Thompson*,[6] that a warranty that the vessel would carry a particular cargo did not preclude the assured from carrying additional cargo.

5.5   Whether the courts could also be assisted by the *de minimis non curat lex* rule in order to mitigate the harsh consequences of strict compliance doctrine was discussed in *Overseas Commodities Ltd v Style*.[7] In commercial law the application of this rule could be observed, particularly when numerical calculations were involved. Accordingly, in cases where this rule applies, non-performance or defective performance of a commercially insignificant amount has no legal consequence.

In the *Overseas* case, the assured shipped two consignments of tinned pork from France to London, under an all risk policy of insurance underwritten by the insurers. The policy contained a warranty that required that all the tins should be marked by the manufacturers verifying the date of manufacture. When the tins were delivered, many of them were found to be rusty or broken and much of the pork was either condemned or sold off cheaply. The assured claimed on the policy, but the insurer rejected the claim on the basis that, as many of the tins did not have the date of manufacture upon them, the warranty was breached. The court ruled that lack of such marks on many of the tins amounted to breach of warranty and, thus, the underwriters were not liable. However, the judgment of McNair J leaves no doubt that the possible application of the *de minimis non curat lex* rule has been considered by the court. Towards the end of his judgment, McNair J stated that:[8]

> Being satisfied that, as regards both policies, a substantial number of tins – well exceeding any tolerance that could be disregarded under the *de minimis* rule – were not marked with a code which enabled the true and correct date of manufacture to be established, I have no option to hold that the breach of the express warranty affords the underwriters a complete defence in this action.

5.6   It is certain from the language adopted that had only one tin out of, say, a thousand not been stamped in accordance with the warranty, by applying the *de minimis* rule McNair J would have held that the warranty was not breached. The application of this rule, especially in cases like the *Overseas* case, is fully justified and there is case law that suggests that such a rule could be applied in all areas of commercial law, including marine insurance. In *Margaronis Navigation Agency Ltd v Henry W Peabody & Co of London Ltd*,[9] Sellers LJ, referring to the rule of *de minimis non curat lex*, said that:[10]

> I think it is a rule of general application. It matters not whether it be a claim or defence. It matters not the nature of the transaction. It seems to me that in all cases the court is called upon to consider the substance of the matter and will not regard or give effect to

---

6   (1811) 2 Camp 610.
7   [1958] 1 Lloyd's Rep 546.
8   *Ibid*, p 558 (emphasis added).
9   [1965] 2 QB 430.
10   *Ibid*, p 444.

what are undoubtedly, in the view of the court, trivialities, matters of little moment, of a trifling and negligible nature.

5.7 In fact, the Malaysia High Court, in *Boon & Cheah Steel Pipes SDN BDH v Asia Insurance Co Ltd*,[11] discussed the application of the *de minimis* rule to a marine insurance contract.[12] In that case, the assured were the owners of 668 steel pipes, which were insured free from particular average and carried from Prai to Brunei by a barge towed by the tug *Selvaliant*. In the course of the voyage, the vessel and cargo were damaged by perils of the sea insured against and only 24 of the pipes were delivered, 12 of them in a damaged condition. The assured sued the insurer on the ground that the cargo was an actual total loss by reason of the *de minimis* rule. The court considering the facts of the case decided that, although the rule has application in marine insurance contracts, it cannot be applied in the present case, since 12 pipes which were delivered in a good condition formed too high a proportion of 668 pipes. Delivering the judgment of the court, Shah J said that:[13]

> It may be that in the case of a single pipe or two out of the whole consignment, the rule would apply, but I fail to see how it is possible to hold that 12 pipes can be ignored or treated as trifling and to be brushed aside.

Therefore, it can be concluded that the *de minimis* rule could be applied to overcome the strictness of strict compliance doctrine to a certain degree. However, the application of this rule is rather limited and the breach should involve only a trivial part of the whole undertaking.

II – NO MATERIALITY AND CAUSAL LINK REQUIRED

5.8 Section 33(3), repeating the rule set by Lord Mansfield,[14] declares that a warranty needs to be complied with, whether it be material to the risk or not. This rule, in fact, implies two things. First, it means that an express warranty might cover anything, even if it be 'absurd' or 'fanciful'.[15] Put another way, the facts warranted may be of a sort that could not affect the risk in any manner. For example, if the assured in a hull policy warrants that the name of the insured vessel shall not be altered, despite the fact that this point could have no effect on the risk insured against, still a warranty of that type must be exactly complied with.

Furthermore, it also implies that, even though the warranted event concerns things which could be material in a general way, whether the particular breach by the assured has any material effect on the case in question is irrelevant. Accordingly, in *Yorkshire Insurance Co Ltd v Campbell*,[16] where the insurance was on a horse, against marine

---

11 [1975] 1 Lloyd's Rep 452.
12 It should be noted that Malaysia is one of the common law countries which has adopted the MIA 1906 into its legal system.
13 [1975] 1 Lloyd's Rep 452, p 460.
14 In *De Hahn v Hartley* (1786) 1 TR 343, p 345, Lord Mansfield said that: 'It is perfectly immaterial for what purpose a warranty is introduced, but, being inserted, the contract does not exist unless it be literally complied with.'
15 See *Farr v Motor Traders' Mutual Insurance Society* [1920] 3 KB 669, p 673, *per* Bankers LJ.
16 [1917] AC 218.

perils and risks of mortality during a sea voyage, and it was described in the proposal form as – 'Bay gelding by Soult X St Paul (mare) five years', the pedigree as stated was incorrect and the Privy Council held that since, on its construction, the description of the horse was a warranty, the inaccuracy provided insurers with a defence to the owner's claim when the horse died on the voyage. It is clear that, in such an insurance policy, the pedigree of the insured horse has a bearing on its temperament and, thus, its ability to withstand a marine voyage, but there was no evidence in the case that the horse's actual pedigree adversely affected it in this regard or had made any difference in the actual circumstances of the loss. However, the fact that there was a breach of warranty in the case was sufficient to discharge the insurer from liability.[17] Similarly, in *Forsikringsaktielselskapet Vesta v Butcher*,[18] it was held that under English law the failure of the assured owner of a fish farm to comply with a warranty whereby a 24-hour watch had to be maintained was fatal to his claim for loss from storm damage. It was conceded that the presence of a watch could not possibly have in any way lessened the likelihood or degree of loss by storm. The absence of a watch, on the other hand, was sufficient to deny the claim of the assured under English law.

5.9   A line of antecedent case law also suggests that, although the loss may not have been in the remotest degree connected with the breach of warranty, the insurer is, nonetheless, discharged on that account from all liability for the loss, if the warranty has, in fact, been broken. Thus, in *Hibbert v Pigou*,[19] where a ship warranted to sail with convoy had, in fact, sailed without it and went down in a storm, the underwriter was held not liable for this loss.[20] Again, in *Foley v Tabor*,[21] Chief Justice Erle's address to the jury on this point stated that:[22]

> It is not necessary for the insurer to make out that the loss was caused by the unseaworthiness relied upon. The question depends upon the state of the ship at the time when she sailed upon her voyage.

5.10   Although no point has been made in the MIA 1906 as to this issue, by virtue of s 91(2) these cases are still good law nowadays[23] and it is an established rule that breach of a marine warranty discharges the insurer from further liability, regardless of the existence of a causal link between the breach and loss. More recently, this rule has been regarded as 'one of the less attractive features of English insurance law', by Lord Griffiths in *Forsikringsaktielselskapet Vesta v Butcher*.[24] Admittedly, allowing the insurer to discharge himself from liability, even in cases where there is no causal link between the loss and breach, creates unfair consequences for the assured and the need for a possible reform in this area will be advocated in the final chapter of this book.

---

17 See, also, *Blackhurst v Cockell* (1789) 3 TR 360 to the same effect.
18 [1989] AC 852.
19 (1783) 3 Doug KB 213.
20 See, also, *Christian v Ditchell* (1797) Peake's Add Cas 141; *Thomson v Weems* (1884) 9 App Cas 671; *Wedderburn v Bell* (1807) 1 Camp 1; *Lane v Nixon* (1866) LR 1 CP 412.
21 (1861) 2 F & F 663.
22 *Ibid*, p 672.
23 Section 91(2) reads as follows: 'The rules of common law including the law merchant, save in so far as they are inconsistent with the express provisions of this Act, shall continue to apply to contracts of marine insurance.'
24 [1989] AC 852, p 893.

III – BREACH OF WARRANTY CANNOT BE REMEDIED

5.11   Section 34(2) reads as follows:

Where a warranty is broken, the assured cannot avail himself of the defence that the breach has been remedied, and the warranty complied with, before loss.

This sub-section has been derived from cases that were decided in the late 18th and early 19th century. In *De Hahn v Hartley*,[25] when the insured vessel commenced the intended voyage the warranted number of crew were not on board. The warranted number of crew had been recruited before the vessel sailed on the leg of the voyage during which the casualty occurred. However, it was held that once the warranty was breached it was immaterial whether it was remedied later. Similarly, in *Quebec Marine Insurance Co v Commercial Bank of Canada*,[26] the vessel was insured for a voyage 'at and from' Montreal to Halifax, Nova Scotia. After leaving Montreal, her boiler, which had been defective from the outset, became unmanageable when seawater entered and she had to seek refuge nearby in order to effect repairs. The repairs were duly made, but soon after resuming her voyage she encountered severe weather and was lost. The Privy Council ruled that the assured were in breach of the implied warranty of seaworthiness and the insurers were not liable under the policy even though the defect was remedied before the loss occurred.

IV – NO EXCUSE FOR BREACH OF A WARRANTY – EXCEPTIONS TO THE GENERAL RULE

5.12   Arnould stated that:[27]

No cause, however sufficient; no motive however good, no necessity, however irresistible, will excuse non-compliance with a warranty.

This principle was declared in the late 18th century and is still good law by virtue of s 91(2). In *Hore v Whitmore*,[28] the insured vessel was warranted to sail on a given day; however, she was prevented from doing so by an embargo imposed by a British governor. It was ruled that this breach of the warranty was sufficient to discharge the insurer from liability, despite the fact that such an embargo came expressly within the words 'restraints and detainment of kings, princes and people', which were perils expressly insured against in the policy. Also, whether the assured is innocent or not is immaterial. In *Douglas v Scougall*,[29] Lord Eldon said that:

It is not necessary to inquire whether the owners acted honestly and fairly in the transaction; for this, it is clear law that, however just and honest the intentions of the owner may be, if he is mistaken in the fact and the vessel is, in fact, not seaworthy, the underwriter is not liable.

---

25   (1786) 1 TR 343.
26   (1870) LR 3 PC 234.
27   Arnould, 1981, para 687.
28   (1778) 2 Cowp 784.
29   (1816) 4 Dow 269, p 276.

This means that if the insured vessel is diverted to a port due to a storm and, by undertaking this diversion, a navigation warranty is breached, the insurer will still be discharged from liability should a loss occur. Similarly, if the master and crew take the insured vessel to a different destination from that ordered by the owner and, during this time, a warranty is breached, the insurer will still be discharged from liability even though 'barratry'[30] is a risk insured against in modern hull cover.

5.13   Although the rule itself has not been expressly spelt out in the MIA 1906, Sir Mackenzie Chalmers felt that it was essential to indicate its exceptions in s 34(1). This was probably done in order to limit the scope of exceptions and prevent courts from adopting new exceptions to the rule by considering the special circumstances of the case in question.

The first case where non-compliance with marine warranties could be excused is when the warranty ceases to be applicable to the circumstances of the contract by reason of a change of circumstances. At first sight, the scope of this exception seems to be extensive. However, by evaluation of the example provided by Sir Mackenzie Chalmers in the commentary for the MIA 1906,[31] it can be observed that it has only a limited application. According to the drafter of the Act, if, during war, a warranty to sail with a convoy at a future time from some foreign station was inserted, the intervention of peace before the period at which the ship was so to sail would excuse the necessity of compliance. Thus, under this sub-section, in cases where a warranty has been incorporated into the policy for a particular reason, the assured will be excused for not complying with it provided that the reason, which made parties agree on such a warranty, ceases to exist after the attachment of the policy. In this respect the exception expressed in s 34(1) seems to derive from the celebrated Latin maxim *cessante ratione, cessat lex*.[32] If this analysis is accurate,[33] then it can be concluded that this exception has no application as far as implied warranties are concerned since it is very unlikely that the reason behind an implied warranty will cease to exist during the currency of the policy.

5.14   According to s 34(1), non-compliance with a warranty is excused in cases where compliance with the warranty is rendered unlawful by any subsequent law. It is an established rule of law that if a man agrees to do a thing which is lawful at the time, but an Act of Parliament comes in and hinders him from doing it, the agreement is repealed.[34] The exception in s 34(1) could be regarded as a reflection of this principle on marine warranties regime. The author believes that this sub-section is essential in order to harmonise the warranty regime with s 41, which imposes an implied

---

30 Rule 11 of the Rules for Construction of Policy reads as follows: 'The term "barratry" includes every wrongful act wilfully committed by the master or crew to the prejudice of the owner, or, as the case may be, the charterer.'

31 Chalmers and Archibald, 1922.

32 With the reason for the law ceasing, the law itself ceases.

33 The decision in *Agapitos v Agnew (The Aegeon) (No 2)* [2002] EWHC 1558, [2003] Lloyd's Rep IR 54, confirms the view that the scope of this exception is rather limited. In that case a warranty, which required Salvage Association's approval of location, fire fighting and mooring arrangements, was breached. The assured sought to argue that the warranty had ceased to apply by reason of the fact that the vessel was moved from the original location to another place. Moore-Bick J disagreed. The circumstances to which the warranty had been directed had not changed irrespective of the vessel's location.

34 *Brewster v Kitchin* (1698) 1 Ld Raym 321.

warranty to the effect that the assured should make sure that the adventure is carried out in a lawful manner, so far as he can control the matter. Without such an exception, the assured could find himself in a 'no win' situation, because he wcould have been in breach of an implied warranty, while trying to comply with another one. Furthermore, expecting the assured to commit illegal activities to comply with the terms of an insurance contract would be against the principles of public policy.

5.15   As was indicated by Clarke,[35] in non-marine insurance, apart from these two exceptions, the assured might be excused for breach of an express warranty if he neither knew of the warranty nor had the opportunity of knowing it. This would be because the warranty was not a term of the contract or was not intended to apply until the terms including warranty had been communicated to the assured.[36] By virtue of s 35(2), which requires all express warranties to be included in or written upon the policy, or contained in some document incorporated by reference into the policy, the assured could not allege that he did not have knowledge about the existence of an express warranty. The formal requirement that all express warranties must be, somehow, incorporated into the policy makes the application of such an exception very difficult as far as marine insurance contracts are concerned.

V – EFFECT OF BREACH OF MARINE INSURANCE WARRANTIES

(A)   Meaning of breach and burden of proof

5.16   The effects of breach of a warranty arise in cases where there is an actual breach. For example, a warranty of locality is breached from the moment the insured vessel travels outside the warranted area. Intention to commit a breach of warranty does not itself constitute a breach. Thus, in *Simpson SS Co Ltd v Premier Underwriting Association Ltd*,[37] where a policy contained a warranty of locality that prevented the vessel from proceeding east of Singapore and she sailed from Cardiff bound for a port east of Singapore, underwriters were not held to be relieved of liability when she sailed as there was at most an intention to breach.[38]

5.17   As the breach of warranty defence is one of the most effective defences for an underwriter, it is understandable that the law has put the onus to prove breach of warranty on the shoulders of the insurer.[39] It is, however, open to the parties to shift the burden of proof by expessing this clearly in their contract. For instance, it may be provided in the policy that, on the happening of certain events, the warranty will be regarded as breached and the assured has to prove that this is not the case.

---

35   Clarke, 2002, para 20-6B2.
36   *Re Coleman's Depositories Ltd and Life & Health Insurance Association* [1907] 2 KB 798, p 805, *per* Vaughan Williams LJ; p 812, *per* Buckby LJ.
37   (1905) 10 Com Cas 198.
38   See, also, *Baines v Holland* (1885) 10 Exch 802 to the same effect.
39   *Barrett v Jermy* (1849) 3 Exch 535; *Stebbing v Liverpool & London & Globe Insurance Co Ltd* [1917] 2 KB 433; *Bonney v Cornhill Insurance Co* (1931) 40 L1L Rep 39; *Bond Air Services Ltd v Hill* [1955] 2 QB 417; *W & J Lane v Spratt* [1970] 2 QB 480; *Soft v Prudential Assurance Co* [1993] 2 Lloyd's Rep 559.

(B)   Legal effect of breach

(a)   Effect of breach of warranties which relate to a period before the attachment of the risk

5.18   As examined in Chapter 1, some warranties relate, in terms of time, to circumstances at the inception of the risk. In such a case, the warranted event or condition must be complied with at some time before the risk attaches. For instance, the MIA 1906 implies a warranty of portworthiness in respect of a voyage policy on hull that attaches 'at and from' the place named in the policy.[40] Section 39(2) requires such a vessel to be reasonably fit to encounter the ordinary perils of the port at the commencement of the risk. Similarly, s 41 implies a warranty of legality in all policies and requires the insured voyage to be a lawful one. Express warranties can also be drafted to cover a period before the attachment of the risk. For instance, an express warranty of neutrality requires the vessel to be warranted neutral, that is to have such a character at the commencement of the risk.[41]

5.19   In cases where the warranty relates in time to circumstances at the inception of the risk, breach will result in the insurer never coming on risk. Compliance with a warranty of this type was considered as 'a condition precedent to the attaching of the risk', in *Thomson v Weems*,[42] by Lord Blackburn. There, the assured had warranted, in a life policy, the accuracy of the statements made by him in the proposal form. When the evidence clearly proved that the assured's statement as to his temperance in his habits was untrue, the policy was held null and void. Accordingly, the validity of the insurance policy depends on the compliance with the warranty and, once the warranty is breached, the contract never comes into existence. The suspensive effect of contingent condition precedents, which may arise in some contracts,[43] therefore has no application in this context due to the special nature of insurance contracts. In such a case, it seems likely that the premium is refundable due to total failure of consideration, unless the breach of warranty is, in fact, fraudulent.[44]

5.20   One may argue that the principle in relation to breach of warranties, which relate to a period before the attachment of the risk, has derived from a non-marine case and, therefore, does not apply in the context of marine insurance. However, this point cannot be argued forcefully for two reasons. First, Lord Blackburn, in *Thomson v Weems*, expressly stated that, in his opinion, as regards the effect of breach of warranty, the same principles applied whether the insurance be marine or not.[45] Secondly, two different judgments of Lord Mansfield in relation to marine warranties delivered in the late 18th century adopt a similar language. In *Woolmer v Muilman*,[46] the insured vessel

---

40   For the nature and scope of this implied warranty see above [4.3] to [4.6].
41   See s 36.
42   (1884) 9 App Cas 671, p 684.
43   *Marten v Whale* [1917] 2 KB 480.
44   See s 84(1).
45   (1884) 9 App Cas 671, p 684. He drew upon the decision of Lord Eldon in *Newcastle Fire Insurance Co v Macmorran & Co* (1815) 3 Dow 255.
46   (1763) 3 Burr 1419.

was warranted neutral and was lost by perils of the sea. At the trial there was evidence to the effect that she was not neutral property and Lord Mansfield CJ said that:[47] 'This was no contract, for the man insured neutral property and this was not neutral property.' Similarly, in *De Hahn v Hartley*,[48] he described a marine warranty which related to a period before the attachment of the risk, in a very similar sense as did Lord Blackburn in *Thomson v Weems*:[49]

> A warranty in a policy of insurance is a condition or contingency, and unless that be performed there is no contract. It is perfectly immaterial for what purpose a warranty is introduced, but, being inserted, the contract does not exist unless it be literally complied with.

Since there is no express provision in the MIA 1906 in relation to the effect of breach of warranties of this type, by virtue of s 91(2), Lord Mansfield's judgments can still be regarded as good law.

(b)   Effect of breach of warranties which relate to a period after the attachment of the risk

5.21   Some warranties concern the assured's future conduct and require him to do or not to do a particular thing, or fulfil some condition at some point after the attachment of the risk.[50] The warranty of seaworthiness that is implied in respect of voyage policies by the MIA 1906[51] and most express warranties, such as locality warranties, institute warranty (as to towage and salvage services) and laid up and out of commission warranties,[52] are examples of warranties of this type. Since the warranted event or condition relates, in time, to a period after the attachment of the risk, breach of a warranty of this type does not have any effect on the existence of the contract, unlike the breach of warranties discussed earlier in previous part. The legal effect of breach for these kinds of warranties is spelt out in s 33(3) as follows: '... the insurer is discharged from liability as from the date of the breach of warranty, but without prejudice to any liability incurred by him before that date.'

5.22   The meaning of this sub-section became the subject of judicial examination in the 1990s in *The Good Luck*.[53] It is to be noted that, though the case was concerned directly with an express warranty, namely, warranty of locality, the principles enunciated therein on the effects of a breach also apply to implied warranties. The facts of the case may be summarised as follows: *The Good Luck* was insured with the defendant club and mortgaged to the plaintiff bank. As required by the mortgage, the benefit of the insurance was assigned to the bank and the club gave a letter of undertaking to the bank, whereby the club promised to advise the bank promptly if they should 'cease to insure' the ship. Diagram 1 shows the relationship between various parties in this case.

---

47   *Ibid*, p 1420.
48   (1786) 1 TR 343.
49   *Ibid*, pp 345–46.
50   See above [1.18].
51   See s 39(1).
52   For a detailed analysis on express warranties of this type, see above [2.33] to [2.51].
53   [1988] 1 Lloyd's Rep 514; [1990] 1 QB 818; [1989] 2 Lloyd's Rep 238 (CA); [1992] 1 AC 233; [1991] 2 Lloyd's Rep 191 (HL).

Diagram 1: The Good Luck

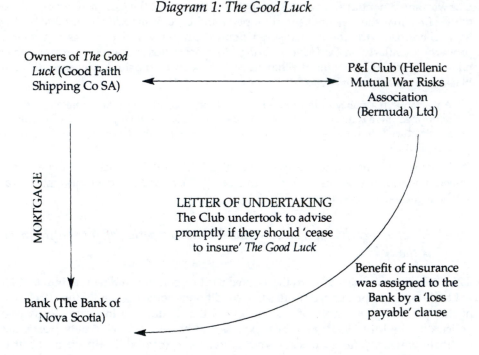

The rules of the relevant club contained an express warranty prohibiting the insured vessel from entering certain declared areas. These areas were areas of such extreme danger that it was not considered acceptable by the club that they should cover vessels entering these areas. If an owner wanted such cover while his vessel was in a prohibited area, special arrangements had to be made. The owners of *The Good Luck* were in the practice of sending the vessel into prohibited areas, but neither the club nor the bank were informed. The managers of the club later discovered what was going on, but they neither took any steps to deter the owners of *The Good Luck* from carrying on nor informed the bank of what they had discovered. On her last voyage *The Good Luck* was sent to part of the Arabian Gulf in breach of warranty. She was hit by Iraqi missiles and became a constructive total loss. Both club and bank knew of the total loss, but, whereas the club discovered the breach of warranty, the bank negligently did not investigate the possibility.[54] In the mistaken belief that the loss was covered, the bank made further loans to the shipowners. In view of the breach of warranty, the insurance could not be enforced, but the bank brought an action against the club for having failed to give prompt notice that they had ceased to insure the ship. Accordingly, it was contended that the club was in breach of the letter of undertaking given by them to the bank.

---

54   The bank was of the opinion that an arrangement was made between the owners and the club to keep the vessel insured while she was in the prohibited areas.

The bank relied on three different grounds. First, they alleged that the club was liable to them for breach of a continuing duty of good faith, as stated in s 17. The existence of such a duty was denied by both the first instance judge, Hobhouse J, and the Court of Appeal. Secondly, it was contended that the club was liable to the bank in tort for 'breach of a duty to speak'. This argument, which was accepted at first instance, was reversed by the Court of Appeal. The third allegation of the bank gave rise to a serious and intense judicial examination of s 33(3), as a result of which the effect of breach for warranties that relate to a period after the attachment of the risk was clarified. The bank contended that, by virtue of s 33(3), the breach of warranty brought the vessel's insurance to an end automatically and, accordingly, the insurer was in breach of the express provisions of the letter of undertaking in failing to notify the bank as to such a breach.

This argument, which was accepted at first instance by Hobhouse J, was challenged by the club in the Court of Appeal. The club supported the view that breach of a warranty does not automatically discharge the insurer from liability, but gives the club a right to elect to terminate it. Since the club elected to terminate the contract for breach, at a time after the loans were made by the bank, the provisions of the letter of undertaking were not breached.[55] Agreeing with the contention of the club, the Court of Appeal held that breach of a warranty did not automatically discharge the insurer from liability and he was required to take active steps to rescind or repudiate the contract as he would have to in the case of a breach of a condition under ordinary principles of contract law. Accordingly, since the club had not taken such steps to repudiate the contract before further loan was given by the bank, they were not in breach of the letter of undertaking they had given to the bank.

When delivering its judgment, the Court of Appeal was influenced by some academic texts relating to insurance law as well as by two different reports, one of which was signed by Lords Jenkins, Parker, Devlin and Diplock, equating breach of warranty with a repudiatory breach.[56] Citing Arnould,[57] the Court of Appeal also found that the 'automatic discharge' remedy in case of breach of a warranty contradicts the possibility of waiver by the insurer of the breach as is expressly contemplated by s 34(3).[58] In the view of the Court of Appeal, a contract that has come

---

55 There is a whole world of difference in saying that a contract is 'void' from saying that the insurer is 'discharged from liability'. In the case of a discharge, under s 33(3), the insurer is discharged from liability only as from the date of the breach; all rights and liabilities accrued before the breach are preserved. When the contract is void, it has no legal consequences from the very beginning.

56 [1990] 1 QB 818, pp 876–77.

57 Arnould, 1981, para 708, fn 18, which reads as follows:

The statement made by Arnould that the breach of warranty avoids the policy is clearly inaccurate, since after it had been avoided it would not be possible for the insurer to affirm it, as he has always been able to do, by waiving the breach. It was no doubt for this reason that the draftsman of the MIA 1906, preferred to use the expression 'discharged from liability'. Strictly speaking, however, this is open to the same objection, since if he had once become 'discharged as from the date of the breach' it would logically become impossible for the insurer to make himself liable by subsequent waiver, unless possibly he could be held estopped from pleading 'the discharge'. The true position appears to be that the breach of warranty gives the insurer the right to avoid the policy, and to make such avoidance operate from the time of breach ...

58 [1990] 1 QB 818, p 880.

to an end cannot be revived by the act of one party, namely the insurer. Revival would require the making of a new contract by both parties. Furthermore, the Court of Appeal found it impossible to reconcile the concepts of 'condition precedent' properly so-called, non-fulfilment of which results in there being no contract, and breach of a promissory warranty, which cannot be contended to have that result.[59]

Reversing the Court of Appeal's decision, the House of Lords held that breach of a warranty of this nature automatically discharges the insurer from liability from the date of breach. Accordingly, the club was in breach of the letter of undertaking since they were automatically discharged from further liability from the moment *The Good Luck* entered the prohibited area. The reasonings of the House of Lords and their accuracy will be discussed in the following part of this chapter.

(i)   Justification of the decision of the House of Lords in The Good Luck

5.23   Unlike the Court of Appeal, which suggested the existence of an irreconcilable contradiction between the concepts of 'condition precedent' and 'breach of a promissory warranty', Lord Goff, in the House of Lords, referring to the wording of s 33(3) held that:[60]

... if a promissory warranty is not complied with, the insurer is discharged from liability as from the date of the breach of warranty, for the simple reason that fulfilment of the warranty is a condition precedent to the liability or further liability of the insurer.

Further, in his judgment Lord Goff made the following remark as to the meaning of the expression 'condition precedent' in the above passage:[61]

In the case of conditions precedent, the word 'condition' is being used in its classical sense in English law, under which the coming into existence of (for example) an obligation, or the duty or further duty to perform an obligation, is dependent upon the fulfilment of the specified condition.

5.24   Despite the fact that no authority has been cited to support the 'condition precedent' analysis in the context of a breach of a warranty, Lord Goff might have

---

59   *Ibid*, p 881. To support their view, the Court of Appeal cited the *dictum* of Donaldson J, in *De Maurier (Jewels) Ltd v Bastion Insurance Co Ltd* [1967] 2 Lloyd's Rep 550, at pp 558–59, where he said as follows:

I also hold, as was ultimately conceded, that the warranty delimits and is part of the description of the risk and is not of a promissory character. By a warranty of a promissory character I mean a warranty by the assured that a particular state of affairs will exist, breach of which destroys a substratum of the contract and entitles the underwriter to decline to come on risk or, as the case may be, to terminate the risk as from the date of breach. In the marine field 'warranted free from capture and seizure' is a warranty of the former character leaving the contract effective in respect of loss by other perils. 'Warranted to sail on or before a particular date' is, however, of a promissory character, breach of which renders the contract voidable. The commercial reasoning behind this legal distinction is clear, namely, that breach of the former type of warranty does not affect the nature or extent of the risks falling outside the terms of the warranty; breach of a promissory warranty may, however, materially affect such risks.

60   [1992] 1 AC 233, pp 262–63.
61   *Ibid*, p 263.

borrowed this idea from Bramwell B in *Jackson v Union Marine Insurance Co Ltd*.[62] In that case, a voyage charterparty was held to be frustrated due to an unreasonable delay in delivering the vessel for the contracted voyage and the charterer was discharged from further performance of his obligations. Bramwell B commented as follows:[63]

> There are the cases which hold that, where the shipowner has not merely broken his contract, but has also broken it that condition precedent is not performed, the charterer is discharged ... Why? Not merely because the contract is broken. If it is not a condition precedent, what matters is whether it is unperformed with or without excuse? Not arriving with due diligence, or at a day named, is the subject of a cross-action only. But not arriving in time for the voyage contemplated, but at such a time that it is frustrated, is not only a breach of contract, but discharges the charterer. And so it should, though he has such an excuse that no action lies.

Accordingly, in a voyage charterparty, delivery of the chartered vessel in reasonable time was held to be a condition precedent to the enforceability of the primary obligations of the charterer. In case of a breach of the condition precedent, the remedy is discharge of the charterer from his further obligations.

5.25 Lord Goff has employed a similar solution for warranties that relate to a period after the attachment of the risk. In this context, fulfilment of the warranty is a condition precedent to the liability of the insurer and, in case of breach, the remedy is automatic discharge of the insurer from his further liabilities. This analysis is not only logical and consistent with the general principles of general contract law, but also has judicial support. Thus, the Court of Appeal's decision that there is an irreconcilable contradiction between concepts of 'condition precedent' and 'breach of warranty' is not an accurate one. At the same time, the *dictum* of Donaldson J, in *De Maurier (Jewels) Ltd v Bastion Insurance Co Ltd*, which was cited to support the Court of Appeal's decision,[64] fails to explain the existence of an irreconcilable contradiction between these two concepts.

5.26 When equating the effect of breach of a marine warranty with breach of a condition in general contract law, the Court of Appeal, in the words of Lord Goff,[65] was 'led astray by passages in certain books and other texts'. Lord Goff has given no explanation regarding the sources which misdirected the Court of Appeal. Thus, a careful examination in respect of the books and texts relied on by the Court of Appeal has to be carried out in order to test the accuracy of Lord Goff's statement.

5.27 Two of the books referred to by the Court of Appeal, namely *A Digest of the Law Relating to Marine Insurance* (1st edn, 1901; 2nd edn, 1903) and *The Marine Insurance Act 1906* (1st edn, 1907; subsequent editions, 1913, 1922 and 1932), were written by Sir Mackenzie Chalmers, one of the co-authors of the draft Bill of the MIA 1906. In all editions of both books the following commentary appears:

---

62   (1874) LR 10 CP 125.
63   *Ibid*, p 147.
64   [1967] 2 Lloyd's Rep 550.
65   [1992] 1 AC 233, p 263.

It is often said that breach of a warranty makes the policy void. But this is not so. A void contract cannot be ratified, but a breach of warranty in insurance law appears to stand on the same footing as the breach of a condition in other branch of contract.

There is no doubt that the case law and especially the *dictum* of Lord Mansfield in *De Hahn v Hartley*[66] that suggested that a breach of warranty entitled the insurer to repudiate was taken into account by Sir Mackenzie. This definitely reflects the legal position prior to the enactment of the MIA 1906. Also, there are cases decided after the enactment of the Act that held that breach of a non-marine warranty entitled the insurer to repudiate the contract.[67] The judges in those cases simply relied on marine cases decided before the enactment of the Act and made no reference to s 33(3) when delivering their judgments. The question which needs to be raised at this stage is whether s 33(3) was intended to alter the legal position in respect of breach of a warranty which relates to a period after the attachment of the risk. If the answer is yes, Sir Mackenzie's commentary in the above mentioned books is misleading since it reflects the position before the enactment of the Act and ignores the new status which was adopted by the MIA 1906.

5.28   It can be argued that the common law position in respect of breach of a warranty has been altered by s 33(3). This argument can be supported by considering various provisions of the Act. Some provisions of the Act use the term 'avoidance'. If, for example, utmost good faith is not observed by either party, the contract may be avoided by the other party by virtue of s 17. Similarly, if the assured fails to disclose a material fact, or makes a material misrepresentation in the course of pre-contract negotiations, the insurer may avoid the contract.[68] A further group of provisions, including s 33(3), on the other hand, speak of discharge from liability.[69] As can be seen, different consequences have been afforded for breach of different provisions of the Act. Therefore, if the parliamentary draftsman had had intentions of retaining the common law position in respect of breach of a warranty, a different wording for s 33(3) would have been adopted. Indeed, at one stage during its chequered passage to the statute book,[70] the second sentence of s 33(3) of the Bill read, '... if it be not so complied with, the insurer may avoid the contract'. The fact that s 33(3) was enacted in the form that it was indicates that the parliamentary draftsman intended to change the common law position in respect of the effect of a breach of warranty.[71] The following speech of Swinfen-Eady LJ, in *Sanday & Co v British & Foreign Marine Insurance Co*,[72] in relation to principles of construing a codifying act, also supports the notion that s 33(3) of the Act altered the common law position:

---

66   *De Hahn v Hartley* (1786) 1 TR 343.

67   See *West v National Motor and Accident Insurance Union Ltd* [1955] 1 All ER 800 and *CTN Cash & Carry Ltd v General Accident Fire & Life Assurance Corp Ltd* [1989] 1 Lloyd's Rep 299.

68   See ss 18(1) and 20(1), respectively. See, also, ss 36(2) and 42(1).

69   See, eg, s 45(2), which provides that, if there is a change of voyage, the insurer is discharged from liability as from the time of change. See, also, ss 46 and 48.

70   The MIA 1906 had been first introduced into Parliament in 1894 and was re-introduced many times thereafter with variations in its language.

71   The intention of Parliament was, presumably, to give a different legal character to marine insurance warranties due to the role they play in assessing the risk undertaken.

72   [1915] 2 KB 781, p 786.

The proper course is in the first instance to examine the language of the statute, and to ask what is its natural meaning, uninfluenced by any considerations derived from the previous state of law, and not to start with inquiring how the law previously stood.

5.29   Presumably, when the Bill was drafted the intention was to retain the common law position for breach of a warranty and, accordingly, give an option to the insurer to elect to terminate the contract in case of breach. This outcome is not at odds with the current wording of s 33(3). Sir Mackenzie, however, paid no attention to this fact when writing the above commentary and relied on the antecedent case law. Accordingly, Lord Goff is accurate to suggest that the Court of Appeal has been misled by Sir Mackenzie.

5.30   The other books cited by the Court of Appeal to support its decision can also be criticised as being 'misleading' in this context. The full title of *MacGillivray and Parkington on Insurance Law*, which was quoted by the Court of Appeal, is *MacGillivray and Parkington on Insurance Law Relating on All Risks Other Than Marine*.[73] It seems that the present editors of the book took only pro-Act non-marine cases, mentioned above, into account when concluding that a breach of warranty entitles the insurer to repudiate the policy. Similarly, in *Chitty on Contract*,[74] another book cited by the Court of Appeal, the authority cited[75] does not support the proposition that a breach of warranty entitles the assured to avoid the contract.

5.31   The reports evaluating different aspects of insurance contracts, namely the Fifth Report of the Law Reform Committee, *Conditions and Exceptions in Insurance Policies*, and the Law Commission Report, *Insurance Law: Non-Disclosure and Breach of Warranty*, were also cited by the Court of Appeal to support the idea that breach of a marine warranty has the same effect as breach of a condition in contract law. Agreeing with Lord Goff, the author believes that, just like the books cited, these reports are misleading in this context as well. The former refers to the common law position on the effect of breach of a warranty before the enactment of the MIA 1906, ignoring the possible effect of s 33(3),[76] while the latter cites the books, which had already been considered above as misleading.[77]

5.32   To sum up, the effect of s 33(3) and, accordingly, the effect of breach of a marine warranty had been considered neither by high minds from the pantheon on common law purity, including Sir Mackenzie Chalmers, nor by academics commenting on the issue for over 70 years. All the commentaries on the topic were based on the antecedent case law and, accordingly, as was accurately stated by Lord Goff, they led the Court of Appeal, which relied on them intensively, to a wrong conclusion.

---

73   MacGillivray, 1988, para 790.
74   Guest, AG, *Chitty on Contracts: Specific Contracts*, Volume 2, 26th edn, 1989.
75   *Equitable Life Assurance Society of the United States v Reed* [1914] AC 587.
76   In the Fifth Report of the Law Reform Committee 1957, para 8, Lord Mansfield's *dicta* in *De Hahn v Hartley* (1786) 1 TR 343 were cited as authority when equating breach of a warranty in insurance law with breach of a condition in general contract law.
77   Law Commission, 1980, para 6.2, refers to *MacGillivray* when commenting on the effect of breach of an insurance warranty.

5.33   Another ground relied on by the Court of Appeal, when denying the automatic discharge remedy for breach of a warranty, was the 'potential difficulties' that may arise in this context.[78] Citing a footnote from Arnould,[79] the Court of Appeal ruled that the remedy of automatic discharge from the contract would be inconsistent with the insurer's right to waive the breach as set out in s 34(3).

On a strict analysis a contract, which has come to an end, cannot be revived by the act of one party alone, revival would require both parties to enter into a new contract. From this point of view, the Court of Appeal's interpretation is accurate since there would be an obvious inconsistency between the concepts of 'termination of contract' and 'waiver of the breach and, accordingly, revival of the contract by the act of one party'. However, Lord Goff, speaking for the House of Lords, made it clear that the Court of Appeal was wrong when suggesting that the contract comes to an end as a result of breach of warranty.[80] He stated the effect of s 33(3) in the following way:

> Certainly, it [s 33(3)] does not have the effect of avoiding the contract *ab initio*. Nor, strictly speaking, does it have the effect of bringing the contract to an end. It is possible that there may be obligations of the assured under the contract, which will survive the discharge of the insurer from liability, as for example a continuing liability to pay a premium. Even if, in the result, no further obligations rest on either party, it is not correct to speak of the contract being avoided: and it is, strictly speaking, more accurate to keep to the carefully chosen words in s 33(3) of the Act, rather than to speak of the contract being brought to an end, though that may be the practical effect.[81]

Thus, under the solution adopted by Lord Goff, there is still an opportunity for the insurer to waive the breach, simply because the contract remains on foot after breach, although the insurer is discharged from further liability.[82]

5.34   For all the arguments advanced above, it can be concluded that Lord Goff's interpretation of the effect of s 33(3) is accurate and full of sense. After almost 75 years from the enactment of the Act, finally the effect of breach of warranty in marine insurance has been clarified. The possible ramifications of Lord Goff's *dicta* in the market practice will be considered next.

---

78 [1990] 1 QB 818, p 880.
79 Arnould, 1981, para 708, fn 18.
80 [1992] 1 AC 233, p 263.
81 He was, of the opinion that the *dicta* of the Court of Appeal caused Lord Justice Kerr to express himself in tentative terms about the effect of breach of an insurance warranty in *State Trading Corp of India Ltd v M Golodetz Ltd* [1989] 2 Lloyd's Rep 277, p 287, where, *obiter dictum*, he said as follows: 'Thus, the correct analysis of breach of warranty in an insurance contract may be that the consequence of the breach is that the cover ceases to be applicable unless the insurer subsequently affirms the contract, rather than to treat the occurrence as a breach of the contract by the insured which the insurer subsequently accepts as a wrongful repudiation.'
82 The effect of *The Good Luck* on the doctrines of waiver and estoppel will be evaluated in detail in the following chapter.

*(ii)   Nature of automatic discharge remedy and its implications in marine insurance
        practice*

5.35   In the wake of the decision of the House of Lords in *The Good Luck*, it is now
clear that the remedy available in case of a breach of a marine insurance warranty is
radically different than remedies for breach of other contractual terms. A breach of
warranty is distinguished from the general conditions in that the latter, if broken, gives
rise to both damages and discharge, but the discharge occurs only on the election of
the innocent party. The marine insurance warranty is also distinguished from the
general warranty in that the latter, if broken, gives rise to damages, but not to
discharge, whether automatic or by election.

5.36   The remedy for breach of a marine warranty is also different than the remedy
available in case of breach of utmost faith obligations.[83] In the latter case, the innocent
party could avoid the contract *ab initio*, but the contract cannot be said to be
automatically avoided by breach of utmost good faith obligations; it remains in force
until avoided by the insurer.[84] Once the innocent party elects to avoid the contract,
however, the avoidance will be effective as of the moment of agreement.

5.37   The automatic discharge remedy is expected to have serious implications on
the position of parties to an insurance contract. Under the automatic discharge rule,
rights and liabilities of the insurer that materialised before the breach remain
unaffected. The insurer is entitled to retain the full amount of the premium, unless the
risk is divisible,[85] as he has been on risk for a while and, therefore, there has not been a
total failure of consideration. Similarly, any liability on the insurer, which had accrued
up to the date of the breach of warranty, remains unaffected. These points have been
illustrated in *JA Chapman & Co Ltd v Kadirga Denizcilik ve Ticaret*,[86] where the assured
had warranted that instalments of the premium would be paid on given dates, but had
fallen behind. It was held that the late payment of a single instalment brought the risk
to an end so that the insurer could never be liable for future losses, whereas the
assured remained under an obligation to continue to make payments.[87]

5.38   Where an underwriter discovers that a breach has taken place without any
claim arising, even though he is discharged from liability automatically in law, he
should still notify the assured that he is minded to regard himself as discharged from
liability. If he does not, he runs the risk of committing an unequivocal conduct, which
could amount to waiver of breach of warranty.[88] The notification, without a doubt,
gives the assured sufficient time to arrange alternative cover.

5.39   The insurer should also be entitled to seek a declaration of non-liability from
the court where he contends that his liability has been discharged by a breach of

---

83 See, ss 17–20 of the MIA 1906.
84 *Holland v Russel* (1863) 4 B & S 14.
85 This issue will later be discussed below at [5.50].
86 [1998] Lloyd's Rep IR 377.
87 This assumes that the risk is indivisible and does not run from instalment to instalment.
88 Waiver of breach of a marine warranty after the occurrence of breach is discussed in detail in
    the following chapter.

warranty.[89] The remedy is, of course, discretionary and will not be granted if it would create substantial inconvenience or injustice.[90]

5.40   Similarly, in cases where a claim is made and the insurer, suddenly discovering a previous breach, refuses to pay, the insurer will be justified in his refusal, provided of course he has not acted in any way since the time of the breach that can be considered as waiver of breach. Finally, in a case where the breach and claim are simultaneous and are related to one another it is still advisable that the insurer notifies the assured that that he regards himself as discharged, in order to disregard the possibility of waiver by an act of affirmative conduct.

5.41   Where a policy of insurance covers risks that are clearly and definitely separate, the courts might be prepared to construe such policy as containing separate contracts so that insurance on one risk is not invalidated by the breach of a provision which applies to the other risk.[91] A similar approach has recently been employed in the context of non-marine warranties. In *Printpak v AGF Insurance*,[92] the assured obtained insurance cover for his business premises. The policy had a number of sections, each of which provided a different form of cover. The precise terms relating to each risk were prescribed in separate schedules, each of which contained section endorsements. Section A covered goods, *inter alia*, against loss or damage by fire. Section B covered theft. The assured suffered loss as a result of fire. At the time of fire the burglar alarm was not operational in breach of a warranty in Section B of the policy. The Court of Appeal held that the policy was divisible and that the warranty did not apply to the fire risk provided by the policy in a different section. Accordingly, the assured was entitled to recovery.

5.42   In the practice of marine insurance, it is possible that various risks are covered by a single policy on certain occasions. For example, in a case where the assured obtains cover for a number of vessels in his fleet, it can forcefully be argued that each vessel constitutes a distinct risk so if a warranty is breached in respect of one of the vessels, this should not have an impact on the cover of other vessels.[93]

5.43   A similar situation could arise in cases where the assured is given a non-obligatory open cover. A cover of this nature does not require the assured to declare all risks and the insurer is not obliged to accept any risk that is declared under the cover.[94] The open cover is, therefore, merely a contract for insurance and each time the underwriter agrees to accept a risk, a contract of insurance is formed in relation to that particular risk. Thus, breach of a warranty in one of the policies underwritten under an

---

89   *Insurance Corporation of Ireland v Strombus International Co Ltd* [1985] 2 Lloyd's Rep 138; *Meadows Co v Insurance Corporation of Ireland* [1989] 2 Lloyd's Rep 298; *St Paul Fire & Marine Insurance Co (UK) Ltd v McConnell Dowell Constructors Ltd* [1995] 2 Lloyd's Rep 116.

90   *Ibid, Insurance Corporation of Ireland v Strombus International Co Ltd*, p 144. Also, r 40.20 of the Civil Procedure Rules reads as follows: 'The court may make binding declarations whether or not any other remedy is claimed.'

91   See, eg, *Arab Bank plc v Zurich Insurance Co* [1999] 1 Lloyd's Rep 262 and *James v CGU Insurance* [2002] Lloyd's Rep IR 206.

92   [1999] Lloyd's Rep IR 542.

93   The position has been clarified in cl 26 of the IHC 2003, which indicates that each vessel is deemed to be seperately insured if more than one vessel is insured under the policy.

94   It is appropriate to regard an agreement of this type as a procedural mechanism for the submission of proposals to the insurer.

open cover of this nature would not have an impact on other policies issued under the same cover.

5.44   As a subsidiary point, it has to be stressed that the adoption of the automatic discharge remedy in case of a breach of a warranty is not expected to have any impact on the position of the assignee. Under s 50(1), a marine policy can be assigned to a third party and s 50(2) provides that, in such a case, the insurer is entitled to use any defence arising out of the contract that he would have been entitled to use if the action had been brought in the name of the person by, or on behalf of, whom the policy was effected. Therefore, in cases where the loss is made payable to a third party (for example, a mortgagee) and, accordingly, a claim is made by this person, the insurer could rely on the automatic discharge remedy to free himself from liability even though the former is in no way responsible for the breach. One way of preventing this harsh consequence, from the assignee's point of view, is to incorporate a clause into the contract to the effect that breach of the warranty shall not afford the insurer any defence to a claim made by a mortgagee who has accepted the insurance without knowledge of such breach.[95]

(C)   Miscellaneous points

(a)   Application of s 33(3) to breach of the warranty of legality that requires the insured adventure to be carried out in a lawful manner

5.45   Due to the special nature of a marine contract, s 41 imposes an implied warranty of legality in respect of all policies. This warranty is twofold and requires both the adventure insured to be a lawful one and the adventure insured to be carried out in a lawful manner, so far as the assured can control the matter. If the adventure insured is not a lawful one, the issue is straightforward. In such a case a warranty that relates to a period before the attachment of the risk is breached and accordingly the risk never attaches.[96] The doubtful issue is the future of a policy where the insured adventure is lawful, but an illegality arises afterwards and within the control of the assured. Will the contract be void *ab initio* or will the discharge remedy spelt out in s 33(3) be applied here as well? If the discharge remedy applies, this means that the insurer will be under an obligation to indemnify the assured for loss which occurs before such a breach occurs.

It is possible to support the view that the marine insurance contract should be void *ab initio*, as illegality is a concept that involves the notion of public policy. However, there is evidence to the contrary. Section 33(3) is drafted to apply to all warranties, whether implied or express, and there is nothing in s 41, which regulates the implied warranty of legality, that prevents the application of s 33(3) to breach of warranty of legality.[97] Furthermore, holding the whole contract void and, accordingly, affording no cover for the assured in a case where the illegality arises only at the final stage of an

---

95 Standard Institute Time Clauses (Hull) include such a clause in respect of the disbursements warranty. See cl 21.2 of the ITCH 1983; cl 22.2 of the ITCH 1995; cl 20.2 of the IVCH 1995; cl 24.2 of the IHC 2003.

96 Section 84(1) precludes the assured from recovery of the premium in such a case.

97 Section 41 reads as follows: 'There is an implied warranty that the adventure insured is a lawful one, and that, as far as the assured can control the matter, the adventure shall be carried out in a lawful manner.'

insured voyage is unfair from the assured's point of view. In such a scenario the assured would be left unprotected for a period when he or his servants are not involved in illegal activities. Support for this contention can be drawn from the Canadian case, *James Yachts v Thames & Mersey Marine Insurance Co Ltd and Others*,[98] where Rutton J[99] had no doubt whatsoever that, pursuant to the equivalent to s 41, the insurers were to be discharged from liability as the plaintiffs had carried out an unlawful business of boatbuilding contrary to the bylaws and regulations of the municipality.

(b)   Modification of the provisions of the MIA 1906 in relation to effect of breach of warranty

5.46   Most provisions of the MIA 1906 are regulatory[100] and they can be contracted out of, if the parties agree. For example, s 39(1) imposes an implied warranty of seaworthiness in respect of voyage policies, but almost all cargo policies have express provisions waiving this obligation.[101] Due to the fact that s 33(3) has no connection with the notion of public policy, there is nothing preventing the parties from replacing the automatic discharge remedy spelt out by this sub-section with a different one. In fact, this is the case in practice, particularly when the market is soft and accordingly the assured is in a better position in terms of negotiating the terms of the contract. Selling hard conditions in a soft market is a difficult thing to do and, to a certain extent, the insurer could sacrifice the automatic discharge remedy afforded by s 33(3).[102]

(c)   Application of the automatic discharge remedy in non-marine insurance

5.47   Before *The Good Luck*, following the trend in the decisions of Lord Mansfield, it was held in a number of non-marine cases that breach of a warranty entitled the insurer to elect to terminate the insurance contract. The question here is whether a distinction between marine and non-marine insurance has been created by *The Good Luck* litigation.

There is nothing in Lord Goff's judgment to support the view that it was intended to create a distinction between marine and non-marine warranties. On the contrary, their Lordships, intentionally, used broad language and implied that breach of an

---

98 [1977] 1 Lloyd's Rep 206.

99 *Ibid*, p 212.

100 Some provisions, on the other hand, relate to public policy grounds and cannot be altered even by agreement of the parties. See, eg, s 4 of the MIA 1906, which regulates wagering or gaming contracts. Provisions of this type in the Act are very rare.

101 See cl 5.2 of the Institute Cargo Clauses (type A, B, C).

102 For example, such a modification in the remedy afforded by s 33(3) could be seen in *Martin Maritime Ltd v Provident Capital Indemnity Fund Ltd (The Lydia Flag)* [1998] 2 Lloyd's Rep 652, where the policy provided *inter alia* that: 'The following are warranties that must be complied with to maintain the insurance in effect. If these warranties are not complied with, the insurance will be suspended until the warranties are complied with. Any claims which occur during any period in which the insurance is suspended for failure to comply with these warranties will not be covered by this insurance.' See, in the non-marine insurance context, *Bennett (t/a Soho Pizzeria) v Axa Insurance Plc* [2004] EWHC 86; [2004] Lloyd's Rep IR 615.

insurance warranty has the same effect in all areas of insurance law. For instance, at one point, Lord Goff said that:[103]

> ... if a promissory warranty is not complied with the insurer is discharged from liability as from the date of breach of warranty ... the rationale of warranties in *insurance law* is that the insurer only accepts the risk provided that the warranty is fulfilled.

5.48   Recently, the Court of Appeal, clarified the position in *Printpak v AGF Insurance Ltd*,[104] where s 33(3) was referred to in order to state the effect of a non-marine insurance warranty in a commercial inclusive policy. Hirst LJ stated that:[105]

> It must be remembered that a continuing warranty is a draconian term. As I have noted, the breach of such a warranty produces an automatic cancellation of the cover, [under s 33(3) of the MIA 1906] and the fact that a loss may have no connection at all with the breach is simply irrelevant.[106]

(D)   Return of the premium in case of breach of a marine warranty

5.49   Whether the assured is entitled to his premium, after the occurrence of breach of a warranty, depends on the nature of the warranty in question. If the warranty in question is one that needs to be complied with before the attachment of the risk, if it is breached the insurer never comes on risk.[107] In such a case it is reasonable to expect the insurer to return the premium since he has never been at risk of indemnifying the assured. Accordingly, s 84(1) provides that:

> Where the consideration for the payment of the premium totally fails, and there has been no fraud or illegality on the part of the assured or his agents, the premium is thereupon returnable to the assured.[108]

5.50   However, if the warranty breached is one that has to be complied with at one certain point after the attachment of the risk, then by virtue of s 84(2) the premium is not returnable at all if the risk insured against is entire and indivisible. Conversely, in cases where the risk is divisible, the assured is entitled to the part of the premium that belongs to the unattached part of the risk. This rule, laid down in s 84, was undoubtedly on the mind of Lord Goff when delivering the judgment of the House of Lords in *The Good Luck*, where he, referring to the effect of breach of a warranty, said that:[109]

> It is possible that there may be obligations of the assured under the contract which will survive the discharge of the insurer from liability, as for example a continuing liability to pay a premium.

---

103 [1992] 1 AC 233, p 262–63 (emphasis added).
104 [1999] 1 Lloyd's Rep IR 542.
105 *Ibid*, p 545.
106 The same view has also been expressed by the Court of Appeal in *HIH Casualty & General Insurance Ltd v New Hampshire Insurance Co and Others* [2001] EWCA Civ 735; [2001] 2 Lloyd's Rep 161.
107 See, *Thomson v Weems* (1884) 9 App Cas 671.
108 By virtue of this section, if the implied warranty of legality is breached because of illegality of the insured adventure, then the assured is not entitled to return of the premium.
109 [1991] 2 Lloyd's Rep 191, p 201.

It should, however, be borne in mind that determining whether the risk is divisible is a rather problematic task and the existence of commercial usage in the relevant area could be a decisive factor. In *Meyer v Gregson*,[110] a ship insured 'at and from Jamaica to Liverpool, warranted to sail on or before 1 August', did not sail till 1 September, so that by virtue this breach of warranty the insurer was off risk. The assured, however, contended that the risk was divisible and the risk had attached upon the ship while she lay in port at Jamaica before 1 August. However, the assured gave no proof of a usage of trade to consider such risks divisible, or to make a rateable return of the premium for the risk after leaving the island. In these circumstances the court held that there could be no apportionment.[111]

110 (1784) 3 Dougl 402.
111 Cf *Gale v Machell* (1785) 2 Park Ins 797, where the risk was held to be divisible in an 'at and from policy' due to the existence of a commercial usage. More recently, the Court of Appeal, in *Chapman v Kadirga Denizcilik ve Ticaret* [1998] Lloyd's Rep IR 377, where the premium was agreed to be paid in instalments, held that the risk was indivisible. Delivering the Court of Appeal's judgment on this point, Chadwick LJ, at page 389, said that: 'The fact that the successive instalments are due and payable on dates which occur at three monthly intervals during the term of the policy does not, in my view, lead to the conclusion that the premium, which comprises the aggregate of those instalments, is itself divisible between successive three mount periods.'

CHAPTER 6

WAIVER OF BREACH OF MARINE INSURANCE WARRANTIES

6.1   'Waiver' is a term that is used loosely to describe a number of legal concepts in all areas of commercial law.[1] In the law of insurance it is generally used to describe an intentional act, which relinquishes a right or privilege otherwise afforded to the insurer, either by statute or contract.[2] A warranty, either express or implied, imposes certain obligations on the part of the assured and in a case of its breach the insurer is either prevented from coming on risk or discharged from liability automatically.[3] The commercial realities may require the insurer to waive the breach of warranty and accordingly forego his right that is afforded by the MIA 1906.[4] This is spelt out in s 34(3) as follows: 'A breach of warranty may be waived by the insurer.' Such a waiver may take place in different forms. It can either be accomplished by the conduct of the insurer or by a term of the insurance contract, that is a held covered clause, before the breach occurs. Waiver of the breach of warranty is also possible, after the loss occurs, by an unequivocal representation of the insurer to this end. This chapter will analyse different forms of waiver in the light of commercial practice and case law.

I – WAIVER OF BREACH OF MARINE INSURANCE WARRANTIES BEFORE THE BREACH IS COMMITTED

6.2   In some cases the insurer may agree, prior to a breach of warranty, not to take any action against the assured in the event of any breach by him. There are three ways of waiving a breach of a warranty before the occurrence of any breach and these will be scrutinised next.

(A)   Waiver of breach by conduct

6.3   Breach of a warranty may be waived in advance, either by an act or statement of the insurer. In either case such conduct must be unequivocal in the true sense of the word. Put another way, the conduct must be of one interpretation only, namely that a

---

1   The word 'commercial' is used in a general sense to cover not only those areas that fall within the jurisdiction of the commercial court, but also those areas that fall outside that jurisdiction, but remain 'commercial' in a loose sense of the word. For the effect and application of the doctrine in different areas of commercial law, such as agency, banking, company, construction, employment, insurance, sale of goods and shipping law, see Wilken and Villiers, 2002, pp 349–504.

2   *Hoxie v Howe Insurance Co* (1864) 32 Conn 21.

3   The former is the case for warranties, which relate to a period before the attachment of the risk, and the latter is the effect of breach of warranties, which relate to a period after the attachment of the risk.

4   Various factors, such as the longevity and strength of the relation between insurer and assured, or the climate in the market, might require the insurer to take such a step.

particular breach of warranty during the currency of the policy will not be relied upon by the insurer. It is a question of fact in each case whether the conduct of the insurer is unequivocal enough to prevent him from relying on a future breach of warranty. For instance, in *Sleigh v Tyser*,[5] where the insured vessel was lost due to unseaworthiness that existed when the voyage began, the assured contended that the insurer was precluded from relying on breach of the warranty of seaworthiness since an inspection as to the vessel's carrying capability by the insurer's agent prior to the voyage amounted to waiver of the breach of such a warranty. The court held that such an inspection was merely an extra precaution for the insurer and there was no intention and unequivocal act of the insurer to waive breach of the implied warranty of seaworthiness.[6]

Conversely, in *Samuel & Co Ltd v Dumas*,[7] a disbursement warranty required the assured not to effect freight insurance under honour policies in excess of £13,730. Insurance for a greater sum was obtained by means of a slip that the hull insurer had itself initialled. The House of Lords did not hesitate to conclude that obtaining extra insurance from the same hull insurers amounted to an unequivocal conduct in the sense that it demonstrated an intention not to enforce a potential breach of the disbursement warranty against the assured.[8]

6.4   The issue may be complicated in cases where the agent of the insurer performs an unequivocal conduct amounting to waiver of the breach of warranty before such a breach is committed. In such a case, the court must examine whether the agent has authority to bind his principal in that respect.[9] In *Fellas v Continental Insurance Co*,[10] the Supreme Court of British Columbia dealt with such a problem. In that case the insurance policy contained a locality warranty, which prohibited the insured vessel from navigating outside certain 'trading limits' laid down in the policy. The assured approached the agent and advised him that he wished to use the boat outside the limits. The agent said this would be all right. The insurer only became aware of the conduct of the agent after the vessel was damaged in a storm outside the trading limits. The court allowed the claim of the assured, finding that the insurer had held out the agent as having the authority to bind him. Berger J said as follows:[11]

> ... the [assured] was led to believe that [the agent] had the power to waive the warranty. The policy itself said it was not valid 'unless countersigned by the duly Authorised Representative of the company'. Facsimiles of the signatures of the president of the

---

5   [1900] 2 QB 333.

6   In fact, such an inspection was essential under the terms of the insurance policy.

7   [1924] AC 431.

8   See, also, *Weir v Aberdeen* (1819) 2 B & Ald 320, to the same effect. Cf *Burridge & Son v Haines & Sons Ltd* [1918] 118 LT 681. Note that previous waivers of breach of warranty are not, however, to be taken as authorising future disregard of that warranty; see, eg, *London & Manchester Plate Glass Co v Heath* [1913] 3 KB 411.

9   The agent might have an actual or ostensible authority in this regard. The meaning of these concepts and their application in this context will be examined later in this chapter.

10   [1973] ILR 558.

11   *Ibid*, p 713.

company and the secretary appear. Then it says, 'Countersigned at Vancouver BC this 28th day of April, 1970'. Over the words 'Authorised Representative', [the agent's] stamp has been imprinted ...

In my view, the company cannot issue a policy to an applicant which on its face declares [the agent] to be its authorised representative, which depends for its validity upon [his] signature, and then turn around and say: [He] was not our agent ...

(B)   Waiver of breach by an express term

6.5   With an express term, which appears in the policy, the insurer may agree in advance not to rely on breach of a warranty as a defence. In marine insurance this kind of clause usually intends to waive breach of implied warranties, that is warranties of seaworthiness and cargoworthiness, which are incorporated into the policy by the MIA 1906.[12] The language employed in a term of this type must be 'express, pertinent and apposite' in order to achieve the desired result.[13] The poor drafting of such a clause was one of the main reasons for litigation in *HIH Casualty v Chase Manhattan Bank*.[14] In that case, the assured was a bank, which insured the loan it provided for a film production company. The insurance was under time variable contingency policies and HIH was the leading insurer. HIH made an application for a decision of the preliminary issue of whether they were entitled to avoid or rescind contracts of or for insurance on the ground of fraudulent or negligent non-disclosure or misrepresentation by the assured's agent. One of the clauses in the policies provided that:

... the insured will not have any duty or obligation to make any representation, warranty or disclosure of any nature, express or implied (such duty and obligation being expressly waived by the insurers) ...

Relying on this clause, the assured contended that the insurer had waived their right to avoid the policy for non-disclosure/misrepresentation. Aikens J, however, had other ideas. He held that the clause in question did not waive breach of the duty of good faith or a breach of warranty. According to Aikens J, the clause attempted to negate a 'duty' to make representations or warranties. However, this had no effect, as there was no such duty on the assured. Of course, if the assured chose to make a representation or create a warranty, that was another matter. Then a statement that there is no 'duty' could not negate the fact that a representation had been made or a warranty had been created voluntarily by the assured; nor could it negate the consequences if the statement amounted to a misrepresentation or if the warranty was breached.[15]

6.6   Conversely, in some cases a waiver clause, which is not drafted clearly, could still assist the assured if the surrounding circumstances, that is, commercial

---

12   Note that breach of the implied warranty of legality cannot be waived as the issue is one of public policy rather than private contract. This issue will be discussed at the end of this chapter.

13   *Quebec Marine Ins Co v Commercial Bank of Canada* (1870) LR 3 PC 234, p 243.

14   [2001] Lloyd's Rep IR 191.

15   *Ibid*, p 213. This part of the judgment was affirmed by the Court of Appeal [2001] EWCA Civ 1250; [2001] 2 Lloyd's Rep 483; and eventually by the House of Lords [2003] UKHL 6; [2003] Lloyd's Rep IR 230.

background, are taken into account. In *Kumar v AGF Insurance Ltd*,[16] on 18 December 1990, Mr Chopra, a solicitor in partnership with the claimant, signed a proposal form for £1m in respect of each and every claim, in excess of the £1m compulsory cover under the Solicitors Indemnity Fund (SIF). A policy was issued on 27 February 1991 by AGF for the period 19 February to 31 August 1991. The proposal form required the firm to give details of all known, but not reported, claims and circumstances which might give rise to a claim. The form required the firm to declare that, after making inquiries, the details given were correct to the best of its knowledge and belief. The proposal form also contained a statement that it was to form the basis of any contract of insurance offered thereon. The policy itself provided that the insurers would not be liable for claims arising from any of the matters reported on the proposal form, and the policy also contained a non-avoidance clause stating that:[17]

> The insurers will not seek to avoid, repudiate or rescind this insurance upon *any ground whatsoever*, including in particular misrepresentation or non-disclosure.

During the currency of the policy, a building society obtained judgment by consent against Kumar for £2m. AGF denied liability to provide indemnity. One of their defences was that the policy contained a warranty that, at the date of the proposal form, Mr Chopra was not aware of any circumstances that might give rise to a claim and that this warranty was breached by non-disclosure. They further argued that the non-avoidance clause had no application because the words used were 'avoid, repudiate or rescind this insurance', none of which were applicable to a breach of warranty. Thomas J rejected this argument. Relying on *Investors Compensation Scheme Ltd v West Bromwich Building Society*,[18] he held that contracts had to be interpreted against their background. The significant background to the agreement in the instant case was the Solicitors' Indemnity Fund Rules, particularly rr 29 and 30, and the fact that the scheme of insurance was meant to provide an indemnity to clients in circumstances where they had been caused loss by a solicitor, a fact that was exemplified in the non-avoidance clause. When the proposal form for the policy was drafted and in use in 1990, the House of Lords had not given its decision in *The Good Luck*,[19] and the precise consequences, and precise analysis of the consequences, of a breach of warranty had not been as fully elucidated then as they now have been by *The Good Luck* decision. This point should be taken into account when the scope of non-avoidance clause is construed. Accordingly, Thomas J said as follows:[20]

> Looking at the words in [the non-avoidance clause] in this context, it is in my judgment clear that the draftsman of the policy and the parties did not intend the words in the first paragraph of the clause to have the precise meaning that might be said to be applicable after *The Good Luck* to the consequences of a breach of warranty, and by the use of terms 'avoid, repudiate or rescind'. In my judgment, it is clear that what the parties were doing in 1990 was stating that, in whatever way insurers sought to escape from liability, they were not entitled to do so. The words were and are, in my judgment, to be read as preventing underwriters escaping from liability either by

16 [1999] Lloyd's Rep IR 147.
17 Emphasis added.
18 [1998] 1 WLR 896.
19 [1992] 1 AC 233.
20 [1999] Lloyd's Rep IR 147, p 153.

repudiating, avoiding or rescinding the policy itself, or being discharged from liability under the insurance because of breach of warranty.

6.7   Fortunately, express clauses that are incorporated into Institute Cargo Clauses (ICC) have the ability to waive breach of warranties of seaworthiness and cargoworthiness and to do so in an unambiguous manner. The reason behind such a practice is clear. A cargo policy is effected between the cargo interests[21] and the insurer. Insisting on the implied warranties of seaworthiness and cargoworthiness creates injustice for the cargo interest as he usually has no means of knowing the state of the vessel carrying his goods. Standard ICCs, accordingly, waive breach of these warranties in the following manner:[22]

> The underwriters waive any breach of the implied warranties of seaworthiness of the ship and fitness of the ship to carry the subject matter insured to destination, unless the assured or their servants are privy to such unseaworthiness or unfitness.

As can be clearly seen, the insurer, with an express term, precludes himself from relying on breach of implied warranties of seaworthiness and cargoworthiness, provided that the cargo interests and their servants are not aware of that state of the vessel. Formerly, a different language had been adopted for this clause. It was as follows:[23]

> ... the seaworthiness of the vessel as between the assured and the underwriters is hereby admitted.

It is noted by Arnould[24] that there is a practical difference between the two types of clauses, even though they both intend to waive breach of the implied warranty of seaworthiness. The modern form operates by dispensing of the need for the insurer to rely on a breach of warranty and, in this respect, creates a consequence only from the insurer's point of view, while the former is binding on the assured just as much as on the insurer.

6.8   It must be borne in mind that, in order to waive implied warranties of seaworthiness and cargoworthiness, an express term worded in a different manner than the one in standard Institute Clauses could be employed. However, such a term must be consistent with the nature of the contract in question and clearly reflect the intention of the insurer to waive the warranty.[25]

---

21 This person is either the cargo-owner or consignee, depending on the terms of the original sales contract.

22 See cl 5.2 of the ICC (type A, B, C).

23 Clause 8 of the ICC 1967.

24 Arnould, 1981, para 709.

25 See *McDermott v National Benefit Life Assurance Co* (1921) 7 L1L Rep 97, where a vessel was insured under a voyage policy and contained, *inter alia*, the ICCs, one of which stated that, as between the insurers and the assured, it was admitted that the vessel was seaworthy. In fact the vessel was unseaworthy and became a total loss. Claiming for the loss, the assured contended that the implied warranty of seaworthiness had been waived by the insertion of the clause mentioned above. The insurers maintained that it was merely by an oversight that the clause had not been struck out from the form. It was held by the Irish Court of Appeal that the assured's contention failed because the ICCs were solely referable to cargo and were inapplicable in the present case.

(C)   Held covered clauses

(a)   Introduction

6.9   The reason for incorporating an express warranty into a marine policy is to give the insurer an opportunity to assess the extent of the risk he underwrites. As breach of a warranty amounts to a serious alteration in the risk underwritten, the insurer is discharged automatically from liability in such a case. The insurer may be willing to provide insurance cover, despite the breach, provided the essential arrangements as to premium or otherwise are made so that the altered risk may be properly underwritten. In contemporary marine insurance practice this is achieved by the use of held covered clauses, which are usually, but not invariably, drafted subject to two conditions: that immediate notice be given to the insurer and that any variation in conditions or additional premium be agreed.[26] Thus, by these clauses the insurer agrees, prior to a breach of warranty, not to take any action against the assured, if the assured chooses to operate the clause by satisfying the conditions stated above. Put another way, the general object of such a clause is to give the assured the right to elect to maintain cover in circumstances when, otherwise, it would be terminated by the insurer.

6.10   The held covered formula has been in common use since the late 19th century[27] and, apart from cases of breach of a warranty, it normally affords protection against the risk of deviation or change of voyage.[28] This part of the chapter focuses on held covered clauses, which intend to keep the insurance relation on foot despite the breach of a warranty by the assured. It is the general belief amongst academics and practitioners that these clauses are not well understood in terms of legal analysis and are likely to cause litigation in the future.[29]

(b)   Held covered clauses in practice

6.11   The held covered clause, which is designed to provide cover in case of breach of a warranty, is identical in any set of Institute Time Clauses (Hull) (ITCH) published for use with the marine form of policy[30] and in the Institute Time Clauses, previously published by the Institute of London Underwriters for use with the SG form of policy. The held covered clause provides that:

---

26 There is no legal ground preventing implied warranties being subject to a held covered clause; however, this is not the case in practice. As examined above, implied warranties in cargo policies are usually waived by an express clause.

27 The earliest cases in the reports date from the 1890s. See *Simon Israel & Co v Sedgwick* [1893] 1 QB 303 and *Hyderabad (Deccan) Co v Willoughby* [1899] 2 QB 530.

28 The best example of what is, in effect, a held covered clause with no additional premium or condition to be agreed is the 'deviation and delay' clause in ICC 1982 (type A, B, C). Clause 8.3 provides that: 'This insurance shall remain in force ... during delay beyond the control of the assured, any deviation, forced discharge, reshipment or transhipment and during any variation of the adventure arising from the exercise of a liberty granted to shipowners or charterers under the contract of affreightment.' The 'change of voyage' clause in the same set of rules (cl 10) requires prompt notice, but does not require agreement to new terms or premium, merely stating that they are 'to be arranged'. Previous editions of this clause, apart from the change of voyage, held covered any omission or error in the description of the interest in vessel or voyage.

29 Thomas, 2002, pp 1–55.

30 See cl 3 of the ITCH 1983; cl 3 of the ITCH 1995; cl 4 of the ITCF 1995; cl 3 of the ITCH (Restricted Perils). Even though navigation provisions are not regulated as warranties in the IHC 2003, a similar provision appears affording cover in case of their breach: cl 11 of the IHC 2003.

Held covered in case of any breach of warranty as to cargo, trade, locality, towage, salvage services or date of sailing provided notice be given to the Underwriters immediately after receipt of advices and any amended term of cover and any additional premium required by them be agreed.[31]

In Institute Voyage Clauses, this provision is incorporated within the 'change of voyage' clause and it holds covered breach of warranty only 'as to towage or salvage services',[32] this being much more limited than the scope of the held covered clause appearing in Institute Time Clauses.

(i)   Scope and nature of the clause

6.12   The clause does not relate to all types of warranties; breach of certain express warranties comes under its scope. Accordingly, the assured is held covered in case of the breach of a warranty that relates to cargo, trade, locality, towage, salvage services or date of sailing, in hull time policies, and towage and salvage services, in hull voyage policies,[33] provided, of course, the conditions as to notice and additional premium are satisfied.

6.13   There is not much to be found in authorities in terms of the legal nature of held covered clauses. What is clear is that the held covered clause initially creates an irrevocable unilateral obligation on the part of the insurer to provide the specified additional cover if demanded by the assured.[34] This obligation does not become one requiring performance until notice is given, and if notice is not given it never becomes an active obligation. However, once notice is given, the insurer is obliged to provide the additional cover promised and the assured is obliged to agree on additional premium and amended terms of cover.[35] There is judicial support to the effect that the additional cover is, in fact, a variation in the contract that creates a distinct agreement.[36]

---

31 Note that a very similar wording has been adopted in American Institute Time (Hull) Clauses (2/7/1977). Lines 67–69 read as follows: 'The vessel is held covered in case of any breach of conditions as to cargo, trade, locality, towage or salvage services, or date of sailing or loading or discharging at sea, provided: (a) notice be given to underwriters immediately following knowledge thereof by the assured and (b) any amendment term of cover and any additional premium required by the underwriter are agreed by the assured.' See also, cl 6 of Canadian Hulls (Pacific) Clauses (1/9/1991) which reads as follows: 'The Vessel is covered in case of any breach of warranty as to cargo, employment, towage, salvage services or date of sailing, provided notice be given to the Underwriters immediately after reciept of advices and any amended terms of cover and any additional premium required by them be agreed.'

32 'Change of Voyage Clause' in IVCH 1995 reads as follows: 'Held covered in case of deviation or change of voyage or any breach of warranty as to towage or salvage services, provided notice be given to the underwriters immediately after receipt of advices and any amended terms of cover and any additional premium required by them be agreed.'

33 The scope of these warranties has been analysed in Chapter 2.

34 *United Dominions Trust (Commercial) Ltd v Eagle Aircraft Services Ltd* [1968] 1 WLR 74, p 86, *per* Diplock LJ.

35 For a detailed analysis on this point, see, Thomas, 2002, [1.141] to [1.152].

36 *Iron Trades Mutual Insurance Co Ltd v Comphanhia de Seguros Imperio* (1990) Unreported (QB); and *The Star Sea* [1997] 1 Lloyd's Rep 360, p 370, *per* Leggatt LJ.

(ii)   Notice requirement

6.14   The assured is under an obligation to give notice in order to activate the held covered clause as giving timeous notice is normally a condition precedent to the liability of the insurer.[37] The exact time for this notice has been judicially considered in numerous cases and it is concluded that, in the absence of any specific provision, notice has to be given within a reasonable time after the facts have come to the knowledge of the assured.[38] What is meant by a reasonable time has been further explained by Donaldson J, in *Liberian Insurance Agency Inc v Mosse*,[39] as follows:

> ... if the assured learns the true facts whilst the risk is still current, a reasonable time will usually be a shorter period than if it occurs when the adventure is already ended. If the assured learns the true facts when the assured property is in the grip of a peril, which is likely to cause loss or damage, a reasonable time will be short indeed.

6.15   This test, however, has no application anymore since the notice requirement has been qualified by the word 'immediately' in the present form of held covered clauses. Thus, the assured is not allowed a reasonable time, but has to give notice 'immediately' to the insurer after the assured becomes aware, or ought to have become aware, of the situation.[40] There appear to be no reported cases on the meaning to be given to the word 'immediate' in the context of a held covered clause, but the expression has been construed in other contexts and its meaning appears to be well settled. The word implies 'prompt, vigorous action, without any delay', after learning of the relevant facts.[41] Therefore, for the operation of the held covered clause, the assured must act promptly after he learns that a warranty is going to be breached, or has already been breached, and must give notice to the underwriter.

6.16   One might wonder whether a held covered clause can be invoked by the assured even after the occurrence of a casualty if he was not aware beforehand of the occurrence of the events in which he is to be held covered under the clause. In *Greenock Steamship Co Ltd v Maritime Insurance Co Ltd*,[42] it was suggested by Bigham J that the

---

37   *Thames & Mersey Marine Insurance Co Ltd v HT Van Laun & Co* [1917] 2 KB 48. Note that, in some policies, notice is not a condition for the operation of the held covered clause. See, eg, *Anz Bank v Compagnie d' Assurances Maritime Aeriennes et Terrestres (The Northern L)* [1996] IVR 561, where the held covered clause stated that: '... continuation and breach of a warranty clause held covered with or without notice.'

38   *Hood v West End Motor Car Packing Co* [1917] 2 KB 38; ibid, *Thames & Mersey Marine Insurance Co Ltd v HT Van Laun & Co*; *Overseas Commodities Ltd v Style* [1958] 1 Lloyd's Rep 546. The term 'knowledge' in this context seems to cover not only actual knowledge, but also 'turning a blind eye knowledge'. On the other hand, the use of the phrase 'on receipt of advices' makes it very difficult to argue that constructive knowledge is in the ambit of this clause.

39   [1977] 2 Lloyd's Rep 560, p 566, *per* Donaldson J.

40   It must be remembered that, if the assured notifies his broker in time, but the broker does not immediately notify the underwriter, the assured cannot claim benefit of a held covered clause if there is breach of a warranty. In such event the assured could bring an action for damages against the broker if the assured could prove that his position had been prejudiced by the broker's negligence; such an action would be pursued under the law of contract or tort.

41   *R v Berkshire Justices* (1878) 4 LR QBD 469, p 476, *per* Cockburn CJ. In other instances 'immediately' has been said to mean 'with all reasonable speed considering the circumstances of the case', see *Re Coleman's Depositories* [1907] 2 KB 798, p 807. More recently, in *Fraser Shipping Ltd v Colton and Another* [1997] 1 Lloyd's Rep 586, it was conceded that a delay, of just under a month, in giving notice of change of voyage failed the immediacy test.

42   [1903] 1 KB 367, p 376.

held covered clause in question could have held good even though the held covered event was not discovered until a loss had occurred.[43] It is submitted that a literal reading of the clause is in line with this approach. The requirement to give notice has not been qualified in a way that would indicate that notice must be given before any loss arises. Therefore, provided the notice is given immediately and there was no way for the assured to learn about the breach at an earlier date, the held covered clause could be invoked.[44]

6.17   Furthermore, it was indicated, in *Overseas Commodities Ltd v Style*,[45] by McNair J that, provided that the assured complies with the other requirements relating to the giving of notice, a held covered clause could be invoked not only after the occurrence of loss, but also after the period of the policy had expired.

6.18   As indicated above, a held covered clause, which is successfully employed, amounts to a variation in the contract and giving of notice by the assured is the initial step which facilitates the whole process. Accordingly, the assured is expected to observe the duty of utmost good faith at the time of giving notice. It was McNair J, in *Overseas Commodities Ltd v Style*, who first indicated the importance of utmost good faith principles in the application of held covered clauses. In this case the insurance was on 'canned pork butts' for shipment from France to Britain. The insurance provided that the tins were to be marked in a particular fashion and there was a warranty that all tins were so marked by the manufacturer. In fact, the tins were not all marked in the stipulated fashion. The goods were condemned on import and the assured sought recovery under the policy. In answer to the underwriter's case that the tins were not marked in the warranted manner, the assured relied upon a held covered clause that provided that goods would be held covered '... at a premium to be arranged in case of ... any omission or error in the description of the interest vessel or voyage ...'. When the underwriters had inquired why the tins had not been correctly marked, the assured obtained from their suppliers two letters containing different reasons. However, only one explanation (the most favourable to the assured) was passed on to the underwriters. McNair J held that the assured could not rely upon the held covered clause because, in order to do so, they must act with the utmost good faith towards the underwriters, '... this being an obligation which rests upon them throughout the currency of the policy'.[46]

    Therefore, the assured is expected to disclose any material facts and not to make material misrepresentations in relation to the events that will be held covered. Put another way, the process is parallel to the presentation of the risk prior to the formation of the contract and in this respect the doctrine of utmost good faith should apply in a similar way. However, the precise content of the duty attaching to the giving of notice must reflect the fact that the contract is not reviewed *in toto*.[47] All that is being requested is the implementation of cover to which the insurer has already agreed, subject to specified conditions. The concept of materiality must, therefore, be

---

43 See, also, *Hewitt v London General Insurance Co* (1925) 23 L1L Rep 243.
44 *Mentz Decker & Co v Maritime Insurance Co* [1910] 1 KB 132.
45 [1958] 1 Lloyd's Rep 546, p 559.
46 *Ibid*, p 559. The same principle was later affirmed by Donaldson J, in *Liberian Insurance Agency Inc v Mosse* [1977] 2 Lloyd's Rep 560, p 568.
47 Bennett, 'Mapping the doctrine of utmost good faith in insurance contract law' [1999] *LMCLQ* 165, p 204.

considered from the point of the variation proposed. Thus, a circumstance that has arisen since the conclusion of the contract that would be material, were the risk being placed for the first time or being renewed, but that is not material to the amendment, does not require disclosure under a held covered clause. Similarly, information relating to whether the additional risk should be accepted is not material, but information which helps the underwriter to decide whether the additional risk falls within the terms of the held covered clause is material. In *The Star Sea*,[48] the need to tailor the utmost good faith duty to its context was stated, in the Court of Appeal by Leggatt LJ, as follows:

> ... there is force in the argument that the scope of the duty of utmost good faith will alter according to whether underwriters have to make a decision under the policy or the assured decides to make a claim, and may also be affected according to the stage of the relationship at which the scope of the duty becomes material.[49]

6.19   There is a further point that needs to be clarified. The remedy afforded in the MIA 1906 for breach of disclosure, misrepresentation and general good faith duty is 'avoidance'. In this respect, if the assured is in breach of any of these duties when invoking the held covered clause, does it mean that the insurer could avoid the whole contract, or should the remedy of avoidance be limited to the endorsement? Put another way, in a case where the assured is in breach of the good faith duty when giving notice in the process of invoking the held covered clause, is it possible to avoid the new part of the contract and require the insurer to indemnify the assured for losses that have occurred before the endorsement of the held covered clause, or should the whole policy be avoided? The answer to this question is not an easy one and arguments for each solution could be advanced. It could be argued that, despite the existence of a new contract by operation of the held covered clause, the whole contract is affected by the wrongful act of the assured. This is the case, mainly, because the contract is one that is based upon the utmost good faith. On the other hand, it could be argued that, permitting avoidance of the entire contract in the event of non-compliance with the duty of utmost good faith that applies to held covered clauses, is not fair. In the absence of a held covered clause, or were the assured to elect not to request extension of cover pursuant to such a clause, the consequence of an alteration of risk would be a purely prospective discharge of liability without prejudice to cover up to that point.[50] The author believes that allowing the insurer to avoid the whole contract *ab initio* could be a quite disproportionate remedy in certain cases, particularly where no fraud on the part of the assured is involved.

---

48   [1997] 1 Lloyd's Rep 360, p 370.
49   In the House of Lords, [2001] UKHL 1; [2003] 1 AC 469, [54], Lord Hobhouse seemed to support such a contention: 'Where the contract is being varied, facts must be disclosed which are material to the additional risk being accepted by the variation. It is not necessary to disclose facts occurring, or discovered, since the original risk was accepted material to the acceptance and rating of that risk.' See, also, *The Mercandian Continent* [2001] EWCA Civ 1275; [2001] 2 Lloyd's Rep 563.
50   See the judgment of the Court of Appeal, delivered by Leggatt LJ, in *The Star Sea* [1997] 1 Lloyd's Rep 360, p 370, where he said that: 'In relation to amendment, a duty of disclosure of facts material to the amendment will exist but the law is not, we think, as to whether the remedy is avoidance of the whole contract or merely the amendment. Since inducement of the actual underwriter is necessary, there seems much to be said for the point of view that avoidance of the amendment is all that should be permitted, but this is not the place to explore that aspect further.' See, also, the judgment of Longmore LJ in *The Mercandian Continent* [2001] EWCA Civ 1275; [2001] 2 Lloyd's Rep 563, [22].

(iii)   Agreement on any additional premium and amended terms of cover

6.20   It is a customary feature of a held covered clause to put the assured under an obligation to agree additional premium and/or any amended terms of cover as a condition of the additional cover.[51] The rest of this part of the chapter intends to offer a more detailed analysis of these points.

6.21   Following the tender of notice, in most instances the additional premium payable will be settled by negotiation. However, there is always a possibility that the parties might fail to agree an additional premium. The issue may then be referred to the court or arbitration,[52] but, of course, it has to be borne in mind that loss following a breach might arise during this period. If it does, due to the initial undertaking of the insurer to provide cover for additional risks, the assured can recover retrospectively following the judgment of the court or arbitration on the issue of premium.

6.22   Section 31(2) indicates that where an insurance is effected on the terms that an additional premium is to be arranged in any given event, and that event happens, but no arrangement is made, then a reasonable additional premium is payable. This provision introduces a conditional implied statutory term to every held covered clause to the effect that where the parties fail to agree an additional premium the assured is under an obligation to pay a reasonable additional premium. It is left to judiciary to decide what the reasonable additional premium is in each case. In principle, the rate of additional premium to which the insurer is entitled under a held covered clause is the rate that would reasonably have been calculated and agreed between the parties had they known the breach of warranty or other circumstances, which is to be held covered, at the time when it happened.[53]

6.23   It might be possible that the court or arbitrator could determine such a high amount of additional premium that the assured ends up receiving nothing for the subsequent loss. In *Greenock SS Co Ltd v Maritime Insurance Co Ltd*, the insured vessel commenced a voyage in an unseaworthy state as she was inadequately coaled. There was a held covered clause that the assured wished to employ, but the parties failed to agree an additional premium. In order to enable the vessel to reach the next port safely, the ship's fittings and spars were burnt and in the litigation the assured sought indemnity for the loss of them. In an attempt to determine the amount of reasonable premium in this case, Bigham J thought it was essential to answer the question, 'What might an underwriter fairly require as a premium for insuring a steamer, which stands on a voyage short of coal?'. He concluded that the underwriter was entitled to charge an additional premium at least equal to the average loss claimed by the assured for ship's fittings and spars burnt. In the event, the claim under the policy was equalled by the entitlement of the underwriter to additional premium, and the claim of the assured, therefore, failed.

---

51   The previous versions of the held covered clauses made no reference to the premium or any other amendments in the policy. See *Liberian Insurance Agency Inc v Mosse* [1977] 2 Lloyd's Rep 560.

52   In that case, until the premium is fixed by the court or arbitrator, the assured cannot compelled to pay any premium: *Kirby v Cosinart SPA* [1969] 1 Lloyd's Rep 75.

53   *Greenock SS Co v Maritime Insurance Co Ltd* [1903] 1 KB 367, p 375; *Mentz Decker & Co v Maritime Insurance Co* [1910] 1 KB 132, p 135; *Hewitt v London General Insurance Co* (1925) 23 LlL Rep 243.

6.24   It should be borne in mind that the additional risk contemplated by a held covered clause must be one that is capable of being placed in the market at a reasonable commercial rate.[54] If not, a held covered clause would find no application. The reason for this is because the undertaking given by the insurer under a held covered clause is subject to an implied condition that the additional risk is one that has a market value.

6.25   In the third volume of Arnould it is submitted that underwriters can still insist upon payment of additional premium where the assured has not sought to invoke the clause.[55] It is believed that such an outcome not only contradicts the nature of held covered clauses, but also creates unfairness. It is clear that, despite its ability to extend the cover under the contract, the additional coverage is at the election of the assured. There is no obligation to trigger the clause on the occurrence of a 'held covered' event. In this respect, if the assured chooses not to rely on the clause and there is a breach of a warranty all the insurer can do is to state that the warranty has been breached and, accordingly, he is discharged from liability. If the underwriters could demand payment of a premium when they were never on risk of having to pay for any loss, this would, as was stated by Hirst J, in *Black King Shipping Corporation & Wayang Panama SA v Mark Ranold Massie (The Litsion Pride)* make the bargain one-sided and unfair.[56] Also, such an outcome would be against the principles of insurance law. Providing indemnity against insured marine risks in return for a payment called a premium is the main concept in insurance relationships. Thus, payment of the premium is the obligation on the part of the assured and, in return, he receives a promise from the insurer that he will be indemnified if a loss arises as a result of perils insured against. If the insurer was allowed to claim premium in cases where the clause had not been invoked, this would entitle the insurer to a payment, although for that part of the risk for which he has not given any promise of indemnity.

6.26   In holding an assured 'held covered' in case of breach of a warranty the underwriter may be entitled to demand amended terms of cover. For instance, if it is intended that the assured will breach a warranty prohibiting the insured vessel to undertake towage services, the underwriter might require that the towage operation be supervised by a surveyor appointed by the Salvage Association. The question that springs to mind is whether there is any restriction on the right of the underwriter to insist on amended terms of cover. Admittedly, s 31(2) has no application in this context. However, the author believes that an implied term of the cover allows the insurer to demand only reasonable amendments. Therefore, the right of the underwriter to request amended terms of cover is qualified by reasonableness. What is reasonable has to be decided taking into account the realities of the market and facts of each individual case.

---

54 *Liberian Insurance Agency Inc v Mosse* [1977] 2 Lloyd's Rep 560, p 568, *per* Donaldson J.
55 Arnould, 1997, pp 39–40.
56 [1985] 1 Lloyd's Rep 437, p 470.

(D)   Waiver of breach of warranty by Inchmaree Clause?

6.27   An Inchmaree Clause[57] significantly expands the hull insurer's undertaking by specifying coverage for a variety of perils in addition to the ones specified in the traditional standard form policy – that is, perils of seas, fire, jettison, piracy. The Inchmaree Clause, which appears in standard Institute Clauses, provides cover for perils, some of which are excluded by s 55(2)(c).[58] However, under the Inchmaree Clause any loss caused by a lack of due diligence on the part of the assured or his servants is excluded from coverage.

6.28   The Inchmaree Clause provides cover for, amongst other perils, loss of or damage to the insured property directly caused by latent defect in the machinery or the hull. Arnould, citing a number of American cases, suggests that, in a case where damage was occasioned by a latent defect whose existence also constituted a breach of warranty of seaworthiness, which is implied in respect of voyage policies, the underwriter cannot rely on breach of warranty to deny liability.[59] Put another way, in so far as unseaworthiness is covered by this clause, the express coverage must prevail over the implied warranty and the underwriter should not be allowed to rely on a latent defect as being a breach of the warranty of seaworthiness.

An alternative view could be that the Inchmaree Clause and implied warranty of seaworthiness are two distinct concepts with different objects. The former determines the extent of the insurer's liability, while the latter illustrates the obligations of the assured. The way to reconcile these two concepts to allow the assured to recover in cases where a latent defect, which also constitutes unseaworthiness, causes a loss, provided that the defect comes into operation after the commencement of voyage. In such a case, even though the latent defect renders the vessel unseaworthy, it has no effect on the implied warranty of seaworthiness because there is no continuing duty to maintain the insured vessel in a seaworthy state after the voyage commences.

6.29   There is, however, evidence to the effect that Arnould's opinion has found support in English courts recently. In *Martin Maritime Ltd v Provident Capital Indemnity Fund Ltd (The Lydia Flag)*,[60] the vessel was insured under a policy incorporating the ITCH and which contained an Inchmaree Clause that stated that:

---

57   This clause derived its name from the vessel of the same name in the case of *Thames and Mersey Marine Insurance Co v Hamilton, Fraser & Co (The Inchmaree)* (1887) 12 AC 484. In marine insurance practice it is sometimes referred to as the 'Liner Clause' or 'Negligence Clause'.

58   For a typical Inchmaree Clause, see cl 4.2 of the IVHC 1995, cl 6.2 of the ITCH 1995 and cl 2.2 of the IHC 2003.

59   Arnould, 1981, para 710. The cases cited in support are: *Ferrante v Detroit Fire & Marine Insurance Co* [1954] AMC 2026; *Tropical Marine Products Inc v Birmingham Fire Ins Co of Pa (The Sea Pak)* [1957] AMC 616; *Saskatchewan Government Insurance Office v Spot Pack Inc* [1957] AMC 655; *Founders' Insurance Co v Rogers* [1963] AMC 116; *Larsen v Insurance Co of North America* [1965] AMC 2576; *Presti v Firemen's Insurance Co of Newark* [1972] AMC 1220; *Parente v Bayville Marine Inc* [1975] 1 Lloyd's Rep 333; *Capital Coastal Shipping Corp v Hartford Fire Insurance Co (The Cristie)* [1975] 2 Lloyd's Rep 100; *Joseph Navigation Corp v Chester* [1976] AMC 1565. More recently, in *Thann Long Partnership v Highlands Insurance Co* 32 F 3d 189 (5th Cir 1994), the US Court of Appeals for the Fifth Circuit discussed the overriding effect of the Inchmaree Clause over the implied warranty of seaworthiness and reached the conclusion that the clause could entitle the assured to recover in cases where the warranty is breached provided, of course, the assured or his employees do not demonstrate a lack of due diligence.

60   [1998] 2 Lloyd's Rep 652, hereafter referred to as *The Lydia Flag*.

This insurance covers loss of or damage to the subject matter insured caused by ... Negligence of repairers ... Provided such loss or damage has not resulted from want of due diligence by the assured ...

Although, the policy in question was a time policy, an express warranty of seaworthiness was included by the following wording:

Warranted that at the inception of this policy the vessel ... shall be in a seaworthy condition and thereafter during the valid period of this policy the insured shall exercise due diligence to keep the vessel seaworthy ...

In August 1996 the insured vessel lost her rudder at Abidjan and sustained damage. It was common ground that the cause of loss was the negligence of ship-repairers who had previously dismantled her rudder in drydock in Piraeus in December 1995 in order to examine the tail shaft. When the assured claimed on the policy under the Inchmaree Clause the insurers refused liability on the basis that, at the time of the inception of the policy in question, the vessel had been unseaworthy and, therefore, the assured was in breach of the express warranty.

The evidence showed that the vessel was unseaworthy due to the negligence of the repairers; and this meant breach of the express warranty of seaworthiness. Accordingly, the insurer could only have been liable had the Inchmaree Clause overridden the express warranty. The judge, Moore-Bick J, gave judgment in favour of the assured. He was of the opinion that the correct way of interpreting the Inchmaree Clause was that it provided exceptions to the express warranty of seaworthiness and the cover could only have been lost had unseaworthiness resulted from want of due diligence on the part of owners or managers. This was not the case. Accordingly, the insurers were entitled to recover.[61]

6.30   Comment is called for on several points relating to this judgment. First, it is clear that not only latent defects, as suggested by Arnould, but also other perils insured under the Inchmaree Clause would have priority over the warranty of seaworthiness. Moore-Bick J evaluating the overriding effect of perils covered by an Inchmaree Clause said as follows:[62]

In this case, it is accepted that the loss of the rudder was caused by negligence on the part of the repairers. It could just as well, of course, have been caused by some latent defect in the mechanism securing the rudder to the rudder stock. One would be surprised to find that, having taken insurance of this kind and the vessel being unseaworthy by reason of a latent defect at the inception of the policy, the owners would be completely without cover if the vessel was lost as a result, for example, of a collision with another vessel for which no fault could be attached to the owners of the vessel simply because there was a latent defect which had not in any way contributed to the casualty.

---

61 [1998] 2 Lloyd's Rep 652, p 656, Moore-Bick J said that: 'In my judgment the only sensible way in which to read these clauses together is in the way suggested by [the assured] and in those circumstances I am satisfied that cover is not lost, in so far as the vessel may be unseaworthy at the inception of the policy as a result of latent defect or negligence, as in this case, of repairers, provided of course that unseaworthiness has not resulted from want of due diligence on the part of the owners or managers.'

62 *Ibid*, p 655.

6.31   Secondly, the warranty in *The Lydia Flag* was specially incorporated into the time policy and, accordingly, comments of Moore-Bick J were made in reference to an express warranty of seaworthiness in a time policy. However, as discussed in earlier parts of this book, unless otherwise stated expressly there is no distinction in the rules that apply to express and implied warranties. Section 34(3), which regulates waiver of breach of warranty, does not make any distinction between express and implied warranties and applies to both equally. Thus, it can be argued that, even though *The Lydia Flag* was concerned with an express warranty, the judgment has applicability to implied warranties as well. By the same token, it is possible to argue that breach of other express warranties, that is, locality warranties could be rendered ineffective by the Inchmaree Clause. For instance, if the insured vessel navigates to an area in breach of a locality warranty and this is occasioned by negligence of the master, the insurance cover should not be affected. The reason for this is that the risk covered by the Inchmaree Clause, namely negligence of the master, is regarded as an exception to the express warranty of locality.

6.32   It would appear that further legal debate is essential in order to clarify the interrelation between the Inchmaree Clause and marine warranties. The law, as it stands, suggests that the Inchmaree Clause has the ability to waive breach of warranty in most cases. This consequence had not been foreseen by the drafter of the clause and surely has an impact on the balance of the relationship between the assured and insurer. In this respect, it will not be a surprise to see an attempt by insurers in the future to alter the wording of the Inchmaree Clause and restrict the scope of the cover provided.

II – WAIVER OF BREACH OF MARINE INSURANCE WARRANTIES AFTER THE BREACH IS COMMITTED

(A)   Legal position in light of *The Good Luck*: a dramatic change in law?

6.33   As s 34(3) imposes no time restriction on the insurer's right to waive a breach of a marine warranty, it is possible that waiver might take place after the occurrence of breach. Traditionally, waiver following a breach of a marine warranty might take two forms: waiver by election and waiver by estoppel (promissory).

6.34   Lord Goff summarised the elements of waiver by election, in a general sense, in *Motor Oil Hellas (Corinth) Refineries SA v Shipping Corp of India (The Kanchenjunga)*[63] in the following speech:[64]

> In particular, where with knowledge of the relevant facts a party has acted in a manner which is consistent only with his having chosen one of the two alternative and inconsistent courses of action then open to him – for example, to determine a contract or alternatively to affirm it – he is held to have made his election accordingly ... It can be communicated to the other party by words or by conduct, though, perhaps because

---

63   [1990] 1 Lloyd's Rep 391, hereafter referred to as *The Kanchenjunga*.
64   *Ibid*, p 398.

a party who elects not to exercise a right which has become available to him is abandoning that right, he will only be held to have done so if he has so communicated his election to the other party in clear and unequivocal terms ...[65]

Applying this to the insurance context, it can be concluded that a breach of warranty could be waived after the occurrence of such beach by an unequivocal representation of the insurer who has knowledge of such breach. The presence of both of these elements is essential for waiver by election. Thus, even if there is a presentation of the most unequivocal kind, if there is nothing to suggest that the insurer possessed the appropriate knowledge, there will be no waiver.[66]

6.35   Promissory estoppel (equitable forbearance) operates where, in a legal relationship, one party (promissor) leads the other party (promisee) to believe that promissor's rights under a contract or other legal relationship will not be enforced.[67] When an insurer is said to be estopped from relying on a breach of a warranty, he, either by conduct or words, leads the assured to believe that he will not rely on the remedy afforded to him by the MIA 1906.

6.36   Following the decision of the House of Lords in *The Good Luck*,[68] some eminent commentators were of the opinion that the legal position in relation to waiver by election had changed dramatically. Both Clarke and the editors of *MacGillivray and Parkington on Insurance Law* suggested that the remedy of automatic discharge employed in *The Good Luck* by Lord Goff made it impossible to apply waiver by election in the context of breach of a marine warranty. An assured who wishes to contend that the insurer has waived a breach of warranty, according to these commentators, must now establish waiver by equitable estoppel. The commentators relied on different grounds to support their argument. Clarke argued that waiver by election could not be applied as a breach of warranty by the assured automatically terminated the contract.[69] It was submitted by the editors of *MacGillivray and Parkington*, on the other hand, that waiver by election was not applicable in this context simply because by the occurrence of the breach the insurer was automatically discharged from liability and accordingly he could not be put to any election.[70]

6.37   In the first edition of this book, these views were contested on various grounds. First, it was argued that a breach of warranty did not have the effect of terminating the

---

65   A similar analysis was also undertaken by Lord Diplock in *Kammins Ballroom Co Ltd v Zenith Investments (Torquay) Ltd (No 1)* [1971] AC 850.

66   See *Samuel & Co Ltd v Dumas* [1924] AC 431, p 483, *per* Lord Sumner. In such a case, the assured might allege that the insurer has been estopped from relying on the breach provided some other conditions, which will be discussed later in this chapter, exist.

67   The doctrine was first created by Lord Cairns in *Hughes v Metropolitan Railway Co* (1877) 2 App Cas 439. It was later adopted by Lord Denning in *Central London Property Trust Ltd v High Trees House Ltd* [1947] KB 130, p 136, who summarised the doctrine in the following way: 'Where a promise was made which was intended to create legal relations and which, to the knowledge of the person making the promise, was going to be acted upon by the person to whom it was made and which was, in fact, so acted on ... the promise must be honoured.'

68   [1992] 1 AC 233; [1991] 2 Lloyd's Rep 191.

69   Clarke, 1997, para 20-7A, p 548 (note that a new edition of this book has been published since then).

70   MacGillivray, 1997, para 10-98, p 254 (note that a new edition of this book has been published since then).

contract.[71] Secondly, it was contended that the remedy of automatic discharge did not mean that the insurer was not required to make an election anymore. It was submitted that the insurer was still put to an election of whether to rely on this defence or not.[72]

6.38   It is, however, clear that the view expressed by Clarke and editors of *MacGillivray*, has found judicial support. In *Kirkaldy (J) & Sons Ltd v Walker*,[73] Longmore J suggested that the doctrine of waiver by election had no application after *The Good Luck* and the assured needed to rely on the doctrine of waiver by estoppel. He commented as follows:[74]

> Section 33 of the MIA 1906 provides for the insurer to be discharged from liability as from the date of breach of warranty. It is, therefore, apparent that no question of election arises although by s 34(3) the insurers may waive the breach. Since the breach of warranty does not give rise to any election by the insurer, eg, to choose to keep the contract on foot, the doctrine of waiver by election has no application.[75]

More recently, in *HIH Casualty & General Insurance Ltd v Axa Corporate Solutions*,[76] Mr Jules Sher QC, sitting as a deputy High Court judge, rejected the insurer's argument that the appropriate doctrine for the purposes of s 34(3) was waiver by election and not waiver by estoppel. He said as follows:[77]

> The plea is put in terms of waiver or estoppel. It is necessary to distinguish two, quite different, concepts that lie behind these words. The first is waiver by election. The second is waiver by estoppel. The traditional common law concept of waiver by election involves a choice by the waiving party between two inconsistent courses of action. Outside the insurance sphere, when there has been a repudiatory breach of a promissory warranty by one party the other has a choice whether to accept the breach as discharging the contract or to waive it and affirm the contract. If he does not accept it the contract continues in force. That is an example of a true election between two inconsistent courses. In the case of an insurance contract, on the other hand, breach of the promissory warranty discharges the cover (though not, technically, the entire contract) automatically, without any action or election on the part of the insurer. There is no choice involved at all. There is no election to be made. So much comes out of the Good Luck and is not disputed before me as applicable to the insurances and reinsurances here. It follows that waiver by election can have no application in such a case and the waiver, therefore, referred to in section 34(3) of the Marine Insurance Act 1906 must encompass waiver by estoppel, the second of the two concepts above-mentioned, rather than waiver by election ...

---

71   See the judgment of Lord Goff on this point in *The Good Luck* [1992] 1 AC 233, p 263. More recently, the Court of Appeal, in *Chapman v Kadirga Denizcilik ve Ticaret* [1998] Lloyd's Rep IR 377, affirmed the position by stating that, although the effect of the breach of warranty is to discharge insurers from liability as from the date of breach, this does not necessarily have the effect of bringing the contract to an end.

72   See, also, Wilken and Villiers, 2002, para 21.36.

73   [1999] Lloyd's Rep IR 410.

74   *Ibid*, p 422.

75   See, also, the judgment of Aikens J in *The Milasan* [2000] 2 Lloyd's Rep 458, p 467.

76   [2002] Lloyd's Rep IR 325, aff'd by the Court of Appeal [2002] EWCA Civ 1253; [2003] 1 Lloyd's Rep IR 1.

77   *Ibid*, [23].

6.39   The current legal position could be summarised in the following manner. At the time when the MIA 1906 was drafted, a number of doctrines were applicable in the context of waiving marine insurance warranties. The term 'waive' in s 34(3) has, therefore, been used in a loose sense of the word, referring not only to an express agreement to waive a breach of a marine warranty, but also to waiver by election and various forms of waiver by estoppel. However, in the light of the automatic discharge remedy adopted by the House of Lords in *The Good Luck*, it is very difficult to argue that the insurer, after the occurrence of breach, is in a position to make an election. This, of course, does not mean that s 34(3) is made redundant. It is still possible to waive a breach of a marine warranty by an express agreement or by estoppel. Waiver of breach by an express term has been considered in the first part of this chapter. The rest of the chapter will, therefore, focus on waiver of breach of a marine warranty by promissory estoppel.

(B)   Application of the promissory estoppel doctrine (equitable forbearance) in the context of breach of a marine warranty

6.40   The elements of waiver by promissory estoppel in this context have been summarised, in *HIH Casualty & General Insurance Ltd v Axa Corporate Solutions*, by deputy judge Sheer QC as follows:[78]

> Waiver by estoppel or promissory estoppel, as it is more commonly described, involves a clear and unequivocal representation that the reinsurer (or insurer) will not stand on its right to treat the cover as having been discharged on which the insurer (or insured) has relied in circumstances in which it would be inequitable to allow the reinsurer (or insurer) to resile from its representation.

Therefore, in order to establish waiver by estoppel, the assured has to demonstrate that the insurer has made an unequivocal representation to the effect that he would not insist on his automatic right to discharge himself from further liability; it would be inequitable, if the assured had relied on this representation, on the part of the insurer to decide to go back on his promise.

(a)   Unequivocal conduct (representation)

6.41   The unequivocal conduct in this context is one that is inconsistent with the insurer's right to be discharged from liability under the contract of insurance. It has to be borne in mind that the required degree of unequivocal conduct in this context may well be different from the one required to establish waiver of the insurer's the right to avoid the contract.[79] Since the legal effect of breach of a warranty was believed to be different in the past, when assessing whether there is an unequivocal conduct or not it would be dangerous to place too much reliance on authorities pre-dating *The Good Luck*.[80]

---

78   *Ibid*, [24].
79   See s 18(3)(c) of the MIA 1906.
80   MacGillivray, 2003, para 10-108.

6.42   For the purposes of waiver by estoppel, the insurer's conduct could amount to an unequivocal representation if, and only if, the assured, by considering the conduct and surrounding circumstances, could draw the conclusion that the insurer wishes to keep the contract intact.[81] This point has been emphasised with an illustration by David Steel J, in *Callaghan and Hedges v Thompson and Others*:[82]

> Approaching the matter without reference to the authorities, it seems to me that an unequivocal demonstration of an intention to proceed with a contract can only be exhibited if the other party appreciates that a choice has been made. It would not, for instance, constitute affirmation if a party learning of a misrepresentation justifying avoidance decides simply in his own mind not to avoid and then be the author of a letter to the other party which is consistent with the contract being alive. That letter would not exhibit to the other party any election or choice at all.

6.43   Payment of premium that becomes due after the breach of a warranty is a clear indication that the insurer wishes to keep the insurance relation on foot.[83] However, it should be borne in mind that not all types of payments made by the insurer after the breach could amount to unequivocal conduct. If the insurer makes a payment in relation to a loss that occurred before the breach, this does not mean that he has an intention of keeping the contractual relation on foot. Similarly, acceptance of a premium by the insurer, which fell due or was earned before the breach, should not amount to an unequivocal representation on his part that he will not rely on breach of warranty defence. Although there is no authority on this point, it is obvious that such conduct shows no intention of the insurer to keep the insurance relation on foot. He is simply collecting a payment that was due for a period when the contract was in force to the fullest extent.

6.44   In similar vein, giving advice as to security measures, which might avoid future loss, might amount to unequivocal conduct on the part of the assured for it would be difficult for the insurer to explain why he would be concerned about the risk of the assured suffering loss in the future if the insurer is discharged from liability under the insurance as a result of a breach of warranty.[84] Another example of conduct that might be regarded as sufficient to found an unequivocal conduct on the part of the insurer is payment of a claim or payment of money into court in response to the assured's claim.[85]

6.45   There is authority to suggest that silence, or delay to act, after a warranty is breached could constitute a sufficiently unequivocal representation so as to found

---

81   The law of estoppel looks chiefly at the situation of the person relying on the estoppel: *Craine v Colonial Mutual Fire Insurance Co* [1920] 28 CLR 305, p 327, *per* Isaacs J.

82   [2000] Lloyd's Rep IR 125, p 134.

83   *Wing v Harwey* (1854) 5 De GM & G 265, pp 269–71, *per* Knight Bruce and Turner LJJ; *Hadenfayre v British National Insurance Ltd* [1984] 2 Lloyd's Rep 393, p 400, *per* Lloyd J; *Stone v Reliance Mutual Insurance Society Ltd* [1972] 1 Lloyd's Rep 469, p 475, *per* Denning LJ.

84   *De Maurier (Jewels) Ltd v Bastion Insurance Co Ltd* [1967] 2 Lloyd's Rep 550, p 559, *per* Donaldson J.

85   *Svenska Handelsbanken v Sun Alliance and London Insurance plc* [1996] 1 Lloyd's Rep 519, p 569, *per* Rix J; *Baghbadrani v Commercial Union Assurance Co plc* [2000] Lloyd's Rep IR 94, p 123, *per* HHJ Gibbs QC.

waiver.[86] However, these decisions were delivered at a time when it was thought that a positive act of repudiation might be required before insurers could take advantage of a breach of a warranty.[87] After the adoption of the remedy of automatic discharge by *The Good Luck*, it can be concluded that these cases are not good law any more. The insurer is now automatically discharged from liability in case of a breach of a warranty and his silence or failure to act shows that he has elected to rely on the defence afforded to him and has no intention of waiving this remedy. It is clear that, after *The Good Luck*, a representation, in the form of an affirmative conduct, is required to found waiver.

6.46   In the light of the above analysis, the insurer must be extremely careful and avoid certain types of conduct after a breach of warranty has occurred, as the conduct may amount to an unequivocal representation that prevents him from relying on the breach of warranty. In order to reduce such a risk, it is quite common to introduce 'non-waiver clauses' in insurance contracts. Clauses of this type provide that certain conduct of the insurer, or in some cases, the assured, would not mean waiver of a certain right. Clause 17 of the ICC (type A, B, C) is a clause of this type and provides that measures taken by the assured or the underwriters with the object of saving, protecting or recovering the subject matter insured shall not be considered as a waiver or acceptance of abandonment, or otherwise prejudice the rights of either party.[88] 'Non-waiver clauses' can be drafted widely enough to assist the insurer in case of a breach of warranty. This is usually the case in protection and indemnity (P&I) practice. The following is a 'non-waiver clause' that appears in most club rules:

> No act, omission, course of dealing, forbearance, delay or indulgence by the club in enforcing any of the club rules or any of the terms or conditions of its contracts with members nor any granting of time by the club shall prejudice or affect the rights and remedies of the club under the club rules or under such contracts, and no such matter shall be treated as any evidence of waiver of the club's rights thereunder, nor shall any waiver of any breach by a member of club rules or contracts operate as a waiver of any subsequent breach thereof .

Thus, if the club requires a contribution from its member[89] after one of the vessels owned by the member has committed a breach of a club warranty, this would not mean waiver of that particular breach in the light of the clause mentioned above. Similarly, in cases where the club grants a letter of security to release the vessel from

---

86   *Allen v Robles (Compagnie Parisiene de Garantie, Third Party)* [1969] 1 WLR 1193 and *Wahbe Tamari & Sons and Jaffa Trading Co v Colprogenca-Socidade General de Fibras Gabes e Products Colonial Ltd* [1969] 2 Lloyd's Rep 18.

87   At that time, breach of a marine warranty was equated with breach of a condition in general contract law.

88   For clauses of similar effect, see cl 12 of the Institute War Clauses (Cargo) and cl 12 of the Institute Strikes Clauses (Cargo).

89   In P&I practice, instead of charging a premium, a system of levying calls is applied. Each member pays an advance call, which is calculated according to the tonnage of his vessels entered in the club. Advance calls, although announced at the beginning of each policy year, are made payable by most clubs by instalments during the year. Club rules, invariably, give the power of levying supplementary, or additional, calls to the committee of directors who also decide upon the percentage to be applied to the advance call, which will be the level of supplementary call. The directors ask for supplementary calls from the members if the claims made by members during that policy year exceed the amount of advance calls that have been collected.

arrest, this will not mean that the club has waived its right to rely on the breach of a warranty committed by that particular vessel before it was arrested.[90]

6.47   There is nothing preventing the insurers from inserting a non-waiver clause in a hull policy, which states that certain acts or conduct of the insurer will not amount to waiver of breach of warranty. It must, however, be borne in mind that clauses of this nature must be drafted as clearly as possible and care must be taken to avoid any ambiguity. The reason for this is that in case of an ambiguity the *contra proferentem* rule may require this kind of clause to be construed against the insurer.

6.48   As estoppel is an equitable remedy, the courts chiefly look at the position of the representee, in this case the assured, in particular how the representation appeared to him. This, however, does not mean that knowledge has no role to play in this context. A representor (insurer) who is unaware that he has a right to be discharged from his liability is unlikely to make a representation that carries with it some apparent awareness that he has such a right. By the same token, a respresentee who is unaware that the representor has a particular right is unlikely to understand the representation to mean that the representor is not going to insist on that right.

The significance of knowledge in this context has been given judicial consideration in *HIH Casualty & General Insurance Ltd v Axa Corporate Solutions*.[91] It was argued by the reassured that the reinsurers were estopped from relying on a breach of a warranty, which required the assured to produce a certain amount of films, because prior to making payment to its assureds the reassured became aware of the fact that an inadequate number of films had been made. It was, however, not until after payment by the reassured that the Court of Appeal decided that there was a warranty as to the number of films, in *HIH Casualty & General Insurance Ltd v New Hampshire Insurance Co*.[92] Therefore, the reinsurers appreciated that they had a defence based on a breach of warranty after the reassured made payment under the original policy. In those circumstances, Deputy High Court Judge Sher QC ruled that there could be no waiver as it was not enough that the reinsurers were aware of the facts that constituted a breach – it was, in addition, necessary for them to be aware of the legal consequences that flowed from that knowledge. The Court of Appeal affirmed the judgment, but indicated that some awareness of a legal right not to pay would suffice in order to establish waiver by estoppel.[93]

---

90   One of the most popular facilities afforded by P&I clubs is their assistance in securing the release of arrested vessels entered in the club. The furnishing of a club letter of undertaking or guarantee is not automatic, nor is it free of conditions. Clubs have adopted certain rules in order to safeguard themselves from having this facility abused. Generally speaking, the following conditions must be satisfied in order to grant a letter of security: (a) the vessel must be an entered vessel; (b) the claim must be part of the club's cover; (c) the calls must be paid fully by the member; (d) a counter-security must be provided by the member, if required by the club.

91   [2002] Lloyd's Rep IR 325, aff'd by the Court of Appeal [2002] EWCA Civ 1253; [2003] 1 Lloyd's Rep IR 1.

92   [2001] EWCA Civ 735.

93   It has been suggested that no knowledge is required when the insurer's words or conduct suggest that he is indifferent to the possibility of breach: Clarke, 2002, at 20-7C.

(b)   Reliance

6.49   In order to establish the existence of promissory estoppel it is essential to show that the assured acted in reliance of the promise of the insurer that the legal right arising from the breach of the warranty would not be enforced.[94] This means that the assured should show that he had attached some significance to the representation in question and acted on it; that is, he had changed his position.[95]

6.50   Reliance must also be reasonable. Whether reliance is reasonable depends on the facts of each case. It is highly unlikely that reliance would be reasonable in cases where the alleged representation was made by an agent of the insurer who lacked both actual and ostensible authority.[96]

6.51   Reliance may be presumed in cases where it can be shown that a representation was calculated to influence the judgment of a reasonable man.[97]

(c)   Being inequitable

6.52   It has been suggested that detriment is an essential ingredient of the promissory estoppel doctrine.[98] It would be much easier for a court to conclude that the insurer's attempt to go back on his promise creates inequality if it can be shown that the assured has altered his position to his own detriment.[99] In the insurance context, not seeking alternative cover was held to be sufficient to establish detriment.[100]

6.53   It should be noted that estoppel is an equitable remedy and equity will not assist a party who is, himself, guilty of continuing misconduct.[101] In practical terms, it is difficult to see how an assured who had defrauded the insurer could establish that he understood the insurer to have knowledge of the fraud.

---

94   *The Kanchenjunga* [1990] 1 Lloyd's Rep 391, p 399, *per* Goff LJ. More recently, the point has been made by Aikens J in *The Milasan* [2000] 2 Lloyd's Rep 458, p 467; by Ward LJ in *Seechurn v Ace Insurance SA-NV* [2002] EWCA Civ 67; [2002] 2 Lloyd's Rep 390, [26]; by Tuckey LJ in *HIH Casualty & General Insurance Ltd v Axa Corporate Solutions* [2002] EWCA Civ 1253, [29].

95   *Lark v Outhwaite* [1991] 2 Lloyd's Rep 132.

96   Ostensible authority is described by Diplock LJ, in *Freeman & Lockyer v Buckhurst Park Properties (Mangal) Ltd* [1964] 2 QB 480, p 503, as follows: '... a legal relationship between the principal and the contractor created by a representation, made by the principal to the contractor, intended to be and in fact acted upon by the contractor, that the agent has authority to enter on behalf of the principal into a contract of a kind within the scope of the "apparent authority" so as to render the principal liable to perform any obligations imposed upon him by such a contract.' Accordingly, ostensible authority can arise from either an express oral or written representation, or by the principal's conduct on which the third party must have relied, or have been induced to act, to its detriment.

97   *Brikom Investments Ltd v Carr* [1979] QB 467, p 483, *per* Lord Denning MR.

98   *Tool Metal Manufacturing Co Ltd v Tungsten Electric Co Ltd* [1955] 1 WLR 761, p 764, *per* Viscount Simonds; *Societe Italo-Belge pour Le Commerce et l'Industrie SA v Palm and Vegetable Oils (Malaysia) sdn Bdh (The Post Chaser)* [1981] 1 All ER 19, 27, *per* Goff J.

99   *Emery v UCB Corporate Services Ltd* [2001] EWCA Civ 675, *per* Gibson LJ, [28] and [36].

100   *Hargett v Gulf Insurance Co* 55 P2d 12.

101   *Baghbadrani v Commercial Union Assurance Co plc* [2000] Lloyd's Rep IR 94.

III – WAIVER AND SPECIAL POSITION OF THE WARRANTY OF LEGALITY

6.54   As s 34(3) is designed to apply to all types of warranties it can be argued that breach of warranty of legality can also be waived. This view can be supported by the fact that s 41, which regulates the implied warranty of legality, does not prevent it from being waived. However, this is not the case. In contract law, a contract that is somehow tainted by illegality cannot be later affirmed by the parties and converted to an enforceable contract;[102] the issue is one of public policy rather than private contract. Similarly, in this context, if the insurer is discharged from liability due to the illegal nature of the adventure insured, he cannot be made liable by a waiver. Such an act would be contrary to public policy. This was expressly stated in *Gedge and Others v Royal Exchange Assurance Corp*,[103] only six years before the enactment of the Act. It might be possible that this decision came too late to attract the attention of the draftsman to include it in the Act.[104] However, by virtue of s 91(2),[105] although expressly not stated in the Act, the judgment in *Gedge v Royal Exchange Assurance Corp* is still good law and a breach of warranty of legality cannot be waived. General contract law principles, mentioned above, also support this conclusion.

---

102 See the *dicta* of Lord Mansfield in *Holman v Johnson* (1775) 1 Cowp 343.

103 [1900] 2 QB 214.

104 The MIA 1906 was first drafted in 1894 and discussions and negotiations went on, in Parliament and sub-commissions, regarding different provisions before it was enacted. During this period (1894–1906), little attention was paid to the cases recently decided as the main concern was to evaluate the accuracy and appropriateness of the sections already drafted.

105 This sub-section reads as follows: 'The rules of common law including the law merchant, save in so far as they are inconsistent with the express provisions of this Act, shall continue to apply to contracts of marine insurance.'

CHAPTER 7

LEGAL POSITION IN RELATION TO WARRANTIES IN SOME OTHER JURISDICTIONS

I – OBJECT AND EXTENT OF A COMPARATIVE STUDY

7.1   Several criticisms have been directed towards the 'warranty regime' adopted by the MIA 1906. Some have focused on the point that the current legal regime does not provide for a fair distribution of rights and obligations between assured and insurer, while others have usually blamed English law for being too formal. Furthermore, the evaluation of the current legal rules on marine warranties in earlier chapters has identified certain deficiencies. All these issues will be taken into account when the need for reform in this area is discussed in the final chapter of the book. However, before questioning the English marine warranty regime, some other legal systems need to be evaluated. It is believed that such a comparative approach will bring an additional dimension to the issues in question and provide the basis for a discussion on possible reform in this area.

7.2   The two legal systems chosen for this comparative study are the German and the Norwegian systems. The choice of these two systems is not just a coincidence. German law represents the traditional continental approach, together with French law, and its influence can be observed on the law and policies of a great number of countries, both inside and outside Europe.[1] Also, the German marine insurance market is one of the largest markets in the world and most of the policies underwritten in this market are subject to German marine insurance conditions and, accordingly, to German law.

7.3   The Norwegian marine insurance plans are one of the most recent and possibly sophisticated codes in the world. Indeed, the United Nations Conference on Trade and Development (UNCTAD) Report recommended the adoption of the Norwegian form when considering reform of the documentary aspects of marine insurance.[2] Since the early 1980s, an extensive and far-reaching internationalisation of the Norwegian marine insurance market has been observed. Today, for example, foreign owned and/or controlled vessels constitute an essential part of many Norwegian insurers' portfolios.[3] It is submitted that the success of the provisions in marine insurance plans, and their ability to create a fair balance between the assured and insurer, played a

---

1   For example, Chapter 14 of the Greek Code of Private Maritime Law of 1958 contains provisions for marine insurance, which were highly influenced by German law. Similarly, the Turkish Commercial Code of 1956, which was drafted by a German professor, Professor Hirsh, contains provisions in its fifth book in relation to marine insurance. Also, the effect of German marine insurance law can be seen in general clauses of hull insurance drafted by Japan Shipping Exchange Inc, which are quite commonly used in the Japanese marine insurance market.

2   UN, *Legal and Documentary Aspects of the Marine Insurance Contract*, 1982, para 226.

3   In 1992, of 1,542 vessels insured in the Norwegian market 63.17% were owned/controlled by non-Norwegian citizens. Statistics also suggest that the amount of non-Norwegian owned/controlled vessels in the Norwegian market has increased by another 2–3% in recent years. All the figures are taken from Marine Insurance Report, Issues No 121, 125 and 139, published by DYP Group Newsletters.

crucial role in the internationalisation process of the Norwegian marine insurance market.[4] Also, the Norwegian marine insurance plans have, to a considerable extent through the years, influenced the drafting of corresponding conditions in some other Nordic countries.[5]

7.4   The legal regime in relation to marine warranties in the German and Norwegian systems will be examined later in this chapter after the legislative context of marine insurance in these jurisdictions is outlined. It should be noted that the comparison will be based on hull practice and other types of insurance, that is energy, cargo insurance, insurance for oilrigs, fishing vessels, will not be taken into account. Since most marine warranties in English law appear in hull policies, it is believed that an intensive study of hull insurance will be sufficient to show the main differences between English law and these legal systems in relation to warranties.[6] One might, at this stage, wonder why American law, given the size and importance of the American marine insurance market, has been excluded from such an intensive study. The reasons behind this exclusion will be summarised briefly.

II – REASONS FOR EXCLUDING AMERICAN LAW FROM COMPARISON

(A)   The *Wilburn Boat* case: a turning point

7.5   Prior to the *Wilburn Boat* case,[7] just like the other areas of marine insurance, there used to be a remarkable uniformity between English and American laws in the context of marine warranties.[8] Indeed, there was a tendency amongst the judges to keep the uniformity between these legal systems.[9] The main reason behind this uniformity was the presumption that federal law would apply, in preference to inconsistent state law, in any action involving marine insurance and English law; the legal regime adopted mainly by the MIA 1906, was regarded as the federal law by the majority of the American courts. However, great changes with numerous judicial

---

4   This view is that of Professor Hans Jacob Bull, who acted as the chairman of the committee that revised the Marine Insurance Plan of 1964, Huybrechts, Hooydonk and Dieryck, 1999, pp 109–22.

5   The first Swedish General Marine Insurance Plan was introduced in 1891, 15 years after the first Norwegian Marine Insurance Plan (NMIP). Similarly, Finnish General Hull Conditions for Vessels were adopted in 1968 with the inspiration taken from the NMIPs.

6   It should also be borne in mind that hull insurance forms the largest part of English, German and Norwegian marine insurance markets' premium income.

7   *Wilburn Boat Co v Fireman's Fund Insurance Co* [1953] AMC 284, reversed [1955] AMC 467.

8   The main divergence between English and American law seems to be in the application of the implied warranty of seaworthiness. American law has adopted, somehow, a continuing warranty status in respect of voyage policies. See *McDowell v General Mutual Insurance Co* 7 Louisiana Annual 684. Also, American law, in relation to time policies, implies a warranty of seaworthiness if the insured vessel is at port at the time of attachment of the policy. See *Union Insurance Co of Philadelphia v Smith* 124 US 405.

9   For example, in *Queen Insurance Co of America v Globe & Rutgers Fire Insurance Co* 263 US 487, the court felt constrained to say that: 'There are special reasons for keeping in harmony with the marine insurance laws of England, the great field of this business.'

implications have occurred in American law following the Supreme Court's decision in the *Wilburn Boat* case. A summary of the facts of this celebrated case follows.[10]

In May 1947, Fireman's Fund Insurance Co issued a marine hull policy on *The Wanderer*, a small houseboat. The policy was issued in Illinois through an Illinois broker to the assureds who also resided in Illinois. The policy, *inter alia*, provided that the vessel could neither be sold nor pledged without the insurer's consent;[11] she could only be used 'solely for private pleasure purposes' and could not be 'hired or chartered' without the insurer's permission.[12] In June 1948, three brothers – Glenn, Frank, and Henry Wilburn – purchased *The Wanderer* for US $9,000. The insurer indorsed the policy in favour of the new owners, who were in business as a partnership known as Wilburn's Boat Company. The Wilburn brothers, who were from Texas, moved the vessel to Lake Texoma, an artificial lake which lies (as its name suggests) on the border between Texas and Oklahoma. A policy indorsement authorised the trip and provided that, after the move, *The Wanderer* would be confined to Lake Texoma.

In September 1948, the brothers sold *The Wanderer* to the Wilburn's Boat Company, an Oklahoma corporation that they owned, without the consent of the insurer. On three occasions the Wilburn brothers or their corporation pledged the vessel to secure promissory notes, again without the consent of the insurer. Finally, the owners had leased the vessel on several occasions and had carried passengers for hire. Undoubtedly, these actions of the Wilburn brothers amounted to several breaches of the policy. On 25 February 1949, a fire destroyed *The Wanderer* while she was moored approximately 90 m off the Oklahoma shore of the lake. The origin of the fire could not be identified, but there was no doubt that the breaches of the policy noted above did not contribute to the loss. The Wilburn brothers made a claim under the policy, but the insurer refused to pay on the ground that several warranties in the policy were breached and the federal law of marine insurance permitted the underwriters to avoid payment for a subsequent loss – even if the breach was unrelated to the loss. The Wilburns, on the other hand, argued that Texas law, rather than the general maritime law, governed the policy. Under Texas law, the policy breaches relating to the sale and use of the vessel would not defeat coverage unless they had contributed to the loss.

In June 1949, the three brothers and their company sued Fireman's Fund Insurance Company in a Texas state court claiming over $40,000 under the insurance contract. The insurer, Fireman's Fund, managed to have the case moved to the Federal District Court the following month by asserting diversity jurisdiction.[13] In December 1951, the District Court ruled that federal maritime law, rather than Texas law, governed the policy, and, due to the 'literal compliance' rule, the Wilburns were not entitled to

---

10 As is commonly the case, the Supreme Court's opinion gives only a bare outline of the facts. More details can be found in some of the lower courts' opinions, The Transcript of Record and in the secondary literature.

11 This clause was worded in the following manner: 'It is also agreed that this insurance shall be void in case this policy or the interest insured thereby shall be sold, assigned, transferred or pledged without consent in writing of the assurers.'

12 The policy provided as follows: 'Warranted by the assured that the within named vessel shall be used solely for private pleasure purposes during the currency of this policy and shall not be hired or chartered unless permission is granted by endorsement hereon.'

13 Diversity jurisdiction gives the Federal Court the power to hear certain cases when the parties are from different states.

recovery. The decision of the District Court was later affirmed by US Court of Appeals for the Fifth Circuit.

Due to the importance of the questions involved, the Supreme Court 'granted *certiorari*', meaning that it agreed to hear the case. On 28 February 1955, almost six years after the loss, the Supreme Court reversed the Fifth Circuit's decision and remanded the case to the District Court 'for a trial under appropriate state law'.[14] The Supreme Court's decision, which was written by Black J, needs to be analysed carefully. The Supreme Court immediately held that there was not a judicially-established federal admiralty rule governing marine insurance warranties. It was further stressed that, in cases where no federal rule existed, state law should be applied. Accordingly, it was decided that the effect of breach of warranties in the policy would be decided by applying the appropriate state law.[15] Moreover, the court discussed whether a 'new federal admiralty rule' in this area should be fashioned and it concluded that this was not necessary for two principal reasons. First, the regulation of insurance has, historically, been a matter for the individual states (even if the federal government does have the power to regulate insurance if it chooses to do so) and Congress has recognised and acted upon this division of responsibility.[16] Secondly, even if the court wished to fashion a new rule, doing so would be a complex and difficult task that courts are poorly equipped to undertake.[17]

7.6   Despite the passage of 50 years, discussions on the actual impact of the *Wilburn Boat* case are still going on in the USA. Most commentators criticise the judgment severely, on the ground that it has a destructive effect on uniformity and certainty of both American marine insurance law and admiralty law.[18] Some, on the other hand, regard the holding in *Wilburn Boat* as a necessary element of the constitutional system of the USA, which seeks to balance federal and state powers by allowing state law to prevail in certain instances.[19] It is beyond the scope of this book to discuss the justification for and evaluate the accuracy of the judgment of the Supreme Court in *Wilburn Boat*. The main concern is the conflicts and difficulties arising from the judgment that prevent us from carrying out a healthy comparison between English and American law in relation to warranties as will be discussed in the following part. In order to complete the picture it is sufficient to state Professor Schoenbaum's view that the real reason for the holding was, presumably, the Supreme Court majority's perception of the rigidity and formalism of English law and the fear of miscarriage of justice if the English law rule was allowed to prevail.[20] Perhaps, the Supreme Court

---

14   On remand, the litigation odyssey continued for slightly more than seven additional years and, finally, the case was resolved by applying Texas law. Ironically, the Supreme Court's decision did not help the Wilburn brothers, who were found guilty of eight material misrepresentations and non-disclosures and their claim was denied even on state law grounds.

15   [1955] AMC 467, pp 472–73.

16   [1955] AMC 467, pp 473–75.

17   *Ibid*, pp 475–76.

18   See McGlore 'Marine insurance and the implied warranty of seaworthiness' (1975) *Loyola Law Review* 960, pp 969–71; Waesche 'Choice and uniformity of law generally' (1991) *Tulane Law Review* 293, pp 303–04 and Waddell 'Current issues and developments in marine insurance' (1993) *University of San Fransisco Maritime Law Journal* 185, p 187.

19   See, 'The general maritime law v State law in maritime cases: which, when and why?' 50 *NWUL Rev* 677, p 682.

20   *Key Divergences between English and American Law of Marine Insurance: A Comparative Study*, (by TJ Schoenbaum) Maryland, 1999, p 37.

was uncomfortable with the 'harsh' literal compliance rule and did not want to deprive the Wilburn brothers of recovery for breaches of warranties that had no causal link with the loss. Deferring the problem to Congress or the states, with their greater expertise and experience, probably seemed much easier than adopting a new rule to replace it.[21]

(B)   Unpredictability of American law

7.7   The judgment of the Supreme Court in *Wilburn Boat* creates problems on many levels, most of which relate to predictability in the law governing marine insurance warranties. The main reason behind this is that the Supreme Court gave virtually no guidance on how to decide whether federal or state law should apply when warranties are concerned, but it, at least, offered the illustrations of its own analysis concerning the 'literal compliance' rule. In this respect, determining the extent of the ruling in *Wilburn Boat* is left to the lower courts and this, inevitably, creates a remarkable degree of uncertainty in law.[22] It is not crystal clear whether *Wilburn Boat* will be applied to all areas as far as marine warranties are concerned, or solely when the 'literal compliance' rule is involved. Similarly, whether the Wilburn rule be applied to all types of warranties, or only to the ones dealt with in the case, is a mystery. For instance, certain courts, despite *Wilburn Boat*, are of the opinion that the 'literal compliance' rule applies to warranties as a matter of federal law. Put another way, they insist on the existence of a federal rule, especially in cases where the 'literal compliance' rule is involved.[23] These courts, apparently, take the view that *Wilburn Boat* should be confined to its particular facts so that non-Wilburn warranties, such as navigational warranties, are subject to federal law.[24]

(C)   Other practical difficulties

7.8   Even though the *Wilburn Boat* decision is interpreted as allowing state law to govern marine insurance warranties, further problems, in terms of a comparative study, are likely to arise. Such an interpretation opens the way for the potential of 50 different rules on marine warranties. For example, Washington law requires a causal connection between a breach of warranty and the cause of loss in order for the breach to avoid coverage.[25] Florida law, on the other hand, provides that a breach of warranty

---

21 Professor Goldstein has found considerable evidence in several of the justices' private papers, which have since become available to scholars, that the result in *Wilburn Boat* was largely driven by the equities of the case. See, Goldstein 'The life and times of Wilburn Boat: A critical guide' (1997) *Journal of Maritime Law and Commerce* 395, pp 410–17.

22 This situation had been foreseen, in a general sense, by Professors Gilmore and Black in the first edition of their treatise, Gilmore and Black, 1957, § 2–8, p 63, where they stated that: 'Wilburn may mean merely that the States are to have a limited competency to regulate certain terms of marine policies. It could as a matter of cold logic be read to mean that there is no federal maritime law at all. It may very well turn out to mean anything between these extremes.'

23 See *Lexington Insurance Co v Cooke's Seafood* 835 F 2d 1364; *Aetna Insurance Co v Dudney* 595 So 2d 238 and *Home Insurance Co v Veron Holdings* [1995] AMC 369.

24 See *Lexington Insurance Co v Cooke's Seafood* 835 F 2d 1364, p 1366.

25 See *Riordan v Commercial Travelers Mutual Insurance Co* 525 P 2d 804; *Port Lynch Inc v New England International Assurety of America Inc* [1992] AMC 225; *Oregon Auto Insurance Co v Salzberg* 535 P 2d 816.

does not void the policy or contract, or constitute a defence to a loss thereon, unless such breach or violation increased the hazard by any means within the control of the assured.[26] In the presence of such a complicated legal regime, it is submitted that it would be unreasonable to attempt to generalise American law and compare it to the MIA 1906.[27]

7.9   Furthermore, the fact that many states explicitly exclude marine insurance from significant proportions of their insurance legislation[28] adds further complexities to such a comparative study. In such states, due to lack of a marine insurance precedent, the courts usually resolve marine disputes with reasoning designed for motor or homeowners' insurance.[29] Therefore, for those states, not only the marine insurance law, but other areas of insurance law need to be explored carefully in order to identify the state law on marine warranties and, naturally, this makes a comparative study not impossible, but very difficult.

III – GENERAL APPROACH IN RELATION TO ALTERATION OF RISK UNDER GERMAN AND NORWEGIAN LAW

7.10   In an insurance relationship it is crucial for the insurer that certain factors affecting the risk will remain unchanged during the currency of the contract because he has based his agreement and rate of the premium on this assumption. In the event that this assumption should not hold true, the insurer requires protection. In English insurance law, the general rule is that if the risk is increased during the currency of the policy, this has no adverse effects on its validity.[30] However, the common law tolerance of post-contractual increases of risk is modified by the MIA 1906 and standard Institute Clauses. Warranties, either express and implied, are the main sanctions used in relation to alteration of risk and, in case of their breach, the insurer is automatically discharged from further liability.[31]

As examined earlier, in the first chapter of this book, the unique nature of warranties in English insurance law was formed by Lord Mansfield and, for this

---

26   See s 627.409(2) of FLA STAT ANN (West 1996) and *Fireman's Fund Insurance Co v Cox* [1990] AMC 908.

27   The number of contradicting judgments, even within the same circuit, makes any generalisation on American law almost an impossible task.

28   See, eg, s 27-14-2(3) of the ALA CODE (1986) (excepting 'wet marine and transportation insurance' from the chapter governing insurance contracts); s 22:611(A) of the LA REV STAT ANN (West 1995) (excepting 'ocean marine and foreign trade insurances' from Pt XIV of the Insurance Code, which governs insurance contracts); s 38.2-300(1) of the VA CODE ANN (1994) (excepting 'ocean marine insurance other than private pleasure vessels', from the chapter governing insurance policies and contracts); s 48.18.010 of the WASH REV CODE ANN (1984) (excepting 'ocean marine and foreign trade insurances', from the chapter governing insurance contracts).

29   In *Associates Ltd (5801) v Continental Insurance Co* [1993] AMC 1453, eg, a decision involving the sinking of a barge in the open seas off the coast of South Carolina, the Federal Court felt compelled to look at the law of Missouri. Finding no marine insurance decision on point, it followed an automobile insurance decision.

30   See *Shaw v Robberds* (1837) 6 Ad & El 75; *Pim v Reid* (1843) 6 Man & G 1; *Mitchell Conveyer & Transport Co Ltd v Pulbrook* (1933) 45 LlL Rep 239.

31   The other main sanctions stated in the MIA 1906 for alteration of risk are: change of voyage clause (s 45); deviation clauses (ss 46 and 49); and delay in voyage clauses (ss 48 and 49).

reason, such 'terms' are unknown in most other legal systems.[32] Being a part of the continental legal system, it is not astonishing to see that there is no concept of warranties in either German or Norwegian marine insurance law. Instead, separate provisions have been provided, both in German and Norwegian law, for matters that are traditionally dealt with as express or implied warranties in English law. These provisions usually afford the insurer protection against post-contractual alterations of risk by the assured.

7.11   There are specific provisions in German and Norwegian marine insurance rules relating to, for example, seaworthiness, maintenance of class, trading limits and legal consequences of breach of them, that have been expressly spelt out in the relevant provisions. If a breach of the insurance contract does not activate any of these specific provisions, then the insurer might seek assistance from a general provision that deals with 'alteration of risk'. Put another way, the specific provisions can be seen as an extension of the duty not to alter the risk insured against. This means that, as far as these issues are concerned, the general provision regarding 'alteration of risk' will not be applied. However, if a certain breach of insurance contract does not amount to breach of any specific provision in the Codes, it might, nevertheless, be caught by the general 'alteration of risk' clause. In cases where breach of the insurance contract neither activates any specific provision in the codes, nor is caught by the general 'alteration of risk' provision, the issue should be resolved by reference to general insurance law principles. Accordingly, such a breach will, presumably, entitle the insurer to damages, but will not give him the opportunity to be discharged from liability under the policy.

The rest of this chapter will discuss the specific and general provisions regarding alteration of risk in German and Norwegian marine insurance law that can be regarded as the equivalent of English marine warranties. Before the comparative position is set out, a brief historical account of the development of marine insurance in these systems will be provided.

IV – GERMAN LAW

(A)   The legislative context of marine insurance law in Germany

7.12   The German Commercial Code of 1867 (*Handelsgesetzbuch*),[33] contains provisions in relation to marine insurance, ss 778–900.[34] However, those legal provisions can be contracted out of and, today, have been almost totally superseded by the General Marine Insurance Terms of 1919 (*Allgemeine Deutsche Seeversicherungs-*

---

32 According to the survey carried out by Prof Wilhelmsen, the concept of warranties, apart from in common law countries, seems to be applied only in Portugal, Spain, Venezuela and China (Wilhemsen 'Duty of disclosure, duty of good faith, alteration of risk and warranties' published in CMI Yearbook 2000, p 239).

33 This Code incorporates the old German Commercial Code of 1861 (*Allgemeines Deutsches Handelsgesetzbuch*) without amendment.

34 Section 186 of the ICA 1908 (*Versicherungsvertragsgesetz*) states that the Act applies to non-marine and inland marine insurance, but excluding expressly ocean marine insurance, that is hull and cargo.

Bedingungen (ADS 1919)).[35] The ADS 1919 was drafted in close co-operation with interested commercial circles (shipowners, traders, insurers, brokers and the Chambers of Commerce in Hamburg and Bremen).[36] The ADS 1919 contains both general principles concerning, for example, insurable interest and value, duties of the assured, premium and special provisions for ship's hull insurance and for cargo insurance. Thus, the ADS 1919 provides a complete regulatory framework for marine insurance and is in harmony with the basic provisions in the German Commercial Code. It is fair to say that the ADS 1919 constitutes a complete contractual codex for marine insurance, on the basis of the German Commercial Code. The ADS 1919 has, in turn, been largely superseded by newer special standard conditions for hull and machinery, as well as for marine cargo insurance. Therefore, the importance today of the ADS 1919 only lies in the fact that it contains the general basic principles of marine insurance.

7.13   As regards marine hull and machinery insurance, the most important regulatory framework is made up of the Hull Clauses of the German Marine Insurance Association 1978 (*Deutscher Transport-Versicherungs-Verband* (DTV 1978)),[37] which take precedence over the ADS 1919.[38] The DTV 1978 was further amended in November 1982. Two later amendments have taken place; first in 1984 and then in 1992. The amendment in 1984 could be regarded as the response of the German market to the adoption of new hull clauses in the London market in 1983. The 1992 amendment made changes in the provisions dealing with liability to third parties (cl 34) and introduced new rules on salvage and classification (cls 36 and 37 respectively). The version of the DTV 1978 (as amended in 1992) will form the basis of the examination that will be carried out in this chapter.[39]

(B)   Main specific provisions regarding alteration of risk in the DTV

(a)   Seaworthiness

7.14   German marine insurance law regards the act of putting the insured vessel to sea in an unseaworthy condition as a serious alteration of the risk and cl 23 of the DTV

---

35 Before the adoption of ADS 1919, two local attempts had been made to codify German marine insurance rules. In 1846, the General Plan of Marine Insurance (*Allgemeiner Plan See-Versicherung*) and, in 1867, the General Conditions of Marine Insurance (*Allgemeine Seeversicherungs-Bedingungen*) were adopted. The former was effective in Hamburg and the Baltic Sea ports, while the latter found application in port cities Emden, Leer, Lubeck, Rostock, Stettin and Stralsund. For more information about the development of German marine insurance law, see Anderson 'The evolution of the implied warranty of seaworthiness in comparative perspective' (1986) *Journal of Maritime Law and Commerce* 1, pp 23–24.
36 *Transportversicherung* (by HJ Enge), Hamburg, 1996, p 37 (original in German).
37 It should be noted that the DTV 1978 has not led to any significant alteration in the original ADS 1919 cover.
38 Clause 1 of the DTV 1978 reads as follows: 'The hull clauses of the German Transport Insurance Association take precedence over the General German Marine Insurance Conditions.'
39 There is no sign in the German marine insurance market of discussions on a further amendment in the DTV 1978. The same, however, cannot be said of the General German Marine Insurance Terms – Special Conditions for Cargo Insurance 1973 (*Allgemeine Deutsche Seeversicherungs-Bedingungen, Besondere Bestimmungen für die Gülterversicherung*) which have recently been changed. The recent change has been the creation of new cargo insurance conditions, in 1999, called Cargo 2000 and consisting of a combination of the general part of the ADS, the 1973 Cargo Conditions and those broker clauses that deserved general recognition – partly for market importance.

1978 provides that the insurer is not liable for any loss caused by this conduct.[40] Therefore, causation plays a crucial role in the application of this sanction and the assured has the burden of proof to show that there is no causal link between the breach and loss.

7.15   There is no attempt to define the meaning of 'unseaworthiness' in the DTV 1978, but some guidelines have been provided in cl 23(1). Accordingly, the vessel will be regarded as 'unseaworthy' particularly if she is not properly equipped, manned, or loaded, or if she sails without the necessary documents required for identification of the ship, crew and cargo, or without the highest category of an approved classification society and without permission to sail given by the Board of Ship Safety and Social Security or, in case of a foreign flag, the competent authorities. The wording of cl 23(1) makes it clear that these guidelines are not restrictive in the definition of 'unseaworthiness'. They are presumably intended to attract the attention of judicial authorities to certain aspects of ship maintenance but the courts have the final say in deciding whether the vessel in question is 'seaworthy' or not.[41]

7.16   Clause 23(2), however, provides that the sanction expressed in cl 23(1), allowing no indemnity for the assured for loss or damage caused by putting the insured vessel to sea in an unseaworthy state, does not apply if the unseaworthiness is due to the reasons beyond the control of the assured. In cases where the assured is a corporate personality, it is safe to assume that factors, which are in the control of the assured company, are those which are in the control of its management team. Therefore, if the vessel is unseaworthy due to the fact that her master is incompetent in using the fire-fighting system, the assured company can still be indemnified for any loss attributable to this unseaworthiness provided that it can be demonstrated that the management team had no knowledge of the particular incompetency of the master and they were in no way negligent in not finding out.

(b)   Change in management of vessel

7.17   The identity of people who are in charge of the management of the insured vessel is fairly important for the insurer because this plays a crucial role in assessing the risk. For this reason, just as in many other legal systems, German law has chosen to make specific provisions in relation to change in management of the insured vessel during the currency of the policy. Accordingly, cl 12(1) of the DTV 1978 puts the assured under an obligation to notify the insurers of a change in the management of

---

40   Clause 23 of the DTV 1978, which replaces Art 58 of the ADS 1919, provides '(1) Underwriters are not liable for loss or damage resulting from the vessel having put to sea in a state of unseaworthiness or from her not having been properly equipped, manned, or loaded, or without the certificates necessary for the vessel, crew, or her cargo. If loss or damage occurs prior to the sailing, underwriters are not liable if the occurrence was due to the vessel being unfit for the service in port. (2) In the event of the vessel being lost or damaged without there being any external event and there being doubt about the courses, the occurrence shall be deemed to have been caused by the circumstances explained in sub-para (1).' (author's translation)

41   It would be a fair comment to say that there is no substantial difference in the definition of seaworthiness between English and German law. Both legal systems set out the general guidelines and give the courts the freedom to determine whether the particular vessel in question is seaworthy or not by evaluating a number of factors, that is, the nature of voyage undertaken, the type of cargo carried, etc.

the insured vessel, before it occurs. If the assured fails to comply with this obligation, the insurers are discharged from liability by virtue of cl 12(5) unless the assured could prove that the infringement of the notification duty was not deliberate. Therefore, negligence, even gross, of the assured in notifying the insurer of a change in management will not be sufficient to deprive him of the insurance cover. After the notification of such a change, the insurer is entitled to terminate the contract within 14 days following the receipt of the notification, subject to 14 days' notice.[42] Change of management of the insured vessel has been treated differently under the standard Institute Hull Clauses. Clause 5.2 of the ITCH 1995 provides that, unless the insurer agrees to the contrary in writing, this insurance shall terminate automatically when a change in management occurs.[43]

(c)   Change of ownership

7.18   In cases where the ownership of the insured vessel changes, the insurance contract terminates automatically by virtue of cl 13 of the DTV 1978. This stringent regulation can be justified on the ground that the risk insured against alters dramatically with change of ownership of the insured vessel. The owners might be engaged in a different type of business or might have a different approach to the safety aspects of the vessel.

This provision resembles cl 5.2 of ITCH (1995 version) in the sense that both afford the remedy of 'automatic termination' in case of change of ownership of the insured vessel. The Institute Clause, however, is more assured-friendly because it provides that, if the vessel has cargo on board and has already sailed from her loading port, or is at sea in ballast, such automatic termination shall, if required, be deferred whilst the vessel continues her planned voyage, until arrival at final port of discharge, if with cargo, or port of destination if in ballast.[44] Clause 13 of the DVT, on the other hand, does not offer any extended coverage to the assured in case of change of ownership.

(d)   Change in class and flag

7.19   Clause 36.1 is a new provision that requires the assured to notify the insurer of any change in the class and flag of the insured vessel. A failure to notify would be treated as an alteration of the risk within the meaning of cl 11 and the insurer will be discharged from liability unless the non-disclosure was not intentional or the increase in risk had no impact on the occurrence of the loss or damage or the extent thereof.[45]

By virtue of cl 36.2, insurance is terminated automatically when the class is withdrawn. In that case, the premium is returned in accordance with cl 13.

---

42   Clause 12(2) of the DTV 1978.
43   See cl 14 of the IHC 2003 to the same effect.
44   See cl 14 of the IHC 2003 to the same effect.
45   *Cf* cls 13 and 14 of the IHC 2003 that call for more draconian remedies in cases of change of class or flag.

(C)   General provisions regarding alteration of risk in the DTV

7.20   After the attachment of the policy, the risk insured against might be altered by reasons either within, or without, the control of the assured. The DTV 1978, by a general provision, cl 11, attempts to regulate alteration of risk by the assured or by a third party who is authorised by the assured. As stated earlier, this provision is a general provision that provides protection for the insurer against post-contractual alterations of the risk that are not covered by any other specific provisions examined above. For example, if the class or classification society of the insured vessel is changed during the currency of the policy by the assured, or by a third party authorised by the assured, this will be dealt with as an ordinary alteration of the risk under cl 11 of the DTV 1978.

7.21   Just like cl 23, which deals with seaworthiness, cl 11 has chosen not to provide a general definition of the term 'alteration of risk', but, instead, gives examples of acts that will be deemed to be alteration of risk.[46] Accordingly, entering the dock or slipway with a cargo, unusual towing or being towed, except in cases of distress at sea,[47] exceeding the agreed voyage boundaries,[48] transhipment between ships on the high seas, and use of the ship for military manoeuvres[49] are all regarded as alteration of risk.

7.22   By virtue of cl 11(2) of the DTV 1978, if the assured alters or becomes aware of an alteration of the risk, he is under an obligation to inform the insurer accordingly. In such a case, the insurer is entitled to an additional premium. The additional premium will not be afforded to the insurer in cases where the aggravation was caused by the insurer's interest or by a humanitarian duty, or was necessary due to an insured event threatening the vessel.[50] On the other hand, if the assured fails to notify an alteration of risk, the insurer will be free of liability if the casualty or the amount of indemnity have been influenced by the alteration of risk. Therefore, the assured will be able to be indemnified despite the fact that he has altered, or agreed to the alteration of, the risk, if there is no causal link between the loss and alteration of risk. Clause 11(3) also provides that the sanction will not be applied in cases where the infringement of the

---

46   See cl 11(5) of the DTV 1978. This approach, not providing a definition, could be seen as a source of uncertainty. It can, however, be argued that the draftsman wished not to restrict the courts on this point with a 'strict' legal definition. The draftsman's approach can be supported on the ground that each marine insurance contract is unique and whether the risk has been altered should be determined by considering the facts and circumstances surrounding each contract.

47   This point is usually regulated with an express warranty in standard Institute Hull Clauses. See, eg, cl 1.1 of the ITCH 1995, which provides that: '... it is warranted that the vessel shall not be towed, except as is customary or to the first safe port or place when in need of assistance ...' This obligation has been regulated as a suspensory provision under the IHC 2003, see, cls 10 and 11.

48   In standard Institute Hull Clauses certain navigation warranties are usually inserted that prevent the vessel from navigating outside the stated areas. See standard Institute Navigation Warranties (1/7/1976) that can be attached to hull policies. Cf cls 11 and 32 of the IHC 2003.

49   These acts are regarded as 'war risks' and are expressly excluded from hull cover. Clause 24 of the ITCH 1995, eg, provides that: 'In no case shall this insurance cover loss damage liability or expense caused by, war, civil war, revolution, rebellion, insurrection, or civil strife arising therefrom, or any hostile act by or against a belligerent power.' See cl 29 of the IHC 2003 to the same effect.

50   See cl 11(4) of the DTV 1978.

notification obligation by the assured was not deliberate. Thus, the insurance cover of the assured will not be jeopardised if he can prove that he has acted negligently and not intentionally in failing to report the alteration of the risk. It is clear from the wording of cl 11 of the DTV 1978 that the burden of proof lies on the assured to show that there is no causal link between the loss and alteration of risk, or that he did not deliberately infringe the notification obligation, if he wishes to be indemnified despite the alteration in the risk.

V – NORWEGIAN LAW

(A)   The legislative context of marine insurance law in Norway

7.23   Just as in German law, in Norway the conditions for marine insurance traditionally have been incorporated into extensive private codifications, which are published as Norwegian Marine Insurance Plans (NMIP).[51] These plans routinely override the provisions of public legislation, apart from the ones which are mandatory. The main public legislation dealing with insurance law is the Insurance Contracts Act (ICA) 1989. This Act is compulsory, but s 1(3), sub-para 2, allows insurance of commercial activity performed by ships that have to be registered according to the Maritime Code of 1994, or commercial activity dealing with international trade, to be written on conditions other than set out in the Act. However, two sections of the Act, ss 7 and 8, cannot be contracted out of. Those two provisions allow an injured party direct action against the insurer of large-sized operations, including ships subject to the provisions of the Norwegian Maritime Code. Accordingly, for marine insurance, there is complete contractual freedom, limited only by general contractual principles against illegal and unfair contracts and mandatory provisions of the ICA 1989.

7.24   The marine insurance plans have been drafted in a co-operative effort between insurers, assureds and other interested parties[52] and, thus, can be described as agreed standardised conditions.[53] They contain comprehensive insurance conditions for different types of marine insurance and are made applicable by direct reference in the relevant insurance contract.

The current NMIP, 1996, which came into force on 1 January 1997, supersedes the 1964 version[54] and will be the main source for the purposes of this chapter. It contains: general provisions which applicable to all types of insurance (Chapters 1–9); special conditions for hull insurance (Chapters 10–13); total loss insurances (Chapter 14) war

---

51 The tradition of such plans dates back to 1876, since which they have been revised at regular intervals.

52 For example, in the drafting process of the NMIP 1996, the Norwegian Shipowners' Association, the Mutual Hull Clubs Committee, the Central Union of Marine Underwriters, the Norwegian Shipowners' Mutual War Risks Association, the P&I insurers, the Federation of Norwegian Engineering Industries, Det Norske Veritas and the Norwegian Average Adjusters took active roles. Two professors from the Scandinavian Institute of Maritime Law, namely, Hans Jacob Bull and Trine-Lise Wilhelmsen, occupied the Chairman and the Secretary posts of the Revision Committee.

53 *Introduction to Norwegian Maritime Law*, (by Falkenger, Bull and Brautaset) Oslo, 1998, p 509.

54 For a detailed analysis of the background and substantial provisions of the NMIP 1996, see, Huybrechts, Hooydonk and Dieryck, Volume 1, 1999, pp 109–22.

risks insurance (Chapter 15); loss of hire insurance (Chapter 16); insurance for fishing vessels (Chapter 17); insurance for offshore structures (Chapter 18) and builders risk insurance (Chapter 19).[55]

The Standing Revision Committee has in the course of its work during 2003 agreed upon minor amendments to the Plan. These amendments primarily relate to Chapter 16, which deals with loss of hire insurance. The Revision Committee has not recommended changes in 2004.

The NMIP 1996, just like the 1964 version, has an extensive Commentary that provides the background to, and explanations of, the individual provisions. The Commentary, which will be relied on heavily in this chapter, constitutes an integral part of the NMIP 1996 and can even be referred to by the courts.[56]

(B) Main specific provisions regarding alteration of risk in the NMIP 1996

7.25   Specific provisions dealing with 'alteration of risk' can be found in Chapter 3 of the NMIP 1996, which broadly regulates the duties of the person effecting the insurance and of the assured. It must be borne in mind that the provisions, which will be evaluated in this part of this chapter, apply not only to hull insurance, but also to war risks insurance, loss of hire insurance, insurance for offshore structures and builder's risk insurance.[57]

(a)   Seaworthiness

7.26   Section 3-22 of the NMIP 1996 reads as follows:

The insurer is not liable for loss that is a consequence of the ship not being in a seaworthy condition, provided that the assured knew or ought to have known of the ship's defects at such a time that it would have been impossible for him to intervene.

For the operation of this defence, therefore, three conditions must be satisfied. First, the insured vessel must be in an unseaworthy condition and by virtue of sub-para 2 of the same section, the insurer has the burden of proving that the vessel is not in a seaworthy condition, unless she springs a leak whilst afloat. If, therefore, the insured vessel springs a leak whilst afloat, the burden to show that she was seaworthy is reversed to the assured by the plan itself.

---

55 In the 1964 version of the plan, P&I insurance was also included. During the considerations for 1996 version, two Norwegian P&I insurers, Gard and Skuld, indicated clearly that the highly international aspect of P&I insurance made it inexpedient to regulate shipowners' liability insurance in the plan and they would continue to effect insurance on their conditions. The Revision Committee accepted this point and the P&I section was removed from the NMIP 1996.

56 The Commentary of the NMIP 1996 can be found on the internet at the following address: http://www.norwegianplan.no/eng/index.htm (last tested on 6 February 2005).

57 There is a separate plan, Norwegian Cargo Clauses: Conditions Relating to Insurance for the Carriage of Goods of 1995 (Cefor Form No 252). This plan has superseded the 1967 Carriage of Goods Plan. The amendment was mainly as a result of the ICA 1989, which is mandatory for insurance concerning national transport of goods. Many clauses of the 1967 plan had to be amended to conform to the requirements of the 1989 Act.

The term 'seaworthiness' has not been defined in the NMIP 1996, but s 2 of the Seaworthiness Act 1903 (*Sjødyktighetsloven*) defines seaworthiness in the following terms:

> A ship shall be deemed unseaworthy when, due to defects in the hull, equipment, machinery or crew or due to overloading or faulty overloading or due to some other reason, it is in such condition that, in light of the intended voyage or activity, there is greater danger to human life than is normal for the operation in question.

This definition of 'seaworthiness' is very broad and flexible, just like the one provided in the MIA 1906.[58] The main criteria in determining seaworthiness of a vessel is the risk associated with sending the vessel out to sea. The vessel needs to be strong and well equipped, so that the risk will not be greater 'than is normal for the operation in question'. In this respect, whether a vessel is seaworthy will depend on a number of relative factors, such as the time of the year, the voyage undertaken and length of the voyage. By considering the relative nature of definitions provided, both in the MIA 1906 and s 2 of the Norwegian Seaworthiness Act 1903, it can be suggested that a vessel that is found to be unseaworthy under English law will probably be regarded as unseaworthy under Norwegian law as well.

7.27   In order to free the insurer from liability due to unseaworthiness of the insured vessel under s 3-22 of the NMIP 1996, there has to be a causal link between the loss and such unseaworthiness. It is suggested in the Commentary to the plan that, due to the relative nature of the term 'seaworthiness', the assessment of whether there is a causal connection between the unseaworthiness and the loss will often go no further than the unseaworthiness assessment. If, following a detailed assessment, a court comes to the conclusion that the ship was unseaworthy, there will be little room left for examining the issue of causation because causation related considerations will have already played a key role in the appraisal of the seaworthiness issue. However, it has to be borne in mind that the assured might still be able to show the lack of a causal link between unseaworthiness and the loss. For example, it is crystal clear that in a case where the vessel is found to be unseaworthy due to undermanning and the loss is caused by lightening, the insurer will not be able to rely on the unseaworthiness defence.

7.28   Finally, the insurer might rely on the unseaworthiness defence if he could show that the assured knew, or ought to have known, of the ship's defects at such time that it would have been possible for him to intervene. Accordingly, the assured will be deprived of indemnity not only if he knew about the ship's defects, but also if he missed the opportunity to be aware of them due to his ignorance or negligence. The wording of the section also suggests that it does not matter whether the unseaworthiness arose before or after the vessel left the port. The criteria for the operation of the defence is whether it is possible for the assured to intervene. With the advanced communication systems now available, it is easy to report defects that allow the assured to intervene, for example, by giving specific orders to the master. If the assured chooses not to act in that case and unseaworthiness causes the casualty, there will be no claim under the policy.

---

58 Section 39(4) reads as follows: 'A ship is deemed to be seaworthy when she is reasonably fit in all respects to encounter the ordinary perils of the seas of the adventure insured.'

It should be noted that if the insured vessel becomes unseaworthy for any reason during the currency of the policy the insurer might terminate the insurance by giving 14 days' notice by virtue of s 3-27(a) of the plan.

(b)   Safety regulations

7.29   A safety regulation has been defined in sub-para 1 of s 3-24 of the NMIP 1996 as 'a rule concerning measures for the prevention of loss issued by public authorities, stipulated in the insurance contract, prescribed by the insurer pursuant to the insurance contract, or issued by the classification society'.[59] Accordingly, a rule can be regarded as a safety regulation within the context of the NMIP 1996, provided that it concerns measures for the prevention of loss. The fact that a term of the insurance contract imposes an obligation on the assured, therefore, would not necessarily mean that it is a 'safety regulation'. A literal interpretation of s 3-24 reveals that a safety regulation might arise in a number of ways. It may be issued by public authorities. The section adopts the term 'public authority'; accordingly, this should mean that, not only regulations issued by local government,[60] but also the ones issued by international bodies, for example the International Maritime Organisation,[61] will be regarded as safety regulations. A safety regulation may also be adopted by the insurer. The insurer may impose this kind of regulation into the contract not only at the time the contract is entered into, but also at a later time.[62] For instance, if it is warranted in a term of the insurance contract that a special type of equipment will exist on board for safety reasons, this will be regarded as a safety regulation. Last, but not least, a safety regulation may be issued by classification societies. By virtue of sub-para 2 of s 3-24, periodic surveys required by public authorities, or the classification society, have been regarded to constitute a safety regulation.

7.30   The sanction for breach of a safety regulation has been spelt out in s 3-25 of the NMIP 1996. Accordingly, if the assured is in breach of a safety regulation, the insurer is not liable for any loss occasioned by such breach. However, the assured, despite the breach, can be entitled to be indemnified if he proves that either there is no causal link between the loss and breach or he is not responsible for the breach.[63] Additionally, the insurer might, under s 3-27(c) of the plan, terminate the insurance by giving 14 days'

---

59 Safety regulation seems to be a Nordic invention, not much used in other civil law countries and certainly not in German law. Danish, Swedish and Finish marine insurance laws seem to have the same legal concept.
60 How a requirement imposed by a government authority has come into existence is of no importance. Accordingly, in the case of RAMFLØY ND 1973 450, it was held that a requirement issued by a government authority could also include rules set out in legislation.
61 Thus, a provision of the Safety of Life at Sea Convention (SOLAS) 1974 that requires each vessel to carry on board certain navigation equipment, eg, radar, can be regarded as a safety regulation.
62 The use of the words 'pursuant to the insurance contract' opens the door to the insurer being able to issue safety requirements at a later time.
63 It should be noted that breach of a safety regulation might also lead to the ship being unseaworthy. For example, if a provision of the SOLAS 1974, which requires the insured vessel to carry specific navigation equipment, is breached, this will presumably render the vessel unseaworthy. In such a case, the insurer might use both ss 3-22 and 3-25 simultaneously. However, since the sanction system adopted by these provisions is the same – not indemnifying the assured for losses caused by breach – the result should be the same whether the insurer chose to invoke one of the provisions or both.

notice if a safety regulation of material significance has been violated 'intentionally, or through gross negligence', by the assured. Therefore, the insurer, in case of a breach of a safety regulation by the assured, is not entitled automatically to terminate the contract. The right to terminate by giving notice arises only in cases where a significant safety regulation, a regulation which is extremely important for the protection of the insured vessel, is breached, by either bad faith or gross negligence of the assured.

(c) Trading limits

7.31   The function of trading warranties in English law is to prevent the insured vessel from navigating in areas where the risk of loss is high. The assured warrants that he will not send the vessel to those areas during the currency of the policy. Breach of such a warranty is held covered, provided immediate notice is given and additional premium and other conditions required by the insurer are agreed by the assured.[64] The NMIP 1996 attempts to provide a similar sort of protection to the insurer, by regulating the navigation limits for the insured vessel. Section 3-15 of the plan makes a tripartite division amongst ordinary trading limits, conditional trading limits and excluded trading limits.

7.32   The first sentence of sub-para 1 of s 3-15 gives a negative delimitation of the ordinary trading limits, which comprise all waters except those which are defined in the Appendix to the Plan as conditional or excluded areas. The vessel is covered against all the named risks when she navigates in the ordinary trading areas. The same sub-paragraph sets out the rule that the assured is under an obligation to notify the insurer whenever the ship is sent beyond the ordinary trading limits. The sanction for failure to notify will depend on which type of trading limit has been exceeded.

7.33   Sub-paragraphs 2 and 3 deal with navigation of the insured vessel in conditional and excluded trading limits. Conditional and excluded trading limits for each insurance policy are stated in the Appendix attached thereto. If the assured gives notice and enters a conditional trading limit area, the insurer might charge an additional premium and impose other conditions. If, however, the insured vessel enters into a conditional area without giving notice, with the consent of the assured, an additional deduction of one-quarter is to be made for each claim, but subject to a maximum of US $150,000.[65] Two points need to be clarified as to the application of this rule. First, the deductible in this provision only applies to damage and not total loss. Secondly, the assured's consent is a precondition for the application of the deduction. Therefore, in cases where the vessel enters into a conditional trading limit area without the consent of the assured, for example as a result of a mistake of the master, any damage occurring will not trigger the extra deductible.

7.34   According to sub-para 3, the insured vessel can only navigate in the excluded trading area if advance permission of the insurer is obtained.[66] If the insured vessel

---

64 See, eg, cl 3 of the ITCH 1995. It should be borne in mind that under the IHC 2003 trading warranties are treated as suspensory provisions.

65 According to the Commentary, the rationale of this deduction is that the assured would have nothing to lose if there had been no sanction for a failure to give notice.

66 Nothing has been stated in the provision as to the requirement for such a permission. It is submitted in the Commentary, however, that there is nothing preventing the insurer from making the permission subject to certain conditions, eg, payment of an additional premium.

enters into an excluded trading limit area despite the lack of permission of the insurer, then the insurance ceases to be in effect while the vessel is in the excluded trading area. The second sentence of the sub-paragraph makes it clear that the insurance shall come back into effect as soon as the vessel leaves the excluded trading area. Thus, entering into an excluded trading limit area without the permission of the insurer will, in no way, have any effect on the validity of the policy. The obligations of the insurer, to indemnify the assured against losses, will be frozen until the vessel leaves the excluded trading area.

(d)   Loss of class or change of classification society

7.35   Section 3-14 of the NMIP 1996 spells out the defence available to the insurer in case of loss of class or change of the classification society of the insured vessel. In order to clarify the extent of the insurer's defence, sub-para 3 sets out what is deemed as a 'loss of class'. Loss of class occurs where the assured, or someone on his behalf, requests that the class be cancelled, or where the class is suspended[67] or withdrawn for reasons other than casualty.[68] In the event of a loss of class or change of classification society, by virtue of sub-para 1, the insurance terminates automatically, although cover would remain in effect until the ship reached port. It has been expressly stated, in the same sub-paragraph, that the insurance cover will not terminate if the insurer expressly consents to the change in the vessel's class status.

(e)   Change of ownership

7.36   Under the NMIP 1996, change in the ownership of the insured vessel during the currency of the policy causes the automatic termination of the insurance cover by virtue of s 3-21. Accordingly, the insurance lapses for casualties that occur after the change in the ownership. The provision is stringent in the sense that no opportunity has been given to the new owner of the vessel to keep the insurance relationship alive, even by obtaining the permission of the insurer. Also, the provision does not provide protection to the new owner until the insured vessel reaches the port of destination, if she is at sea at the time the transfer of ownership occurs.

(f)   Illegal activities

7.37   Section 3-16 of the NMIP 1996 deals with illegal activities carried out during the currency of the insurance policy. According to the Commentary of the NMIP 1996, an activity is regarded as illegal not only when it violates the laws of the flag state, but also when it is unlawful under the laws of the state that has authority over the

---

67   The trend among classification societies is to introduce rules on automatic suspension of class when the assured has failed to carry out one of the three periodic surveys: Renewal Survey (every five years); Intermediate Survey (every second or third year); and the Annual Survey. Therefore, class can be suspended without a formal decision on the part of the administration in the classification society.

68   It was felt necessary by the draftsman to state that the loss of class resulting from a 'casualty which has occurred', is not deemed a loss of class due to the practice of some classification societies to cancel the vessel's class when a casualty has occurred.

ship in the situation in question. A distinction has been made in s 3-16 between using the insured vessel principally for the purposes of illegal activities and using the insured vessel for illegal purposes on some occasions. In the former case, if the insured vessel is essentially put into illegal activities, for example smuggling traffic, with the consent of the assured, the insurance terminates automatically.[69] On the other hand, if the ship is used for illegal purposes occasionally and the assured knew or ought to have known of the facts at such a time that it would have been possible for him to intervene, then the insurer is free from liability for loss that is a consequence of the ship being used for illegal purposes.[70] In this way, the assured is protected if the crew uses the insured vessel for illegal purposes without his knowledge. The causation issue may give rise to difficulty in the application of this provision. In order to discharge the insurer from liability, the loss must, to a certain extent, be a foreseeable consequence of the illegal act.

(C)   General provisions regarding alteration of risk in the NMIP 1996

7.38   Just like the DTV 1978, the NMIP 1996 has adopted provisions, ss 3-8–3-13, dealing generally with alteration of risk that occurs during the currency of the policy. These provisions can be regarded as a safety net from the insurer's point of view because they can be invoked in cases where specific provisions regulating particular types of alteration of risk (the provisions examined above) cannot be applied. The term 'alteration of risk' has been defined in sub-para 1 of s 3-8.[71] There is an alteration of risk if two conditions are satisfied. First of all, there must have been a change in the factual circumstances that affect the nature of the risk and this change in the factual circumstances must amount to a breach of the implied conditions upon which the contract was based.[72] It must, therefore, be determined in each case whether these conditions are satisfied. For instance, since there is no specific provision in the NMIP 1996 dealing with the issue of the insured vessel undertaking towage services,[73] the practice of the assured of entering into towage contracts without the consent of the insurer could be regarded as an 'alteration of risk' under the scope of s 3-8. Sub-paragraph 2 of the same section, by way of example, indicates that a change of the

---

69 See sub-para 3 of s 3-16. It should be noted that, in such a case, it does not matter that the insured vessel also carries some legal cargo. The decisive factor is whether she is used principally for the purposes of the illegal undertaking.

70 See sub-para 1 of s 3-16. By virtue of sub-para 2 of the same section, once the assured learns of the matter he should intervene promptly. If he fails to do so, the insurer may terminate the contract on 14 days' notice.

71 According to the Commentary to the NMIP 1996, in this sub-paragraph the draftsman has chosen to adopt the expression 'alteration of risk' and not 'increase of risk' because of consideration for situations where there is clearly a change in the risk due to evolving external circumstances, but it is difficult to determine whether the risk has, in fact, become demonstrably greater.

72 There is absolutely no limitation in the NMIP 1996 concerning what kind of circumstances the insurer may claim to be a basis of the insurance, or which alterations may be contrary to the implied conditions of the contract. Therefore, each factual change will be interpreted by considering the surrounding circumstances and intentions of parties.

73 This issue is regulated with an express warranty in English law. For example, cl 1.1 of the ITCH 1995 reads as follows: '... it is warranted that the vessel shall not be towed ... or undertake towage ... services under a contract previously arranged ...'

state of registration, the manager of the ship or the company, shall be deemed to be alteration of the risk.[74]

7.39   The sanctions that can be used by the insurer in case of alteration of the risk have been spelt out in ss 3-9-3-11 of the NMIP 1996. Accordingly, in case the assured intentionally altered the risk, agreed to such alteration, or neglected to notify the insurer about an alteration,[75] the insurer is free of any liability, provided that the insurer would not have effected the insurance had he known at the time the contract was concluded that the risk would have been altered. However, if the insurer would have accepted the insurance on other conditions, for example an increased premium, had he known about the possibility of alteration at the time the contract was concluded, he is only liable to the extent that the loss is not caused by the alteration of the risk. In either case, the insurer might terminate the contract by giving 14 days' notice. It appears from the wording of these sections that the insurer is under an obligation to show that either he would not have accepted the insurance, or would have accepted it with different conditions, had he known, during the formation of the contract, that the assured would have altered the risk.[76] The insurer has been prevented from invoking the alteration of risk defence when such alteration has ceased to be material to him and if the alteration has occurred for the purpose of saving human life, or while salving or attempting to salve ships or goods during the voyage.[77]

VI – SUNDRY CONSIDERATIONS

7.40   The specific and general provisions in relation to 'alteration of risk' in German and Norwegian hull insurance, which can be regarded as the equivalent of English marine warranties, have been examined in this chapter. The findings of this comparative study reveal that the approach of the MIA 1906 to this issue is severe from the assured's point of view. In fact, the study affirms the views of some sceptics of the MIA 1906, that English marine insurance law is geared to protect the interests of the insurers only.

Breach of the specific and general provisions in the DTV 1978 and NMIP 1996, apart from the ones dealing with change of ownership and the ones in the NMIP 1996 that are related to class of the vessel and illegal activities, do not have any effect on the validity of the insurance contract. The usual remedy is to preclude the assured from recovery in relation to loss that occurs as a result of a breach of the relevant provision. Even this remedy does not operate automatically. There must be a causal link between the breach and loss. However, despite the existence of a causal link between breach

---

74   In the original version of the Plan, only a change in the management of the ship and/or company amounted to an alteration of the risk. This provision was amended in 2003 by the addition of the words 'a change of the state of registration'. The alteration intends to bring the Plan in line with standard provisions used in the London market and a number of continental conditions. The words added clearly refer to the state in which the ship is registered. Naturally, a change from one register to another register within the same state would not amount to breach of this provision.

75   By virtue of s 3-11 the assured is not deemed to have altered the risk in cases where there is a justifiable reason for not notifying the insurer.

76   Proving the actual state of mind at the time the contract was formed could be quite problematic for the insurer.

77   See s-12 of the NMIP 1996.

and loss, the assured in many cases could recover provided that breach occurred for reasons other than those in his control.

It is possible to argue that both German and Norwegian legal systems attempt to keep the balance between the sides of a marine insurance contract. The insurer is protected against alteration of risk during the currency of the policy by a wide range of specific and general provisions. However, the sanctions expressed in these provisions can only be invoked in cases where there is a causal link between breach of these provisions and loss.

7.41   By evaluating the solutions offered by these two advanced legal systems against alteration of risk, English marine warranties can be criticised on two grounds. First, it looks unfair that breach of a marine warranty, even though it does not lead to any loss, releases the insurer from further liability. Releasing the insurer from liability in relation to loss, which has occurred as a result of breach of warranty, seems a fair remedy. Secondly, leaving the assured unprotected, even where the breach of warranty occurs for reasons beyond his control, is rather harsh. At least a chance to prove that the breach has occurred for reasons other than his control and he had no means of intervening, should be given to the assured.

CHAPTER 8

A CASE FOR REFORM?

I – THE NEED FOR REFORM

(A) A different legal regime for non-marine insurance warranties: a model for marine insurance warranties?

8.1   Certain aspects of 'insurance warranties' have been the main topic of numerous debates over the years. In particular, the pleas of assureds for a more equitable legal regime have prompted the Law Commission to prepare a report highlighting the defects of the present legal regime and to request Parliament to adopt legislation, which distributes the rights and obligations of parties fairly,[1] in this area. The striking point of this report is the exclusion of marine insurance from the scope of possible reform.[2] According to the Law Commission, it would be clearly undesirable to disturb the basis of legal certainty in English law by making substantial changes to the Marine Insurance Act (MIA) 1906 in view of London's position as a leading centre for marine insurance in a competitive international market. The Law Commission was also of the opinion that marine insurance contracts are generally effected by 'professionals' – that is to say, persons whose everyday business dealings involve the making and carrying out of insurance contracts – so they can be reasonably expected to be aware of the niceties of insurance law.

8.2   Although a draft Bill was introduced in Parliament for the reform of non-marine warranties and non-disclosure by the assured, it did not come to fruition. In fact, the draft Bill was withdrawn after the government reached agreement with the Association of British Insurers (ABI) to the effect that the Association would take up the Law Commission's recommendations on a self-regulatory basis. This was to be achieved by an amendment to the existing Statement of Insurance Practice, which had been accepted in 1977 in exchange for exclusion of insurance contracts from the Unfair Contract Terms Act 1977.[3] The nature and features of Statements of Insurance Practice will be examined later in this chapter when they are considered as an alternative to legislative reform. At this stage, it is sufficient to state that they are adopted by the ABI for their members and imply no duty of compliance. They also lack legal force and,

---

1   Law Commission, 1980. This was not the first time that the defects of the warranty regime were brought under spotlight. Reference was made to certain problematic areas in *Conditions and Exceptions in Insurance Policies* (Law Reform Committee, 1957). A similar development was, also, observed in Australia where the Law Reform Commission (1982) adopted a similar report entitled *Insurance Contracts* (Rep No 20).

2   *Ibid*, para 2.8, p 14.

3   This Act contains a number of provisions limiting the extent to which it is possible to 'exclude or restrict liability'. Its title is misleading because the Act applies, not only to liability arising both in contract and tort, but also to exclusion clauses contained in any contractual term or notice.

accordingly, cannot be relied upon in court proceedings. They only have the force of their prestige and inherent wisdom.[4]

8.3   Section 2(b)(iii) of the Statement of General Insurance Practice 1986 provides that non-marine insurers will not repudiate liability to indemnify a policy holder:

> ... on the grounds of breach of warranty or condition where the circumstances of the loss are unconnected with the breach unless fraud is involved.

The effect of this clause is that the insurer is prevented from relying on a breach of warranty defence unless there is a causal connection between breach and loss.[5] It should be noted that nothing in the clause prevents the insurer from relying upon a breach of warranty in cases where the breach had occurred before the loss.

In practice, non-marine insurers usually comply with s 2(b)(iii) of the Statement of General Insurance Practice and do not rely on a breach of warranty defence in cases where the breach has not contributed to the loss. It should be stressed that the Insurance Ombudsman Bureau (IOB), an institution formed by insurers to deal with complaints about insurers' handling of claims and 'reliance on the fine print' to avoid losses,[6] takes the Statements, especially s 2(b)(iii), into account when deciding on disputes brought to it.[7]

8.4   The current position in non-marine insurance, therefore, is that insurers are precluded, by a voluntary code, the Statement of General Insurance Practice 1986, from relying on the breach of warranty defence in cases where there is no causal link between the loss and breach. The general belief in the market is that insurers, despite the lack of its legal force, comply with the requirements of this Statement and in cases where they do not, the IOB has the power to force them to do so. It is a fair comment to say that the insurers, by self-regulation, have managed to overcome the criticisms of

---

4   Recently, the ABI arranged procedures to monitor the compliance of its members with the Statements.

5   However, if fraud on the part of the assured is ascertained, the insurer could rely on the breach, regardless of the existence of any causal link.

6   The IOB was founded in March 1981 by a small number of leading insurance companies, which funded the operation of the Bureau. Since those days, the membership of the Bureau has grown to encompass almost all of the leading insurers in the UK, including Lloyd's. The ombudsman's jurisdiction now extends to about 70% of the domestic market. According to the ombudsman's Terms of Reference, the ombudsman has jurisdiction over the disputes if the following conditions are satisfied: (a) the assured's main or principal residence is the UK, the Isle of Man or the Channel Islands; (b) the complainant must be the assured or assignee; (c) the policy must have been effected for a natural person or persons, and not a company; (d) the insurer's obligations under the policy must be performed in the UK; (e) the claim relates only to a claim under the policy or to the marketing or administration of the policy.

7   The ombudsman's Terms of Reference provide that, in making a decision or award, the ombudsman:

> ... shall have regard to the terms of the contract and act in conformity with any applicable rule of law or relevant judicial authority, with general principles of good insurance, investment or marketing practice, with these Terms of Reference, with *the Statements of Insurance Practice* and Codes of Practice issued from time to time by the Association of British Insurers and with Rules made from time to time by the Boards of Directors of the Life Assurance and Unit Trust Regulatory Organisation Ltd and the Investment Management Regulatory Organisation Ltd. (emphasis added)

assureds in relation to the 'harshness' of the warranty regime, to a certain degree, and avoid a statutory regime in this area – what they call government 'interference' – at the same time.[8]

8.5   There are indications that winds of change are on the way, partly due to the extensive pressure from the EU demanding member states to afford more protection for consumers in their jurisdictions. In 2001, the British Insurance Law Association (BILA) appointed a sub-committee with a view to the sub-committee examining areas of insurance law causing concern in the insurance market and in insurance disputes and making recommendations to the Law Commission as to the desirability of drafting a new Insurance Contracts Act in respect of marine and non-marine insurance and/or other reforms to current legislation.[9] The areas specifically examined by the sub-committee were: utmost good faith, reinsurance, marine insurance, claims and intermediaries. In essence, the Report, as far as warranties are concerned, supports the changes proposed by the Law Commission in 1980. However, it recommends that marine, aviation and transport should be excluded from reforms, apart from the possible inclusion of private yacht owners or aircraft owners, on the basis that long processes of consultation with these markets are likely to delay the implementation of a possible law reform in this area.

8.6   It is obvious why the sub-committee is not in favour of extending reforms to cover marine insurance warranties. The sub-committee is probably aware that it would be rather difficult to convince the marine insurance sector to accept governmental interference. However, the analysis carried on throughout this book demonstrates that certain aspects of the warranty regime are in need of urgent reform. It is submitted that the marine insurance sector has a lot to gain in terms of achieving a competitive edge against rival markets if the reforms are carried out. The rest of this part of this chapter will argue that a reform, similar to the ones intended for non-marine warranties, is required in this area. Several justifications will be put forward to support this argument.

(B)   The changing nature of marine insurance relationship

8.7   In the first chapter, when evaluating the historical development of warranty regime, it was observed that the current legal status of marine warranties was

---

8   The Australian insurers, on the other hand, were not as lucky as their English counterparts. Partly due to the fact that the Australian insurance market's political strength is not as great as the London market's, the recommendations of the Law Reform Commission, including the ones on warranties, were adopted in the Insurance Contracts Act (ICA) 1984. This Act, which applies to all insurance contracts apart from marine, has brought a different regime for warranties. Section 54(1) of the ICA denies the insurer a right to avoid liability simply by relying on a breach of warranty or some other condition of the insurance contract. Instead, this section provides that the insurer is limited to a reduction in liability to the assured by an amount representing the extent to which the insurer's interests were prejudiced. Termination is available under s 54(2), where the breach could reasonably be regarded as being capable of causing or contributing to a loss. Section 54(3) denies the insurer the right to terminate where the act was necessary to protect a person or property, or where it was not reasonably possible for the assured not to do the act.

9   The sub-committee was chaired by Adrian Hamilton QC.

developed by Lord Mansfield in the late 18th century.[10] In those days, particularly as far as marine insurance contracts were concerned, the assured's promise or undertaking as to a certain event was extremely significant for the insurer, as the means of communication were very restricted and the insurer had to rely largely on the initial promise of the assured when deciding to accept the risk, or even when determining the rate of the premium. For instance, if the assured warranted that the insured vessel would sail on a certain day, it would have been very difficult, or even impossible, considering the efficiency of communication in the 18th century, to inform the insurer in cases where this promise had not been kept. In such a case, even if the promise was not kept for reasons beyond the control of the assured, the risk insured against would have been altered and the insurer would have been exposed to a risk that was completely different to the one agreed.

Moreover, at that time, the insurer was dependent on the word of the assured when determining the scope of the risk – more than today – since the insurer did not have access to numerous databases that would have provided him with information about the insured vessel or the nature of the assured. For instance, in a case where the assured warranted that the company, that owned the insured vessel had a certain nationality, the insurer would have limited means of checking the accuracy of the statement.

Bearing in mind the realities of the 18th century, it could easily be understood why Lord Mansfield chose to attach such a strict legal character to marine warranties. The 'promise' given by the assured meant a lot to the insurer in assessing the scope of the risk in those days. He expected the assured to comply with the promise, literally, and afforded no excuse for its breach. The MIA 1906, which was designed to codify the existing case law in marine insurance, did little more than enshrine in law the doctrines formulated by Lord Mansfield as they existed in the latter part of the 18th century.

8.8   Circumstances, however, have changed dramatically since the times of Lord Mansfield. Of course, it is understandable that the insurer in an insurance contract, which is based upon utmost good faith, expects the assured to keep his promises. The remedy of automatic discharge from liability, regardless of existence of a causal link between the breach and loss, on the other hand, seems harsh in the realities of the 21st century for two reasons. First, communications have advanced so much that it is possible to be in touch with the insured vessel all the time during the currency of the policy. The insurer, therefore, can be informed about the recent state of the vessel and, if the need to breach certain warranties occurs, the parties might negotiate an amendment in the cover.[11] In this respect, the assured's 'promise' still plays an important role in assessing the scope of the risk, but it is not as crucial as it used to be in the 18th century since the parties, in most cases, have the opportunity to negotiate an amendment in the cover when it becomes obvious that the assured will not be able to keep his promise.

---

10 See [1.11] to [1.15].
11 As examined in Chapter 6, the use of held covered clauses is quite common in modern marine insurance policies. Under these clauses, as soon as the assured becomes aware of breach of a warranty, he gives immediate notice to the insurer. After the receipt of the notice, the insurer waives breach of warranty and keeps the insurance contract alive, provided the assured agrees to pay an additional premium.

8.9   Also, nowadays, the insurer is often in a more powerful position, especially with the significant advantages he receives from having access to sophisticated data and information. For instance, the insurer may obtain the inspection records held by different port authorities about the vessels owned by a specific shipowner and identify points which are relevant to the insurance cover.[12] For this reason, it seems that the presumed equality of bargaining power on the part of the assured and insurer has changed swiftly in favour of the insurer, and allowing him to discharge himself from further liability on the occurrence of minor, inconsequential or non-causative breach of a warranty would cause even more injustice for the assured.

(C)   Unfairness arising from the harshness of remedy and further complexities of law

8.10   The remedy afforded by s 33(3) in case of a breach of a marine warranty – automatic discharge from further liability without the need for a causal link between the loss and breach – has been the target of the assured and academics dealing with marine insurance over the years.[13] When the insurance literature is examined, numerous articles criticising the harshness and unfairness of this remedy can easily be spotted. It would be a quite simple task to justify these criticisms with a hypothetical example. Let us assume that hull cover is provided for a vessel for a certain period of time and the policy in its fine print has a clause, which reads as follows:

> Warranted that the assured shall exercise due diligence to keep the navigational equipment of the vessel in working condition during the currency of the policy.

When in port, it is realised that the radar of the vessel is not working. The master instructs a repairer to fix the defect. The contracted repairer observes that the problem with the radar is more serious than he anticipated and informs the master that he will not be able to sort it out unless certain equipment, which will cost extra money, is provided for his use. In order not to spend more money, the master orders the engineer of the vessel to assist the contractor with the problem. Meanwhile, a fire breaks out while the vessel is receiving fuel and, in a couple of hours, she becomes a total loss. There is no doubt that the express warranty in the policy is breached, since the master has failed to exercise due diligence to keep the radar in working condition. Such a warranty is clearly intended to prevent an increase of risk of casualties whilst the vessel is being navigated and its breach has no effect whatsoever on the occurrence of loss. Put another way, the loss would still have occurred, even if the master had exercised due diligence to keep the radar in working condition. However, when the assured makes a claim for total loss, it is likely that he will receive notification from his insurer rejecting his claim upon grounds of breach of warranty.

8.11   The unfairness of the remedy afforded by the Act in the case of a breach of a marine warranty becomes more obvious after considering the findings of the analysis

---

12   The significance of Port State Control is increasing and recently a European Community Directive, which requires the Member States to carry out intensive inspections on vessels visiting their ports, has been brought into force. This Directive was adopted into English law by the Merchant Shipping (Port State Control) Regulations 1995 SI 1995/3128, as amended by SI 1998/1433, SI 2001/2349 and SI 2003/1636.

13   See, eg, Schoenbaum, 'Warranties in the law of marine insurance: some suggestions for reform of English and American law' (1999) *Tulane Maritime Law Journal* 267.

carried out in Chapter 7 as to the approach of some other legal systems to the issue. A similar clause, for example, would have been regarded as a 'safety regulation' under Norwegian law and in a case of its breach the insurer would only have been entitled to damages by way of reduction of liability and nothing else since breach of this clause did not contribute to the loss.[14] The assured would, naturally, expect a similar treatment from English law and, when he did not receive it under the current warranty regime, he would blame English law for not being fair and for protecting the interests of the insurer more than the interests of the assured.

8.12   The harshness of the remedy in case of a breach of a marine warranty has also led the judicial authorities to seek alternative interpretations of the clauses in question and this adds further legal complexities. Such an attempt by the Canadian Supreme Court could be observed in *The Bamcell II*,[15] where the court held that a clause which read, 'Warranted that a watchman is stationed on board *The Bamcell II* each night from 2200 hours to 0600 hours with instructions for shutting down all equipment in an emergency', was a clause delimiting the risk and not a warranty.[16] When the judgment of the court is carefully analysed, that the 'justice instincts' of the judges led them to decide in that direction could easily be sensed.[17] It is submitted that the judges were fully aware of the fact that the above mentioned clause carried a warranty status.[18] However, had they conceded this, the assured would not have been allowed an indemnity under the policy since there was no watchman stationed on board between 10 pm and 6 am the night before the casualty and breach of this obligation would have discharged the insurer from all liability automatically. In order to avoid this harsh consequence, they preferred to classify the clause as a clause delimiting the risk and allowed recovery because the casualty occurred during daytime when there was no obligation on the part of the assured to station a watchman on board *The Bamcell II*.[19]

---

14   The damages in such a case would presumably be nominal damages, since it is difficult to show that any loss has occurred as a result of breach of the clause in question.

15   [1983] 2 SCR 47. This case has been analysed in depth in Chapter 2, when express warranties are identified as distinct from other terms of the marine insurance contract.

16   As examined in Chapter 2, in case of breach of a clause that delimits the risk, the insurance cover is suspended while the breach continues. As soon as the breach terminates, the insurance cover becomes effective.

17   For example, in a desperate attempt to show that the clause in question was not a warranty, by considering the presumed intentions of the parties, in (1980) 133 DLR (3d) 727, pp 740–41, Lambert JA, in the Court of Appeal said that: 'The parties cannot have intended that, if the watchman was late one night, or even missed a night, then the insurers should be discharged from liability for the remainder of the term of the policy.'

18   It was suggested by Lambert JA that the existence of the watchman borne no relationship whatever to the risk. With respect, it is submitted that exitence of the watchman with responsibility on safety of the vessel should be at least a relevant factor in the assessment of the risk by the insurer.

19   The same attitude, challenging the legal character of a clause in question for the sake of justice, can also be observed in a number of non-marine cases: *Roberts v Anglo Saxon Insurance Co* (1927) 27 LIL Rep 313; *Farr v Motor Traders' Mutual Insurance Society Ltd* [1920] 3 KB 669; *De Maurier (Jewels) Ltd v Bastion Insurance Co Ltd & Coronet Insurance Co Ltd* [1967] 2 Lloyd's Rep 550; *CTN Cash & Carry v General Accident Fire & Life Assurance Corp* [1989] 1 Lloyd's Rep 299.

Thus, it can be concluded that the justice instinct of the judges, in *The Bamcell II*, played a crucial role when assessing the legal character of the clause in question. However, in reaching the conclusion that the clause was not a warranty, they have, unintentionally, harmed the fine distinction between express warranties and other terms of a marine insurance contract. Identifying the legal status of certain clauses in marine insurance policies has now become more problematic in the light of decision in *The Bamcell*, since a weapon has been given to the assured to challenge the warranty status of certain clauses in question.[20] Without doubt, this situation creates an uncertainty in law and the unfairness of the remedy afforded by s 33(3), in a case of breach of a warranty, is an accessory to crime that might force the judges to pull the trigger.

(D) Position of the London marine insurance market and some other rival markets: significance of legal rules in competition

8.13   Statistics reveal that the London market's leading position in the marine insurance business has been under threat for some time. While 31.2% of the world's marine insurance business was written in London market in 1991, this figure came down to 27% in 1994. The drop continued and by 1999 the London market's share of world marine insurance business was down to 21%.[21] Figures in the first few years of the new millenium do not suggest any signs of recovery.

8.14   There are a number of factors behind this decline. One reason is that many countries today prevent direct insurance business from being placed outside their own national markets for foreign exchange reasons.[22] This is particularly the case for cargo insurance and, as a result of this, more business has been retained by local markets.[23] Another reason is the cautiousness of the underwriters in the London market after the bad underwriting years of the late 1980s. Numerous catastrophes, which occurred during those years,[24] made the underwriters a bit more selective in accepting insurance risks. In the early 1990s, underwriters in the London market chose not to provide cover for certain types of vessels, usually those that involved high risks. In this way the market missed the opportunity of expanding its capacity to the developing

---

20   In a recent non-marine insurance case, *Kler Knitwear Ltd v Lombard General Insurance Co Ltd* [2000] Lloyd's Rep IR 47, *The Bamcell II* [1983] 2 SCR 47 was used by the court to hold that a clause in which the assured warranted that the sprinkler systems would be installed was not an express warranty, but a clause delimiting risk. There is no doubt that *The Bamcell II* could also be applied in marine insurance cases, particularly, where the judges feel that it is not fair to adopt the 'draconian' remedy of automatic discharge.

21   These figures have been obtained from Association of British Insurers, *Insurance: Facts, Figures and Trends* (1997, 1998, 1999 and 2000).

22   See the paper delivered by Jenkins, 'Forecasting changes in the world's marine insurance market and predicting London's place in the long term', at a conference on the Marine Insurance Market organised by IIR Ltd in 1996.

23   For example, in the Hong Kong marine insurance market, in a country that with strict regulations prevents certain types of insurance being placed in other markets, cargo business has increased by HK$362.5 m between 1991 and 1993. The figures are taken from DYP Group Newsletters, *Marine Business From Around the World*, (1995) Marine Insurance Report No 136, p 125.

24   The losses of Piper Alpha, Exxon Valdez, Hurricane Hugo, Philips Petroleum and Arca Baker occurred in 1988 and 1989.

countries.[25] However, the main reason for the London market losing its market share is intense competition coming from some other markets. The German and Norwegian markets, whose marine warranty regime in relation to hull insurance has been examined in the previous chapter, are amongst those markets, according to the recent Annual Report on the London market published by the ABI.[26]

8.15   The success of these markets lies mainly in the fact that they have succeeded in developing strong links with different interests around the world and attracting a great deal of foreign business.[27] Why were they so successful in attracting foreign business? Without a doubt, the hesitation of the English market in underwriting insurance for high risks in the early 1990s played a crucial role in the success of the German and Norwegian markets; however, it is submitted that their main advantage was the assured-friendly legal rules that they adopted in their policies.[28] Marine insurance business has an international character and the figures, which compose the demand side of this business, are quite flexible in choosing the market in which they will obtain cover. Their main interest lies in obtaining the lowest available market rate on the best terms possible. In this respect, provided that the premium rate is compatible with other rival markets, insurance conditions are an important element in the competition for market shares.

A recent example, which shows the relation between insurance conditions and marine business underwritten, can be given from hull practice. In 1995, the Institute of London Underwriters published the new version of Institute Time Clauses (Hull) (ITCH). These clauses contain more stringent provisions, from the assured's point of view, and offer a better regime for underwriters than the 1983 version. However, mainly due to the current soft nature of the London market, these clauses have not been popular. The insurers cannot insist on these clauses because the assured usually threatens to go to an alternative market that offers better conditions. Today, a large number of policies in the London market are still written or renewed on the 1983 version of the clauses. Therefore, it can be concluded that selling harder conditions in a soft market is a difficult thing to do and, by analogy, it could be argued that the nature of insurance conditions is quite significant in the marine insurance business. They can, indeed, be used as a tool to attract more business to a market.

---

25 For example, according to the statistics compiled by the UNCTAD secretariat on the basis of data supplied by Lloyd's Maritime Information Services (London), the gross tonnage of vessels owned by developing countries of Asia has increased by 44.8 m (an increase of 279.2%) in 16 years, from 1980–96. During the same period, the gross tonnage of vessels owned by developing countries in Central America and eastern Europe has shown an increase of 7.2 m and 0.5 m, respectively (Source: United Nations, 1997).

26 Association of British Insurers, *Insurance: Facts, Figures and Trends*, 1999, p 32.

27 Marine insurance markets, which intend to extend their market share, usually attempt to attract foreign business. For example, the French market is examining the ways of attracting more foreign brokers in order to be able to reach different parts of the world. See, Bonnaud, *Paris as an International Centre*, 1994 (original in French).

28 This point has been stressed on numerous occasions both by Dr Klaus Kostka (for the German market) and Prof Hans Jacob Bull (for the Norwegian market), when the author found an opportunity to consult them during the Marine Insurance Conference organised by The European Institute of Maritime and Transport Law at Antwerp in November 1999.

8.16   After examining the warranty regime adopted by the German and Norwegian hull clauses in the previous chapter, it is fair to say that they provide a more equitable solution for the assured than does English law. The same is true for cargo insurance. Also, the good faith duty of the assured is less stringent in the German and Norwegian clauses than English law.[29] Accordingly, it will not be an overstatement to suggest that their marine insurance provisions – the fact that they protect the assured's interest more than English law does, both in terms of marine warranties and in other areas – helped the German and Norwegian marine insurance markets to increase their market shares dramatically and retain them over the years. This situation had been foreseen long ago by Antony Diamond QC, in his lecture delivered at the Third Annual Lecture of the Institute of Maritime Law of the University of Southampton on 31 October 1985 where, after examining the current regime of English marine warranties, he concluded as follows:[30]

> I referred at the beginning of this lecture to the common interest of all three groups, the marketplace, the academics and the legal practitioners that the law of insurance should develop so that it meets the needs of the present and future and so that it provides for a fair distribution of rights and obligations as between assured and insurer. If the law fails to do this, then other rival centres of insurance will undoubtedly succeed where we have failed.

(E)   National developments and winds of change in some other common law jurisdictions

8.17   One might be tempted to argue along the lines that the London market has finally responded to the needs of the international community and its clients by introducing the IHC 2003.[31] There is no doubt that the IHC 2003 is a more balanced product than its predecessors as it provides significant improvements in the position of the assured. Most notably, some obligations that have traditionally been regulated by the warranty regime, that is Institute navigation warranties (1/1/76), are now treated as suspensory provisions.[32] It is submitted that transforming some warranties into suspensory provisions is a self-admission by the market that the warranty regime is in need of reform. However, perhaps the market, with this modification, was trying to send a message to the government that it is capable of addressing its problems without governmental interference.

8.18   The approach adopted by the IHC 2003 is certainly a step in the right direction. However, it is submitted that in a competitive market more needs to be done to attract new business to the market, and even to retain existing business. There are still numerous warranties that are in use in marine insurance practice. Even the IHC 2003 itself contains other warranties.[33] Therefore, contractual arrangements might not be

---

29 See the paper delivered by Wilhelmsen, 'The marine insurance system in civil countries' at the Marine Insurance Symposium, 1998 (published in 1998 *Mar Ins* 242, p 15).
30 Diamond, 'The law of marine insurance – has it a future' (1985) *LMCLQ* 24, p 42.
31 For a detailed anaysis of these clauses, see, Soyer, 'A survey of new International Hull Clauses 2002' (2003) *JIML* 256.
32 See, cls 10 and 11 of the IHC 2003.
33 See, eg, cl 24 of the IHC 2003.

sufficient in giving security to the potential assureds that their interests will be well looked after by the English legal system.

8.19   There is evidence to suggest that the 'harshness' of the warranty regime, adopted by the MIA 1906, is gradually being softened to a certain extent in some areas in some common law jurisdictions. This is clearly the case as far as pleasure crafts (yachts) are concerned. Despite the fact that insurance on these vessels is regarded as a type of marine insurance and made subject to the MIA 1906, the owners of these crafts are usually non-professional individuals. These people are not aware of the particularities of marine insurance law and, quite rightly so, expect the legal nature of the insurance cover they obtain for their pleasure crafts to be similar to the legal nature of the cover they obtain for their houses and cars.[34]

8.20   After numerous debates, Australia has responded to the requests of pleasure-craft owners by removing these crafts from the MIA 1909 and treating insurance on these craft as a matter of general insurance.[35] Accordingly, breach of a warranty in a yacht policy does not automatically discharge the insurer from further liability anymore.[36] The same result is obtained in the Canadian marine insurance market, though a different way. When insurance policies are effected for pleasure crafts, certain modifications are made and many provisions of the MIA 1993, including the one on breach of warranty, are contracted out. The same practice can also be observed in the USA. Consultation with the American Insurer's Association shows that yacht insurers in the USA deal with the problem in two ways. They either incorporate a clause in the policy to the effect that a breach of a warranty will not afford a defence to the insurer unless there is a causal link between the loss and breach[37] or, alternatively, they insert a choice of law clause and make the contract subject to a state law where breach of warranty does not automatically discharge the insurer from liability.[38]

8.21   More significantly, in Australia, in January 2000, the Attorney-General asked the Law Reform Commission to review the Marine Insurance Act, and to take into account the desirability of having a regime consistent with international practice in marine insurance, and to consider whether any change might result in a competitive disadvantage for the Australian insurance industry. The Commission was also required to draft any appropriate new legislation and an explanatory memorandum to give effect to its recommendations. The Commission responded with a report published on 30 April 2001.[39] This report recommends reform in many areas of marine

---

34 In fact, it was highlighted in the Report prepared by the Law Commission (1980), p 15, that a number of policy holders were in need of greater protection than that afforded under current legislation, such as the MIA 1906. These persons included persons who own sailing boats and similar pleasure craft. The Law Commission recommended that the Secretary of State be empowered to exclude certain classes of crafts from MIA 1906, as may appear appropriate following consultation with the industry. Unfortunately, nothing has been done since then and, due to the exclusion of marine and aviation insurance from the ambit of the Statement of General Insurance Practice, insurance on these crafts cannot receive the protection provided in the area of warranties and non-disclosure by this Statement.

35 See s 9(A) of the ICA 1984, which applies to contracts of insurance entered into on or after 30 April 1998.

36 See s 54 of the ICA 1984.

37 In this way, the effect of breach of a warranty afforded by law has been qualified.

38 As was stated in the Chapter 7, state laws of Texas, Florida, Hawaii and Washington do not discharge the insurer from liability automatically in case of breach of a warranty.

39 The Australian Law Reform Commission, *Review of the Marine Insurance Act 1909*, Report No 91, 2001.

insurance, and marine warranties are on the top of the reform list.[40] No step has yet been taken to implement these proposals. In essence, there is a concern that the proposed changes would move Australian law too significantly away from its major trading partners.[41]

8.22   All these international developments confirm that there is a consensus on the need for reform as far as the warranty regime is concerned. However, it is abundantly clear that no common law jurisdiction would be prepared to take the brave step of reforming their law unless the law of the state, which is a dominant force in international marine insurance business, goes down the same route. As England is the nation that created one of the most impressive codified acts in the area of marine insurance, the author is of the opinion that England and Wales is under a moral obligation to take the first step and correct the parts of this Act that do not comply with the realities of the 21st century and create unfairness. Surely, the marine warranties regime is one of the areas that is in need of reform. A reform in English law will, without a doubt, be followed by other common law countries since the resistance of the marine insurance industries in those countries, which are against a change in law, will be broken. Put another way, a reform in English and Welsh law in this area will have a dual role. It will not only correct the deficiencies in its legal system, but show the way forward to other jurisdictions which adopted its law.

II – THE FORM OF REFORM

8.23   It has been considered in detail, in the earlier part of the chapter, why there is a need for reform in the warranty regime adopted by the MIA 1906. In this part, the possible methods in which such a reform could be carried out will be discussed. First, the possibility of legislative reform and the problems that are likely to occur during this process will be considered. Then, the alternatives to legislative reform will be highlighted. At the end of this part of the chapter, it is intended to indicate the form which reform should take in order to achieve the best possible results.

(A)   Legislative reform and possible obstacles

8.24   The author believes that the defects in the current warranty regime could be best corrected through statutory reform. Such reform would not only balance the relation between the assured and insurer, but also be quite effective in showing the shift in the attitude of English marine insurance law towards the assured to the rest of the marine insurance world. In this way, it would assist English marine insurance law to retain the reputation, which it has gained over many years.

8.25   There are, however, certain obstacles facing legislative reform. It is a known fact that different elements in the marketplace, underwriters, assureds, brokers, do not

---

40 The Report also recommends subtantial reforms on the duty of utmost good faith, insurable interest and subrogation.
41 Recommendations of the Commission on warranties will be examined later in this chapter.

like governmental interference in market practice. Every time the possibility of such interference arises, they immediately forget their differences and agree on one thing if nothing else; namely, that parliamentary interference in commercial affairs is likely to be ill formed at worst, or irrelevant at best, and is always unjustified.[42] Accordingly, legislative reform in this area is possible only if the market elements change their attitudes and welcome governmental interference. It is clear that certain market elements, particularly assureds and underwriters, have reasons to accept governmental interference. The assureds would surely welcome a reform that would afford them a better position and the underwriters would not wish to lose ground in the competition with other rival markets.

There is, however, as indicated by Clarke,[43] a further problem that has to be overcome in order to achieve legislative reform in this area. Parliament, with Members who are subject to re-election, prefers to spend time and energy on legislation that is attractive to a significant section of the electorate. Put another way, there is almost no political will to force reform in the area of marine warranties, which is seen as something not all that relevant to the person in the street. However, the insurance industry, especially a large group of insurers who see their long term benefit in reform, possesses the political power to inspire parliament to put such a reform on its agenda.[44]

(B)   Alternatives to legislative reform

8.26   One alternative to legislative reform in the area of marine warranties is to declare a Statement of Practice, similar to the one declared for non-marine insurance, and require the insurers underwriting policies in the market to comply with it. Such a Statement would be regarded as a self-regulatory code, since its designer, namely the insurer, is also the party who would be bound by it. A Statement of Practice does not have legal force, but implies a communal obligation of observance for the insurers who operate in the market. With such a Statement, certain alterations to the current marine warranty regime could be imposed.

8.27   There are certain advantages of carrying out a reform in this area through a Statement of Practice. Since such a document does not require the approval of parliament, it can be updated more easily. Also, it can be argued that the industry itself is in the best position to spot breaches of the code and to take effective enforcement action against recalcitrant members.[45] However, such a method is not free from problems. It has been observed that monitoring whether the provisions of a self-regulatory code are adhered to by insurers in practice is a very difficult thing to do.[46] Furthermore, certain doubts as to the effectiveness of a reform, which will be inserted in a self-regulatory code, could arise. In an international business such as marine insurance, will it be satisfactory for the foreign assured if the insurers, with a voluntary

---

42 See, Diamond, 'The law of marine insurance – has it a future?' (1985) *LMCLQ* 24, p 28.

43 See Clarke, 'The marine insurance system in common law countries – statutes and problems', paper delivered at Marine Insurance Symposium, 1998 (published in 1998 *Mar Ins* 242, p 63).

44 The Financial Services and Markets Act 2000 is a recent example illustrating how the commercial interest could accelerate the decision making process.

45 See, Hamilton, 'The duty of disclosure in law: the effectiveness of self-regulation' (1995) *Australian Business Law Review* 359, pp 363–64.

46 *Ibid*, p 366.

code that has no legal effect, declare that certain provisions of the MIA 1906 in relation to warranties will not be relied on or will be modified? Will a reform, which will be carried out in this way, be sufficient to protect the interest of the assured and, more importantly, attract more foreign business to the market? The problem is not that the insurers will have a tendency not to comply with such a Statement of Practice. It is a known fact that the reputation of insurers is a significant factor in the market. However, the doubtful point is whether their promise, which is not supported by any legal instrument, will be sufficient for the foreign assured.

8.28   Another alternative to legislative reform is to amend standard Institute Clauses in a way in which all the agreed reforms in the area of marine insurance are covered. For instance, it could be stated in the standard Institute Clauses that the sections of the MIA 1906 that regulate marine warranties are replaced with the provisions[47] provided in another part of the Clauses.[48] The Technical and Clauses Committee of the London market could, surely, be engaged in such a task and this Committee, by wearing the shoes of parliament, could achieve a reform through amendment of Institute Clauses.[49]

8.29   Without doubt, a reform, carried out in this way would be quite effective in attracting the attention of foreign assureds. However, such a process could take more time than it is expected because a large number of clauses need to be evaluated and modified. Also, the pressure of drafting a huge number of clauses in a short period could increase the possibility of litigation in the long term.

(C)   The way forward

8.30   As stated at the beginning of this part of the chapter, the author is of the opinion that the most convenient form of reform in this area is through legislation. It is acknowledged that political will for such a reform could be lacking in parliament, but it is also believed that a desirous market could use its political force to prompt the Parliament to take the necessary steps. In case of failure of this option, the best alternative to legislative reform is an amendment in the standard Institute Clauses. This method is, at least, as effective as legislative reform. The market might prefer this option because, in this way, it does not lose the initiative to parliament to determine the extent of the reform. A reform through a voluntary code – a Statement of Practice – should be at the bottom of the list. A reform based on an agreement without any legal

---

47   As discussed in Chapter 6, s 41 of the MIA 1906, which imposes implied warranty of legality, cannot be contracted out of.

48   It is not uncommon to contract out of certain parts of an Act by way of express provisions being added to the policy. For example, as was examined in the Chapter 9, ss 778–900 of the German Commercial Code 1867, which regulate marine insurance, have been almost superseded by the General Marine Insurance Terms 1919.

49   When the Technical & Clauses Committee is instructed to draft clauses, legal advice on specific matters is usually sought from solicitors in London and American markets. However, the representation of assureds in this Committee is very limited. The author believes that, if it is decided to carry out a reform of this area in this way, the views of assureds need to be taken into account. It should be remembered that the success of the Norwegian Marine Insurance Plans lies in the fact that the full participation of assureds is secured during the drafting process.

force is bound to be an ineffective one. When the extent of a possible reform in this area is considered in the final part of this chapter, all the discussions will be based on the assumption that legislation should be the form of a possible reform.

III – THE EXTENT OF REFORM

(A)   Option 1: scrapping the warranty regime from the MIA 1906

8.31   Certain authorities regard the warranty regime adopted by the MIA 1906 as 'toxic' and suggest that it should be removed from English marine insurance law completely.[50] This view has been endorsed by the Australian Law Reform Commission in its recent report. The Commission recommends that the concept of warranties, both express and implied, as used in the law of marine insurance should be abolished.

8.32   In place of warranties, the amended Act should permit the parties to include a term that the insurer is discharged from liability to indemnify the assured for loss proximately caused by a breach by the assured of an express term of the contract. In the absence of such a term, breach of the contract will entitle the insurer only to such relief as may be available under the general law of contract, which would generally be the award of damages.

8.33   Since implied warranties would be repealed under the proposed regime, obligations of seaworthiness should also be dealt with as express terms of the contract. Insurers will be at liberty to include an express term in the contract stipulating that the insurer will be discharged from liability to indemnify the assured for any loss attributable to the unseaworthiness of the vessel where the assured knew or ought to have known of that unseaworthiness and failed to take such steps as were reasonably available to render the vessel seaworthy.[51]

8.34   Similarly, the insurer will be permitted, due to the fact that implied warranties are repealed, to include in any contract of marine insurance terms to the following effect and in the following terms:

> So far as the assured can control the matter, the insured adventure shall have no unlawful purpose. If there is a breach of such a term, the insurer is automatically discharged from all liability under the policy.
>
> So far as the assured can control the matter, the insured adventure shall be carried out in a lawful manner. If there is a breach of such a term, the insurer is not liable to indemnify the assured for any loss that is attributable to the breach.

---

50 See, for example, Hare, 'The omnipotent warranty: England v the world', paper delivered at the International Marine Insurance Conference, 1999 (published in Huybrechts, Hooydonk and Dieryck, Volume 2, 1999, p 37).

51 The Commission stipulates that the proposed contractual term may be continuous. However, unseaworthiness that develops during a voyage will not generally prejudice an assured unless he ought to have been aware of that unseaworthiness.

8.35 Even though the proposed changes could be regarded as an improvement compared to the current warranty regime, the author is of the opinion that a reform advocated by the Australian Law Reform Commission is not one that would be welcomed by the London insurance market for two reasons. First, such a reform requires drafting of a large number of clauses, which could be a lengthy process causing uncertainties in the market. More significantly, the proposed regime puts serious restrictions on the freedom of contract principle as the parties are prevented from drafting clauses in the way they deem appropriate. In a commercial setting, a code restricting parties' freedom of contract to that extent has little chance of success.

8.36 A close scrutiny of the proposed changes reveals further complexities. It is hard to justify why regulation of the concept of legality, which has public policy implications, is left to the parties. Furthermore, it is submitted that the proposed changes could be more detrimental for the assured than the current warranty regime. For instance, if the parties fail to put an express provision in their contract dealing with the possibility that the insured adventure is carried out in an unlawful manner after the attachment of the risk, the general principles of contract law would possibly not allow any recovery even if the matter is outside the control of the assured.[52]

(B) Option 2: regulating all warranties as suspensory provisions

8.37 A straightforward way of reforming the warranty regime would seem to be the deletion of s 34(2) of the MIA 1906,[53] and making other changes to the Act so as to change the present position of warranties to one where they become suspensory provisions. Therefore, a breach of warranty would result in the cover being suspended for the duration thereof, but the cover would then be reinstated once the infringement ceased.

8.38 Admittedly, this is a very simple solution that might find support in the market.[54] However, this solution has the potential of creating unfairness from the assured's point of view as suspensory provisions, in fact operate similarly to exclusion clauses without taking into account whether the breach has caused, or contributed to, the loss. This can be illustrated by borrowing some of the facts from *Forsikringsaktielselskapet Vesta v Butcher*.[55] Let us assume that the owner of a fish farm obtains insurance cover against marine perils for his farm. The contract includes a warranty that requires the owner to have a watchman on the premises for 24 hours a day. During a period when the watchman is away, as a result of a storm the fish farm is destroyed. If the effect of a breach of a warranty is equated with the effect of breach of a suspensory provision, it is clear that in this case the assured could not recover for his loss even though absence of the watchman had, in all probability, no impact on the loss.[56]

---

52 *Gray v Barr* [1971] 2 QB 554.
53 This sub-section reads as follows: 'Where a warranty is broken, the assured cannot avail himself of the defence that the breach has been remedied, and the warranty complied with, before loss.'
54 As illustrated earlier [2.39], navigation warranties in hull policies have already been transformed into suspensory provisions in the IHC 2003.
55 [1989] AC 852.
56 See, also, Longmore, 'Good faith and breach of warranty: are we moving forwards or backwards?' (2004) *LMCLQ* 158.

(C)   Option 3: establishing a link between the breach and loss

8.39   Another way of reforming the warranty regime would be to restrict the insurer's right to rely on the breach of warranty defence by requiring him to demonstrate some kind of link between the breach and loss. One could object to such a reform on the basis that the reform would result in the erosion of safety standards by removing or reducing the incentive for compliance with warranties, many of which are in the nature of undertakings on the part of the assured to observe precautions. Such an argument could be disputed on three grounds. First, many assureds observe prescribed precautions not out of any considerations relevant to their rights against the insurers, but simply because they wish to preserve their property from loss or damage. Secondly, in most cases, observing prescribed precautions and protecting the subject-matter insured could be cheaper for the assured rather than facing litigation. Finally, it is not appropriate to make any direct link between public policy issues, such as erosion of safety standards, and the contents of private marine insurance contracts. Such public policy considerations are better left to national and international regulation.

8.40   A detailed analysis of other legal systems reveals that there are two possible ways of establishing a link between the loss and the breach. One is that the insurer could be requested to demonstrate that the breach of warranty has increased the risk (increase of risk criteria).[57] The other is that the breach of warranty must contribute to the loss if the breach is going to afford the insurer a defence. Put another way, a causal link between the breach and the loss needs to be established (causal link criteria).[58] It is submitted that adoption of the latter approach is likely to achieve the desired results in a less problematic manner. The reasons for choosing this measure over the 'increase of risk' criteria need to be evaluated a bit further.

8.41   Adoption of increase of risk criteria could cause further complexities. First of all, there could be a problem in identifying the meaning of 'increase of risk'. Does the term 'risk' refer to a net risk, in which case an increase from the specified circumstances constituting a violation may be offset by decreases achieved? Or does it instead refer only to the effects of breach, without regard to offsetting changes of circumstances? Presumably, a narrower meaning than the total of all risks under the policy is intended. The kinds of change in circumstances that an assured might raise in mitigation of a breach are countless, and case-by-case comparative evaluation of total risk would be extremely expensive and wasteful. Furthermore, such an approach would make law fairly unpredictable.

Even though it is assumed that the concern is with only substantial increases in risk that arise from specific breaches regardless of changes in net risk from all

---

57 In some USA states, breach of warranty does not afford a defence for the insurer unless it increases the risk: *Windward Traders Ltd v Fred S James & Co of NY* 855 F 2d 814 (11th Circuit 1988); *Fireman's Fund Insurance Co v Cox* 742 F Supp 609 (MD Fla 1989) (Florida Law); *United States Fire Insurance Co v Liberati* [1989] AMC 1436 (ND Cal 1989) (California Law).

58 Some American courts, when construing marine insurance policies, apply the rule that for breach of warranty to afford a defence to the insurer, the breach must be a proximate cause of loss: *Thann Long Partnership v Highlands Insurance Co* [1955] AMC 203 (5th Circuit 1994); *Home Insurance Co v Ciconnett* 179 F 2d 892 (6th Circuit 1950); *Coffey v Indiana Lumberman's Mutual Insurance Co* 372 F 2d 646 (6th Circuit 1967).

circumstances, the core question still needs to be answered. Is an increase of risk to be determined from the point of view of a standard or typical effect of a specific breach upon the risk assumed under policies of a given type, or from the point of view of the effect of a breach upon the risk assumed under the individual policy, taking into account all the particulars of the situation of that policyholder. While the latter seems like a more appropriate approach, as it incorporates subjective measures into the test, there could still be some situations where determining whether the risk has increased would not be an easy question to answer. For instance, suppose in a hull policy there is an express warranty that requires the insured vessel to be surveyed by the London Salvage Association within 30 days after the inception. If the vessel is made subject to survey by another association and is lost a day after the survey due to severe weather conditions, would the insurer be entitled to resist the claim on the grounds of breach of warranty? Even though the insurer succeeds in demonstrating an increase of risk arising as a result of breach of a warranty, this time another problem arises. Is a short period of increase sufficient to give the insurer a right to rely on the breach of warranty defence or should the increase persist some substantial period of time? In the hypothetical scenario illustrated above, would a delay of one day in having the survey made be sufficient for the insurer to activate the breach of warranty defence? If this were the case, then the solution would be very similar to the current regime, as the insurer would be given an opportunity to rely on a technical ground to deny liability. If, on the other hand, the increase should persist for some substantial amount of time, litigation is bound to arise as to the meaning of the term 'substantial amount of time'. Could we, for example, assume that the risk has increased for a substantial amount of time if the survey was delayed for four days?

8.42   As can be seen, adoption of 'increase of risk' criteria is not an ideal solution to establish a link between breach and loss. The author believes that a fairer warranty regime could be achieved by adopting the causal link criteria. In the final part of the book, therefore, a reform will be advocated placing the causal link criteria in the heart of the proposals.

(D)   Provisions of the MIA 1906 that are in need of modification

(a)   The effect of breach of a marine warranty (s 33)

8.43   The second part of s 33(3) regulates the effect of a breach of a marine warranty. Accordingly, in such a case, regardless of the type of warranty breached, the insurer is automatically discharged from further liability, whether the breach has any causative effect on the loss or not.[59] Most of the criticisms made about the current warranty regime could be avoided were the insurer not allowed to rely on this defence in cases where there is no causal link between the breach and loss. This could be achieved by amending s 33 to read that, in cases where breach of a warranty is followed by a loss, the insurer is precluded from relying on s 33(3) if the assured, on a balance of

---

59   The exact meaning and effect of this sub-section has been clarified by the House of Lords in *The Good Luck* [1992] 1 AC 233. See Chapter 5 for a detailed analysis of the decision of the House of Lords.

probabilities, proves that the loss in respect of which he seeks to be indemnified was not caused or contributed to by the breach.[60]

8.44   Such an amendment in s 33 would distribute the rights and obligations of the parties fairly. The insurer, in cases where the breach of warranty has caused or contributed to loss, would be discharged from further liability and, in this way, would be protected against serious alterations of the agreed coverage. The assured, on the other hand, would be given an opportunity to be indemnified, despite the breach of the warranty, in cases where he could show that there was no causal link between the breach and loss. It has been submitted that, in practice, particularly in hull insurance, insurers have a tendency to waive breaches of warranty where the breach has not affected the claim.[61] Therefore, the new sub-section would provide a legal basis for this market practice and, accordingly, protect the interests of the assured by means of legal rules.

8.45   It should be noted that the proposed amendment to s 33 would have no impact on cases where the breach of warranty did not cause any loss. However, in that case it is highly probable that the insurer might not wish to continue to provide insurance cover to the assured in question. Therefore, it may be essential to include a new provision in s 33, stipulating the insurer's right of cancellation. This solution does not create any 'unfairness' from the assured's point of view because, after he receives notification from the insurer stating that he wishes to terminate the insurance relation, the assured has time to arrange new insurance cover.

8.46   One might be tempted to criticise the suggested modification of s 33 on three grounds. First, it could be argued that such an alteration would cause further complexities in law and prolong the cases because the courts would be asked to identify the causal link between breach and loss. Admittedly, this would impose an extra task on the parties and the courts; however, it is submitted that such a price is not too high, considering that the modifications would lead to a fairer warranty regime. Furthermore, case law suggests that, during the application of some other defences, for example ss 55(2)(a) and 39(5), where the courts are asked to determine whether the loss is attributable to a certain act (wilful misconduct of the assured), or to a certain state (unseaworthiness), they have not experienced any serious difficulties in dealing with the causation issue.[62]

Secondly, the proposal could be criticised on the ground that the reform would not be extended to cover contractual terms other than warranties. It is, therefore, possible that insurers might find ways of drafting clauses which would achieve consequences similar to the current warranty regime. This is certainly a valid point. However, it should be borne in mind that freedom of contract is the underlying principle in commercial law. Therefore, any attempt to regulate and restrict freedom of contract is bound to create problems of its own. The author is of the opinion that all can be offered

---

60   A similar solution has been adopted by s 11 of the New Zealand Insurance Law Reform Act (ILRA) 1977, which applies to non-marine insurance.

61   *Marine Insurance: Hull Practice*, Volume 3, 2nd edn, (by RH Brown) London, 1993, p 427.

62   For example, in the application of s 39(5) the main problem is proving that the assured had knowledge about the unseaworthiness; identifying whether that particular unseaworthiness has caused loss is usually more straightforward.

to the market is a better warranty regime that protects the interests of all parties; the manner how the parties then choose to regulate their relationship is up to them.

Last but not least, one could argue that, since the assured is under the burden of proof to show that breach has not caused or contributed to loss in order to preclude the insurer from relying on s 33(3), this would cause a flood of litigation because the insurer would deny liability, even in cases where the loss was not connected to the breach. Anybody who brings such an argument is completely unaware of the realities of the market practice. The marine insurance market is a place where the insurer's reputation is largely dependent on the way he treats the assured. Without doubt, any insurer who prefers to adopt such a course of action will not be on the top of any broker's shopping list. Also, there is evidence to suggest that a flood of litigation has not resulted in New Zealand from the passage of the ILRA 1977, which adopted a similar solution.

(b) Further clarification of s 33 of the MIA 1906

8.47   In an attempt to define the nature of a marine warranty, the first sentence of s 33(3) provides that:

> A warranty, as above defined, is a condition which must be exactly complied with, whether it be material to the risk or not.

The use of the term 'condition' has led to confusion, simply because it has different meanings both in general contract law and insurance law and it is not clear in which sense it has been used in this sub-section. It can be argued that the meaning of this term has been clarified by Lord Goff in *The Good Luck*.[63] If a reform in this area is going to be carried out, the complex wording of this sub-section should be simplified with a view to reflecting the judgment of Lord Goff and avoiding further disputes regarding the nature of warranties. It is suggested that this part of s 33 should be amended in the following way:

> A warranty, as above defined, is a condition precedent to the attachment of risk or to further liability of the insurer ...

Such a provision would reflect the nature of marine insurance warranties accurately. If a marine warranty is a type of warranty that needs to be complied with before the risk attaches, then it is a condition precedent to the 'attachment of risk' and, in cases where it is breached, the insurer never comes on risk. Conversely, if a warranty, like most of the warranties, needs to be satisfied at some point after the attachment of the risk, it is a condition precedent to the 'liability of the insurer'. It should be borne in mind that the new sub-section, which would be added to s 33 to give an opportunity for the assured to show that there was no causal link between the loss and breach, would not change the nature of marine warranties. Breach of a warranty, still, would have the effect of discharging the insurer from liability automatically when it is relied on by the insurer; however, the new sub-section would

---

63   See Lord Goff's judgment, [1992] 1 AC 233, p 263, where he said that: 'In the case of conditions precedent, the word "condition" is being used in its classical sense in English law, under which the coming into existence of (for example) an obligation, or the duty or further duty to perform an obligation, is dependent upon the fulfilment of the special condition.'

give the assured a lifeline against insurers who rely on this defence in cases where there is no causal link between the breach and loss.

8.48   Some further modifications would need to be made in s 33(3) in order to clarify the law on this point and accommodate the causal link requirement, which is adopted by the subsequent sub-section. Section 33(3), as it stands, requires exact compliance with a warranty, whether it be material to the risk or not. It has been noted earlier that the words 'material to the risk' imply two things.[64] First, they imply that the facts warranted by an express warranty may be of a sort which could not affect the risk in any manner. They, also, suggest that, even though the warranted event concerns things which could be material in a general way, whether the particular breach by the assured has material effect on the case in question is irrelevant to the invocation the warranty defence. The author believes that the latter implication of these words would have no effect once the causal link requirement was introduced. If the particular breach by the assured had no material effect on the case in question, then it could not, surely, be causative of the loss or contribute to it.

8.49   It is also suggested that this sub-subsection is not the proper place to accommodate the first implication of these words. Section 33(3) regulates the nature of marine warranties, whether express or implied, and a principle that gives freedom to the parties to adopt an express warranty, even though it could not affect the risk in any manner, should be placed somewhere else in the Act. For instance, s 35(1), which regulates express warranties, is appropriate for this purpose and it could be altered to read as follows:

> An express warranty may be in any form of words from which the intention of warrant is to be inferred and it need not be material to the risk insured against.

Thus, after emphasising the first implication of the words – 'whether it be material to the risk or not' – in s 35(1), a further amendment needs to be made in s 33(3) and, accordingly, the words 'whether it be material to the risk or not' should be removed. Such a modification would not only serve the purpose of clarifying the meaning of this sub-section, but also would be a step which would bring this sub-section into line with the new sub-section added.

(c)   Repeal of s 34(2) of the MIA 1906

8.50   Section 34(2) provides that once a warranty is breached it is not a defence to the assured that the breach has been remedied before a loss has occurred. There is no doubt that this provision is in harmony with the automatic discharge rule adopted by s 33(3). However, once the automatic discharge rule was modified, to the extent that the insurer is precluded from relying on it in cases where there was no causal link between the breach and loss, it is obvious that s 34(2) would be redundant. In a case where a breach of warranty was remedied before loss, the assured would be able to recover in the absence of a causal link between remedied breach and loss. In this respect, adoption of causal link requirement would render s 34(2) superfluous.

---

64 See Chapter 5.

(d) The position of the implied warranty of legality

8.51   The *sui generis* nature of the implied warranty of legality has been the topic of a detailed examination earlier, in Chapter 4. Since this warranty has the notions of public policy, it has been stressed, in the light of case law,[65] that its breach could not be waived, although this has not been stated expressly in the Act. This situation could be clarified by inserting a new sub-section to s 34.

Also, for the same reason, the implied warranty should be excluded from the suggested modification of s 33. It is an established contract law principle that a contract that is tainted by illegality cannot be modified to provide a benefit to the party who is involved in this illegality.[66] In order to achieve this end, a final sub-section should be added to s 33. Accordingly, if a loss occurs on a voyage that, with the consent of the assured, is carried out in an unlawful manner, the insurer should be discharged from liability, regardless of a causal link between breach and loss.

(e) The seaworthiness obligation in time policies (s 39(5))

8.52   Finally, the author believes that a reform in the area should also be extended to s 39(5), which occasionally creates problems due to its complicated nature. The justification behind s 39(5) and the reason for not incorporating an implied warranty of seaworthiness into time policies has been examined earlier in Chapter 3. However, the alternative defence to an implied warranty of seaworthiness, which is stated in s 39(5), is far from being convincing. A careful analysis of this sub-section reveals that this provision, in practice, is very difficult to operate. The insurer has to show not only that the vessel was sent to sea in an unseaworthy state, but also that the assured had, either actual or constructive, knowledge about this unseaworthiness and, furthermore, that the loss was attributable to the unseaworthiness of which the assured had knowledge. In particular, demonstrating that the assured had knowledge about the unseaworthiness that caused the loss has been problematic.[67]

Also, identifying whose knowledge, within the company structure of the assured, will be attributable to the knowledge of the assured is another difficult task, especially in cases where numerous individuals are involved in the decision-making process.[68]

It has been submitted that proving the assured's knowledge in relation to a particular unseaworthiness would be easier after the ISM code, but the way in which

---

65 *Gedge and Others v Royal Exchange Assurance Corp* [1900] 2 QB 214.

66 *Holman v Johnson* (1775) 1 Cowp 341.

67 For example, in the Court of Appeal, in *The Star Sea* [1997] 1 Lloyd's Rep 360, the insurer had failed to show that the assured had knowledge about the factors that rendered the vessel unseaworthy, that is incompetence of the master, despite the fact that two of the assured's vessels had been lost earlier, in the same fashion and due to similar defects. The decision of the Court of Appeal on this point has recently been approved by the House of Lords [2001] UKHL 1; [2003] 1 AC 469; [2001] 1 Lloyd's Rep 389.

68 See *Meridian Global Funds Management Asia Ltd v The Securities Commission* [1995] 2 AC 500, where the court was asked to fashion a special rule of attribution to determine whose act or knowledge would be attributable to the act of the assured.

courts would interpret this Code would have to be seen in order to confirm whether such a statement is correct.[69]

8.53   In addition to the problems that might arise in the application of s 39(5), it could be argued that, especially after the insured vessel has returned to the control of her owner or manager, or of those who are in other respects acting as his agents in her management, it is unfair for the insurer to be deprived of the protection that he would enjoy if the vessel were insured voyage by voyage. It should be borne in mind that, even in time policies, the assured, through his agents, is in a position to access the requirements in order to render the vessel seaworthy for each voyage that will be taken after the attachment of the risk.[70]

8.54   An implied warranty of seaworthiness could be imposed on time policies in a way that the interests of both the assured and insurer are protected. In this respect, attention should be directed to the suggestion made by one of the most celebrated authors of the early 20th century, namely William Gow.[71] He suggested that the assured might be subject to an implied warranty of seaworthiness in time policies with a wording as follows:

> A time policy shall be subject to the same warranty of seaworthiness as if the vessel were insured separately for each voyage.[72]

By virtue of such a wording, the owner of a vessel that has commenced the voyage in a seaworthy condition and on which his old policy lapses and the new one commences is effectually protected to the end of that voyage. This point can be highlighted with a couple of hypothetical examples. Let us assume a vessel commences a journey in a seaworthy condition and, while she is at sea, her insurance policy lapses and a new one commences; but, just after the commencement of the new policy, she becomes unseaworthy. In this case, the assured will be able to be indemnified in respect of the losses occurring during the first policy, as she commenced the voyage in a seaworthy state. The assured will also be able to recover in respect of the losses occurring during the second policy, as she commenced the voyage in a seaworthy state and the unseaworthiness that occurred after the commencement of the voyage does not have any effect on the implied warranty of seaworthiness. On the other hand, if the vessel was unseaworthy at the commencement of the voyage and the first policy lapses and the second commences when she is at sea, the assured will not be protected for losses which occurred either during the first or the second policy.

---

69 See Chapter 3 where the potential implications of the ISM Code on s 39(5) have been considered.

70 It is quite common, in practice, to see that an express warranty of seaworthiness has been incorporated into time policies. Usually, in such a case, the remedy available to the insurer, in case of a breach of this warranty, is modified. For instance, in *The Lydia Flag* [1998] 2 Lloyd's Rep 652, an express warranty of seaworthiness had been imposed into the policy in the following way: 'Warranted that at the inception of this policy the vessel ... shall be in a seaworthy condition and thereafter during the valid period of this policy the insured shall exercise due diligence to keep the vessel seaworthy.' However, the remedy afforded in case of breach of this warranty was the suspension of the cover, until the warranty was complied with. This indicates that the assured is prepared to have an express warranty of seaworthiness in time policies, provided, of course, the remedy available in case of its breach is not 'draconian'.

71 *Sea Insurance*, (by W Gow) London, 1914, p 272.

72 It is clear that each marine adventure carried out, whether the vessel is in ballast, or carries cargo, or performs a particular task, during the currency of the policy, is regarded as a separate voyage within the meaning of this regulation.

8.55   It is obvious that this kind of warranty status in respect of time policies serves the interests of both the assured and insurer. The assured is only precluded from recovery for something that was in his control. He is not expected to guarantee the seaworthy state of the vessel during the continuation of the voyage. Similarly, the insurer is assured of the proper information and control of the owner or manager at the commencement of that voyage by means of an implied warranty of seaworthiness.

The rewording of s 39(5) and imposing a warranty status in respect of time policies, assuming that the vessel is insured separately for each voyage, as suggested by Gow, is a reform that would bring a degree of certainty to this area. Also, the assured could not argue that his position had been worsened by this amendment, considering that, under the proposed new warranty regime, a causal link between the breach and loss would be required in order to deny liability.[73]

(f)   The MIA 1906 after the reform: the draft provisions

8.56   In this final part of the book, the author wishes to formulate the suggested reform by redrafting the provisions of the MIA 1906 that would be affected. Provided a reform in this area, as suggested by the author, is carried out, ss 33, 34, 35 and 39 of the MIA 1906 would read as follows:[74]

33.   Nature of warranty

(1)   A warranty, in the following sections relating to warranties, means a promissory warranty, that is to say, a warranty by which the assured undertakes that some particular thing shall or shall not be done, or that some condition shall be fulfilled, or whereby he affirms or negatives the existence of a particular state of facts.

(2)   A warranty may be express or implied.

(3)   *A warranty, as above defined, is a condition precedent to the attachment of risk or to further liability of the insurer, and must be exactly complied with.* If it be not so complied with, then, subject to any express provision in the policy, the insurer is discharged from liability as from the date of breach of warranty, but without prejudice to any liability incurred by him before that date.

(3A)   *Where the breach of warranty is followed by a loss, the insurer cannot rely on s 33(3) if the assured on a balance of probabilities proves that the loss in respect of which he seeks to be indemnified was not caused or contributed to by the breach.*

(3B)   *Where no loss follows the breach of warranty, the insurer may cancel the contract by giving notice in writing as soon as he becomes aware of the breach.*

(3C)   *Section 33(3A) does not apply when the implied warranty of legality is breached.*

---

73   There have been a number of criticisms aboutnadopting a warranty status to seaworthiness obligation in marine insurance. It is clear that the harshness of the remedy afforded by the MIA 1906 in case of breach of a warranty was the main reason behind these criticisms and, provided that this remedy is modified by adopting a causal link requirement, there is no reason to consider a change in the legal status of implied warranty of seaworthiness. The adoption of a causal link requirement in case of a breach of warranty will bring the law on this point into line with other jurisdictions and distribute the rights and obligations of the parties fairly.

74   The parts in italics are the parts that have been inserted or altered.

34.   When breach of warranty excused

(1)   Non-compliance with a warranty is excused when, by reason of a change of circumstances, the warranty ceases to be applicable to the circumstances of the contract, or when compliance with the warranty is rendered unlawful by any subsequent law.

(3)   A breach of warranty may be waived by the insurer.

(3A)   *The previous sub-section does not apply when the implied warranty of legality is breached.*

35.   Express warranties

(1)   An express warranty may be in any form of words from which the intention to warrant is to be inferred *and it needs not be material to the risk insured against.*

(2)   An express warranty must be included in, or written upon, the policy, or must be contained in some document incorporated by reference into the policy.

(3)   An express warranty does not exclude an implied warranty, unless it be inconsistent therewith.

39   Warranty of seaworthiness of ship

(1)   In a voyage policy there is an implied warranty that at the commencement of the voyage the ship shall be seaworthy for the purpose of the particular adventure insured.

(2)   Where the policy attaches while the ship is in port, there is also an implied warranty that she shall, at the commencement of the risk, be reasonably fit to encounter the ordinary perils of the port.

(3)   Where the policy relates to a voyage which is performed in different stages, during which the ship requires different kinds of or further preparation or equipment, there is an implied warranty that at the commencement of each stage the ship is seaworthy in respect of such preparation or equipment for the purposes of that stage.

(4)   A ship is deemed to be seaworthy when she is reasonably fit in all respects to encounter the ordinary perils of the seas of the adventure insured.

(5)   *A time policy shall be subject to the same warranty of seaworthiness as if the vessel were insured separately for each voyage.*

SELECT BIBLIOGRAPHY

Books

Abbott, C, *A Treatise of the Law Relative to Merchant Ships and Seamen*, 2nd American edn, 1810, Newburyport: Edward Little

Anderson, P, *ISM Code: A Practical Guide To the Legal and Insurance Implications*, 1998, London: LLP

Ashburner, W, *The Rhodian Sea Law*, 1909, Oxford: Clarendon

Atkins, H (ed), *Eldridge on Marine Policies*, 3rd edn, 1938, London: Butterworths

Bennett, H, *Law of Marine Insurance*, 1996, Oxford: Clarendon

Birds, J and Hird, N, *Birds' Modern Insurance Law*, 6th edn, 2004, London: Sweet & Maxwell

Brown, RH, *Analysis of Marine Insurance Clauses, Book Two: The Institute Time Clauses – Hulls (1983)*, 1993a, London: Witherby

Brown, RH, *Marine Insurance: Hull Practice*, Vol 3, 2nd edn, 1993b, London: Witherby

Brown, RH and Wormell, J, *Lloyd's Market Practice*, 2nd edn, 1992, London: Witherby

Buglass, LJ, *Marine Insurance and General Average in the United States*, 2nd edn, 1991, Maryland: Cornell Maritime Press

Buglass, LJ, *Marine Insurance Claims*, 2nd edn, 1972, Maryland: Cornell Maritime Press

Chalmers, MD and Archibald, JG, *The Marine Insurance Act 1906*, 3rd edn, 1922, London: Butterworths

Chalmers, MD and Owen, D, *The Marine Insurance Act 1906*, 1907, London: Williams Clowes

Chalmers, MD and Owen, D, *A Digest of the Law Relating to Marine Insurance*, 2nd edn, 1903, London: Williams Clowes

Chalmers, MD and Owen, D, *A Digest of the Law Relating to Marine Insurance*, 1901, London: Williams Clowes

Chorley of Kendal (Lord) (ed), *Arnould on the Law of Marine Insurance and Average*, Vols 1 and 2, 14th edn, 1954, London: Stevens

Clarke, M, *The Law of Insurance Contracts*, 4th edn, 2002, London: LLP

Clarke, M, *Policies and Perceptions of Insurance: An Introduction to Insurance Law*, 1997, Oxford: Clarendon

Colinvaux, R, *Law of Insurance*, 5th edn, 1984, London: Sweet & Maxwell

Det Norske Veritas (ed), *Commentary to Norwegian Marine Insurance Plan 1996, Version 1997*, 1997, Oslo: Elan ders Publishing Association

Enge, HJ, *Transportversicherung*, 3rd edn, 1996, Hamburg: Gabler (original in German)

Egger, PM, Picken, S and Foss, P, *Good Faith and Insurance Contracts*, 2nd edn, 2004, London: LLP

Falkanger, T, Bull, HJ and Brautaset, L, *Introduction to Norwegian Maritime Law*, 1998, Oslo: Tano Aschehoug

Fernandes, RM, *Marine Insurance Law of Canada*, 1987, Toronto: Butterworths

Goodacre, JK, *Goodbye to the Memorandum: An In-depth Study of the Standard Cargo, War and Strikes Clauses*, 1988, London: Witherby

Goodacre, JK, *Marine Insurance Claims*, 1981, London: Witherby

Gow, W, *Sea Insurance*, 1914, London: Macmillan

Gow, W, *Marine Insurance – A Handbook*, 1895, London: Macmillan

Hare, J, *Shipping Law and Admiralty Jurisdiction in South Africa*, 1999, Kenwyn: Juta

Hazelwood, SJ, *P&I Clubs Law and Practice*, 3rd edn, 2000, London: LLP

Hill, J (ed), *O'May on Marine Insurance Law and Policy*, 1993, London: Sweet & Maxwell

Hilyard, F (ed), *Park: A System of the Law of Marine Insurances*, 8th edn, 1832, London: Saunders & Benning

Hodges, S, *Cases and Materials on Marine Insurance Law*, 1999, London: Cavendish Publishing

Hodges, S, *Law of Marine Insurance*, 1996, London: Cavendish Publishing

Hudson, NG, *The Institute Clauses*, 2nd edn, 1995, London: LLP

Hurd, HB, *The Law and Practice of Marine Insurance: Relating to Collision Damages and Other Liabilities to Third Parties*, 2nd edn, 1952, London: Pitman

Hurd, HB, *Marine Insurance*, 1922, London: Effingham Wilson

Huybrechts, M, Hooydonk, EV and Dieryck, C (eds), *Marine Insurance at the Turn of the Millennium*, Vols 1 and 2, 1999, Antwerp: Intersantia

Ivamy, ERH, *General Principles of Insurance Law*, 6th edn, 1993, London: Butterworths

Ivamy, ERH, *Law of Marine Insurance*, 8th edn, 1988, London: Butterworths

Ivamy, ERH, *Marine Insurance*, 4th edn, 1985, London: Butterworths

Ivamy, ERH (ed), *Chalmers' Marine Insurance Act 1906*, 9th edn, 1983, London: Butterworths

Kelly, DSL and Ball, ML, *Principles of Insurance Law in Australia and New Zealand*, 1991, Sydney: Butterworths

Lambeth, RJ (ed), *Templeman on Marine Insurance*, 6th edn, 1986, London: Pitman

Legh-Jones, N, Birds, J and Owen, D (ed), *MacGillivray on Insurance Law*, 10th edn, 2002, London: Sweet & Maxwell

Lewison, K, *The Interpretation of Contracts*, 3rd edn, 2004, London: Sweet & Maxwell

Martin, F, *The History of Lloyd's and of Marine Insurance in Great Britain*, 1876, London: MacMillan

Merkin, RM, *Annotated Marine Insurance Legislation*, 1997, London: LLP

Merkin, RM (ed), *Colinvaux's Law of Insurance*, 7th edn, 1997, London: Sweet & Maxwell

Miller, MV, *Marine War Risks*, 2nd edn, 1990, London: LLP

Mitchel, K, *War, Terror and Carriage by Sea*, 2004, London: LLP

Mustill, MJ and Gilman, JCB (eds), *Arnould's Law of Marine Insurance and Average*, Vol 3, 1997, London: Stevens

Mustill, MJ and Gilman, JCB (eds), *Arnould's Law of Marine Insurance and Average*, Vols 1 and 2, 16th edn, 1981, London: Stevens

Pawlowski, M, *The Doctrine of Proprietary Estoppel*, 1996, London: Sweet & Maxwell

Preston, S and Colinvaux, RP, *The Law of Insurance*, 2nd edn, 1961, London: Sweet & Maxwell

Rose, F, *Marine Insurance Law and Practice*, 2004, London: LLP

Schoenbaum, TJ, *Key Divergences Between English and American Law of Marine Insurance: A Comparative Study*, 1999, Maryland: Cornell Maritime Press

Sharp, DW, *Offshore Oil and Gas Insurance*, 1994, London: Witherby

Strathy, GR and Moore GC, *Law & Practice of Marine Insurance in Canada*, 2003, Toronto: LexisNexis Canada

Thomas, DR (ed), *The Modern Law of Marine Insurance*, Volume 2, 2002, London: LLP

Thomas, DR (ed), *The Modern Law of Marine Insurance*, 1996, London: LLP

Treitel, GH, *The Law of Contract*, 11th edn, 2003, London: Sweet & Maxwell

Van Niekerk, *The Development and Principles of Insurance Law in the Netherlands from 1500 to 1800*, 1999, Kenwyn: Juta

Vyleden, F, Goovaerts, M and Haezendonck, J (eds), *Premium Calculation in Insurance*, 1983, Dordrecht: D Reidel

Wilken, S (ed), *Wilken and Villiers The Law of Waiver, Variation And Estoppel*, 2002, Oxford: OUP

Articles

Anderson, CB, 'The evolution of the implied warranty of seaworthiness in comparative perspective' (1986) *Journal of Maritime Law and Commerce* 1

Arjunan, K, 'Waiver and estoppel – distinction without a difference?' (1993) *Australian Business Law Review* 182

Bennett, HN, 'Mapping the doctrine of utmost good faith in insurance contract law' (1999) *Lloyd's Maritime and Commercial Law Quarterly* 165

Birds, J, 'The effect of breach of warranty' (1991) *Law Quarterly Review* 540

Birds, J, 'Warranties in insurance proposal forms' (1977) *Journal of Business Law* 231

Brice, G, 'Unexplained losses in marine insurance' (1991) *Tulane Maritime Law Journal* 105

Carter, JW, 'Conditions and conditions precedent' (1990) *Journal of Contract Law* 90

Cattell, J and Edward, V, 'A comparison of USA law to the MIA of 1906' (1995) *Tulane Maritime Law Journal* 1

Clarke, M, 'Waiver, estoppel and election' (1993) *British Insurance Law Association* 5

Clarke, M, 'The nature of warranty in contracts of insurance' (1991) *Cambridge Law Journal* 393

Davenport, BJ, 'The duty of disclosure' (1990) *Lloyd's Maritime and Commercial Law Quarterly* 251

Diamond, A, 'The law of marine insurance – has it a future?' (1986) *Lloyd's Maritime and Commercial Law Quarterly* 25

Donaldson, Lord of Lymington, 'The ISM Code: the road to discovery?' (1998) *Lloyd's Maritime and Commercial Law Quarterly* 526

Ellis, H, 'Insurance law: special warranties' (1986) *Dublin University Law Journal* 91

Ellis, H, 'Insurance law: express warranties' (1985) *Dublin University Law Journal* 130

Fawlk, C, 'The meaning and effect of s 33 of the MIA of 1906' (1991) *Insurance Law and Practice* 98

Goldman, S, 'Marine insurance – the literal compliance rule applies to breaches of trading and navigational warranties' (1995) *Journal of Maritime Law and Commerce* 315

Goldman, S, 'Breach of warranty in American marine insurance' (1985) *Insurance Council Journal* 60

Goldstein, JK, 'The life and times of *Wilburn Boat*: a critical guide' (1997) *Maritime Law and Commerce* 395

Goodacre, SB, 'To err is human: an appraisal of some possible effects of ISM Code on the English marine hull policy' (1997) *International Maritime Law* 263

Gregory, M, 'Legal implications of the ISM Code: new impediments to sea fever' (1996) *University of San Francisco Maritime Law Journal* 37

Hamilton, J, 'The duty of disclosure in law: the effectiveness of self-regulation' (1995) *Australian Business Law Review* 359

Hayden, RP and Balic, S, 'Marine insurance: varieties, combinations and coverages' (1991) *Tulane Law Review* 311

Henley, C, 'Waiver, affirmation, election and estoppel: the worst is over' (1993) *Insurance Law and Practice* 71

Hird, NJ, 'Warranties – better in the future?' (1996) *Journal of Business Law* 405

Hodges, S, 'Seaworthiness and safe ship management' (1998) *International Journal of Insurance Law* 162

Leeming, M, 'Discharge for breach of warranty in contract of marine insurance' (1992) *Journal of Contract Law* 163

Males, S and Kenny, J, 'Unseaworthiness, the Institute Cargo Clauses and the ISM Code' (1999) *International Trade Law Quarterly* 136

McGlore, K, 'Marine Insurance and implied warranty of seaworthiness' (1975) *Loyola Law Review* 960

Mustill, JM, 'Fault and marine losses' (1988) *Lloyd's Maritime and Commercial Law Quarterly* 310

Nicoll, CC, 'Marine insurance: reformed or deformed' (1994) *Lloyd's Maritime and Commercial Law Quarterly* 256

Ogg, T, 'IMO's International Safety Management (The ISM Code)' (1996) *International Law of Shipping Law* 143

O'Sullivan, BP, 'The scope of the sue and labour clause' (1990) *Journal of Maritime Law and Commerce* 545

Owles, D, 'The meaning of "Seaworthy"' (1984) *New Law Journal* 825

Pamborides, GP, 'The ISM Code: potential legal implications' (1996) *International Maritime Law* 56

Powles, DG, 'Insured perils, unseaworthiness and causation' (1988) *Journal of Business Law* 83

Pritchett, RW, 'The implied warranty of seaworthiness in time policies: the American view' (1983) *Lloyd's Maritime and Commercial Law Quarterly* 195

Roger, W, 'Human factor in unseaworthiness claims' (1993) *Lloyd's Maritime and Commercial Law Quarterly* 345

Salter, R, 'Marine insurance – wilful misconduct of the assured' (1985) *Lloyd's Maritime and Commercial Law Quarterly* 415

Schmidt, R and Johannsen, R, 'Some considerations on the practice of insurance law in Germany' (1996) *International Journal of Insurance Law* 3

Schoenbaum, TJ, 'Warranties in the law of marine insurance: some suggestions for reform of English and American law' (1999) *Tulane Maritime Law Journal* 267

Soyer, B, 'Potential legal implications of the ISMC for marine insurance' (1998) *International Journal of Insurance Law* 268

Soyer, B, 'A Survey of the new International Hull Clauses 2002' (2003) *Journal of International Maritime Law*, 256

Thompson, GA, 'Perils of the seas: burden of proof and causation' (1991) *Insurance Law Journal* 113

Thompson, M, 'Reform of the law of marine insurance' (1993) *Insurance Law Journal* 195

Treitel, GH, 'Conditions and condition precedent' (1990) *Law Quarterly Review* 185

Vance, WR, 'The history of the development of the warranty in insurance law' (1911) *Yale Law Journal* 521

Waddell, G, 'Current issues and developments in marine insurance' (1993) *University of San Francisco Maritime Law Journal* 185

Waesche, AJ, 'Choice and uniformity of law generally' (1991) *Tulane Law Review* 293

Ward, RDP, 'Strict compliance with marine insurance contracts' (1995) *Washington Law Review* 519

White, R, 'The human factor in unseaworthiness claims' (1995) *Lloyd's Maritime and Commercial Law Quarterly* 221

White, R, 'Human unseaworthiness' (1996) *Lloyd's Maritime and Commercial Law Quarterly* 24

Papers

Aikens, R, 'Star Sea: continuing duty of utmost good faith', paper delivered at Insurance and Law Conference, 1999, organised by St John's College

Bull, HJ, 'Norwegian Marine Insurance Plan of 1996', paper delivered at International Marine Insurance Conference, 1999, organised by The European Institute of Maritime and Transport Law (published in Huybrechts, M, Hooydonk, EV and Dieryck, C (eds), *Marine Insurance at the Turn of the Millennium*, Vol 1, 1999, Antwerp: Intersantia, p 109)

Cadwallader, FJJ, 'Instant death (breach of an underwriter's warranty)', paper delivered at the Second International Maritime Law Seminar, 1981, Vancouver

Cadwallader, FJJ, 'Unseaworthiness: Manning, competence and carriage by sea', paper delivered at International Conference on Seaworthiness, Fitness for Sea, 1980, organised by Newcastle University

Cedric, B, 'Technical aspects of unseaworthiness', paper delivered at Cargo Claims Seminar, 1975, organised by LLP

Clarke, AP, 'Seaworthiness: the resolution of disputes', paper delivered at Mariner and the Maritime Law, 1992, organised by the Nautical Institute

Clarke, M, 'The marine insurance system in common law countries – status and problems', paper delivered at Marine Insurance Symposium, 1998, organised jointly by Comité Maritime International, Norwegian Maritime Law Association and Scandinavian Institute of Maritime Law at Oslo (published in 1998 *Mar Ins* 242, p 63)

Corbett, HS, 'The importance of seaworthiness', paper delivered at Voyage and Time Charterer's Conference, 1996, organised by the IBC

Griggs, P, 'Summing up: towards harmonisation of marine insurance conditions – the role of the CMI', paper delivered at Marine Insurance Symposium, 1998, organised jointly by Comité Maritime International, Norwegian Maritime Law Association and Scandinavian Institute of Maritime Law, Oslo (published in 1998 *Mar Ins* 242, p 239)

Hare, J, 'The omnipotent warranty: England v the world', paper delivered at International Marine Insurance Conference, 1999, organised by the European Institute of Maritime and Transport Law (published in Huybrechts, M, Hooydonk, EV and Dieryck, C (eds), *Marine Insurance at the Turn of the Millennium*, Vol 2, 1999, Antwerp: Intersantia, p 37)

Hilton, C, 'Seaworthiness: a legal perspective', paper delivered at Mariner and the Maritime Law conference, 1992, organised by the Nautical Institute

Honka, H, 'Harmonisation of hull insurance contracts in the light of seaworthiness and safety regulations', paper delivered at Marine Insurance Symposium, 1998, organised jointly by Comité Maritime International, Norwegian Maritime Law Association and Scandinavian Institute of Maritime Law, Oslo (published in 1998 *Mar Ins* 242, p 165)

Jenkins, N, 'Forecasting changes in the world of marine insurance market and predicting London's place in it in the long term', paper delivered at Marine Insurance Market Conference, 1996, organised by IIR Ltd, London

Kostka, K, 'Marine transport insurance in Germany: the General German Cargo Conditions in comparison to the Institute Cargo Clauses and recent German court decisions', paper delivered at International Marine Insurance Conference, 1999, organised by the European Institute of Maritime and Transport Law (published in Huybrechts, M, Hooydonk, EV and Dieryck, C (eds), *Marine Insurance at the Turn of the Millennium*, Vol 2, 1999, Antwerp: Intersantia, p 361)

Lowry, PD, 'Perils of the seas and warranties – a case for the assured', paper delivered in the Third International Maritime Law Conference, 1986, Vancouver

McEven, DF, 'Perils of the sea and warranties – the underwriter's perspective', paper delivered in the Third International Maritime Law Conference, 1986, Vancouver

Redmond, S, 'The London marine hull market – past, present, future', paper delivered at Marine Insurance Market Conference, 1996, organised by IIR Ltd, London

Remé, T, 'The CMI working group on marine insurance: challenges for the future', paper delivered at International Marine Insurance Conference, 1999, organised by the European Institute of Maritime and Transport Law (published in Huybrechts, M, Hooydonk, EV and Dieryck, C (eds), *Marine Insurance at the Turn of the Millennium*, Vol 1, 1999, Antwerp: Intersantia, p 399)

Sturley, M, 'Marine insurance in the United States: the US Supreme Court's *Wilburn Boat* decision and its impact on marine insurance', paper delivered at International Marine Insurance Conference, 1999, organised by the European Institute of Maritime and Transport Law (published in Huybrechts, M, Hooydonk, EV and Dieryck, C (eds), *Marine Insurance at the Turn of the Millennium*, Vol 1, 1999, Antwerp: Intersantia, p 145)

Thomas, DR, 'Cargo insurance: issues arising from the standard cover provided by the London Institute Cargo Clauses', paper delivered at International Marine Insurance Conference, 1999, organised by the European Institute of Maritime and Transport Law (published in Huybrechts, M, Hooydonk, EV and Dieryck, C (eds), *Marine Insurance at the Turn of the Millennium*, Vol 1, 1999, Antwerp: Intersantia, p 325)

Wilhelmsen, TL, 'The Norwegian Marine Insurance Plan and sub-standard ships', paper delivered at International Marine Insurance Conference, 1999, organised by the European Institute of Maritime and Transport Law (published in Huybrechts, M, Hooydonk, EV and Dieryck, C (eds), *Marine Insurance at the Turn of the Millennium*, Vol 1, 1999, Antwerp: Intersantia, p 123)

Wilhelmsen, TL, 'The marine insurance system in civil law countries', paper delivered at Marine Insurance Symposium, 1998, organised jointly by Comité Maritime International, Norwegian Maritime Law Association and Scandinavian Institute of Maritime Law, Oslo (published in 1998 *Mar Ins* 242, p 15)

Reports

Association of British Insurers, *Insurance: Facts, Figures and Trends*, November 1999, London

Association of British Insurers, *Insurance: Facts, Figures and Trends*, October 1998, London

Association of British Insurers, *Insurance: Facts, Figures and Trends*, September 1997, London

Bonnaud, M (chair), *Paris as an International Centre*, 1994, prepared by a group of experts, Paris: Hachette (original in French)

British Insurance Law Association, *Insurance Contract Law Reform*, 2002, London: Centre for Financial Regulation Studies

Bryants, DT, De Bievre, A and Dyer-Smith, M, *The Human Element in Shipping Casualties*, 1988, London: Tavistock Institute of Human Relations

Carter, RL and Falush, P, *The London Insurance Market*, 1998, London: Association of British Insurers, Institute of London Underwriters, London International Insurance and Reinsurance Market Association, Lloyd's, Lloyd's Insurance Broker's Committee

Official reports

UK

Donaldson, Lord, *Safer Ships, Cleaner Seas: Report of Lord Donaldson's Inquiry into the Prevention of Pollution from Merchant Shipping*, Cm 2560, 1994, presented to the Parliament by the Secretary of State for transport by Command of Her Majesty, 1994

Law Commission, *Insurance Law: Non-disclosure and breach of warranty*, Law Com No 104, 1980, London: HMSO

Law Reform Committee, Fifth Report, *Conditions and Exceptions in Insurance Policies*, Cmnd 62, 1957, London: HMSO

Australia

Commonwealth Attorney General's Department, *The Marine Insurance Act 1909*, Issues Paper 1997, Canberra: International Trade and Environment Law Branch

Community Law Reform Program, First Report, Insurance Contracts – Non-disclosure and misrepresentation, 1983, Sydney: New South Wales Law Reform Commission

Law Reform Commission, *Insurance Contracts*, Report No 20, 1982, Canberra: Australian Government Publishing Service

Law Reform Commission, *Review of the Marine Insurance Act 1909*, Report No 91, 2001, Canberra: Australian Government Publishing Service

International

United Nations, *Legal and Documentary Aspects of the Marine Insurance Contract*, 1982, United Nations Conference on Trade and Development, (UNCTAD) TD/B/C.4/ISL 27 New York

United Nations, *Review of Maritime Transport*, 1997, United Nations Conference on Trade and Development, UNCTAD/RMT(97/1) New York

APPENDICES

LEGISLATION

1   Marine Insurance Act 1906

DOCUMENTS*

2   Institute Time Clauses Hulls (1 November 1995)
3   Institute Voyage Clauses Hulls (1 November 1995)
4   International Hull Clauses (1 November 2003)
5   Institute Cargo Clauses (A) (1 January 1982)
6   Institute Cargo Clauses (B) (1 January 1982)
7   Institute Cargo Clauses (C) (1 January 1982)
8   Institute Warranties (1 July 1976)

---

*   These documents have been reproduced by kind permission of The Institute of London Underwriters and Witherby & Co Ltd.

APPENDIX 1

MARINE INSURANCE ACT 1906

An Act to codify the Law relating to Marine Insurance.   [21 December 1906]

BE it enacted by the King's most Excellent Majesty, by and with the advice and consent of the Lords Spiritual and Temporal, and Commons, in this present Parliament assembled, and by the authority of the same, as follows:

MARINE INSURANCE

1   Marine insurance defined

A contract of marine insurance is a contract whereby the insurer undertakes to indemnify the assured, in manner and to the extent thereby agreed, against marine losses, that is to say, the losses incident to marine adventure.

2   Mixed sea and land risks

(1)   A contract of marine insurance may, by its express terms, or by usage of trade, be extended so as to protect the assured against losses on inland waters or on any land risk which may be incidental to any sea voyage.

(2)   Where a ship in course of building, or the launch of a ship, or any adventure analogous to a marine adventure, is covered by a policy in the form of a marine policy, the provisions of this Act, in so far as applicable, shall apply thereto; but, except as by this section provided, nothing in this Act shall alter or affect any rule of law applicable to any contract of insurance other than a contract of marine insurance as by this Act defined.

3   Marine adventure and maritime perils defined

(1)   Subject to the provisions of this Act, every lawful marine adventure may be the subject of a contract of marine insurance.

(2)   In particular there is a marine adventure where—

  (a)   Any ship, goods or other moveables are exposed to maritime perils. Such property is in this Act referred to as 'insurable property';

  (b)   The earning or acquisition of any freight, passage money, commission, profit. Or other pecuniary benefit, or the security for any advances, loan, or disbursements, is endangered by the exposure of insurable property to maritime perils;

  (c)   Any liability to a third party may be incurred by the owner of, or other person interested in or responsible for, insurable property, by reason of maritime perils.

'Maritime perils' means the perils consequent on, or incidental to, the navigation of the sea, that is to say, perils of the seas, fire, war perils, pirates, rovers, thieves, captures, seizures, restraints, and detainments of princes and peoples, jettisons, barratry, and any other perils, either of the like kind or which may be designated by the policy.

INSURABLE INTEREST

4   Avoidance of wagering or gaming contracts

(1)   Every contract of marine insurance by way of gaming or wagering is void.

(2)   A contract of marine insurance is deemed to be a gaming or wagering contract—

  (a)   Where the assured has not an insurable interest as defined by this Act, and the contract is entered into with no expectation of acquiring such an interest; or

  (b)   Where the policy is made 'interest or no interest,' or 'without further proof of interest than the policy itself,' or 'without benefit of salvage to the insurer,' or subject to any other like term:

Provided that, where there is no possibility of salvage, a policy may be effected without benefit of salvage to the insurer.

5   Insurable interest defined

(1)   Subject to the provisions of this Act, every person has an insurable interest who is interested in a marine adventure.

(2)   In particular a person is interested in a marine adventure where he stands in any legal or equitable relation to the adventure or to any insurable property at risk therein, in consequence of which he may benefit by the safety or due arrival of insurable property, or may be prejudiced by its loss, or damage thereto, or by the detention thereof, or may incur liability in respect thereof.

6   When interest must attach

(1)   The assured must be interested in the subject-matter insured at the time of the loss though he need not be interested when the insurance is effected:

        Provided that where the subject-matter is insured 'lost or not lost,' the assured may recover although he may not have acquired his interest until after the loss, unless at the time of effecting the contract of insurance the assured was aware of the loss, and the insurer was not.

(2)   Where the assured has no interest at the time of the loss, he cannot acquire interest by any act or election after he is aware of the loss.

7   Defeasible or contingent interest

(1)   A defeasible interest is insurable, as also is a contingent interest.

(2)   In particular, where the buyer of goods has insured them, he has an insurable interest, notwithstanding that he might, at his election, have rejected the goods, or have treated them as at the seller's risk, by reason of the latter's delay in making delivery or otherwise.

8   Partial interest

A partial interest of any nature is insurable.

9   Re-insurance

(1)   The insurer under a contract of marine insurance has an insurable interest in his risk, and may re-insure in respect of it.

(2)   Unless the policy otherwise provides, the original assured has no right or interest in respect of such re-insurance.

10   Bottomry

The lender of money on bottomry or respondentia has an insurable interest in respect of the loan.

11   Master's and seamen's wages

The master or any member of the crew of a ship has an insurable interest in respect of his wages.

12   Advance freight

In the case of advance freight, the person advancing the freight has an insurable interest, in so far as such freight is not repayable in case of loss.

13   Charges of insurance

The assured has an insurable interest in the charges of any insurance which he may effect.

14   Quantum of interest

(1)   Where the subject-matter insured is mortgaged, the mortgagor has an insurable interest in the full value thereof, and the mortgagee has an insurable interest in respect of any sum due or to become due under the mortgage.

(2)   A mortgagee, consignee, or other person having an interest in the subject-matter insured may insure on behalf and for the benefit of other persons interested as well as for his own benefit.

(3)   The owner of insurable property has an insurable interest in respect of the full value thereof, notwithstanding that some third person may have agreed, or be liable, to indemnify him in case of loss.

15   Assignment of interest

Where the assured assigns or otherwise parts with his interest in the subject-matter insured, he does not thereby transfer to the assignee his rights under the contract of insurance, unless there be an express or implied agreement with the assignee to that effect.

But the provisions of this section do not affect a transmission of interest by operation of law.

INSURABLE VALUE

16   Measure of insurable value

Subject to any express provision or valuation in the policy, the insurable value of the subject-matter insured must be ascertained as follows:—

(1)   In insurance on ship, the insurable value is the value, at the commencement of the risk, of the ship, including her outfit, provisions and stores for the officers and crew, money advanced for seamen's wages, and other disbursements (if any) incurred to make the ship fit for the voyage or adventure contemplated by the policy, plus the charges of insurance upon the whole:

The insurable value, in the case of a steamship, includes also the machinery, boilers, and coals and engine stores if owned by the assured, and, in the case of a ship engaged in a special trade, the ordinary fittings requisite for that trade:

(2)   In insurance on freight, whether paid in advance or otherwise, the insurable value is the gross amount of the freight at the risk of the assured, plus the charges of insurance:

(3)   In insurance on goods or merchandise, the insurable value is the prime cost of the property insured, plus the expenses of and incidental to shipping and the charges of insurance upon the whole:

(4)   In insurance on any other subject-matter, the insurable value is the amount at the risk of the assured when the policy attaches, plus the charges of insurance.

DISCLOSURE AND REPRESENTATIONS

17   Insurance is *uberrimae fidei*

A contract of marine insurance is a contract based upon the utmost good faith, and, if the utmost good faith be not observed by either party, the contract may be avoided by the other party.

18   Disclosure by assured

(1)   Subject to the provisions of this section, the assured must disclose to the insurer, before the contract is concluded, every material circumstance which is known to the assured, and the assured is deemed to know every circumstance which, in the ordinary course of business, ought to be known by him. If the assured fails to make such disclosure, the insurer may avoid the contract.

(2)   Every circumstance is material which would influence the judgment of a prudent insurer in fixing the premium, or determining whether he will take the risk.

(3)   In the absence of inquiry the following circumstances need not be disclosed, namely:—

    (a)   Any circumstance which diminishes the risk;

    (b)   Any circumstance which is known or presumed to be known to the insurer.

    The insurer is presumed to know matters of common notoriety or knowledge, and matters which an insurer in the ordinary course of his business, as such, ought to know;

    (c)   Any circumstance as to which information is waived by the insurer;

    (d)   Any circumstance which it is superfluous to disclose by reason of any express or implied warranty.

(4)   Whether any particular circumstance, which is not disclosed, be material or not is, in each case, a question of fact.

(5)   The term 'circumstance' includes any communication made to, or information received by, the assured.

19   Disclosure by agent effecting insurance

Subject to the provisions of the preceding section as to circumstances which need not be disclosed, where an insurance is effected for the assured by an agent, the agent must disclose to the insurer—

    (a)   Every material circumstance which is known to himself, and an agent to insure is deemed to know every circumstance which in the ordinary course of business ought to be known by, or to have been communicated to, him; and

    (b)   Every material circumstance which the assured is bound to disclose, unless it come to his knowledge too late to communicate it to the agent.

20   Representations pending negotiation of contract

(1)   Every material representation made by the assured or his agent to the insurer during the negotiations for the contract, and before the contract is concluded, must be true. If it be untrue the insurer may avoid the contract.

(2)   A representation is material which would influence the judgment of a prudent insurer in fixing the premium, or determining whether he will take the risk.

(3)   A representation may be either a representation as to a matter of fact, or as to a matter of expectation or belief.

(4)   A representation as to matter of fact is true, if it be substantially correct, that is to say, if the difference between what is represented and what is actually correct would not be considered material by a prudent insurer.

(5)   A representation as to a matter of expectation or belief is true if it be made in good faith.

(6)   A representation may be withdrawn or corrected before the contract is concluded.

(7)   Whether a particular representation be material or not is, in each case, a question of fact.

21   When contract is deemed to be concluded

A contract of marine insurance is deemed to be concluded when the proposal of the assured is accepted by the insurer, whether the policy be then issued or not; and, for the purpose of showing when the proposal was accepted, reference may be made to the slip or covering note or other customary memorandum of the contract.

ANNOTATION:

Words omitted repealed by the Finance Act 1959, s 37(5), Sched 8, Pt II.

THE POLICY

22 Contract must be embodied in policy

Subject to the provisions of any statute, a contract of marine insurance is inadmissible in evidence unless it is embodied in a marine policy in accordance with this Act. The policy may be executed and issued either at the time when the contract is concluded, or afterwards.

23 What policy must specify

A marine policy must specify—

(1) The name of the assured, or of some person who effects the insurance on his behalf:

(2)–(5) ...

ANNOTATION:

Words omitted repealed by the Finance Act 1959, ss 30(5), (7), 37(5), Sched 8, Pt II.

24 Signature of insurer

(1) A marine policy must be signed by or on behalf of the insurer, provided that in the case of a corporation the corporate seal may be sufficient, but nothing in this section shall be construed as requiring the subscription of a corporation to be under seal.

(2) Where a policy is subscribed by or on behalf of two or more insurers, each subscription, unless the contrary be expressed, constitutes a distinct contract with the assured.

25 Voyage and time policies

(1) Where the contract is to insure the subject-matter 'at and from', or from one place to another or others, the policy is called a 'voyage policy', and where the contract is to insure the subject-matter for a definite period of time the policy is called a 'time policy'. A contract for both voyage and time may be included in the same policy.

(2) ...

ANNOTATION:

Sub-section (2): repealed by the Finance Act 1959, ss 30(5), (7), 37(5), Sched 8, Pt II.

26 Designation of subject matter

(1) The subject matter insured must be designated in a marine policy with reasonable certainty.

(2) The nature and extent of the interest of the assured in the subject matter insured need not be specified in the policy.

(3) Where the policy designates the subject matter insured in general terms, it shall be construed to apply to the interest intended by the assured to be covered.

(4) In the application of this section regard shall be had to any usage regulating the designation of the subject matter insured.

27 Valued policy

(1) A policy may be either valued or unvalued.

(2) A valued policy is a policy which specifies the agreed value of the subject-matter insured.

(3) Subject to the provisions of this Act, and in the absence of fraud, the value fixed by the policy is, as between the insurer and assured, conclusive of the insurable value of the subject intended to be insured, whether the loss be total or partial.

(4) Unless the policy otherwise provides, the value fixed by the policy is not conclusive for the purpose of determining whether there has been a constructive total loss.

28   Unvalued policy

An unvalued policy is a policy which does not specify the value of the subject-matter insured, but, subject to the limit of the sum insured, leaves the insurable value to be subsequently ascertained, in the manner hereinbefore specified.

29   Floating policy by ship or ships

(1)   A floating policy is a policy which describes the insurance in general terms, and leaves the name of the ship or ships and other particulars to be defined by subsequent declaration.

(2)   The subsequent declaration or declarations may be made by indorsement on the policy, or in other customary manner.

(3)   Unless the policy otherwise provides, the declarations must be made in the order of dispatch or shipment. They must, in the case of goods, comprise all consignments within the terms of the policy, and the value of the goods or other property must be honestly stated, but an omission or erroneous declaration may be rectified even after loss or arrival, provided the omission or declaration was made in good faith.

(4)   Unless the policy otherwise provides, where a declaration of value is not made until after notice of loss or arrival, the policy must be treated as an unvalued policy as regards the subject-matter of that declaration.

30   Construction of terms in policy

(1)   A policy may be in the form in the First Schedule to this Act.

(2)   Subject to the provisions of this Act, and unless the context of the policy otherwise requires, the terms and expressions mentioned in the First Schedule to this Act shall be construed as having the scope and meaning in that schedule assigned to them.

31 Premium to be arranged

(1)   Where an insurance is effected at a premium to be arranged, and no arrangement is made, a reasonable premium is payable.

(2)   Where an insurance is effected on the terms that an additional premium is to be arranged in a given event, and that event happens but no arrangement is made, then a reasonable additional premium is payable.

DOUBLE INSURANCE

32   Double insurance

(1)   Where two or more policies are effected by or on behalf of the assured on the same adventure and interest or any part thereof, and the sums insured exceed the indemnity allowed by this Act, the assured is said to be over-insured by double insurance.

(2)   Where the assured is over-insured by double insurance—

(a)   The assured, unless the policy otherwise provides, may claim payment from the insurers in such order as he may think fit, provided that he is not entitled to receive any sum in excess of the indemnity allowed by this Act;

(b)   Where the policy under which the assured claims is a valued policy, the assured must give credit as against the valuation for any sum received by him under any other policy without regard to the actual value of the subject-matter insured;

(c)   Where the policy under which the assured claims is an unvalued policy he must give credit, as against the full insurable value, for any sum received by him under any other policy;

(d)   Where the assured receives any sum in excess of the indemnity allowed by this Act, he is deemed to hold such sum in trust for the insurers, according to their right of contribution among themselves.

WARRANTIES, ETC

33　Nature of warranty

(1)　A warranty, in the following sections relating to warranties, means a promissory warranty, that is to say, a warranty by which the assured undertakes that some particular thing shall or shall not be done, or that some condition shall be fulfilled, or whereby he affirms or negatives the existence of a particular state of facts.

(2)　A warranty may be express or implied.

(3)　A warranty, as above defined, is a condition which must be exactly complied with, whether it be material to the risk or not. If it be not so complied with, then, subject to any express provision in the policy, the insurer is discharged from liability as from the date of the breach of warranty, but without prejudice to any liability incurred by him before that date.

34　When breach of warranty excused

(1)　Non-compliance with a warranty is excused when, by reason of a change of circumstances, the warranty ceases to be applicable to the circumstances of the contract, or when compliance with the warranty is rendered unlawful by any subsequent law.

(2)　Where a warranty is broken, the assured cannot avail himself of the defence that the breach has been remedied, and the warranty complied with, before loss.

(3)　A breach of warranty may be waived by the insurer.

35　Express warranties

(1)　An express warranty may be in any form of words from which the intention to warrant is to be inferred.

(2)　An express warranty must be included in, or written upon, the policy, or must be contained in some document incorporated by reference into the policy.

(3)　An express warranty does not exclude an implied warranty, unless it be inconsistent therewith.

36　Warranty of neutrality

(1)　Where insurable property, whether ship or goods, is expressly warranted neutral, there is an implied condition that the property shall have a neutral character at the commencement of the risk, and that, so far as the assured can control the matter, its neutral character shall be preserved during the risk.

(2)　Where a ship is expressly warranted 'neutral' there is also an implied condition that, so far as the assured can control the matter, she shall be properly documented, that is to say, that she shall carry the necessary papers to establish her neutrality, and that she shall not falsify or suppress her papers, or use simulated papers. If any loss occurs through breach of this condition, the insurer may avoid the contract.

37　No implied warranty of nationality

There is no implied warranty as to the nationality of a ship, or that her nationality shall not be changed during the risk.

38　Warranty of good safety

Where the subject-matter insured is warranted 'well' or 'in good safety' on a particular day, it is sufficient if it be safe at any time during that day.

39　Warranty of seaworthiness of ship

(1)　In a voyage policy there is an implied warranty that at the commencement of the voyage the ship shall be seaworthy for the purpose of the particular adventure insured.

(2)   Where the policy attaches while the ship is in port, there is also an implied warranty that she shall, at the commencement of the risk, be reasonably fit to encounter the ordinary perils of the port.

(3)   Where the policy relates to a voyage which is performed in different stages, during which the ship requires different kinds of or further preparation or equipment, there is an implied warranty that at the commencement of each stage the ship is seaworthy in respect of such preparation or equipment for the purposes of that stage.

(4)   A ship is deemed to be seaworthy when she is reasonably fit in all respects to encounter the ordinary perils of the seas of the adventure insured.

(5)   In a time policy there is no implied warranty that the ship shall be seaworthy at any stage of the adventure, but where, with the privity of the assured, the ship is sent to sea in an unseaworthy state, the insurer is not liable for any loss attributable to unseaworthiness.

40   No implied warranty that goods are seaworthy

(1)   In a policy on goods or other moveables there is no implied warranty that the goods or moveables are seaworthy.

(2)   In a voyage policy on goods or other moveables there is an implied warranty that at the commencement of the voyage the ship is not only seaworthy as a ship, but also that she is reasonably fit to carry the goods or other moveables to the destination contemplated by the policy.

41   Warranty of legality

There is an implied warranty that the adventure insured is a lawful one, and that, so far as the assured can control the matter, the adventure shall be carried out in a lawful manner.

THE VOYAGE

42   Implied condition as to commencement of risk

(1)   Where the subject matter is insured by a voyage policy 'at and from' or 'from' a particular place, it is not necessary that the ship should be at that place when the contract is concluded, but there is an implied condition that the adventure shall be commenced within a reasonable time, and that if the adventure be not so commenced the insurer may avoid the contract.

(2)   The implied condition may be negatived by showing that the delay was caused by circumstances known to the insurer before the contract was concluded, or by showing that he waived the condition.

43   Alteration of port of departure

Where the place of departure is specified by the policy, and the ship instead of sailing from that place sails from any other place, the risk does not attach.

44   Sailing for different destination

Where the destination is specified in the policy, and the ship, instead of sailing for that destination, sails for any other destination, the risk does not attach.

45   Change of voyage

(1)   Where, after the commencement of the risk, the destination of the ship is voluntarily changed from the destination contemplated by the policy, there is said to be a change of voyage.

(2)   Unless the policy otherwise provides, where there is a change of voyage, the insurer is discharged from liability as from the time of change, that is to say, as from the time when

the determination to change it is manifested; and it is immaterial that the ship may not in fact have left the course of voyage contemplated by the policy when the loss occurs.

46 Deviation

(1) Where a ship, without lawful excuse, deviates from the voyage contemplated by the policy, the insurer is discharged from liability as from the time of deviation, and it is immaterial that the ship may have regained her route before any loss occurs.

(2) There is a deviation from the voyage contemplated by the policy—

(a) Where the course of the voyage is specifically designated by the policy, and that course is departed from; or

(b) Where the course of the voyage is not specifically designated by the policy, but the usual and customary course is departed from.

(3) The intention to deviate is immaterial; there must be a deviation in fact to discharge the insurer from his liability under the contract.

47 Several ports of discharge

(1) Where several ports of discharge are specified by the policy, the ship may proceed to all or any of them, but, in the absence of any usage or sufficient cause to the contrary, she must proceed to them, or such of them as she goes to, in the order designated by the policy. If she does not there is a deviation.

(2) Where the policy is to 'ports of discharge', within a given area, which are not named, the ship must, in the absence of any usage or sufficient cause to the contrary, proceed to them, or such of them as she goes to, in their geographical order. If she does not there is a deviation.

48 Delay in voyage

In the case of a voyage policy, the adventure insured must be prosecuted throughout its course with reasonable dispatch, and, if without lawful excuse it is not so prosecuted, the insurer is discharged from liability as from the time when the delay became unreasonable.

49 Excuses for deviation or delay

(1) Deviation or delay in prosecuting the voyage contemplated by the policy is excused—

(a) Where authorised by any special term in the policy; or

(b) Where caused by circumstances beyond the control of the master and his employer; or

(c) Where reasonably necessary in order to comply with an express or implied warranty; or

(d) Where reasonably necessary for the safety of the ship or subject-matter insured; or

(e) For the purpose of saving human life, or aiding a ship in distress where human life may be in danger; or

(f) Where reasonably necessary for the purpose of obtaining medical or surgical aid for any person on board the ship; or

(g) Where caused by the barratrous conduct of the master or crew, if barratry be one of the perils insured against.

(2) When the cause excusing the deviation or delay ceases to operate, the ship must resume her course, and prosecute her voyage, with reasonable dispatch.

ASSIGNMENT OF POLICY

50 When and how policy is assignable

(1) A marine policy is assignable unless it contains terms expressly prohibiting assignment. It may be assigned either before or after loss.

(2)   Where a marine policy has been assigned so as to pass the beneficial interest in such policy, the assignee of the policy is entitled to sue thereon in his own name; and the defendant is entitled to make any defence arising out of the contract which he would have been entitled to make if the action had been brought in the name of the person by or on behalf of whom the policy was effected.

(3)   A marine policy may be assigned by indorsement thereon or in other customary manner.

51   Assured who has no interest cannot assign

Where the assured has parted with or lost his interest in the subject matter insured, and has not, before or at the time of so doing, expressly or impliedly agreed to assign the policy, any subsequent assignment of the policy is inoperative:

Provided that nothing in this section affects the assignment of a policy after loss.

THE PREMIUM

52   When premium payable

Unless otherwise agreed, the duty of the assured or his agent to pay the premium, and the duty of the insurer to issue the policy to the assured or his agent, are concurrent conditions and the insurer is not bound to issue the policy until payment or tender of the premium.

53   Policy effected through broker

(1)   Unless otherwise agreed, where a marine policy is effected on behalf of the assured by a broker, the broker is directly responsible to the insurer for the premium, and the insurer is directly responsible to the assured for the amount which may be payable in respect of losses, or in respect of returnable premium.

(2)   Unless otherwise agreed, the broker has, as against the assured, a lien upon the policy for the amount of the premium and his charges in respect of effecting the policy; and, where he has dealt with the person who employs him as a principal, he has also a lien on the policy in respect of any balance on any insurance account which may be due to him from such person, unless when the debt was incurred he had reason to believe that such person was only an agent.

54   Effect of receipt on policy

Where a marine policy effected on behalf of the assured by a broker acknowledges the receipt of the premium, such acknowledgment is, in the absence of fraud, conclusive as between the insurer and the assured, but not as between the insurer and broker.

LOSS AND ABANDONMENT

55   Included and excluded losses

(1)   Subject to the provisions of this Act, and unless the policy otherwise provides, the insurer is liable for any loss proximately caused by a peril insured against, but, subject as aforesaid, he is not liable for any loss which is not proximately caused by a peril insured against.

(2)   In particular,—

    (a)   The insurer is not liable for any loss attributable to the wilful misconduct of the assured, but, unless the policy otherwise provides, he is liable for any loss proximately caused by a peril insured against, even though the loss would not have happened but for the misconduct or negligence of the master or crew;

    (b)   Unless the policy otherwise provides, the insurer on ship or goods is not liable for any loss proximately caused by delay, although the delay be caused by a peril insured against;

(c) Unless the policy otherwise provides, the insurer is not liable for ordinary wear and tear, ordinary leakage and breakage, inherent vice or nature of the subject-matter insured, or for any loss proximately caused by rats or vermin, or for any injury to machinery not proximately caused by maritime perils.

56 Partial and total loss

(1) A loss may be either total or partial. Any loss other than a total loss, as hereinafter defined, is a partial loss.

(2) A total loss may be either an actual total loss, or a constructive total loss.

(3) Unless a different intention appears from the terms of the policy, an insurance against total loss includes a constructive, as well as an actual, total loss.

(4) Where the assured brings an action for a total loss and the evidence proves only a partial loss, he may, unless the policy otherwise provides, recover for a partial loss.

(5) Where goods reach their destination in specie, but by reason of obliteration of marks, or otherwise, they are incapable of identification, the loss, if any, is partial, and not total.

57 Actual total loss

(1) Where the subject-matter insured is destroyed, or so damaged as to cease to be a thing of the kind insured, or where the assured is irretrievably deprived thereof, there is an actual total loss.

(2) In the case of an actual total loss no notice of abandonment need be given.

58 Missing ship

Where the ship concerned in the adventure is missing, and after the lapse of a reasonable time no news of her has been received, an actual total loss may be presumed.

59 Effect of transhipment, etc

Where, by a peril insured against, the voyage is interrupted at an intermediate port or place, under such circumstances as, apart from any special stipulation in the contract of affreightment, to justify the master in landing and re-shipping the goods or other moveables, or in transhipping them, and sending them on to their destination, the liability of the insurer continues, notwithstanding the landing or transhipment.

60 Constructive total loss defined

(1) Subject to any express provision in the policy, there is a constructive total loss where the subject-matter insured is reasonably abandoned on account of its actual total loss appearing to be unavoidable, or because it could not be preserved from actual total loss without an expenditure which would exceed its value when the expenditure had been incurred.

(2) In particular, there is a constructive total loss—

(i) Where the assured is deprived of the possession of his ship or goods by a peril insured against, and (a) it is unlikely that he can recover the ship or goods, as the case may be, or (b) the cost of recovering the ship or goods, as the case may be, would exceed their value when recovered; or

(ii) In the case of damage to a ship, where she is so damaged by a peril insured against that the cost of repairing the damage would exceed the value of the ship when repaired.

In estimating the cost of repairs, no deduction is to be made in respect of general average contributions to those repairs payable by other interests, but account is to be taken of the expense of future salvage operations and of any future general average contributions to which the ship would be liable if repaired; or

(iii)   In the case of damage to goods, where the cost of repairing the damage and forwarding the goods to their destination would exceed their value on arrival.

61   Effect of constructive total loss

Where there is a constructive total loss the assured may either treat the loss as a partial loss, or abandon the subject-matter insured to the insurer and treat the loss as if it were an actual total loss.

62   Notice of abandonment

(1)   Subject to the provisions of this section, where the assured elects to abandon the subject-matter insured to the insurer, he must give notice of abandonment. If he fails to do so the loss can only be treated as a partial loss.

(2)   Notice of abandonment may be given in writing, or by word of mouth, or partly in writing and partly by word of mouth, and may be given in terms which indicate the intention of the assured to abandon his insured interest in the subject-matter insured unconditionally to the insurer.

(3)   Notice of abandonment must be given with reasonable diligence after the receipt of reliable information of the loss, but where the information is of a doubtful character the assured is entitled to a reasonable time to make inquiry.

(4)   Where notice of abandonment is properly given, the rights of the assured are not prejudiced by the fact that the insurer refuses to accept the abandonment.

(5)   The acceptance of an abandonment may be either express or implied from the conduct of the insurer. The mere silence of the insurer after notice is not an acceptance.

(6)   Where a notice of abandonment is accepted the abandonment is irrevocable. The acceptance of the notice conclusively admits liability for the loss and the sufficiency of the notice.

(7)   Notice of abandonment is unnecessary where, at the time when the assured receives information of the loss, there would be no possibility of benefit to the insurer if notice were given to him.

(8)   Notice of abandonment may be waived by the insurer.

(9)   Where an insurer has re-insured his risk, no notice of abandonment need be given by him.

63   Effect of abandonment

(1)   Where there is a valid abandonment the insurer is entitled to take over the interest of the assured in whatever may remain of the subject-matter insured, and all proprietary rights incidental thereto.

(2)   Upon the abandonment of a ship, the insurer thereof is entitled to any freight in course of being earned, and which is earned by her subsequent to the casualty causing the loss, less the expenses of earning it incurred after the casualty; and, where the ship is carrying the owner's goods, the insurer is entitled to a reasonable remuneration for the carriage of them subsequent to the casualty causing the loss.

PARTIAL LOSSES (INCLUDING SALVAGE AND GENERAL AVERAGE AND PARTICULAR CHARGES)

64   Particular average loss

(1)   A particular average loss is a partial loss of the subject-matter insured, caused by a peril insured against, and which is not a general average loss.

(2)   Expenses incurred by or on behalf of the assured for the safety or preservation of the subject-matter insured, other than general average and salvage charges, are called particular charges. Particular charges are not included in particular average.

65 Salvage charges

(1) Subject to any express provision in the policy, salvage charges incurred in preventing a loss by perils insured against may be recovered as a loss by those perils.

(2) 'Salvage charges' means the charges recoverable under maritime law by a salvor independently of contract. They do not include the expenses of services in the nature of salvage rendered by the assured or his agents, or any person employed for hire by them, for the purpose of averting a peril insured against. Such expenses, where properly incurred, may be recovered as particular charges or as a general average loss, according to the circumstances under which they were incurred.

66 General average loss

(1) A general average loss is a loss caused by or directly consequential on a general average act. It includes a general average expenditure as well as a general average sacrifice.

(2) There is a general average act where any extraordinary sacrifice or expenditure is voluntarily and reasonably made or incurred in time of peril for the purpose of preserving the property imperilled in the common adventure.

(3) Where there is a general average loss, the party on whom it falls is entitled, subject to the conditions imposed by maritime law, to a rateable contribution from the other parties interested, and such contribution is called a general average contribution.

(4) Subject to any express provision in the policy, where the assured has incurred a general average expenditure, he may recover from the insurer in respect of the proportion of the loss which falls upon him; and, in the case of a general average sacrifice, he may recover from the insurer in respect of the whole loss without having enforced his right of contribution from the other parties liable to contribute.

(5) Subject to any express provision in the policy, where the assured has paid, or is liable to pay, a general average contribution in respect of the subject insured, he may recover therefor from the insurer.

(6) In the absence of express stipulation, the insurer is not liable for any general average loss or contribution where the loss was not incurred for the purpose of avoiding, or in connexion with the avoidance of, a peril insured against.

(7) Where ship, freight, and cargo, or any two of those interests, are owned by the same assured, the liability of the insurer in respect of general average losses or contributions is to be determined as if those subjects were owned by different persons.

MEASURE OF INDEMNITY

67 Extent of liability of insurer for loss

(1) The sum which the assured can recover in respect of a loss on a policy by which he is insured, in the case of an unvalued policy to the full extent of the insurable value, or, in the case of a valued policy to the full extent of the value fixed by the policy, is called the measure of indemnity.

(2) Where there is a loss recoverable under the policy, the insurer, or each insurer if there be more than one, is liable for such proportion of the measure of indemnity as the amount of his subscription bears to the value fixed by the policy in the case of a valued policy, or to the insurable value in the case of an unvalued policy.

68 Total loss

Subject to the provisions of this Act and to any express provision in the policy, where there is a total loss of the subject-matter insured,—

(1) If the policy be a valued policy, the measure of indemnity is the sum fixed by the policy:

(2) If the policy be an unvalued policy, the measure of indemnity is the insurable value of the subject-matter insured.

69 Partial loss of ship

Where a ship is damaged, but is not totally lost, the measure of indemnity, subject to any express provision in the policy, is as follows:—

(1) Where the ship has been repaired, the assured is entitled to the reasonable cost of the repairs, less the customary deductions, but not exceeding the sum insured in respect of any one casualty:

(2) Where the ship has been only partially repaired, the assured is entitled to the reasonable cost of such repairs, computed as above, and also to be indemnified for the reasonable depreciation, if any, arising from the unrepaired damage, provided that the aggregate amount shall not exceed the cost of repairing the whole damage, computed as above.

(3) Where the ship has not been repaired, and has not been sold in her damaged state during the risk, the assured is entitled to be indemnified for the reasonable depreciation arising from the unrepaired damage, but not exceeding the reasonable cost of repairing such damage, computed as above.

70 Partial loss of freight

Subject to any express provision in the policy, where there is a partial loss of freight, the measure of indemnity is such proportion of the sum fixed by the policy in the case of a valued policy, or of the insurable value in the case of an unvalued policy, as the proportion of freight lost by the assured bears to the whole freight at the risk of the assured under the policy.

71 Partial loss of goods, merchandise, etc

Where there is a partial loss of goods, merchandise, or other moveables, the measure of indemnity, subject to any express provision in the policy, is as follows:—

(1) Where part of the goods, merchandise or other moveables insured by a valued policy is totally lost, the measure of indemnity is such proportion of the sum fixed by the policy as the insurable value of the part lost bears to the insurable value of the whole, ascertained as in the case of an unvalued policy:

(2) Where part of the goods, merchandise, or other moveables insured by an unvalued policy is totally lost, the measure of indemnity is the insurable value of the part lost, ascertained as in case of total loss:

(3) Where the whole or any part of the goods or merchandise insured has been delivered damaged at its destination, the measure of indemnity is such proportion of the sum fixed by the policy in the case of a valued policy, or of the insurable value in the case of an unvalued policy, as the difference between the gross sound and damaged values at the place of arrival bears to the gross sound value:

(4) 'Gross value' means the wholesale price or, if there be no such price, the estimated value, with, in either case, freight, landing charges. and duty paid beforehand, provided that, in the case of goods or merchandise customarily sold in bond, the bonded price is deemed to be the gross value. 'Gross proceeds' means the actual price obtained at a sale where all charges on sale are paid by the sellers.

72 Apportionment of valuation

(1) Where different species of property are insured under a single valuation, the valuation must be apportioned over the different species in proportion to their respective insurable values, as in the case of an unvalued policy. The insured value of any part of a species is such proportion of the total insured value of the same as the insurable value of the part bears to the insurable value of the whole, ascertained in both cases as provided by this Act.

(2) Where a valuation has to be apportioned, and particulars of the prime cost of each separate species, quality, or description of goods cannot be ascertained, the division of the valuation may be made over the net arrived sound values of the different species, qualities, or descriptions of goods.

73 General average contributions and salvage charges

(1) Subject to any express provision in the policy, where the assured has paid, or is liable for, any general average contribution, the measure of indemnity is the full amount of such contribution, if the subject-matter liable to contribution is insured for its full contributory value; but, if such subject-matter be not insured for its full contributory value, or if only part of it be insured, the indemnity payable by the insurer must be reduced in proportion to the under insurance, and where there has been a particular average loss which constitutes a deduction from the contributory value, and for which the insurer is liable, that amount must be deducted from the insured value in order to ascertain what the insurer is liable to contribute.

(2) Where the insurer is liable for salvage charges the extent of his liability must be determined on the like principle.

74 Liabilities to third parties

Where the assured has effected an insurance in express terms against any liability to a third party, the measure of indemnity, subject to any express provision in the policy, is the amount paid or payable by him to such third party in respect of such liability.

75 General provisions as to measure of indemnity

(1) Where there has been a loss in respect of any subject-matter not expressly provided for in the foregoing provisions of this Act, the measure of indemnity shall be ascertained, as nearly as may be, in accordance with those provisions, in so far as applicable to the particular case.

(2) Nothing in the provisions of this Act relating to the measure of indemnity shall affect the rules relating to double insurance, or prohibit the insurer from disproving interest wholly or in part, or from showing that at the time of the loss the whole or any part of the subject-matter insured was not at risk under the policy.

76 Particular average warranties

(1) Where the subject-matter insured is warranted free from particular average, the assured cannot recover for a loss of part, other than a loss incurred by a general average sacrifice, unless the contract contained in the policy be apportionable; but, if the contract be apportionable, the assured may recover for a total loss of any apportionable part.

(2) Where the subject-matter insured is warranted free from particular average, either wholly or under a certain percentage, the insurer is nevertheless liable for salvage charges, and for particular charges and other expenses properly incurred pursuant to the provisions of the suing and labouring clause in order to avert a loss insured against.

(3) Unless the policy otherwise provides, where the subject-matter insured is warranted free from particular average under a specified percentage, a general average loss cannot be added to a particular average loss to make up the specified percentage.

(4) For the purpose of ascertaining whether the specified percentage has been reached, regard shall be had only to the actual loss suffered by the subject-matter insured. Particular charges and the expenses of and incidental to ascertaining and proving the loss must be excluded.

77 Successive losses

(1) Unless the policy otherwise provides, and subject to the provisions of this Act, the insurer is liable for successive losses, even though the total amount of such losses may exceed the sum insured.

(2) Where, under the same policy, a partial loss, which has not been repaired or otherwise made good, is followed by a total loss, the assured can only recover in respect of the total loss:

Provided that nothing in this section shall affect the liability of the insurer under the suing and labouring clause.

78   Suing and labouring clause

(1)   Where the policy contains a suing and labouring clause, the engagement thereby entered into is deemed to be supplementary to the contract of insurance, and the assured may recover from the insurer any expenses properly incurred pursuant to the clause, notwithstanding that the insurer may have paid for a total loss, or that the subject-matter may have been warranted free from particular average, either wholly or under a certain percentage.

(2)   General average losses and contributions and salvage charges, as defined by this Act, are not recoverable under the suing and labouring clause.

(3)   Expenses incurred for the purpose of averting or diminishing any loss not covered by the policy are not recoverable under the suing and labouring clause.

(4)   It is the duty of the assured and his agents, in all cases, to take such measures as may be reasonable for the purpose of averting or minimising a loss.

RIGHTS OF INSURER ON PAYMENT

79   Right of subrogation

(1)   Where the insurer pays for a total loss, either of the whole, or in the case of goods of any apportionable part, of the subject-matter insured, he thereupon becomes entitled to take over the interest of the assured in whatever may remain of the subject-matter so paid for, and he is thereby subrogated to all the rights and remedies of the assured in and in respect of that subject-matter as from the time of the casualty causing the loss.

(2)   Subject to the foregoing provisions, where the insurer pays for a partial loss, he acquires no title to the subject-matter insured, or such part of it as may remain, but he is thereupon subrogated to all rights and remedies of the assured in and in respect of the subject-matter insured as from the time of the casualty causing the loss, in so far as the assured has been indemnified, according to this Act, by such payment for the loss.

80   Right of contribution

(1)   Where the assured is over-insured by double insurance, each insurer is bound, as between himself and the other insurers, to contribute rateably to the loss in proportion to the amount for which he is liable under his contract.

(2)   If any insurer pays more than his proportion of the loss, he is entitled to maintain an action for contribution against the other insurers, and is entitled to the like remedies as a surety who has paid more than his proportion of the debt.

81   Effect of under insurance

Where the assured is insured for an amount less than the insurable value or, in the case of a valued policy, for an amount less than the policy valuation, he is deemed to be his own insurer in respect of the uninsured balance.

RETURN OF PREMIUM

82   Enforcement of return

Where the premium or a proportionate part thereof is, by this Act, declared to be returnable,—

(a)   If already paid, it may be recovered by the assured from the insurer; and

(b)   If unpaid, it may be retained by the assured or his agent.

83   Return by agreement

Where the policy contains a stipulation for the return of the premium, or a proportionate part thereof, on the happening of a certain event, and that event happens, the premium, or, as the case may be, the proportionate part thereof, is thereupon returnable to the assured.

84   Return for failure of consideration

(1)   Where the consideration for the payment of the premium totally fails, and there has been no fraud or illegality on the part of the assured or his agents, the premium is thereupon returnable to the assured.

(2)   Where the consideration for the payment of the premium is apportionable and there is a total failure of any apportionable part of the consideration, a proportionate part of the premium is, under the like conditions, thereupon returnable to the assured.

(3)   In particular—

    (a)   Where the policy is void, or is avoided by the insurer as from the commencement of the risk, the premium is returnable, provided that there has been no fraud or illegality on the part of the assured; but if the risk is not apportionable, and has once attached, the premium is not returnable;

    (b)   Where the subject-matter insured, or part thereof, has never been imperilled, the premium, or, as the case may be, a proportionate part thereof, is returnable:

    (c)   Provided that where the subject-matter has been insured 'lost or not lost' and has arrived in safety at the time when the contract is concluded, the premium is not returnable unless, at such time, the insurer knew of the safe arrival.

    (d)   Where the assured has no insurable interest throughout the currency of the risk, the premium is returnable, provided that this rule does not apply to a policy effected by way of gaming or wagering;

    (e)   Where the assured has a defeasible interest which is terminated during the currency of the risk, the premium is not returnable;

    (f)   Where the assured has over-insured under an unvalued policy, a proportionate part of the premium is returnable;

Subject to the foregoing provisions, where the assured has over-insured by double insurance, a proportionate part of the several premiums is returnable:

Provided that, if the policies are effected at different times, and any earlier policy has at any time borne the entire risk, or if a claim has been paid on the policy in respect of the full sum insured thereby, no premium is returnable in respect of that policy, and when the double insurance is effected knowingly by the assured no premium is returnable.

MUTUAL INSURANCE

85   Modification of Act in case of mutual insurance

(1)   Where two or more persons mutually agree to insure each other against marine losses there is said to be a mutual insurance.

(2)   The provisions of this Act relating to the premium do not apply to mutual insurance, but a guarantee, or such other arrangement as may be agreed upon, may be substituted for the premium.

(3)   The provisions of this Act, in so far as they may be modified by the agreement of the parties, may in the case of mutual insurance be modified by the terms of the policies issued by the association, or by the rules and regulations of the association.

(4)   Subject to the exceptions mentioned in this section, the provisions of this Act apply to a mutual insurance.

SUPPLEMENTAL

86 Ratification by assured

Where a contract of marine insurance is in good faith effected by one person on behalf of another, the person on whose behalf it is effected may ratify the contract even after he is aware of a loss.

87 Implied obligations varied by agreement or usage

(1) Where any right, duty, or liability would arise under a contract of marine insurance by implication of law, it may be negatived or varied by express agreement, or by usage, if the usage be such as to bind both parties to the contract.

(2) The provisions of this section extend to any right, duty, or liability declared by this Act which may be lawfully modified by agreement.

88 Reasonable time, etc, a question of fact

Where by this Act any reference is made to reasonable time, reasonable premium, or reasonable diligence, the question what is reasonable is a question of fact.

89 Slip as evidence

Where there is a duly stamped policy, reference may be made, as heretofore, to the slip or covering note, in any legal proceeding.

90 Interpretation of terms

In this Act, unless the context or subject matter otherwise requires,—

'Action' includes counterclaim and set off;

'Freight' includes the profit derivable by a shipowner from the employment of his ship to carry his own goods or moveables, as well as freight payable by a third party, but does not include passage money;

'Moveables' means any moveable tangible property, other than the ship, and includes money, valuable securities, and other documents;

'Policy' means a marine policy.

91 Savings

(1) Nothing in this Act, or in any repeal effected thereby, shall affect—

(a) The provisions of the Stamp Act 1891, or any enactment for the time being in force relating to the revenue;

(b) The provisions of the Companies Act 1862, or any enactment amending or substituted for the same;

(c) The provisions of any statute not expressly repealed by this Act.

(2) The rules of the common law including the law merchant, save in so far as they are inconsistent with the express provisions of this Act, shall continue to apply to contracts of marine insurance.

92 Repeals

The enactments mentioned in the Second Schedule to this Act are hereby repealed to the extent specified in that schedule.

93 Commencement

This Act shall come into operation on the first day of January one thousand nine hundred and seven.

94 Short title

This Act may be cited as the Marine Insurance Act 1906.

SCHEDULE 1 (s 30)

The SG Form

Form of policy

BE IT KNOWN THAT .... as well in .... own name as for and in the name and names of all and every other person or persons to whom the same doth, may, or shall appertain, in part or in all doth make assurance and cause .... and them, and every one of them, to be insured lost or not lost, at and from ....

Upon any kind of goods and merchandise, and also upon the body, tackle, apparel, ordnance, munition, artillery, boat, and other furniture, of and in the good ship or vessel called the .... whereof is master under God, for this present voyage, ... or whosoever else shall go for master in the said ship, or by whatsoever other name or names the said ship, or the master thereof, is or shall be named or called; beginning the adventure upon the said goods and merchandises from the loading thereof aboard the said ship.

upon the said ship, etc.

and so shall continue and endure, during her abode there, upon the said ship, etc.

And further, until the said ship, with all her ordnance, tackle, apparel, etc., and goods and merchandises whatsoever shall be arrived at ....

upon the said ship, etc., until she hath moored at anchor twenty-four hours in good safety; and upon the goods and merchandises, until the same be there discharged and safely landed. And it shall be lawful for the said ship, etc., in this voyage to proceed and sail to and touch and stay at any ports or places whatsoever.

without prejudice to this insurance. The said ship, etc., goods and merchandises, etc., for so much as concerns the assured by agreement between the assured and assurers in this policy, are and shall be valued at ....

Touching the adventures and perils which we the assurers are contented to bear and do take upon us in this voyage: they are of the seas, men of war, fire, enemies, pirates, rovers, thieves, jettisons, letters of mart and countermart, surprisals, takings at sea, arrests, restraints, and detainments of all kings, princes, and people, of what nation, condition, or quality soever, barratry of the master and mariners, and of all other perils, losses, and misfortunes, that have or shall come to the hurt, detriment, or damage of the said goods and merchandises, and ship, etc., or any part thereof. And in case of any loss or misfortune it shall be lawful to the assured, their factors, servants and assigns, to sue, labour, and travel for, in and about the defence, safeguards, and recovery of the said goods and merchandises, and ship, etc, or any part thereof, without prejudice to this insurance; to the charges whereof we, the assurers, will contribute each one according to the rate and quantity of his sum herein assured. And it is especially declared and agreed that no acts of the insurer or insured in recovering, saving, or preserving the property insured shall be considered as a waiver, or acceptance of abandonment. And it is agreed by us, the insurers, that this writing or policy of assurance shall be of as much force and effect as the surest writing or policy of assurance heretofore made in Lombard Street, or in the Royal Exchange, or elsewhere in London. And so we, the assurers, are contented, and do hereby promise and bind ourselves, each one for his own part, our heirs, executors, and goods to the assured, their executors, administrators, and assigns, for the true performance of the premises, confessing ourselves paid the consideration due unto us for this assurance by the assured, at and after the rate of ....

IN WITNESS whereof we, the assurers, have subscribed our names and sums assured in London.

NB—Corn, fish, salt, fruit, flour, and seed are warranted free from average, unless general, or the ship be stranded—sugar, tobacco, hemp, flax, hides and skins are warranted free from average, under five pounds per cent., and all other goods, also the ship and freight, are warranted free from average, under three pounds per cent. unless general, or the ship be stranded.

Rules for construction of policy

The following are the rules referred to by this Act for the construction of a policy in the above or other like form, where the context does not otherwise require:—

1   Lost or not lost

Where the subject-matter is insured 'lost or not lost,' and the loss has occurred before the contract is concluded, the risk attaches, unless at such time the assured was aware of the loss, and the insurer was not.

2   From

Where the subject-matter is insured 'from' a particular place, the risk does not attach until the ship starts on the voyage insured.

3   At and from [ship]

(a)   Where a ship is insured 'at and from' a particular place, and she is at that place in good safety when the contract is concluded, the risk attaches immediately.

(b)   If she be not at that place when the contract is concluded, the risk attaches as soon as she arrives there in good safety, and, unless the policy otherwise provides, it is immaterial that she is covered by another policy for a specified time after arrival.

(c)   Where chartered freight is insured 'at and from' a particular place, and the ship is at that place in good safety when the contract is concluded the risk attaches immediately. If she be not there when the contract is concluded, the risk attaches as soon as she arrives there in good safety.

(d)   Where freight, other than chartered freight, is payable without special conditions and is insured 'at and from' a particular place, the risk attaches *pro rata* as the goods or merchandise are shipped; provided that if there be cargo in readiness which belongs to the shipowner, or which some other person has contracted with him to ship, the risk attaches as soon as the ship is ready to receive such cargo.

4   From the loading thereof

Where goods or other moveables are insured 'from the loading thereof,' the risk does not attach until such goods or moveables are actually on board, and the insurer is not liable for them while in transit from the shore to ship.

5   Safely landed

Where the risk on goods or other moveables continues until they are 'safely landed,' they must be landed in the customary manner and within a reasonable time after arrival at the port of discharge, and if they are not so landed the risk ceases.

6   Touch and stay

In the absence of any further licence or usage, the liberty to touch and stay 'at any port or place whatsoever' does not authorise the ship to depart from the course of her voyage from the port of departure to the port of destination.

7   Perils of the seas

The term 'perils of the seas' refers only to fortuitous accidents or casualties of the seas. It does not include the ordinary action of the winds and waves.

8   Pirates

The term 'pirates' includes passengers who mutiny and rioters who attack the ship from the shore.

9   Thieves

The term 'thieves' does not cover clandestine theft or a theft committed by any one of the ship's company, whether crew or passengers.

10   Restraint of princes

The term 'arrests, etc. of kings, princes, and people' refers to political executive acts, and does not include a loss caused by riot or by ordinary judicial process.

11   Barratry

The term 'barratry' includes every wrongful act wilfully committed by the master or crew to the prejudice of the owner, or, as the case may be, the charterer.

12   All other perils

The term 'all other perils' includes only perils similar in kind to the perils specifically mentioned in the policy.

13   Average unless general

The term 'average unless general' means a partial loss of the subject-matter insured other than a general average loss, and does not include 'particular charges.'

14   Stranded

Where the ship has stranded, the insurer is liable for the excepted losses, although the loss is not attributable to the stranding, provided that when the stranding takes place the risk has attached and, if the policy be on goods, that the damaged goods are on board.

15   Ship

The term 'ship' includes the hull, materials and outfit, stores and provisions for the officers and crew, and, in the case of vessels engaged in a special trade, the ordinary fittings requisite for the trade, and also, in the case of a steamship, the machinery, boilers, and coals and engine stores, if owned by the assured.

16   Freight

The term 'freight' includes the profit derivable by a shipowner from the employment of his ship to carry his own goods or moveables, as well as freight payable by a third party, but does not include passage money.

17   Goods

The term 'goods' means goods in the nature of merchandise, and does not include personal effects or provisions and stores for use on board.

In the absence of any usage to the contrary, deck cargo and living animals must be insured specifically, and not under the general denomination of goods.

SCHEDULE 2 (s 92)

Enactments Repealed

Session and Chapter	Title or Short Title	Extent of Repeal
19 Geo 2 c 37	An Act to regulate insurance on ships belonging to the subjects of Great Britain, and on merchandizes or effects laden thereon.	The whole Act.
28 Geo 3 c 56	An Act to repeal an Act made in the twenty-fifth year of the reign of his present Majesty, intituled 'An Act for regulating Insurances on Ships, and on goods, merchandizes, or effects,' and for substituting other provisions for the like purpose in lieu thereof.	The whole Act so far as it relates to marine insurance.
31 & 32 Vict c 86	The Policies of Marine Assurance Act 1868	The whole Act.

APPENDIX 2

INSTITUTE TIME CLAUSES HULLS
(1 November 1995)

(for use only with the current mar policy form)
This insurance is subject to English law and practice

1   NAVIGATION

1.1   The Vessel is covered subject to the provisions of this insurance at all times and has leave to sail or navigate with or without pilots, to go on trial trips and to assist and tow vessels or craft in distress, but it is warranted that the Vessel shall not be towed, except as is customary or to the first safe port or place when in need of assistance, or undertake towage or salvage services under a contract previously arranged by the Assured and/or Owners and/or Managers and/or Charterers. This Clause 1.1 shall not exclude customary towage in connection with loading and discharging.

1.2   This insurance shall not be prejudiced by reason of the Assured entering into any contract with pilots or for customary towage which limits or exempts the liability of the pilots and/or tugs and/or towboats and/or their owners when the Assured or their agents accept or are compelled to accept such contracts in accordance with established local law or practice.

1.3   The practice of engaging helicopters for the transportation of personnel, supplies and equipment to and/or from the Vessel shall not prejudice this insurance.

1.4   In the event of the Vessel being employed in trading operations which entail cargo loading or discharging at sea from or into another vessel (not being a harbour or inshore craft) no claim shall be recoverable under this insurance for loss of or damage to the Vessel or liability to any other vessel arising from such loading or discharging operations, including whilst approaching, lying alongside and leaving, unless previous notice that the Vessel is to be employed in such operations has been given to the Underwriters and any amended terms of cover and any additional premium required by them have been agreed.

1.5   In the event of the Vessel sailing (with or without cargo) with an intention of being (a) broken up, or (b) sold for breaking up, any claim for loss of or damage to the Vessel occurring subsequent to such sailing shall be limited to the market value of the Vessel as scrap at the time when the loss or damage is sustained unless previous notice has been given to the Underwriters and any amendments to the terms of cover, insured value and premium required by them have been agreed. Nothing in this Clause 1.5 shall affect claims under Clauses 8 and/or 10.

2   CONTINUATION

Should the Vessel at the expiration of this insurance be at sea and in distress or missing, she shall, provided notice be given to the Underwriters prior to the expiration of this insurance, be held covered until arrival at the next port in good safety, or if in port and in distress until the Vessel is made safe, at a pro rata monthly premium.

3   BREACH OF WARRANTY

Held covered in case of any breach of warranty as to cargo, trade, locality, towage, salvage services or date of sailing provided notice be given to the Underwriters immediately after receipt of advices and any amended terms of cover and any additional premium required by them be agreed.

4   CLASSIFICATION

4.1   It is the duty of the Assured, Owners and Managers at the inception of and throughout the period of this insurance to ensure that

  4.1.1   the Vessel is classed with a Classification Society agreed by the Underwriters and that her class within that Society is maintained,

4.1.2 any recommendations requirements or restrictions imposed by the Vessel's Classification Society which relate to the Vessel's seaworthiness or to her maintenance in a seaworthy condition are complied with by the dates required by that Society.

4.2 In the event of any breach of the duties set out in Clause 4.1 above, unless the Underwriters agree to the contrary in writing, they will be discharged from liability under this insurance as from the date of the breach provided that if the Vessel is at sea at such date the Underwriters' discharge from liability is deferred until arrival at her next port.

4.3 Any incident condition or damage in respect of which the Vessel's Classification Society might make recommendations as to repairs or other action to be taken by the Assured, Owners or Managers must be promptly reported to the Classification Society.

4.4 Should the Underwriters wish to approach the Classification Society directly for information and/or documents, the Assured will provide the necessary authorization.

5   TERMINATION

This Clause 5 shall prevail notwithstanding any provision whether written typed or printed in this insurance inconsistent therewith.

Unless the Underwriters agree to the contrary in writing, this insurance shall terminate automatically at the time of

5.1 change of the Classification Society of the Vessel, or change, suspension, discontinuance, withdrawal or expiry of her Class therein, or any of the Classification Society's periodic surveys becoming overdue unless an extension of time for such survey be agreed by the Classification Society, provided that if the Vessel is at sea such automatic termination shall be deferred until arrival at her next port. However where such change, suspension, discontinuance or withdrawal of her Class or where a periodic survey becoming overdue has resulted from loss or damage covered by Clause 6 of this insurance or which would be covered by an insurance of the Vessel subject to current Institute War and Strikes Clauses Hulls – Time such automatic termination shall only operate should the Vessel sail from her next port without the prior approval of the Classification Society or in the case of a periodic survey becoming overdue without the Classification Society having agreed an extension of time for such survey,

5.2 any change, voluntary or otherwise, in the ownership or flag, transfer to new management, or charter on a bareboat basis or requisition for title or use of the Vessel, provided that, if the Vessel has cargo on board and has already sailed from her loading port or is at sea in ballast, such automatic termination shall if required be deferred, whilst the Vessel continues her planned voyage, until arrival at final port of discharge if with cargo or at port of destination if in ballast. However, in the event of requisition for title or use without the prior execution of a written agreement by the Assured, such automatic termination shall occur fifteen days after such requisition whether the Vessel is at sea or in port.

A pro rata daily net return of premium shall be made provided that a total loss of the Vessel, whether by insured perils or otherwise, has not occurred during the period covered by this insurance or any extension thereof.

6   PERILS

6.1 This insurance covers loss of or damage to the subject matter insured caused by

6.1.1 perils of the seas rivers lakes or other navigable waters

6.1.2 fire, explosion

6.1.3 violent theft by persons from outside the Vessel

6.1.4 jettison

6.1.5 piracy

6.1.6 contact with land conveyance, dock or harbour equipment or installation

6.1.7 earthquake volcanic eruption or lightning

6.1.8 accidents in loading discharging or shifting cargo or fuel.

6.2 This insurance covers loss of or damage to the subject matter insured caused by

6.2.1   bursting of boilers breakage of shafts or any latent defect in the machinery or hull

6.2.2   negligence of Master Officers Crew or Pilots

6.2.3   negligence of repairers or charterers provided such repairers or charterers are not an Assured hereunder

6.2.4   barratry of Master Officers or Crew

6.2.5   contact with aircraft, helicopters or similar objects, or objects falling therefrom

provided that such loss or damage has not resulted from want of due diligence by the Assured, Owners, Managers or Superintendents or any of their onshore management.

6.3   Masters Officers Crew or Pilots not to be considered Owners within the meaning of this Clause 6 should they hold shares in the Vessel.

7   POLLUTION HAZARD

This insurance covers loss of or damage to the Vessel caused by any governmental authority acting under the powers vested in it to prevent or mitigate a pollution hazard or damage to the environment, or threat thereof, resulting directly from damage to the Vessel for which the Underwriters are liable under this insurance, provided that such act of governmental authority has not resulted from want of due diligence by the Assured, Owners or Managers to prevent or mitigate such hazard or damage, or threat thereof. Master Officers Crew or Pilots not to be considered Owners within the meaning of this Clause 7 should they hold shares in the Vessel.

8   3/4ths COLLISION LIABILITY

8.1   The Underwriters agree to indemnify the Assured for three-fourths of any sum or sums paid by the Assured to any other person or persons by reason of the Assured becoming legally liable by way of damages for

8.1.1   loss of or damage to any other vessel or property on any other vessel

8.1.2   delay to or loss of use of any such other vessel or property thereon

8.1.3   general average of, salvage of, or salvage under contract of, any such other vessel or property thereon,

where such payment by the Assured is in consequence of the Vessel hereby insured coming into collision with any other vessel.

8.2   The indemnity provided by this Clause 8 shall be in addition to the indemnity provided by the other terms and conditions of this insurance and shall be subject to the following provisions:

8.2.1   where the insured Vessel is in collision with another vessel and both vessels are to blame then, unless the liability of one or both vessels becomes limited by law, the indemnity under this Clause 8 shall be calculated on the principle of cross-liabilities as if the respective Owners had been compelled to pay to each other such proportion of each other's damages as may have been properly allowed in ascertaining the balance or sum payable by or to the Assured in consequence of the collision,

8.2.2   in no case shall the Underwriters' total liability under Clauses 8.1 and 8.2 exceed their proportionate part of three-fourths of the insured value of the Vessel hereby insured in respect of any one collision.

8.3   The Underwriters will also pay three-fourths of the legal costs incurred by the Assured or which the Assured may be compelled to pay in contesting liability or taking proceedings to limit liability, with the prior written consent of the Underwriters.

EXCLUSIONS

8.4   Provided always that this Clause 8 shall in no case extend to any sum which the Assured shall pay for or in respect of

8.4.1   removal or disposal of obstructions, wrecks, cargoes or any other thing whatsoever

8.4.2   any real or personal property or thing whatsoever except other vessels or property on other vessels

8.4.3 the cargo or other property on, or the engagements of, the insured Vessel

8.4.4 loss of life, personal injury or illness

8.4.5 pollution or contamination, or threat thereof, of any real or personal property or thing whatsoever (except other vessels with which the insured Vessel is in collision or property on such other vessels) or damage to the environment, or threat thereof, save that this exclusion shall not extend to any sum which the Assured shall pay for or in respect of salvage remuneration in which the skill and efforts of the salvors in preventing or minimising damage to the environment as is referred to in Article 13 paragraph l(b) of the International Convention on Salvage, 1989 have been taken into account.

9 SISTERSHIP

Should the Vessel hereby insured come into collision with or receive salvage services from another vessel belonging wholly or in part to the same Owners or under the same management, the Assured shall have the same rights under this insurance as they would have were the other vessel entirely the property of Owners not interested in the Vessel hereby insured: but in such cases the liability for the collision or the amount payable for the services rendered shall be referred to a sole arbitrator to be agreed upon between the Underwriters and the Assured.

10 GENERAL AVERAGE AND SALVAGE

10.1 This insurance covers the Vessel's proportion of salvage, salvage charges and/or general average, reduced in respect of any under-insurance. but in case of general average sacrifice of the Vessel the Assured may recover in respect of the whole loss without first enforcing their right of contribution from other parties.

10.2 Adjustment to be according to the law and practice obtaining at the place where the adventure ends, as if the contract of affreightment contained no special terms upon the subject; but where the contract of affreightment so provides the adjustment shall be according to the York-Antwerp Rules.

10.3 When the Vessel sails in ballast, not under charter, the provisions of the York-Antwerp Rules 1994 (excluding Rules XI(d), XX and XXI) shall be applicable, and the voyage for this purpose shall be deemed to continue from the port or place of departure until the arrival of the Vessel at the first port or place thereafter other than a port or place of refuge or a port or place of call for bunkering only. If at any such intermediate port or place there is an abandonment of the adventure originally contemplated the voyage shall thereupon be deemed to be terminated.

10.4 No claim under this Clause 10 shall in any case be allowed where the loss was not incurred to avoid or in connection with the avoidance of a peril insured against.

10.5 No claim under this Clause 10 shall in any case be allowed for or in respect of

10.5.1 special compensation payable to a salvor under Article 14 of the International Convention on Salvage, 1989 or under any other provision in any statute, rule, law or contract which is similar in substance

10.5.2 expenses or liabilities incurred in respect of damage to the environment, or the threat of such damage, or as a consequence of the escape or release of pollutant substances from the Vessel, or the threat of such escape or release.

10.6 Clause 10.5 shall not however exclude any sum which the Assured shall pay to salvors for or in respect of salvage remuneration in which the skill and efforts of the salvors in preventing or minimising damage to the environment as is referred to in Article 13, paragraph 1(b) of the International Convention on Salvage, 1989 have been taken into account.

11 DUTY OF ASSURED (SUE AND LABOUR)

11.1 In case of any loss or misfortune it is the duty of the Assured and their servants and agents to take such measures as may be reasonable for the purpose of averting or minimising a loss which would be recoverable under this insurance.

11.2 Subject to the provisions below and to Clause 12 the Underwriters will contribute to charges properly and reasonably incurred by the Assured their servants or agents for such measures. General average, salvage charges (except as provided for in Clause 11.5), special compensation and expenses as referred to in Clause 10.5 and collision defence or attack costs are not recoverable under this Clause 11.

11.3 Measures taken by the Assured or the Underwriters with the object of saving, protecting or recovering the subject matter insured shall not be considered as a waiver or acceptance of abandonment or otherwise prejudice the rights of either party.

11.4 When expenses are incurred pursuant to this Clause 11 the liability under this insurance shall not exceed the proportion of such expenses that the amount insured hereunder bears to the value of the Vessel as stated herein or to the sound value of the Vessel at the time of the occurrence giving rise to the expenditure if the sound value exceeds that value. Where the Underwriters have admitted a claim for total loss and property insured by this insurance is saved, the foregoing provisions shall not apply unless the expenses of suing and labouring exceed the value of such property saved and then shall apply only to the amount of the expenses which is in excess of such value.

11.5 When a claim for total loss of the Vessel is admitted under this insurance and expenses have been reasonably incurred in saving or attempting to save the Vessel and other property and there are no proceeds, or the expenses exceed the proceeds, then this insurance shall bear its pro rata share of such proportion of the expenses, or of the expenses in excess of the proceeds, as the case may be, as may reasonably be regarded as having been incurred in respect of the Vessel, excluding all special compensation and expenses as referred to in Clause 10.5; but if the Vessel be insured for less than its sound value at the time of the occurrence giving rise to the expenditure, the amount recoverable under this clause shall be reduced in proportion to the under-insurance.

11.6 The sum recoverable under this Clause 11 shall be in addition to the loss otherwise recoverable under this insurance but shall in no circumstances exceed the amount insured under this insurance in respect of the Vessel.

12 DEDUCTIBLE

12.1 No claim arising from a peril insured against shall be payable under this insurance unless the aggregate of all such claims arising out of each separate accident or occurrence (including claims under Clauses 8, 10 and 11) exceeds the deductible amount agreed in which case this sum shall be deducted. Nevertheless the expense of sighting the bottom after stranding, if reasonably incurred specially for that purpose, shall be paid even if no damage be found. This Clause 12.1 shall not apply to a claim for total or constructive total loss of the Vessel or, in the event of such a claim, to any associated claim under Clause 11 arising from the same accident or occurrence.

12.2 Claims for damage by heavy weather occurring during a single sea passage between two successive ports shall be treated as being due to one accident. In the case of such heavy weather extending over a period not wholly covered by this insurance the deductible to be applied to the claim recoverable hereunder shall be the proportion of the above deductible that the number of days of such heavy weather falling within the period of this insurance bears to the number of days of heavy weather during the single sea passage. The expression 'heavy weather' in this Clause 12.2 shall be deemed to include contact with floating ice.

12.3 Excluding any interest comprised therein. recoveries against any claim which is subject to the above deductible shall be credited to the Underwriters in full to the extent of the sum by which the aggregate of the claim unreduced by any recoveries exceeds the above deductible.

12.4 Interest comprised in recoveries shall be apportioned between the Assured and the Underwriters, taking into account the sums paid by the Underwriters and the dates when such payments were made, notwithstanding that by the addition of interest the Underwriters may receive a larger sum than they have paid.

13 NOTICE OF CLAIM AND TENDERS

13.1 In the event of accident whereby loss or damage may result in a claim under this insurance, notice must be given to the Underwriters promptly after the date on which the Assured, Owners or Managers become or should have become aware of the loss or damage and prior to survey so that a surveyor may be appointed if the Underwriters so desire. If notice is not given to the Underwriters within twelve months of that date unless the Underwriters agree to the contrary in writing, the Underwriters will be automatically discharged from liability for any claim under this insurance in respect of or arising out of such accident or the loss or damage.

13.2 The Underwriters shall be entitled to decide the port to which the Vessel shall proceed for docking or repair (the actual additional expense of the voyage arising from compliance with the Underwriters' requirements being refunded to the Assured) and shall have a right of veto concerning a place of repair or a repairing firm.

13.3 The Underwriters may also take tenders or may require further tenders to be taken for the repair of the Vessel, Where such a tender has been taken and a tender is accepted with the approval of the Underwriters, an allowance shall be made at the rate of 30% per annum on the insured value for time lost between the despatch of the invitations to tender required by the Underwriters and the acceptance of a tender to the extent that such time is lost solely as the result of tenders having been taken and provided that the tender is accepted without delay after receipt of the Underwriters' approval. Due credit shall be given against the allowance as above for any amounts recovered in respect of fuel and stores and wages and maintenance of the Master Officers and Crew or any member thereof, including amounts allowed in general average, and for any amounts recovered from third parties in respect of damages for detention and/or loss of profit and/or running expenses, for the period covered by the tender allowance or any part thereof. Where a part of the cost of the repair of damage other than a fixed deductible is not recoverable from the Underwriters the allowance shall be reduced by a similar proportion.

13.4 In the event of failure by the Assured to comply with the conditions of Clauses 13.2 and/or 13.3 a deduction of 15% shall be made from the amount of the ascertained claim.

14 NEW FOR OLD

Claims payable without deduction new for old.

15 BOTTOM TREATMENT

In no case shall a claim be allowed in respect of scraping gritblasting and/or other surface preparation or painting of the Vessel's bottom except that

15.1 gritblasting and/or other surface preparation of new bottom plates ashore and supplying and applying any 'shop' primer thereto,

15.2 gritblasting and/or other surface preparation of: the butts or area of plating immediately adjacent to any renewed or refitted plating damaged during the course of welding and/or repairs, areas of plating damaged during the course of fairing, either in place or ashore,

15.3 supplying and applying the first coat of primer/anti-corrosive to those particular areas mentioned in 15.1 and 15.2 above,

shall be allowed as part of the reasonable cost of repairs in respect of bottom plating damaged by an insured peril.

16 WAGES AND MAINTENANCE

No claim shall be allowed, other than in general average, for wages and maintenance of the Master Officers and Crew or any member thereof, except when incurred solely for the necessary removal of the Vessel from one port to another for the repair of damage covered by the Underwriters, or for trial trips for such repairs, and then only for such wages and maintenance as are incurred whilst the Vessel is under way.

17 AGENCY COMMISSION

In no case shall any sum be allowed under this insurance either by way of remuneration of the Assured for time and trouble taken to obtain and supply information or documents or in respect of the commission or charges of any manager, agent, managing or agency company or the like, appointed by or on behalf of the Assured to perform such services.

18 UNREPAIRED DAMAGE

18.1 The measure of indemnity in respect of claims for unrepaired damage shall be the reasonable depreciation in the market value of the Vessel at the time this insurance terminates arising from such unrepaired damage, but not exceeding the reasonable cost of repairs.

18.2 In no case shall the Underwriters be liable for unrepaired damage in the event of a subsequent total loss (whether or not covered under this insurance) sustained during the period covered by this insurance or any extension thereof.

18.3 The Underwriters shall not be liable in respect of unrepaired damage for more than the insured value at the time this insurance terminates.

19 CONSTRUCTIVE TOTAL LOSS

19.1 In ascertaining whether the Vessel is a constructive total loss, the insured value shall be taken as the repaired value and nothing in respect of the damaged or break-up value of the Vessel or wreck shall be taken into account.

19.2 No claim for constructive total loss based upon the cost of recovery and/or repair of the Vessel shall be recoverable hereunder unless such cost would exceed the insured value. In making this determination, only the cost relating to a single accident or sequence of damages arising from the same accident shall be taken into account.

20 FREIGHT WAIVER

In the event of total or constructive total loss no claim to be made by the Underwriters for freight whether notice of abandonment has been given or not.

21 ASSIGNMENT

No assignment of or interest in this insurance or in any moneys which may be or become payable thereunder is to be binding on or recognised by the Underwriters unless a dated notice of such assignment or interest signed by the Assured, and by the assignor in the case of subsequent assignment, is endorsed on the Policy and the Policy with such endorsement is produced before payment of any claim or return of premium thereunder.

22 DISBURSEMENTS WARRANTY

22.1 Additional insurances as follows are permitted:

22.1.1 *Disbursements, Managers' Commissions, Profits or Excess or Increased Value of Hull and Machinery.* A sum not exceeding 25% of the value stated herein.

22.1.2 *Freight, Chartered Freight or Anticipated Freight, insured for time.* A sum not exceeding 25% of the value as stated herein less any sum insured, however described, under 22.1.1.

22.1.3 *Freight or Hire, under contracts for voyage.* A sum not exceeding the gross freight or hire for the current cargo passage and next succeeding cargo passage (such insurance to include, if required, a preliminary and an intermediate ballast passage) plus the charges of insurance. In the case of a voyage charter where payment is made on a time basis, the sum permitted for insurance shall be calculated on the estimated duration of the voyage, subject to the limitation of two cargo passages as laid down herein. Any sum insured under 22.1.2 to be taken into account and only the excess thereof may be insured, which excess shall be reduced as the freight or hire is advanced or earned by the gross amount so advanced or earned.

22.1.4 *Anticipated Freight if the Vessel sails in ballast and not under Charter.* A sum not exceeding the anticipated gross freight on next cargo passage, such sum to be reasonably estimated on the basis of the current rate of freight at time of insurance plus the charges of insurance. Any sum insured under 22.1.2 to be taken into account and only the excess thereof may be insured.

22.1.5 *Time Charter Hire or Charter Hire for Series of Voyages.* A sum not exceeding 50% of the gross hire which is to be earned under the charter in a period not exceeding 18 months. Any sum insured under 22.1.2 to be taken into account and only the excess thereof may be insured, which excess shall be reduced as the hire is advanced or earned under the charter by 50% of the gross amount so advanced or earned but the sum insured need not be reduced while the total of the sums insured under 22.1.2 and 22.1.5 does not exceed 50% of the gross hire still to be earned under the charter. An insurance under this Section may begin on the signing of the charter.

22.1.6 *Premiums.* A sum not exceeding the actual premiums of all interests insured for a period not exceeding 12 months (excluding premiums insured under the foregoing sections but including, if required, the premium or estimated calls on any Club or War etc. Risk insurance) reducing pro rata monthly.

22.1.7 *Returns of Premium.* A sum not exceeding the actual returns which arc allowable under any insurance but which would not be recoverable thereunder in the event of a total loss of the Vessel whether by insured perils or otherwise.

22.1.8 *Insurance irrespective of amount against:* Any risks excluded by Clauses 24, 25, 26 and 27 below.

22.2 Warranted that no insurance on any interests enumerated in the foregoing 22.1.1 to 22.1.7 in excess of the amounts permitted therein and no other insurance which includes total loss of the Vessel P.P.I., F.I.A. or subject to any other like term, is or shall be effected to operate during the currency of this insurance by or for account of the Assured, Owners, Managers or Mortgagees. Provided always that a breach of this warranty shall not afford the Underwriters any defence to a claim by a Mortgagee who has accepted this insurance without knowledge of such breach.

23 RETURNS FOR LAY-UP AND CANCELLATION

23.1 To return as follows:

23.1.1 pro rata monthly net for each uncommenced month if this insurance be cancelled by agreement,

23.1.2 for each period of 30 consecutive days the Vessel may be laid up in a port or in a lay-up area provided such port or lay-up area is approved by the Underwriters

(a) .... per cent net not under repair

(b) .... per cent net under repair.

23.1.3 The Vessel shall not be considered to be under repair when work is undertaken in respect of ordinary wear and tear of the Vessel and/or following recommendations in the Vessel's Classification Society survey, but any repairs following loss of or damage to the Vessel or involving structural alterations, whether covered by this insurance or otherwise shall be considered as under repair.

23.1.4 If the Vessel is under repair during part only of a period for which a return is claimable, the return shall be calculated pro rata to the number of days under 23.1.2 (a) and (b) respectively.

23.2 PROVIDED ALWAYS THAT

23.2.1 a total loss of the Vessel, whether by insured perils or otherwise, has not occurred during the period covered by this insurance or any extension thereof

23.2.2 in no case shall a return be allowed when the Vessel is lying in exposed or unprotected waters, or in a port or lay-up area not approved by the Underwriters

23.2.3 loading or discharging operations or the presence of cargo on board shall not debar returns but no return shall be allowed for any period during which the Vessel is being used for the storage of cargo or for lightering purposes

23.2.4 in the event of any amendment of the annual rate, the above rates of return shall be adjusted accordingly

23.2.5 in the event of any return recoverable under this Clause 23 being based on 30 consecutive days which fall on successive insurances effected for the same Assured, this insurance shall only be liable for an amount calculated at pro rata of the period rates 23.1.2(a) and/or (b) above for the number of days which come within the period of this insurance and to which a return is actually applicable. Such overlapping period shall run, at the option of the Assured, either from the first day on which the Vessel is laid up or the first day of a period of 30 consecutive days as provided under 23.1.2(a) or (b) above.

The following clauses shall be paramount and shall override anything contained in this insurance inconsistent therewith.

24 WAR EXCLUSION

In no case shall this insurance cover loss damage liability or expense caused by

24.1 war civil war revolution rebellion insurrection, or civil strife arising therefrom, or any hostile act by or against a belligerent power

24.2 capture seizure arrest restraint or detainment (barratry and piracy excepted), and the consequences thereof or any attempt thereat

24.3 derelict mines torpedoes bombs or other derelict weapons of war.

25 STRIKES EXCLUSION

In no case shall this insurance cover loss damage liability or expense caused by

25.1 strikers, locked-out workmen, or persons taking part in labour disturbances, riots or civil commotions

25.2 any terrorist or any person acting from a political motive.

26 MALICIOUS ACTS EXCLUSION

In no case shall this insurance cover loss damage liability or expense arising from

26.1 the detonation of an explosive

26.2 any weapon of war

and caused by any person acting maliciously or from a political motive.

27 RADIOACTIVE CONTAMINATION EXCLUSION CLAUSE

In no case shall this insurance cover loss damage liability or expense directly or indirectly caused by or contributed to by or arising from

27.1 ionising radiations from or contamination by radioactivity from any nuclear fuel or from any nuclear waste or from the combustion of nuclear fuel

27.2 the radioactive, toxic, explosive or other hazardous or contaminating properties of any nuclear installation, reactor or other nuclear assembly or nuclear component thereof

27.3 any weapon of war employing atomic or nuclear fission and/or fusion or other like reaction or radioactive force or matter.

APPENDIX 3

INSTITUTE VOYAGE CLAUSES HULLS
(1 November 1995)

(for use only with the current mar policy form)
This insurance is subject to English law and practice

1 NAVIGATION

1.1 The Vessel is covered subject to the provisions of this insurance at all times and has leave to sail or navigate with or without pilots, to go on trial trips and to assist and tow vessels or craft in distress, but it is warranted that the Vessel shall not be towed, except as is customary or to the first safe port or place when in need of assistance, or undertake towage or salvage services under a contract previously arranged by the Assured and/or Owners and/or Managers and/or Charterers. This Clause 1.1 shall not exclude customary towage in connection with loading and discharging.

1.2 This insurance shall not be prejudiced by reason of the Assured entering into any contract with pilots or for customary towage which limits or exempts the liability of the pilots and/or tugs and/or towboats and/or their owners when the Assured or their agents accept or are compelled to accept such contracts in accordance with established local law or practice.

1.3 The practice of engaging helicopters for the transportation of personnel, supplies and equipment to and/or from the Vessel shall not prejudice this insurance.

1.4 In the event of the Vessel being employed in trading operations which entail cargo loading or discharging at sea from or into another vessel (not being a harbour or inshore craft) no claim shall be recoverable under this insurance for loss of or damage to the Vessel or liability to any other vessel arising from such loading or discharging operations, including whilst approaching, lying alongside and leaving, unless previous notice that the Vessel is to be employed in such operations has been given to the Underwriters and any amended terms of cover and any additional premium required by them have been agreed.

2 CHANGE OF VOYAGE

Held covered in case of deviation or change of voyage or any breach of warranty as to towage or salvage services, provided notice be given to the Underwriters immediately after receipt of advices and any amended terms of cover and any additional premium required by them be agreed.

3 CLASSIFICATION

3.1 It is the duty of the Assured, Owners and Managers at the inception of and throughout the period of this insurance to ensure that

    3.1.1 the Vessel is classed with a Classification Society agreed by the Underwriters and that her class within that Society is maintained,

    3.1.2 any recommendations requirements or restrictions imposed by the Vessel's Classification Society which relate to the Vessel's seaworthiness or to her maintenance in a seaworthy condition are complied with by the dates required by that Society.

3.2 In the event of any breach of the duties set out in Clause 3.1 above, unless the Underwriters agree to the contrary in writing, they will be discharged from liability under this insurance as from the date of the breach provided that if the Vessel is at sea at such date the Underwriters' discharge from liability is deferred until arrival at her next port.

3.3 Any incident condition or damage in respect of which the Vessel's Classification Society might make recommendations as to repairs or other action to be taken by the Assured, Owners and Managers must be promptly reported to the Classification Society.

3.4 Should the Underwriters wish to approach the Classification Society directly for information and/or documents, the Assured will provide the necessary authorization.

4   PERILS

4.1   This insurance covers loss of or damage to the subject-matter insured caused by

     4.1.1   perils of the seas rivers lakes or other navigable waters

     4.1.2   fire, explosion

     4.1.3   violent theft by persons from outside the Vessel

     4.1.4   jettison

     4.1.5   piracy

     4.1.6   contact with land conveyance, dock or harbour equipment or installation

     4.1.7   earthquake volcanic eruption or lightning

     4.1.8   accidents in loading discharging or shifting cargo or fuel.

4.2   This insurance covers loss of or damage to the subject-matter insured caused by

     4.2.1   bursting of boilers breakage of shafts or any latent defect in the machinery or hull

     4.2.2   negligence of Master Officers Crew or Pilots

     4.2.3   negligence of repairers or charterers provided such repairers or charterers are not an Assured hereunder

     4.2.4   barratry of Master Officers or Crew

     4.2.5   contact with aircraft, helicopters or similar objects, or objects falling therefrom

     provided such loss or damage has not resulted from want of due diligence by the Assured, Owners, Managers or Superintendents or any of their onshore management.

4.3   Master Officers Crew or Pilots not to be considered Owners within the meaning of this Clause 4 should they hold shares in the Vessel.

5   POLLUTION HAZARD

This insurance covers loss of or damage to the Vessel caused by any governmental authority acting under the powers vested in it to prevent or mitigate a pollution hazard or damage to the environment, or threat thereof, resulting directly from damage to the Vessel for which the Underwriters are liable under this insurance, provided that such act of governmental authority has not resulted from want of due diligence by the Assured, Owners or Managers to prevent or mitigate such hazard or damage, or threat thereof. Master Officers Crew or Pilots not to be considered Owners within the meaning of this Clause 5 should they hold shares in the Vessel.

6   3/4ths COLLISION LIABILITY

6.1   The Underwriters agree to indemnify the Assured for three-fourths of any sum or sums paid by the Assured to any other person or persons by reason of the Assured becoming legally liable by way of damages for

     6.1.1   loss of or damage to any other vessel or property on any other vessel

     6.1.2   delay to or loss of use of any such other vessel or property thereon

     6.1.3   general average of, salvage of, or salvage under contract of, any such other vessel or property thereon, where such payment by the Assured is in consequence of the Vessel hereby insured coming into collision with any other vessel.

6.2   The indemnity provided by this Clause 6 shall be in addition to the indemnity provided by the other terms and conditions of this insurance and shall be subject to the following provisions:

     6.2.1   where the insured Vessel is in collision with another vessel and both vessels are to blame then, unless the liability of one or both vessels becomes limited by law, the indemnity under this Clause 6 shall be calculated on the principle of cross-liabilities as if the respective Owners had been compelled to pay to each other such proportion of each other's damages as may have been properly allowed in ascertaining the balance or sum payable by or to the Assured in consequence of the collision,

6.2.2   in no case shall the Underwriters' total liability under Clauses 6.1 and 6.2 exceed their proportionate part of three-fourths of the insured value of the Vessel hereby insured in respect of any one collision.

6.3   The Underwriters will also pay three-fourths of the legal costs incurred by the Assured or which the Assured may be compelled to pay in contesting liability or taking proceedings to limit liability, with the prior written consent of the Underwriters.

EXCLUSIONS

6.4   Provided always that this Clause 6 shall in no case extend to any sum which the Assured shall pay for or in respect of

6.4.1   removal or disposal of obstructions, wrecks, cargoes or any other thing whatsoever

6.4.2   any real or personal property or thing whatsoever except other vessels or property on other vessels

6.4.3   the cargo or other property on, or the engagements of, the insured Vessel

6.4.4   loss of life, personal injury or illness

6.4.5   pollution or contamination, or threat thereof, of any real or personal property or thing whatsoever (except other vessels with which the insured Vessel is in collision or property on such other vessels) or damage to the environment, or threat thereof, save that this exclusion shall not extend to any sum which the Assured shall pay for or in respect of salvage remuneration in which the skill and efforts of the salvors in preventing or minimising damage to the environment as is referred to in Article 13 paragraph 1(b) of the International Convention on Salvage 1989 have been taken into account.

7   SISTERSHIP

Should the Vessel hereby insured come into collision with or receive salvage services from another vessel belonging wholly or in part to the same Owners or under the same management, the Assured shall have the same rights under this insurance as they would have were the other vessel entirely the property of Owners not interested in the Vessel hereby insured, but in such cases the liability for the collision or the amount payable for the services rendered shall be referred to a sole arbitrator to be agreed upon between the Underwriters and the Assured.

8   GENERAL AVERAGE AND SALVAGE

8.1   This insurance covers the Vessel's proportion of salvage, salvage charges and/or general average, reduced in respect of any under-insurance, but in case of general average sacrifice of the Vessel the Assured may recover in respect of the whole loss without first enforcing their right of contribution from other parties.

8.2   Adjustment to be according to the law and practice obtaining at the place where the adventure ends, as if the contract of affreightment contained no special terms upon the subject; but where the contract of affreightment so provides the adjustment shall be according to the York-Antwerp Rules.

8.3   When the Vessel sails in ballast, not under charter the provisions of the York-Antwerp Rules 1994 (excluding Rules XI(d), XX and XXI) shall be applicable, and the voyage for this purpose shall be deemed to continue from the port or place of departure until the arrival of the Vessel at the first port or place thereafter other than a port or place of refuge or a port or place of call for bunkering only. If at any such intermediate port or place there is an abandonment of the adventure originally contemplated the voyage shall thereupon be deemed to be terminated.

8.4   No claim under this Clause 8 shall in any case be allowed where the loss was not incurred to avoid or in connection with the avoidance of a peril insured against.

8.5   No claim under this Clause 8 shall in any case be allowed for or in respect of

8.5.1   special compensation payable to a salvor under Article 14 of the International Convention on Salvage, 1989 or under any other provision in any statute, rule, law or contract which is similar in substance

8.5.2   expenses or liabilities incurred in respect of damage to the environment, or the threat of such damage, or as a consequence of the escape or release of pollutant substances from the Vessel, or the threat of such escape or release.

8.6   Clause 8.5 shall not however exclude any sum which the Assured shall pay to salvors for or in respect of salvage remuneration in which the skill and efforts of the salvors in preventing or minimising damage to the environment as is referred to in Article 13 paragraph 1(b) of the International Convention on Salvage, 1989 have been taken into account.

9   DUTY OF ASSURED (SUE AND LABOUR)

9.1   In case of any loss or misfortune it is the duty of the Assured and their servants and agents to take such measures as may be reasonable for the purpose of averting or minimising a loss which would be recoverable under this insurance.

9.2   Subject to the provisions below and to Clause 10 the Underwriters will contribute to charges properly and reasonably incurred by the Assured their servants or agents for such measures. General average, salvage charges (except as provided for in Clause 9.5), special compensation and expenses as referred to in Clause 8.5, and collision defence or attack costs are not recoverable under this Clause 9.

9.3   Measures taken by the Assured or the Underwriters with the object of saving, protecting or recovering the subject-matter insured shall not be considered as a waiver or acceptance of abandonment or otherwise prejudice the rights of either party.

9.4   When expenses are incurred pursuant to this Clause 9 the liability under this insurance shall not exceed the proportion of such expenses that the amount insured hereunder bears to the value of the Vessel as stated herein, or to the sound value of the Vessel at the time of the occurrence giving rise to the expenditure if the sound value exceeds that value. Where the Underwriters have admitted a claim for total loss and property insured by this insurance is saved, the foregoing provisions shall not apply unless the expenses of suing and labouring exceed the value of such property saved and then shall apply only to the amount of the expenses which is in excess of such value.

9.5   When a claim for total loss of the Vessel is admitted under this insurance and expenses have been reasonably incurred in saving or attempting to save the Vessel and other property and there are no proceeds, or the expenses exceed the proceeds, then this insurance shall bear its pro rata share of such proportion of the expenses, or of the expenses in excess of the proceeds, as the case may be, as may reasonably be regarded as having been incurred in respect of the Vessel, excluding all special compensation and expenses as referred to in Clause 8.5; but if the Vessel be insured for less than its sound value at the time of the occurrence giving rise to the expenditure, the amount recoverable under this clause shall be reduced in proportion to the under-insurance.

9.6   The sum recoverable under this Clause 9 shall be in addition to the loss otherwise recoverable under this insurance but shall in no circumstances exceed the amount insured under this insurance in respect of the Vessel.

10   DEDUCTIBLE

10.1   No claim arising from a peril insured against shall be payable under this insurance unless the aggregate of all such claims arising out of each separate accident or occurrence (including claims under Clauses 6, 8 and 9) exceeds the deductible amount agreed in which case this sum shall be deducted. Nevertheless the expense of sighting the bottom after stranding, if reasonably incurred specially for that purpose shall be paid even if no damage be found. This Clause 10.1 shall not apply to a claim for total or constructive total loss of the Vessel or, in the event of such a claim, to any associated claim under Clause 9 arising from the same accident or occurrence.

10.2   Claims for damage by heavy weather occurring during a single sea passage between two successive ports shall be treated as being due to one accident. In the case of such heavy weather extending over a period not wholly covered by this insurance the deductible to be applied to the claim recoverable hereunder shall be the proportion of the above deductible that the number of days of such heavy weather falling within the period of this insurance bears to the number of days of heavy weather during the single sea passage. The expression 'heavy weather' in this Clause 10.2 shall be deemed to include contact with floating ice.

10.3 Excluding any interest comprised therein, recoveries against any claim which is subject to the above deductible shall be credited to the Underwriters in full to the extent of the sum by which the aggregate of the claim unreduced by any recoveries exceeds the above deductible.

10.4 Interest comprised in recoveries shall be apportioned between the Assured and the Underwriters, taking into account the sums paid by the Underwriters and the dates when such payments were made, notwithstanding that by the addition of interest the Underwriters may receive a larger sum than they have paid.

11 NOTICE OF CLAIM AND TENDERS

11.1 In the event of accident whereby loss or damage may result in a claim under this insurance, notice must be given to the Underwriters promptly after the date on which the Assured, Owners or Managers become or should have become aware of the loss or damage and prior to survey and so that a surveyor may be appointed if the Underwriters so desire.

If notice is not given to the Underwriters within twelve months of that date, unless the Underwriters agree to the contrary in writing, the Underwriters will be automatically discharged from liability for any claim under this insurance in respect of or arising out of such accident or the loss or damage.

11.2 The Underwriters shall be entitled to decide the port to which the Vessel shall proceed for docking or repair (the actual additional expense of the voyage arising from compliance with the Underwriters' requirements being refunded to the Assured) and shall have a right of veto concerning a place of repair or a repairing firm.

11.3 The Underwriters may also take tenders or may require further tenders to be taken for the repair of the Vessel. Where such a tender has been taken and a tender is accepted with the approval of the Underwriters, an allowance shall be made at the rate of 30% per annum on the insured value for time lost between the despatch of the invitations to tender required by the Underwriters and the acceptance of a tender to the extent that such time is lost solely as the result of tenders having been taken and provided that the tender is accepted without delay after receipt of the Underwriters' approval.

Due credit shall be given against the allowance as above for any amounts recovered in respect of fuel and stores and wages and maintenance of the Master Officers and Crew or any member thereof, including amounts allowed in general average, and for any amounts recovered from third parties in respect of damages for detention and/or loss of profit and/or running expenses, for the period covered by the tender allowance or any part thereof.

Where a part of the cost of the repair of damage other than a fixed deductible is not recoverable from the Underwriters the allowance shall be reduced by a similar proportion.

11.4 In the event of failure by the Assured to comply with the conditions of Clauses 11.2 and/or 11.3 a deduction of 15% shall be made from the amount of the ascertained claim.

12 NEW FOR OLD

Claims payable without deduction new for old.

13 BOTTOM TREATMENT

In no case shall a claim be allowed in respect of scraping gritblasting and/or other surface preparation or painting of the Vessel's bottom except that

13.1 gritblasting and/or other surface preparation of new bottom plates ashore and supplying and applying any 'shop' primer thereto,

13.2 gritblasting and/or other surface preparation of:
the butts or area of plating immediately adjacent to any renewed or refitted plating damaged during the course of welding and/or repairs,

areas of plating damaged during the course of fairing, either in place or ashore,

13.3 supplying and applying the first coat of primer/anti-corrosive to those particular areas mentioned in 13.1 and 13.2 above,

shall be allowed as part of the reasonable cost of repairs in respect of bottom plating damaged by an insured peril.

14 WAGES AND MAINTENANCE

No claim shall be allowed, other than in general average, for wages and maintenance of the Master Officers and Crew or any member thereof, except when incurred solely for the necessary removal of the Vessel from one port to another for the repair of damage covered by the Underwriters, or for trial trips for such repairs, and then only for such wages and maintenance as are incurred whilst the Vessel is under way.

15 AGENCY COMMISSION

In no case shall any sum be allowed under this insurance either by way of remuneration of the Assured for time and trouble taken to obtain and supply information or documents or in respect of the commission or charges of any manager, agent, managing or agency company or the like, appointed by or on behalf of the Assured to perform such services.

16 UNREPAIRED DAMAGE

16.1 The measure of indemnity in respect of claims for unrepaired damage shall be the reasonable depreciation in the market value of the Vessel at the time this insurance terminates arising from such unrepaired damage, but not exceeding the reasonable cost of repairs.

16.2 In no case shall the Underwriters be liable for unrepaired damage in the event of a subsequent total loss (whether or not covered under this insurance) sustained during the period covered by this insurance or any extension thereof.

16.3 The Underwriters shall not be liable in respect of unrepaired damage for more than the insured value at the time this insurance terminates.

17 CONSTRUCTIVE TOTAL LOSS

17.1 In ascertaining whether the Vessel is a constructive total loss, the insured value shall be taken as the repaired value and nothing in respect of the damaged or break-up value of the Vessel or wreck shall be taken into account.

17.2 No claim for constructive total loss based upon the cost of recovery and/or repair of the Vessel shall be recoverable hereunder unless such cost would exceed the insured value. In making this determination only the cost relating to a single accident or sequence of damages arising from the same accident shall be taken into account.

18 FREIGHT WAIVER

In the event of total or constructive total loss no claim to be made by the Underwriters for freight whether notice of abandonment has been given or not.

19 ASSIGNMENT

No assignment of or interest in this insurance or in any moneys which may be or become payable thereunder is to be binding on or recognised by the Underwriters unless a dated notice of such assignment or interest signed by the Assured, and by the assignor in the case of subsequent assignment, is endorsed on the Policy and the Policy with such endorsement is produced before payment of any claim or return of premium thereunder.

20 DISBURSEMENTS WARRANTY

20.1 Additional insurances as follows are permitted:

20.1.1 *Disbursements, Managers' Commissions, Profits or Excess or Increased Value of Hull and Machinery.* A sum not exceeding 25% of the value stated herein.

20.1.2 *Freight, Chartered Freight or Anticipated Freight, insured for time.* A sum not exceeding 25% of the value as stated herein less any sum insured, however described, under 20.1.1.

20.1.3 *Freight or Hire, under contracts for voyage.* A sum not exceeding the gross freight or hire for the current cargo passage and next succeeding cargo passage (such insurance to include, if required, preliminary and an intermediate ballast passage) plus the charges of insurance. In the case of a voyage charter where payment is made on a time basis, the sum permitted for insurance shall be calculated on the estimated duration of the voyage, subject to the limitation of two cargo passages as laid down herein. Any sum insured under 20.1.2 to be taken into account and only the excess thereof may be insured, which excess shall be reduced as the freight or hire is advanced or earned by the gross amount so advanced or earned.

20.1.4 *Anticipated Freight if the Vessel sails in ballast and not under Charter.* A sum not exceeding the anticipated gross freight on next cargo passage, such sum to be reasonably estimated on the basis of the current rate of freight at time of insurance plus the charges of insurance. Any sum insured under 20.1.2 to be taken into account and only the excess thereof may be insured.

20.1.5 *Time Charter Hire or Charter Hire for Series of Voyages.* A sum not exceeding 50% of the gross hire which is to be earned under the charter in a period not exceeding 18 months. Any sum insured under 20.1.2 to be taken into account and only the excess thereof may be insured, which excess shall be reduced as the hire is advanced or earned under the charter by 50% of the gross amount so advanced or earned but the sum insured need not be reduced while the total of the sums insured under 20.1.2 and 20.1.5 does not exceed 50% of the gross hire still to be earned under the charter. An insurance under this Section may begin on the signing of the charter.

20.1.6 *Premiums.* A sum not exceeding the actual premiums of all interests insured for a period not exceeding 12 months (excluding premiums insured under the foregoing sections but including, if required, the premium or estimated calls on any Club or War etc. Risk insurance) reducing pro rata monthly.

20.1.7 *Returns of Premium.* A sum not exceeding the actual returns which are allowable under any insurance but which would not be recoverable thereunder in the event of a total loss of the Vessel whether by insured perils or otherwise.

20.1.8 *Insurance irrespective of amount against*: Any risks excluded by Clauses 21, 22, 23 and 24 below.

20.2 Warranted that no insurance on any interests enumerated in the foregoing 20.1.1 to 20.1.7 in excess of the amounts permitted therein and no other insurance which includes total loss of the Vessel P.P.I., F.I.A., or subject to any other like term, is or shall be effected to operate during the currency of this insurance by or for account of the Assured, Owners, Managers or Mortgagees. Provided always that a breach of this warranty shall not afford the Underwriters any defence to a claim by a Mortgagee who has accepted this insurance without knowledge of such breach.

The following clauses shall be paramount and shall override anything contained in this insurance inconsistent therewith.

21 WAR EXCLUSION

In no case shall this insurance cover loss damage liability or expense caused by

21.1 war civil war revolution rebellion insurrection, or civil strife arising therefrom, or any hostile act by or against a belligerent power

21.2 capture seizure arrest restraint or detainment (barratry and piracy excepted), and the consequences thereof or any attempt thereat

21.3   derelict mines torpedoes bombs or other derelict weapons of war.

22   STRIKES EXCLUSION

In no case shall this insurance cover loss damage liability or expense caused by

22.1   strikers, locked-out workmen, or persons taking part in labour disturbances, riots or civil commotions

22.2   any terrorist or any person acting from a political motive.

23   MALICIOUS ACTS EXCLUSION

In no case shall this insurance cover loss damage liability or expense arising from

23.1   the detonation of an explosive

23.2   any weapon of war and caused by any person acting maliciously or from a political motive.

24   RADIOACTIVE CONTAMINATION EXCLUSION CLAUSE

In no case shall this insurance cover loss damage liability or expense directly or indirectly caused by or contributed to by or arising from

24.1   ionising radiations from or contamination by radioactivity from any nuclear fuel or from any nuclear waste or from the combustion of nuclear fuel

24.2   the radioactive, toxic, explosive or other hazardous or contaminating properties of any nuclear installation, reactor or other nuclear assembly or nuclear component thereof

24.3   any weapon of war employing atomic or nuclear fission and/or fusion or other like reaction or radioactive force or matter.

APPENDIX 4

"These clauses are purely illustrative. Different policy conditions may be agreed. The specimen clauses are available to any interested person upon request. In particular:

(a)   in relation to any clause which excludes losses from the cover, insurers may agree a separate insurance policy covering such losses or may extend the clause to cover such events;

(b)   In relation to clauses making cover of certain risks subject to specific conditions each insurer may alter the said conditions."

INTERNATIONAL HULL CLAUSES
(1 November 2003)

(for use with the current mar policy form)

PART 1 – PRINCIPAL INSURING CONDITIONS

1   GENERAL

1.1   Part 1, Clauses 32-36 of Part 2 and Part 3 apply to this insurance. Parts 2 and 3 shall be those current at the date of inception of this insurance. Clauses 37-41 of Part 2 shall only apply where the Underwriters have expressly so agreed in writing.

1.2   This insurance is subject to English law and practice.

1.3   This insurance is subject to the exclusive jurisdiction of the English High Court of Justice, except as may be expressly provided herein to the contrary.

1.4   If any provision of this insurance is held to be invalid or unenforceable, such invalidity or unenforceability will not affect the other provisions of this insurance, which shall remain in full force and effect.

2   PERILS

2.1   This insurance covers loss of or damage to the subject-matter insured caused by

    2.1.1   perils of the seas, rivers, lakes or other navigable waters

    2.1.2   fire, explosion

    2.1.3   violent theft by persons from outside the vessel

    2.1.4   jettison

    2.1.5   piracy

    2.1.6   contact with land conveyance, dock or harbour equipment or installation

    2.1.7   earthquake, volcanic eruption or lightning

    2.1.8   accidents in loading, discharging or shifting cargo, fuel, stores or parts

    2.1.9   contact with satellites, aircraft, helicopters or similar objects, or objects falling therefrom.

2.2   This insurance covers loss of or damage to the subject matter insured caused by

    2.2.1   bursting of boilers or breakage of shafts but does not cover any of the costs of repairing or replacing the boiler which bursts or the shaft which breaks

    2.2.2   any latent defect in the machinery or hull, but does not cover any of the costs of correcting the latent defect

    2.2.3   negligence of Master, Officers, Crew or Pilots

    2.2.4   negligence of repairers or charterers provided such repairers or charterers are not an Assured under this insurance

    2.2.5   barratry of Master, Officers or Crew

    provided that such loss or damage has not resulted from want of due diligence by the Assured, Owners or Managers.

2.3   Where there is a claim recoverable under Clause 2.2.1, this insurance shall also cover one half of the costs common to the repair of the burst boiler or the broken shaft and to the repair of the loss or damage caused thereby.

2.4   Where there is a claim recoverable under Clause 2.2.2, this insurance shall also cover one half of the costs common to the correction of the latent defect and to the repair of the loss or damage caused thereby.

2.5   Master, Officers, Crew or Pilots shall not be considered Owners within the meaning of Clause 2.2 should they hold shares in the vessel.

3   LEASED EQUIPMENT

3.1   This insurance covers loss of or damage to equipment and apparatus not owned by the Assured but installed for use on the vessel and for which the Assured has assumed contractual liability, where such loss or damage is caused by a peril insured under this insurance.

3.2   The liability of the Underwriters shall not exceed the lesser of the contractual liability of the Assured for loss of or damage to such equipment or apparatus or the reasonable cost of their repair or their replacement value. All such equipment and apparatus are included in the insured value of the vessel.

4   PARTS TAKEN OFF

4.1   This insurance covers loss of or damage to parts taken off the vessel, where such loss or damage is caused by a peril insured under this insurance.

4.2   Where the parts taken off the vessel are not owned by the Assured but where the Assured has assumed contractual liability for such parts, the liability of the Underwriters for such parts taken off shall not exceed the lesser of the contractual liability of the Assured for loss of or damage to such parts or the reasonable cost of their repair or their replacement value.

4.3   If at the time of loss of or damage to the parts taken off the vessel, such parts are covered by any other insurance or would be so covered but for this Clause 4, then this insurance shall only be excess of such other insurance.

4.4   Cover in respect of parts taken off the vessel shall be limited to 60 days whilst not on board the vessel. Periods in excess of 60 days shall be held covered provided notice is given to the Underwriters prior to the expiry of the 60 day period and any amended terms of cover and any additional premium required are agreed.

4.5   In no case shall the total liability of the Underwriters under this Clause 4 exceed 5% of the insured value of the vessel.

5   POLLUTION HAZARD

This insurance covers loss of or damage to the vessel caused by any governmental authority acting under the powers vested in it to prevent or mitigate a pollution hazard or damage to the environment or threat thereof, resulting directly from damage to the vessel for which the Underwriters are liable under this insurance, provided that such act of governmental authority has not resulted from want of due diligence by the Assured, Owners or Managers to prevent or mitigate such hazard or damage or threat thereof. Master, Officers, Crew or Pilots shall not be considered Owners within the meaning of this Clause 5 should they hold shares in the vessel.

6   3/4THS COLLISION LIABILITY

6.1   The Underwriters agree to indemnify the Assured for three fourths of any sum or sums paid by the Assured to any other person or persons by reason of the Assured becoming legally liable by way of damages for

    6.1.1   loss of or damage to any other vessel or property thereon

    6.1.2   delay to or loss of use of any such other vessel or property thereon

    6.1.3   general average of, salvage of, or salvage under contract of, any such other vessel or property thereon,

             where such payment by the Assured is in consequence of the insured vessel coming into collision with any other vessel.

6.2 The indemnity provided by this Clause 6 shall be in addition to the indemnity provided by the other terms and conditions of this insurance and shall be subject to the following provisions

    6.2.1 where the insured vessel is in collision with another vessel and both vessels are to blame then, unless the liability of one or both vessels becomes limited by law, the indemnity under this Clause 6 shall be calculated on the principle of cross-liabilities as if the respective Owners had been compelled to pay to each other such proportion of each other's damages as may have been properly allowed in ascertaining the balance or sum payable by or to the Assured in consequence of the collision

    6.2.2 in no case shall the total liability of the Underwriters under Clauses 6.1 and

6.2 exceed their proportionate part of three fourths of the insured value of the insured vessel in respect of any one collision.

6.3 The Underwriters shall also pay three fourths of the legal costs incurred by the Assured or which the Assured may be compelled to pay in contesting liability or taking proceedings to limit liability, provided always that their prior written consent to the incurring of such costs shall have been obtained and that the total liability of the Underwriters under this Clause 6.3 shall not (unless the Underwriters' specific

written agreement shall have been obtained) exceed 25% of the insured value of the insured vessel.

EXCLUSIONS

6.4 In no case shall the Underwriters indemnify the Assured under this Clause 6 for any sum, which the Assured shall pay for or in respect of

    6.4.1 removal or disposal of obstructions, wrecks, cargoes or any other thing whatsoever

    6.4.2 any real or personal property or thing whatsoever except other vessels or property on other vessels

    6.4.3 the cargo or other property on, or the engagements of, the insured vessel

    6.4.4 loss of life, personal injury or illness

    6.4.5 pollution or contamination, or threats thereof, of any real or personal property or thing whatsoever (except other vessels with which the insured vessel is in collision or property on such other vessels) or damage to the environment, or threat thereof, save that this exclusion shall not exclude any sum which the Assured shall pay for or in respect of salvage remuneration in which the skill and efforts of the salvors in preventing or minimising damage to the environment as referred to in Article 13 paragraph l(b) of the International Convention on Salvage, 1989 have been taken into account.

7 SISTERSHIP

Should the insured vessel come into collision with or receive salvage services from another vessel belonging wholly or in part to the same Owners or under the same management, the Assured shall have the same rights under this insurance as they would have were the other vessel entirely the property of Owners not interested in the insured vessel; but in such cases the liability for the collision or the amount payable for the services rendered shall be referred to a sole arbitrator to be agreed upon between the Underwriters and the Assured.

8 GENERAL AVERAGE AND SALVAGE

8.1 This insurance covers the vessel's proportion of salvage, salvage charges and/or general average, without reduction in respect of any under-insurance, but in case of general average sacrifice of the vessel the Assured may recover in respect of the whole loss without first enforcing their right of contribution from other parties.

8.2 General average shall be adjusted according to the law and practice obtaining at the place where the adventure ends, as if the contract of affreightment contained no special terms upon the subject; but where the contract of affreightment so provides the adjustment shall be according to the York-Antwerp Rules.

8.3   When the vessel sails in ballast, not under charter, the provisions of the York-Antwerp Rules, 1994 (excluding Rules XX and XXI) shall be applicable, and the voyage for this purpose shall be deemed to continue from the port or place of departure until the arrival of the vessel at the first port or place thereafter other than a port or place of refuge or a port or place of call for bunkering only. If at any such intermediate port or place there is an abandonment of the adventure originally contemplated, the voyage shall thereupon be deemed to be terminated.

8.4   The Underwriters shall not be liable under this Clause 8 where the loss was not incurred to avoid or in connection with the avoidance of a peril insured under this insurance.

8.5   The Underwriters shall not be liable under this Clause 8 for or in respect of

8.5.1   special compensation payable to a salvor under Article 14 of the International Convention on Salvage, 1989 or under any other provision in any statute, rule, law or contract which is similar in substance

8.5.2   expenses or liabilities incurred in respect of damage to the environment, or the threat of such damage, or as a consequence of the escape or release of pollutant substances from the vessel, or the threat of such escape or release.

8.6   Clause 8.5 shall not however exclude any sum which the Assured shall pay

8.6.1   to salvors for or in respect of salvage remuneration in which the skill and efforts of the salvors in preventing or minimising damage to the environment as referred to in Article 13 paragraph l(b) of the International Convention on Salvage, 1989 have been taken into account

8.6.2   as general average expenditure allowable under Rule Xl(d) of the York-Antwerp Rules 1994, but only where the contract of affreightment provides for adjustment according to the York-Antwerp Rules 1994.

9   DUTY OF THE ASSURED (SUE AND LABOUR)

9.1   In case of any loss or misfortune it is the duty of the Assured and their servants and agents to take such measures as may be reasonable for the purpose of averting or minimising a loss which would be recoverable under this insurance.

9.2   Subject to the provisions below and to Clause 15, the Underwriters shall contribute to charges properly and reasonably incurred by the Assured their servants or agents for such measures. General average, salvage charges (except as provided for in Clause 9.4), special compensation and expenses as referred to in Clause 8.5 and collision defence or attack costs are not recoverable under this Clause 9.

9.3   Measures taken by the Assured or the Underwriters with the object of saving, protecting or recovering the subject-matter insured shall not be considered as a waiver or acceptance of abandonment or otherwise prejudice the rights of either party.

9.4   When the Underwriters have admitted a claim for total loss of the vessel under this insurance and expenses have been reasonably incurred in saving or attempting to save the vessel and other property and there are no proceeds, or the expenses exceed the proceeds, then this insurance shall bear its pro rata share of such proportion of the expenses, or of the expenses in excess of the proceeds, as the case may be, as may reasonably be regarded as having been incurred in respect of the vessel, excluding all special compensation and expenses as referred to in Clause 8.5.

9.5   The sum recoverable under this Clause 9 shall be in addition to the loss otherwise recoverable under this insurance but shall in no circumstances exceed the insured value of the vessel.

10   NAVIGATION PROVISIONS

Unless and to the extent otherwise agreed by the Underwriters in accordance with Clause 11

10.1   the vessel shall not breach any provisions of this insurance as to cargo, trade or locality (including, but not limited to, Clause 32)

10.2   the vessel may navigate with or without pilots, go on trial trips and assist and tow vessels or craft in distress, but shall not be towed, except as is customary (including customary towage in connection with loading or discharging) or to the first safe port or place when in need of assistance, or undertake towage or salvage services under a contract previously arranged by the Assured and/or Owners and/or Managers and/or Charterers

10.3   the Assured shall not enter into any contract with pilots or for customary towage which limits or exempts the liability of the pilots and/or tugs and/or towboats and/or their owners except where the Assured or their agents accept or are compelled to accept such contracts in accordance with established local law or practice

10.4   the vessel shall not be employed in trading operations which entail cargo loading or discharging at sea from or into another vessel (not being a harbour or inshore craft).

11   BREACH OF NAVIGATION PROVISIONS

In the event of any breach of any of the provisions of Clause 10, the Underwriters shall not be liable for any loss, damage, liability or expense arising out of or resulting from an accident or occurrence during the period of breach, unless notice is given to the Underwriters immediately after receipt of advices of such breach and any amended terms of cover and any additional premium required by them are agreed.

12   CONTINUATION

Should the vessel at the expiration of this insurance be at sea and in distress or missing, she shall be held covered until arrival at the next port in good safety, or if in port and in distress until the vessel is made safe, at a pro rata monthly premium, provided that notice be given to the Underwriters as soon as possible.

These Clauses 13 and 14 shall prevail notwithstanding any provision whether written typed or printed in this insurance inconsistent therewith.

13   CLASSIFICATION AND ISM

13.1   At the inception of and throughout the period of this insurance and any extension thereof

   13.1.1   the vessel shall be classed with a Classification Society agreed by the Underwriters

   13.1.2   there shall be no change, suspension, discontinuance, withdrawal or expiry of the vessel's class with the Classification Society

   13.1.3   any recommendations, requirements or restrictions imposed by the vessel's Classification Society which relate to the vessel's seaworthiness or to her maintenance in a seaworthy condition shall be complied with by the dates required by that Society

   13.1.4   the Owners or the party assuming responsibility for operation of the vessel from the Owners shall hold a valid Document of Compliance in respect of the vessel as required by chapter IX of the International Convention for the Safety of Life at Sea (SOLAS) 1974 as amended and any modification thereof

   13.1.5   the vessel shall have in force a valid Safety Management Certificate as required by chapter IX of the International Convention for the Safety of Life at Sea (SOLAS) 1974 as amended and any modification thereof.

13.2   Unless the Underwriters agree to the contrary in writing, in the event of any breach of any of the provisions of Clause 13.1, this insurance shall terminate automatically at the time of such breach, provided

   13.2.1   that if the vessel is at sea at such date, such automatic termination shall be deferred until arrival at her next port

   13.2.2   where such change, suspension, discontinuance or withdrawal of her class under Clause 13.1.2 has resulted from loss or damage covered by Clause 2 or by Clause 5 or by Clause 41.1.3 (if applicable) or which would be covered by an insurance of the vessel subject to current Institute War and Strikes Clauses Hulls-Time, such automatic termination shall only operate should the vessel sail from her next port without the prior approval of the Classification Society.

A pro rata daily net return of premium shall be made provided that a total loss of the vessel, whether by perils insured under this insurance or otherwise, has not occurred during the period of this insurance or any extension thereof.

14   MANAGEMENT

14.1   Unless the Underwriters agree to the contrary in writing, this insurance shall terminate automatically at the time of

14.1.1   any change, voluntary or otherwise, in the ownership or flag of the vessel

14.1.2   transfer of the vessel to new management

14.1.3   charter of the vessel on a bareboat basis

14.1.4   requisition of the vessel for title or use

provided that, if the vessel has cargo on board and has already sailed from her loading port or is at sea in ballast, such automatic termination shall if required be deferred, whilst the vessel continues her planned voyage, until arrival at final port of discharge if with cargo or at port of destination if in ballast. However, in the event of requisition for title or use without the prior execution of a written agreement by the Assured, such automatic termination shall occur fifteen days after such requisition whether the vessel is at sea or in port.

14.2   Unless the Underwriters agree to the contrary in writing, this insurance shall terminate automatically at the time of the vessel sailing (with or without cargo) with an intention of being broken up, or being sold for breaking up.

14.3   In the event of termination under Clause 14.1 or Clause 14.2, a pro rata daily net return of premium shall be made provided that a total loss of the vessel, whether by perils insured under this insurance or otherwise, has not occurred during the period of this insurance or any extension thereof.

14.4   It is the duty of the Assured, Owners and Managers at the inception of and throughout the period of this insurance and any extension thereof to

14.4.1   comply with all statutory requirements of the vessel's flag state relating to construction, adaptation, condition, fitment, equipment, operation and manning of the vessel

14.4.2   comply with all requirements of the vessel's Classification Society regarding the reporting to the Classification Society of accidents to and defects in the vessel.

In the event of any breach of any of the duties in this Clause 14.4, the Underwriters shall not be liable for any loss, damage, liability or expense attributable to such breach.

15   DEDUCTIBLE(S)

15.1   Subject to Clause 15.2, no claim arising from a peril insured under this insurance shall be payable under this insurance unless the aggregate of all such claims arising out of each separate accident or occurrence (including claims under Clauses 2, 3, 4, 5, 6 (including, if applicable, Clause 6 as amended by Clauses 37 or 38), Clauses 8 and 9 and, if applicable, Clause 41 exceeds the deductible amount agreed in which case this sum shall be deducted. Nevertheless the expense of sighting the bottom after stranding, if reasonably incurred specially for that purpose, shall be paid even if no damage is found.

15.2   No claim for loss of or damage to any machinery, shaft, electrical equipment or wiring, boiler, condenser, heating coil or associated pipework, arising under Clauses 2.2.1 to 2.2.5 and Clause 41 (if applicable) or from fire or explosion when either has originated in a machinery space, shall be payable under this insurance unless the aggregate of all such claims arising out of each separate accident or occurrence exceeds the additional machinery damage deductible amount agreed (if any) in which case that amount shall be deducted. Any balance remaining, after application of this deductible, with any other claim arising from the same accident or occurrence, shall then be subject to the deductible referred to in Clause 15.1.

15.3 Clauses 15.1 and 15.2 shall not apply to a claim for total or constructive total loss of the vessel or, in the event of such a claim, to any associated claim under Clause 9 arising from the same accident or occurrence.

15.4 Claims for damage by heavy weather occurring during a single sea passage between two successive ports shall be treated as being due to one accident. In the case of such heavy weather extending over a period not wholly covered by this insurance the deductible to be applied to the claim recoverable under this insurance shall be the proportion of the deductible in Clause 15.1 that the number of days of such heavy weather falling within the period of this insurance and any extension thereof bears to the number of days of heavy weather during the single sea passage. The expression "heavy weather" in this Clause 15.4 shall be deemed to include contact with floating ice.

15.5 Claims for damage occurring during each separate lightening operation and/or each separate cargo loading or discharging operation from or into another vessel at sea, where recoverable under this insurance, shall be treated as being due to one accident.

16 NEW FOR OLD

Claims recoverable under this insurance shall be payable without deduction on the basis of new for old.

17 BOTTOM TREATMENT

The Underwriters shall not be liable in respect of scraping, gritblasting and/or other surface preparation or painting of the vessel's bottom except that

17.1 gritblasting and/or other surface preparation of new bottom plates ashore and supplying and applying any "shop" primer thereto

17.2 gritblasting and/or other surface preparation of

17.2.1 the butts or area of plating immediately adjacent to any renewed or refitted plating damaged during the course of welding and/or repairs

17.2.2 areas of plating damaged during the course of fairing, either in place or ashore

17.3 supplying and applying the first coat of primer/anti-corrosive to those particular areas mentioned in Clauses 17.1 and 17.2

17.4 supplying and applying anti-fouling coatings to those particular areas mentioned in Clauses 17.1 and 17.2,

shall be included as part of the reasonable cost of repairs in respect of damage to bottom plating caused by a peril insured under this insurance.

18 WAGES AND MAINTENANCE

Other than in general average, the Underwriters shall not be liable for wages and maintenance of the Master, Officers and Crew or any member thereof, except when incurred solely for the necessary removal of the vessel from one port to another for the repair of damage covered by the Underwriters, or for trial trips for such repairs, and then only for such wages and maintenance as are incurred whilst the vessel is under way.

19 AGENCY COMMISSION

No sum shall be recoverable under this insurance either by way of remuneration of the Assured for time and trouble taken to obtain and supply information or documents or in respect of the commission or charges of any manager, agent, managing or agency company or the like, appointed by or on behalf of the Assured to perform such services.

20 UNREPAIRED DAMAGE

20.1 The measure of indemnity in respect of claims for unrepaired damage shall be the reasonable depreciation in the market value of the vessel at the time this insurance terminates arising from such unrepaired damage, but not exceeding the reasonable cost of repairs.

20.2   In no case shall the Underwriters be liable for unrepaired damage in the event of a subsequent total loss of the vessel (whether by perils insured under this insurance or otherwise) sustained during the period of this insurance or any extension thereof.

20.3   The Underwriters shall not be liable in respect of unrepaired damage for more than the insured value of the vessel at the time this insurance terminates.

21   CONSTRUCTIVE TOTAL LOSS

21.1   In ascertaining whether the vessel is a constructive total loss, 80% of the insured value of the vessel shall be taken as the repaired value and nothing in respect of the damaged or break-up value of the vessel or wreck shall be taken into account.

21.2   No claim for constructive total loss of the vessel based upon the cost of recovery and/or repair of the vessel shall be recoverable hereunder unless such cost would exceed 80% of the insured value of the vessel. In making this determination, only the cost relating to a single accident or sequence of damages arising from the same accident shall be taken into account.

22   FREIGHT WAIVER

If a total or constructive total loss of the vessel has been admitted by the Underwriters, they shall make no claim for freight whether notice of abandonment has been given or not.

23   ASSIGNMENT

No assignment of or interest in this insurance or in any moneys which may be or become payable under this insurance is to be binding on or recognised by the Underwriters unless a dated notice of such assignment or interest signed by the Assured, and by the assignor in the case of subsequent assignment, is endorsed on the policy and the policy with such endorsement is produced before payment of any claim or return of premium under this insurance.

24   DISBURSEMENTS WARRANTY

24.1   Additional insurances as follows are permitted by the Underwriters:

24.1.1   *Disbursements, Managers' Commissions, Profits or Excess or Increased Value of Hull and Machinery.* A sum not exceeding 25% of the value stated herein.

24.1.2   *Freight, Chartered Freight or Anticipated Freight, insured for time.* A sum not exceeding 25% of the value as stated herein less any sum insured, however described, under Clause 24.1.1

24.1.3   *Freight or Hire, under contracts for voyage.* A sum not exceeding the gross freight or hire for the current cargo passage and next succeeding cargo passage (such insurance to include, if required, a preliminary and an intermediate ballast passage) plus the charges of insurance. In the case of a voyage charter where payment is made on a time basis, the sum permitted for insurance shall be calculated on the estimated duration of the voyage, subject to the limitation of two cargo passages as laid down herein. Any sum insured under Clause 24.1.2 to be taken into account and only the excess thereof may be insured, which excess shall be reduced as the freight or hire is advanced or earned by the gross amount so advanced or earned.

24.1.4   *Anticipated Freight if the vessel sails in ballast and not under Charter.* A sum not exceeding the anticipated gross freight on next cargo passage, such sum to be reasonably estimated on the basis of the current rate of freight at time of insurance plus the charges of insurance. Any sum insured under Clause 24.1.2 to be taken into account and only the excess thereof may be insured.

24.1.5   *Time Charter Hire or Charter Hire for Series of Voyages.* A sum not exceeding 50% of the gross hire which is to be earned under the charter in a period not exceeding 18 months. Any sum insured under Clause 24.1.2 to be taken into account and only the excess thereof may be insured, which excess shall be reduced as the hire is advanced or earned under the charter by 50% of the gross amount so advanced or earned but the sum insured need not be reduced while the total of the sums insured under Clause 24.1.2 and Clause

24.1.5 does not exceed 50% of the gross hire still to be earned under the charter. An insurance under this Clause may begin on the signing of the charter.

24.1.6 *Premiums*. A sum not exceeding the actual premiums of all interests insured for a period not exceeding 12 months (excluding premiums insured under the foregoing sections but including, if required, the premium or estimated calls on any Club or War etc. Risk insurance) reducing pro rata monthly.

24.1.7 *Returns of Premium*. A sum not exceeding the actual returns which are allowable under any insurance but which would not be recoverable thereunder in the event of a total loss of the vessel whether by perils insured under this insurance or otherwise.

24.1.8 *Insurance irrespective of amount against. Any risks excluded by Clauses 29, 30 and 31.*

24.2 It is warranted that no insurance on any interests enumerated in the foregoing Clauses 24.1.1 to 24.1.7 in excess of the amounts permitted therein and no other insurance which includes total loss of the vessel P.P.I., F.I.A., or subject to any other like term, is or shall be effected to operate during the period of this insurance or any extension thereof by or for account of the Assured, Owners, Managers or Mortgagees. Provided always that a breach of this warranty shall not afford the Underwriters any defence to a claim by a Mortgagee who has accepted this insurance without knowledge of such breach.

25   CANCELLING RETURNS

If this insurance shall be cancelled by agreement, the Underwriters shall pay a pro rata monthly net return of premium for each uncommenced month, provided always that a total loss of the vessel, whether by perils insured under this insurance or otherwise, has not occurred during the period of this insurance or any extension thereof.

26   SEPARATE INSURANCES

If more than one vessel is insured under this insurance, each vessel insured is deemed to be separately insured, as if a separate policy had been issued in respect of each vessel.

27   SEVERAL LIABILITY

The Underwriters' obligations are several and not joint and are limited solely to the extent of their individual subscriptions. The Underwriters are not responsible for the subscription of any co-subscribing Underwriter who for any reason does not satisfy all or part of its obligations.

28   AFFILIATED COMPANIES

In the event of the vessel being chartered by an associated, subsidiary or affiliated company of the Assured, and in the event of loss of or damage to the vessel by perils insured under this insurance, the Underwriters waive their rights of subrogation against such charterers, except to the extent that any such charterer has the benefit of liability cover for such loss or damage.

These Clauses 29, 30 and 31 shall be paramount and shall override anything contained in this insurance inconsistent therewith.

29   WAR & STRIKES EXCLUSION

In no case shall this insurance cover loss, damage, liability or expense caused by

29.1 war, civil war, revolution, rebellion, insurrection, or civil strife arising therefrom, or any hostile act by or against a belligerent power

29.2 capture, seizure, arrest, restraint or detainment (barratry and piracy excepted), and the consequences thereof or any attempt thereat

29.3 derelict mines, torpedoes, bombs or other derelict weapons of war.

29.4 strikers, locked-out workmen, or persons taking part in labour disturbances, riots or civil commotions.

30   TERRORIST, POLITICAL MOTIVE AND MALICIOUS ACTS EXCLUSION

In no case shall this insurance cover loss, damage, liability or expense arising from

30.1 any terrorist

30.2 any person acting from a political motive

30.3 the use of any weapon or the detonation of an explosive by any person acting maliciously or from a political motive.

31   RADIOACTIVE CONTAMINATION, CHEMICAL, BIOLOGICAL, BIOCHEMICAL AND ELECTROMAGNETIC WEAPONS EXCLUSION

In no case shall this insurance cover loss, damage, liability or expense directly or indirectly caused by or contributed to by or arising from

31.1 ionising radiations from or contamination by radioactivity from any nuclear fuel or from any nuclear waste or from the combustion of nuclear fuel

31.2 the radioactive, toxic, explosive or other hazardous or contaminating properties of any nuclear installation, reactor or other nuclear assembly or nuclear component thereof

31.3 any weapon or device employing atomic or nuclear fission and/or fusion or other like reaction or radioactive force or matter

31.4 the radioactive, toxic, explosive or other hazardous or contaminating properties of any radioactive matter. The exclusion in this Clause 31.4 does not extend to radioactive isotopes, other than nuclear fuel, when such isotopes are being prepared, carried, stored, or used for commercial, agricultural, medical, scientific or other similar peaceful purposes

31.5 any chemical, biological, bio-chemical or electromagnetic weapon.

PART 2 – ADDITIONAL CLAUSES (01/11/03)

32   NAVIGATING LIMITS

Unless and to the extent otherwise agreed by the Underwriters in accordance with Clause 33, the vessel shall not enter, navigate or remain in the areas specified below at any time or, where applicable, between the dates specified below (both days inclusive):

Area 1 – Arctic

(a) North of 70° N. Lat.

(b) Barents Sea

except for calls at Kola Bay, Murmansk or any port or place in Norway, provided that the vessel does not enter, navigate or remain north of 72°30'N. Lat. or east of 35° E. Long.

Area 2 – Northern Seas

(a) White Sea.

(b) Chukchi Sea

Area 3 – Baltic

(a) Gulf of Bothnia north of a line between Umea (63°50'N. Lat.) and Vasa (63°06'N. Lat.) between 10th December and 25th May.

(b) Where the vessel is equal to or less than 90,000 DWT, Gulf of Finland east of 28°45'E.Long. between 15th December and 15th May.

(c) Vessels greater than 90,000 DWT may not enter, navigate or remain in the Gulf of Finland east of 28°45'E. Long. at any time.

(d)   Gulf of Bothnia, Gulf of Finland and adjacent waters north of 59°24'N. Lat. between 8th January and 5th May, except for calls at Stockholm, Tallinn or Helsinki.

(e)   Gulf of Riga and adjacent waters east of 22°E. Long. and south of 59°N. Lat. between 28th December and 5th May.

Area 4 – Greenland

Greenland territorial waters.

Area 5 – North America (east)

(a)   North of 52°10'N. Lat. and between 50°W. Long. and 100°W. Long.

(b)   Gulf of St. Lawrence, St. Lawrence River and its tributaries (east of Les Escoumins), Strait of Belle Isle (west of Belle Isle), Cabot Strait (west of a line between Cape Ray and Cape North) and Strait of Canso (north of the Canso Causeway), between 21st December and 30th April.

(c)   St. Lawrence River and its tributaries (west of Les Escoumins) between 1st December and 30th April.

(d)   St. Lawrence Seaway

(e)   Great Lakes.

Area 6 – North America (west)

(a)   North of 54°30'N. Lat. and between 100°W. Long. and 170°W. Long.

(b)   Any port of place in the Queen Charlotte Islands or the Aleutian Islands

Area 7 – Southern Ocean

South of 50°S. Lat. except within the triangular area formed by rhumb lines drawn between the following points

(a)   50°S. Lat.; 50°W. Long

(b)   57₀S. Lat.; 67°30'W. Long.

(c)   50°S Lat.; 160°W. Long.

Area 8 – Kerguelen/Crozet

Territorial waters of Kerguelen Islands and Crozet Islands.

Area 9 – East Asia

(a)   Sea of Okhotsk north of 55°N. Lat. and east of 140°E. Long. between 1st November and 1st June.

(b)   Sea of Okhotsk north of 53°N. Lat. and west of 140°E. Long. between 1st November and 1st June.

(c)   East Asian waters north of 46°N. Lat. and west of the Kurile Islands and west of the Kamchatka Peninsula between 1st December and 1st May.

Area 10 – Bering Sea

Bering Sea except on through voyages and provided that

(a)   vessel does not enter, navigate or remain north of 54°30'N. Lat.; and

(b)   the vessel enters and exits west of Buldir Island or through the Amchitka, Amukta or Unimak passes; and

(c)   the vessel is equipped and properly fitted with two independent marine radar sets, a global positioning system receiver (or Loran-C radio positioning receiver), a radio transceiver and GMDSS, a weather facsimile recorder (or alternative equipment for the receipt of weather and routing information) and a gyrocompass, in each case to be fully operational and manned by qualified personnel; and

(d)   the vessel is in possession of appropriate navigational charts corrected up to date, sailing directions and pilot books.

33   PERMISSION FOR AREAS SPECIFIED IN NAVIGATING LIMITS

The vessel may breach Clause 32 and Clause 11 shall not apply, provided always that the Underwriters' prior permission shall have been obtained and any amended terms of cover and any additional premium required by the Underwriters are agreed.

34   RECOMMISSIONING CONDITION

As a condition precedent to the liability of the Underwriters, the vessel shall not leave her lay-up berth under her own power or navigate following a lay-up period of more than 180 consecutive days unless the Assured has arranged for the Classification Society or a surveyor agreed by the Underwriters to examine the vessel and has carried out any repairs or requirements recommended by the Classification Society or such surveyor.

35   PREMIUM PAYMENT

35.1   The Assured undertakes that the premium shall be paid

    35.1.1   in full to the Underwriters within 45 days (or such other period as may be agreed) of inception of this insurance; or

    35.1.2   where payment by instalment premiums has been agreed

        (a)   the first instalment premium shall be paid within 45 days (or such other period as may be agreed) of inception of this insurance, and

        (b)   the second and subsequent instalments shall be paid by the date they are due.

35.2   If the premium (or the first instalment premium) has not been so paid to the Underwriters by the 46_{th} day (or the day after such period as may have been agreed) from the inception of this insurance (and, in respect of the second and subsequent instalment premiums, by the date they are due), the Underwriters shall have the right to cancel this insurance by notifying the Assured via the broker in writing.

35.3   The Underwriters shall give not less than 15 days prior notice of cancellation to the Assured via the broker. If the premium or instalment premium due is paid in full to the Underwriters before the notice period expires, notice of cancellation shall automatically be revoked. If not, this insurance shall automatically terminate at the end of the notice period.

35.4   In the event of cancellation under this Clause 35, premium is due to the Underwriters on a pro rata basis for the period that the Underwriters are on risk but the full premium shall be payable to the Underwriters in the event of loss, damage, liability or expense arising out of or resulting from an accident or occurrence prior to the date of termination which gives rise to a recoverable claim under this insurance.

35.5   Unless otherwise agreed, the Leading Underwriter(s) designated in the slip or policy are authorised to exercise rights under this Clause 35 on their own behalf and on behalf of all cosubscribing Underwriters. Nothing in this Clause 35.5 shall, however, prevent any co-subscribing Underwriter from exercising rights under this Clause 35 on its own behalf.

35.6   Where the premium is to be paid through a Market Bureau, payment to the Underwriters will be deemed to occur on the day of delivery of a premium advice note to the Bureau.

36   CONTRACTS (RIGHTS OF THIRD PARTIES) ACT 1999

36.1   No benefit of this insurance is intended to be conferred on or enforceable by any party other than the Assured, save as may be expressly provided herein to the contrary.

36.2   This insurance may by agreement between the Assured and the Underwriters be rescinded or varied without the consent of any third party to whom the enforcement of any terms has been expressly provided for.

37   FIXED AND FLOATING OBJECTS

If the Underwriters have expressly agreed in writing, then Clauses 6 and 7 are amended to read as follows

6.1 The Underwriters agree to indemnify the Assured for three fourths of any sum or sums paid by the Assured to any other person or persons by reason of the Assured becoming legally liable by way of damages for

    6.1.1 loss of or damage to any other vessel or fixed or floating object or property thereon

    6.1.2 delay to or loss of use of any such other vessel or fixed or floating object or property thereon

    6.1.3 general average of, salvage of, or salvage under contract of, any such other vessel or property thereon,

    where such payment by the Assured is in consequence of the insured vessel coming into collision with any other vessel or striking any fixed or floating object.

6.2 The indemnity provided by this Clause 6 shall be in addition to the indemnity provided by the other terms and conditions of this insurance and shall be subject to the following provisions

    6.2.1 where the insured vessel is in collision with another vessel and both vessels are to blame then, unless the liability of one or both vessels becomes limited by law, the indemnity under this Clause 6 shall be calculated on the principle of cross-liabilities as if the respective Owners had been compelled to pay to each other such proportion of each other's damages as may have been properly allowed in ascertaining the balance or sum payable by or to the Assured in consequence of the collision

    6.2.2 in no case shall the total liability of the Underwriters under Clauses

    6.1 and 6.2 exceed their proportionate part of three fourths of the insured value of the insured vessel in respect of any one collision.

6.3 The Underwriters shall also pay three fourths of the legal costs incurred by the Assured or which the Assured may be compelled to pay in contesting liability or taking proceedings to limit liability, provided always that their prior written consent to the incurring of such costs shall have been obtained and that the total liability of the Underwriters under this Clause 6.3 shall not (unless the Underwriters' specific written agreement shall have been obtained) exceed 25% of the insured value of the insured vessel.

EXCLUSIONS

6.4 In no case shall the Underwriters indemnify the Assured under this Clause 6 for any sum which the Assured shall pay for or in respect of

    6.4.1 removal or disposal of obstructions, wrecks, cargoes or any other thing whatsoever

    6.4.2 any real or personal property or thing whatsoever except other vessels or any fixed or floating object struck by the insured vessel or property on other vessels or any such fixed or floating object

    6.4.3 the cargo or other property on, or the engagements of, the insured vessel

    6.4.4 loss of life, personal injury or illness

    6.4.5 pollution or contamination, or threats thereof, of any real or personal property or thing whatsoever (except other vessels with which the insured vessel is in collision or property on such other vessels) or damage to the environment, or threat thereof, save that this exclusion shall not exclude any sum which the Assured shall pay for or in respect of salvage remuneration in which the skill and efforts of the salvors in preventing or minimising damage to the environment as referred to in Article 13 paragraph l(b) of the International Convention on Salvage, 1989 have been taken into account.

7. Should the insured vessel come into collision with another vessel or fixed or floating object belonging wholly or in part to the same owners or under the same management or receive salvage services from another vessel belonging wholly or in part to the same owners or under the same management, the assured shall have the same rights under this insurance as they would have were the other vessel or the fixed or floating object entirely the property of owners not interested in the insured vessel; but in such cases the liability for the collision or the amount payable for the services rendered shall be referred to a sole arbitrator to be agreed upon between the underwriters and the assured.

38   4/4THS COLLISION LIABILITY

If the Underwriters have expressly agreed in writing, then Clause 6 is amended such that the words "three fourths of" are deleted on each occasion in which they appear in Clause 6.

39   RETURNS FOR LAY-UP

39.1   If the Underwriters have expressly agreed in writing, such percentage of the net premium as agreed by the Underwriters shall be returned for each period of 30 consecutive days the vessel may be laid up, not under repair, in a port or in a lay-up area provided such port or lay-up area is approved by the Underwriters.

39.2   The vessel shall not be considered to be under repair when work is undertaken in respect of ordinary wear and tear of the vessel and/or following recommendations in the vessel's Classification Society survey, but in the case of any repairs following loss of or damage to the vessel or involving structural alterations, whether covered by this insurance or otherwise, shall be considered as under repair.

39.3   PROVIDED ALWAYS THAT

      39.3.1   a total loss of the vessel, whether by perils insured under this insurance or otherwise, has not occurred during the period of this insurance or any extension thereof

      39.3.2   a return of premium shall not be allowed when the vessel is lying in exposed or unprotected waters, or in a port or lay-up area not approved by the Underwriters

      39.3.3   loading or discharging operations or the presence of cargo on board shall not debar a return of premium but no return shall be allowed for any period during which the vessel is being used for the storage of cargo or for lightering purposes

      39.3.4   in the event of any return of premium recoverable under this Clause 39 being based on 30 consecutive days which fall on successive insurances effected for the same Assured, this insurance shall only be liable for an amount calculated at pro rata of the agreed percentage net for the number of days which come within the period of this insurance or any extension thereof and to which a return is actually applicable. Such overlapping period shall run, at the option of the Assured, either from the first day on which the vessel is laid up or the first day of a period of 30 consecutive days as provided under Clause 39.1 above.

40   GENERAL AVERAGE ABSORBTION

40.1   If the Underwriters have expressly agreed in writing and subject to the provisions of Clause 8, the following shall apply in the event of an accident or occurrence giving rise to a general average act under the York-Antwerp Rules 1994 or under the provisions of the general average clause in the contract of affreightment.

40.2   The Assured shall have the option of claiming the total general average, salvage and special charges up to the amount expressly agreed by the Underwriters, without claiming general average, salvage or special charges from cargo, freight, bunkers, containers or any property not owned by the Assured on board the vessel (hereinafter the "Property Interests").

40.3   The Underwriters shall also pay the reasonable fees and expenses of the average adjuster for calculating claims under this Clause 40, in addition to any payment made under Clause 40.2.

40.4   If the Assured claims under this Clause 40, the Assured shall not claim general average, salvage or special charges against the Property Interests.

40.5   Claims under this Clause 40 shall be adjusted in accordance with the York-Antwerp Rules 1994, excluding the first paragraph of Rule XX and Rule XXI, relating to commission and interest.

40.6   Claims under this Clause 40 shall be payable without the application of the deductible(s) in Clause 15.

40.7   Without prejudice to any other defences that the Underwriters may have under this insurance or at law, the Underwriters waive any defences to payment under this Clause 40 which would have been available to the Property Interests, if the Assured had claimed general average, salvage or special charges from the Property Interests.

40.8 In respect of payments made under this Clause 40, the Underwriters waive their rights of subrogation against the Property Interests, save where the accident or occurrence giving rise to such payment is attributable to fault on the part of the Property Interests or any of them.

40.9 Claims under this Clause 40 shall be payable without reduction in respect of any under-insurance.

40.10 For the purposes of this Clause 40, special charges shall mean charges incurred by the Assured on behalf of or for the benefit of a particular interest to the adventure, for which charges the Assured is not responsible under the contract of affreightment.

41   ADDITIONAL PERILS

41.1 If the Underwriters have expressly agreed in writing, this insurance covers

41.1.1   the costs of repairing or replacing any boiler which bursts or shaft which breaks, where such bursting or breakage has caused loss of or damage to the subject matter insured covered by Clause 2.2.1, and that half of the costs common to the repair of the burst boiler or the broken shaft and to the repair of the loss or damage caused thereby which is not covered by Clause 2.3

41.1.2   the costs of correcting a latent defect where such latent defect has caused loss of or damage to the subject matter insured covered by Clause 2.2.2, and that half of the costs common to the correction of the latent defect and to the repair of the loss or damage caused thereby which is not covered by Clause 2.4

41.1.3   loss of or damage to the vessel caused by any accident or by negligence, incompetence or error of judgment of any person whatsoever

provided that such loss or damage has not resulted from want of due diligence by the Assured, Owners or Managers.

41.2 Master, Officers, Crew or Pilots shall not be considered Owners within the meaning of Clause 41.1 should they hold shares in the vessel.

PART 3 – CLAIMS PROVISIONS (01/11/03)

42   LEADING UNDERWRITER(S)

42.1 Where there is co-insurance in respect of this insurance, all subscribing Underwriters agree that the Leading Underwriter(s) designated in the slip or policy may act on their behalves so as to bind them for their respective several proportions in respect of the following matters (in addition to Clause 35.5)

42.1.1   the appointment of surveyors, experts, average adjusters and lawyers, in relation to matters which may give rise to a claim under this insurance

42.1.2   the duties and obligations to be undertaken by the Underwriters including, but not limited to, the provision of security

42.1.3   claims procedures, the handling of any claim (including, but not limited to, agreements under Clause 43.2) and the pursuit of recoveries

42.1.4   all payments or settlements to the Assured or to third parties under this insurance other than those agreed on an 'ex-gratia' basis.

Notwithstanding the above, the Leading Underwriter(s), or any of them, may require any such matters to be referred to the co-subscribing Underwriters.

42.2. The co-subscribing Underwriters shall, to the extent of their respective several proportions, indemnify and hold harmless the Leading Underwriter(s) in respect of all liabilities, costs or expenses incurred by the Leading Underwriter(s) in respect of the matters in Clause 42.1.

42.2 If the Leading Underwriter(s) require expenses incurred for or on behalf of the Underwriters to be collected for a party instructed by the Leading Underwriter(s), the collecting party shall be entitled to charge 5% of the amount collected for this service or such other amount as may be agreed in advance by the Leading Underwriter(s), such fee to be paid by the Underwriters.

42.3 The agreement in this Clause 42 between the Leading Underwriter(s) and co-subscribing Underwriters is subject to the exclusive jurisdiction of the English High Court of Justice and is subject to English law and practice.

43   NOTICE OF CLAIMS

43.1 In the event of an accident or occurrence whereby loss, damage, liability or expense may result in a claim under this insurance, notice must be given to the Leading Underwriter(s) as soon as possible after the date on which the Assured, Owners or Managers become aware of such loss, damage, liability or expense so that a surveyor may be appointed if the Leading Underwriter(s) so desire.

43.2 If notice is not given to the Leading Underwriter(s) within 180 days of the Assured, Owners or Managers becoming aware of such loss, damage, liability or expense, no claim shall be recoverable under this insurance in respect of such loss, damage, liability or expense, unless the Leading Underwriter(s) agree to the contrary in writing.

44   TENDER PROVISIONS

44.1 The Leading Underwriter(s) shall be entitled to decide the port to which the vessel shall proceed for docking or repair (the actual additional expense of the voyage arising from compliance with the Leading Underwriter(s)' requirements being refunded to the Assured) and shall have a right of veto concerning a place of repair or a repairing firm.

44.2 The Leading Underwriters(s) may also take tenders or may require further tenders to be taken for the repair of the vessel. Where such a tender has been taken and a tender is accepted with the approval of the Leading Underwriter(s), an allowance shall be made at the rate of 30% per annum on the insured value for the time lost between the despatch of the invitations to tender required by the Underwriters and the acceptance of a tender to the extent that such time is lost solely as the result of tenders having been taken and provided that the tender is accepted without delay after receipt of the Leading Underwriter's approval.

44.3 Due credit shall be given against the allowance in Clause 44.2 for any amounts recovered in respect of fuel, stores, wages and maintenance of the Master, Officers and Crew or any member thereof, including amounts allowed in general average, and for any amounts recovered from third parties in respect of damages for detention and/or loss of profit and/or running expenses, for the period covered by the tender allowance or any part thereof.

44.4 Where a part of the cost of the repair of damage other than a fixed deductible is not recoverable from the Underwriters the allowance shall be reduced by a similar proportion.

44.5 If the Assured fails to comply with this Clause 44, a deduction of 15% shall be made from the amount of the ascertained net claim.

45   DUTIES OF THE ASSURED

45.1 The Assured shall, upon request and at their own expense, provide the Leading Underwriter(s) with all relevant documents and information that they might reasonably require to consider any claim.

45.2 Upon reasonable request, the Assured shall also assist the Leading Underwriter(s) or their authorised agents in the investigation of any claim, including, but not limited to

45.2.1 interview(s) of any employee, ex-employee or agent of the Assured

45.2.2 interview(s) of any third party whom the Leading Underwriter(s) consider may knowledge of matters relevant to the claim

45.2.3 survey(s) of the subject-matter insured

45.2.4 inspection(s) of the classification records of the vessel.

45.3 It shall be a condition precedent to the liability of the Underwriters that the Assured shall not at any stage prior to the commencement of legal proceedings knowingly or recklessly

45.3.1 mislead or attempt to mislead the Underwriters in the proper consideration of a claim or the settlement thereof by relying on any evidence which is false

45.3.2 conceal any circumstance or matter from the Underwriters material to the proper consideration of a claim or a defence to such a claim.

45.4 Clause 45.3 does not require the Assured at any stage to disclose to the Underwriters any document or matter which under English law is protected from disclosure by legal advice privilege or by litigation privilege.

46   DUTIES OF THE UNDERWRITERS IN RELATION TO CLAIMS

46.1 The Leading Underwriter(s) may, at their sole discretion, upon the notification of loss, damage, liability or expense arising from an accident or occurrence which may result in a claim under this insurance

46.1.1 instruct a surveyor who shall report to the Leading Underwriter(s) concerning the cause and extent of damage, the necessary repairs and the fair and reasonable cost thereof and any other matter which the Leading Underwriter(s) or the surveyor consider relevant

46.1.2 confirm the appointment of an independent average adjuster to assist the Assured in the preparation of the claim. If not already agreed, the Assured shall propose the average adjuster to be appointed who may be a Fellow of the Association of Average Adjusters of the United Kingdom or any other average adjuster mutually acceptable to the Assured and the Leading Underwriter(s).

46.2 Where such appointments are made, the Underwriters shall be responsible for payment of reasonable fees directly to the surveyor and the average adjuster irrespective of whether a claim ultimately arises under this insurance. However, the Underwriters' liability for the fees of the appointed average adjuster shall cease no later than at such time as the Underwriters pay, settle or communicate their intention to deny the claim under this insurance or when it becomes apparent that any claim is unlikely to exceed the relevant deductible(s) in Clause 15.

46.3 The making of such appointments is not an admission by the Underwriters that the accident, occurrence or resulting claim is covered under this insurance or a waiver of any rights or defences that the Underwriters may have under this insurance or at law.

46.4 The reports of the surveyor shall, subject to no conflict of interest being identified by the Leading Underwriter(s), be released without delay to the Assured and the appointed average adjuster.

46.5 The Leading Underwriter(s) shall be entitled to request the appointed average adjuster to provide status reports at any stage.

46.6 The Leading Underwriter(s) shall give prompt consideration to the making of a payment on account upon the recommendation of the appointed average adjuster or, if no adjuster is appointed, upon the request of the Assured supported by appropriate documentation.

46.7 The Leading Underwriter(s) shall make a decision in respect of any claim within 28 days of receipt by them of the appointed average adjuster's final adjustment or, if no adjuster is appointed, a fully documented claim presentation sufficient to enable the Underwriters to determine their liability in relation to coverage and quantum. If the Leading Underwriter(s) request additional documentation or information to make a decision, they shall make a decision within a reasonable time after receipt of the

additional documents or information requested, or of a satisfactory explanation as to why such documents and information are not available.

47   PROVISION OF SECURITY

If the Assured is obliged to provide security to a third party in order to prevent the arrest of, or to obtain the release of, the vessel, due to an accident or occurrence giving rise to a claim alleged to be covered under this insurance, the Underwriters shall give due consideration to assisting the

Assured by providing security on behalf of the Assured or counter-security in a form to be determined by the Leading Underwriter(s).

48   PAYMENT OF CLAIMS

Claims payable under this insurance shall, subject to the terms of any assignment, be paid to the loss payee or, if no loss payee has been agreed, to the Assured or as they may direct in writing. Such payment, whether in account or otherwise, when made shall be a complete discharge of the Underwriters' obligations under this insurance in respect of the amount so paid.

49   RECOVERIES

49.1   The Assured shall, whether or not the Underwriters have paid a claim or agreed to pay a claim or potential claim under this insurance, take reasonable steps to

    49.1.1   assess as soon as possible whether there are any prospects of a recovery from third parties in respect of matters giving rise to a claim or to a potential claim under this insurance

    49.1.2   protect any claims against such third parties if necessary by the commencement of proceedings and the taking of appropriate steps to obtain security for the claim from third parties

    49.1.3   keep the Leading Underwriter(s) and the appointed average adjuster (if any) advised of the recovery prospects and any action taken against third parties

    49.1.4   co-operate with the Leading Underwriter(s) in the taking of such steps as may be reasonably required to pursue any claims against third parties.

49.2   Underwriters shall pay the reasonable costs incurred by the Assured pursuant to this Clause 49 in the same proportion as the insured losses bear to the total of the insured and uninsured losses (as defined in Clause 49.4.2).

49.3   Where the Assured have incurred reasonable costs pursuant to Clause 49.1.2 and where no claim is recoverable under this insurance, provided always that the Underwriters' written agreement to the reimbursement of such costs shall have been obtained prior to the incurring of such costs, the Underwriters shall reimburse such costs to the extent agreed, notwithstanding that no claim is recoverable under this insurance.

49.4   In the event of recoveries from third parties in respect of claims which have been paid in whole or in part under this insurance, such recoveries shall be distributed between the Underwriters and the Assured as follows

    49.4.1   the reasonable costs and expenses incurred in making such recoveries from the third party shall be deducted first and returned to the paying party

    49.4.2   the balance shall be apportioned between the Underwriters and the Assured in the same proportion that the insured losses and uninsured losses bear to the total of the insured and uninsured losses. For the purposes of Clause 49.2 and this Clause 49.4.2, uninsured losses shall mean loss of or damage to the subject-matter insured and any liability or expense which would have been recoverable under this insurance, but for the application of deductible(s) under Clause 15 and the limits of this insurance

49.5   In the event that under this insurance coverage is not provided in accordance with Clause 6, the following shall apply

    49.5.1   Where the insured vessel is in collision with another vessel and both vessels are to blame then, unless the liability of one or both vessels becomes limited by law, any recovery due to the Underwriters shall be calculated on the principle of cross-liabilities as if the respective Owners had been compelled to pay to each other such proportion of each other's damages as may have been properly allowed in ascertaining the balance or sum payable by or to the Assured in consequence of the collision.

50   DISPUTE RESOLUTION

Subject to the overriding provisions of Clause 1.3, disputes between the Assured and the Underwriters may, if not settled amicably by negotiation, be referred at the request of the Assured or the Underwriters to mediation or other form of alternative dispute resolution and, in default of agreement as to the procedure to be adopted, any such mediation or other form of alternative dispute resolution shall be in accordance with the current CEDR Solve model procedures.

APPENDIX 5

INSTITUTE CARGO CLAUSES (A)
(1 January 1982)

RISKS COVERED

1   This insurance covers all risks of loss of or damage to the subject matter insured except as provided in Clauses 4, 5, 6 and 7 below.

2   This insurance covers general average and salvage charges, adjusted or determined according to the contract of affreightment and/or the governing law and practice, incurred to avoid or in connection with the avoidance of loss from any cause except those excluded in Clauses 4, 5, 6 and 7 or elsewhere in this insurance.

3   This insurance is extended to indemnify the Assured against such proportion of liability under the contract of affreightment 'Both to Blame Collision' Clause as is in respect of a loss recoverable hereunder. In the event of any claim by shipowners under the said Clause the Assured agree to notify the Underwriters who shall have the right, at their own cost and expense, to defend the Assured against such claim.

EXCLUSIONS

4   In no case shall this insurance cover
   4.1   loss damage or expense attributable to wilful misconduct of the Assured
   4.2   ordinary leakage, ordinary loss in weight or volume, or ordinary wear and tear of the subject matter insured
   4.3   loss damage or expense caused by insufficiency or unsuitability of packing or preparation of the subject matter insured (for the purpose of this Clause 4.3 'packing' shall be deemed to include stowage in a container or liftvan but only when such stowage is carried out prior to attachment of this insurance or by the Assured or their servants)
   4.4   loss damage or expense caused by inherent vice or nature of the subject matter insured
   4.5   loss damage or expense proximately caused by delay, even though the delay be caused by a risk insured against (except expenses payable under Clause 2 above)
   4.6   loss damage or expense arising from insolvency or financial default of the owners managers charterers or operators of the vessel
   4.7   loss damage or expense arising from the use of any weapon of war employing atomic or nuclear fission and/or fusion or other like reaction or radioactive force or matter.

5   5.1   In no case shall this insurance cover loss damage or expense arising from
unseaworthiness of vessel or craft,
unfitness of vessel craft conveyance container or liftvan for the safe carriage of the subject matter insured,
where the Assured or their servants are privy to such unseaworthiness or unfitness, at the time the subject matter insured is loaded therein.
   5.2   The Underwriters waive any breach of the implied warranties of seaworthiness of the ship and fitness of the ship to carry the subject matter insured to destination, unless the Assured or their servants are privy to such unseaworthiness or unfitness.

6   In no case shall this insurance cover loss damage or expense caused by
   6.1   war civil war revolution rebellion insurrection, or civil strife arising therefrom, or any hostile act by or against a belligerent power
   6.2   capture seizure arrest restraint or detainment (piracy excepted), and the consequences thereof or any attempt thereat
   6.3   derelict mines torpedoes bombs or other derelict weapons of war.

7   In no case shall this insurance cover loss damage or expense

7.1   caused by strikers, locked-out workmen, or persons taking part in labour disturbances, riots or civil commotions

7.2   resulting from strikes, lock-outs, labour disturbances, riots or civil commotions

7.3   caused by any terrorist or any person acting from a political motive.

DURATION

8   8.1   This insurance attaches from the time the goods leave the warehouse or place of storage at the place named herein for the commencement of the transit, continues during the ordinary course of transit and terminates either

8.1.1 on delivery to the Consignees' or other final warehouse or place of storage at the destination named herein,

8.1.2 on delivery to any other warehouse or place of storage, whether prior to or at the destination named herein, which the Assured elect to use either

8.1.2.1   for storage other than in the ordinary course of transit or

8.1.2.2   for allocation or distribution,

or

8.1.3 on the expiry of 60 days after completion of discharge overside of the goods hereby insured from the oversea vessel at the final port of discharge,

whichever shall first occur.

8.2   If, after discharge overside from the oversea vessel at the final port of discharge, but prior to termination of this insurance, the goods are to be forwarded to a destination other than that to which they are insured hereunder, this insurance, whilst remaining subject to termination as provided for above, shall not extend beyond the commencement of transit to such other destination.

8.3   This insurance shall remain in force (subject to termination as provided for above and to the provisions of Clause 9 below) during delay beyond the control of the Assured, any deviation, forced discharge, reshipment or transhipment and during any variation of the adventure arising from the exercise of a liberty granted to shipowners or charterers under the contract of affreightment.

9   If owing to circumstances beyond the control of the Assured either the contract of carriage is terminated at a port or place other than the destination named therein or the transit is otherwise terminated before delivery of the goods as provided for in Clause 8 above, then this insurance shall also terminate unless prompt notice is given to the Underwriters and continuation of cover is requested when the insurance shall remain in force, subject to an additional premium if required by the Underwriters, either

9.1   until the goods are sold and delivered at such port or place, or, unless otherwise specially agreed, until the expiry of 60 days after arrival of the goods hereby insured at such port or place, whichever shall first occur, or

9.2   if the goods are forwarded within the said period of 60 days (or any agreed extension thereof) to the destination named herein or to any other destination, until terminated in accordance with the provisions of Clause 8 above.

10   Where, after attachment of this insurance, the destination is changed by the Assured, held covered at a premium and on conditions to be arranged subject to prompt notice being given to the Underwriters.

CLAIMS

11   11.1   In order to recover under this insurance the Assured must have an insurable interest in the subject matter insured at the time of the loss.

11.2   Subject to 11.1 above, the Assured shall be entitled to recover for insured loss occurring during the period covered by this insurance, notwithstanding that the loss occurred before the contract of insurance was concluded, unless the Assured were aware of the loss and the Underwriters were not.

12   Where, as a result of the operation of a risk covered by this insurance, the insured transit is terminated at a port or place other than that to which the subject matter is covered under

this insurance, the Underwriters will reimburse the Assured for any extra charges properly and reasonably incurred in unloading storing and forwarding the subject matter to the destination to which it is insured hereunder.

This Clause 12, which does not apply to general average or salvage charges, shall be subject to the exclusions contained in Clauses 4, 5, 6 and 7 above, and shall not include charges arising from the fault negligence insolvency or financial default of the Assured or their servants.

13   No claim for Constructive Total Loss shall be recoverable hereunder unless the subject matter insured is reasonably abandoned either on account of its actual total loss appearing to be unavoidable or because the cost of recovering, reconditioning and forwarding the subject matter to the destination to which it is insured would exceed its value on arrival.

14   14.1   If any Increased Value insurance is effected by the Assured on the cargo insured herein the agreed value of the cargo shall be deemed to be increased to the total amount insured under this insurance and all Increased Value insurances covering the loss, and liability under this insurance shall be in such proportion as the sum insured herein bears to such total amount insured.

In the event of claim the Assured shall provide the Underwriters with evidence of the amounts insured under all other insurances.

14.2   **Where this insurance is on Increased Value the following clause shall apply:**

The agreed value of the cargo shall be deemed to be equal to the total amount insured under the primary insurance and all Increased Value insurances covering the loss and effected on the cargo by the Assured, and liability under this insurance shall be in such proportion as the sum insured herein bears to such total amount insured.

In the event of claim the Assured shall provide the Underwriters with evidence of the amounts insured under all other insurances.

BENEFIT OF INSURANCE

15   This insurance shall not inure to the benefit of the carrier or other bailee.

MINIMISING LOSSES

16   It is the duty of the Assured and their servants and agents in respect of loss recoverable hereunder
16.1   to take such measures as may be reasonable for the purpose of averting or minimising such loss, and
16.2   to ensure that all rights against carriers, bailees or other third parties are properly preserved and exercised
and the Underwriters will, in addition to any loss recoverable hereunder, reimburse the Assured for any charges properly and reasonably incurred in pursuance of these duties.

17   Measures taken by the Assured or the Underwriters with the object of saving, protecting or recovering the subject matter insured shall not be considered as a waiver or acceptance of abandonment or otherwise prejudice the rights of either party.

AVOIDANCE OF DELAY

18   It is a condition of this insurance that the Assured shall act with reasonable despatch in all circumstances within their control.

LAW AND PRACTICE

19   This insurance is subject to English law and practice.

NOTE—*It is necessary for the Assured when they become aware of an event which is 'held covered' under this insurance to give prompt notice to the Underwriters and the right to such cover is dependent upon compliance with this obligation.*

APPENDIX 6

INSTITUTE CARGO CLAUSES (B)
(1 January 1982)

RISKS COVERED

1   This insurance covers, except as provided in Clauses 4, 5, 6 and 7 below,

    1.1   loss of or damage to the subject matter insured reasonably attributable to

        1.1.1 fire or explosion

        1.1.2 vessel or craft being stranded grounded sunk or capsized

        1.1.3 overturning or derailment of land conveyance

        1.1.4 collision or contact of vessel craft or conveyance with any external object other than water

        1.1.5 discharge of cargo at a port of distress

        1.1.6 earthquake volcanic eruption or lightning,

    1.2   loss of or damage to the subject matter insured caused by

        1.2.1 general average sacrifice

        1.2.2 jettison or washing overboard

        1.2.3 entry of sea lake or river water into vessel craft hold conveyance container liftvan or place of storage,

    1.3   total loss of any package lost overboard or dropped whilst loading on to, or unloading from, vessel or craft.

2   This insurance covers general average and salvage charges, adjusted or determined according to the contract of affreightment and/or the governing law and practice, incurred to avoid or in connection with the avoidance of loss from any cause except those excluded in Clauses 4, 5, 6 and 7 or elsewhere in this insurance

3   This insurance is extended to indemnify the Assured against such proportion of liability under the contract of affreightment 'Both to Blame Collision' Clause as is in respect of a loss recoverable hereunder. In the event of any claim by shipowners under the said Clause the Assured agree to notify the Underwriters who shall have the right, at their own cost and expense, to defend the Assured against such claim.

EXCLUSIONS

4   In no case shall this insurance cover

    4.1   loss damage or expense attributable to wilful misconduct of the Assured

    4.2   ordinary leakage, ordinary loss in weight or volume, or ordinary wear and tear of the subject matter insured

    4.3   loss damage or expense caused by insufficiency or unsuitability of packing or preparation of the subject matter insured (for the purpose of this Clause 4.3 'packing' shall be deemed to include stowage in a container or liftvan but only when such stowage is carried out prior to attachment of this insurance or by the Assured or their servants)

    4.4   loss damage or expense caused by inherent vice or nature of the subject matter insured

    4.5   loss damage or expense proximately caused by delay, even though the delay be caused by a risk insured against (except expenses payable under Clause 2 above)

    4.6   loss damage or expense arising from insolvency or financial default of the owners managers charterers or operators of the vessel

    4.7   deliberate damage to or deliberate destruction of the subject matter insured or any part thereof by the wrongful act of any person or persons

    4.8   loss damage or expense arising from the use of any weapon of war employing atomic or nuclear fission and/or fusion or other like reaction or radioactive force or matter.

5   5.1   In no case shall this insurance cover loss damage or expense arising from unseaworthiness of vessel or craft, unfitness of vessel craft conveyance container or liftvan for the safe carriage of the subject matter insured, where the Assured or their servants are privy to such unseaworthiness or unfitness, at the time the subject matter insured is loaded therein.

      5.2   The Underwriters waive any breach of the implied warranties of seaworthiness of the ship and fitness of the ship to carry the subject matter insured to destination, unless the Assured or their servants are privy to such unseaworthiness or unfitness.

6   In no case shall this insurance cover loss damage or expense caused by

      6.1   war civil war revolution rebellion insurrection, or civil strife arising therefrom, or any hostile act by or against a belligerent power

      6.2   capture seizure arrest restraint or detainment, and the consequences thereof or any attempt thereat

      6.3   derelict mines torpedoes bombs or other derelict weapons of war.

7   In no case shall this insurance cover loss damage or expense

      7.1   caused by strikers, locked-out workmen, or persons taking part in labour disturbances, riots or civil commotions

      7.2   resulting from strikes, lock-outs, labour disturbances, riots or civil commotions

      7.3   caused by any terrorist or any person acting from a political motive.

DURATION

8   8.1   This insurance attaches from the time the goods leave the warehouse or place of storage at the place named herein for the commencement of the transit, continues during the ordinary course of transit and terminates either

         8.1.1   on delivery to the Consignees' or other final warehouse or place of storage at the destination named herein,

         8.1.2   on delivery to any other warehouse or place of storage, whether prior to or at the destination named herein, which the Assured elect to use either

           8.1.2.1   for storage other than in the ordinary course of transit or

           8.1.2.2   for allocation or distribution,

           or

         8.1.3   on the expiry of 60 days after completion of discharge overside of the goods hereby insured from the oversea vessel at the final port of discharge, whichever shall first occur.

      8.2   If, after discharge overside from the oversea vessel at the final port of discharge, but prior to termination of this insurance, the goods are to be forwarded to a destination other than that to which they are insured hereunder, this insurance, whilst remaining subject to termination as provided for above, shall not extend beyond the commencement of transit to such other destination.

      8.3   This insurance shall remain in force (subject to termination as provided for above and to the provisions of Clause 9 below) during delay beyond the control of the Assured, any deviation, forced discharge, reshipment or transhipment and during any variation of the adventure arising from the exercise of a liberty granted to shipowners or charterers under the contract of affreightment.

9   If owing to circumstances beyond the control of the Assured either the contract of carriage is terminated at a port or place other than the destination named therein or the transit is otherwise terminated before delivery of the goods as provided for in Clause 8 above, then this insurance shall also terminate unless prompt notice is given to the Underwriters and continuation of cover is requested when the insurance shall remain in force, subject to an additional premium if required by the Underwriters, either

      9.1   until the goods are sold and delivered at such port or place, or, unless otherwise specially agreed, until the expiry of 60 days after arrival of the goods hereby insured at such port or place, whichever shall first occur,

         or

9.2   if the goods are forwarded within the said period of 60 days (or any agreed extension thereof) to the destination named herein or to any other destination, until terminated in accordance with the provisions of Clause 8 above.

10   Where, after attachment of this insurance, the destination is changed by the Assured, held covered at a premium and on conditions to be arranged subject to prompt notice being given to the Underwriters.

CLAIMS

11   11.1   In order to recover under this insurance the Assured must have an insurable interest in the subject matter insured at the time of the loss.

11.2   Subject to 11.1 above, the Assured shall be entitled to recover for insured loss occurring during the period covered by this insurance, notwithstanding that the loss occurred before the contract of insurance was concluded, unless the Assured were aware of the loss and the Underwriters were not.

12   Where, as a result of the operation of a risk covered by this insurance, the insured transit is terminated at a port or place other than that to which the subject matter is covered under this insurance, the Underwriters will reimburse the Assured for any extra charges properly and reasonably incurred in unloading storing and forwarding the subject matter to the destination to which it is insured hereunder.

This Clause 12, which does not apply to general average or salvage charges, shall be subject to the exclusions contained in Clauses 4, 5, 6 and 7 above, and shall not include charges arising from the fault negligence insolvency or financial default of the Assured or their servants.

13   No claim for Constructive Total Loss shall be recoverable hereunder unless the subject matter insured is reasonably abandoned either on account of its actual total loss appearing to be unavoidable or because the cost of recovering, reconditioning and forwarding the subject matter to the destination to which it is insured would exceed its value on arrival.

14   14.1   If any Increased Value insurance is effected by the Assured on the cargo insured herein the agreed value of the cargo shall be deemed to be increased to the total amount insured under this insurance and all Increased Value insurances covering the loss, and liability under this insurance shall be in such proportion as the sum insured herein bears to such total amount insured.

In the event of claim the Assured shall provide the Underwriters with evidence of the amounts insured under all other insurances.

14.2   Where this insurance is on Increased Value the following clause shall apply:

The agreed value of the cargo shall be deemed to be equal to the total amount insured under the primary insurance and all Increased Value insurances covering the loss and effected on the cargo by the Assured, and liability under this insurance shall be in such proportion as the sum insured herein bears to such total amount insured.

In the event of claim the Assured shall provide the Underwriters with evidence of the amounts insured under all other insurances.

BENEFIT OF INSURANCE

15   This insurance shall not inure to the benefit of the carrier or other bailee.

MINIMISING LOSSES

16   It is the duty of the Assured and their servants and agents in respect of loss recoverable hereunder

16.1   to take such measures as may be reasonable for the purpose of averting or minimising such loss, and

16.2   to ensure that all rights against carriers, bailees or other third parties are properly preserved and exercised and the Underwriters will, in addition to any loss recoverable hereunder, reimburse the Assured for any charges properly and reasonably incurred in pursuance of these duties.

17   Measures taken by the Assured or the Underwriters with the object of saving, protecting or recovering the subject matter insured shall not be considered as a waiver or acceptance of abandonment or otherwise prejudice the rights of either party.

AVOIDANCE OF DELAY

18   It is a condition of this insurance that the Assured shall act with reasonable despatch in all circumstances within their control.

LAW AND PRACTICE

19   This insurance is subject to English law and practice.

NOTE—*It is necessary for the Assured when they become aware of an event which is 'held covered' under this insurance to give prompt notice to the Underwriters and the right to such cover is dependent upon compliance with this obligation.*

INSTITUTE CARGO CLAUSES (C)
(1 January 1982)

RISKS COVERED

1   This insurance covers, except as provided in Clauses 4, 5, 6 and 7 below,

    1.1   loss of or damage to the subject matter insured reasonably attributable to

        1.1.1 fire or explosion

        1.1.2 vessel or craft being stranded grounded sunk or capsized

        1.1.3 overturning or derailment of land conveyance

        1.1.4 collision or contact of vessel craft or conveyance with any external object other than water

        1.1.5 discharge of cargo at a port of distress,

    1.2   loss of or damage to the subject matter insured caused by

        1.2.1 general average sacrifice

        1.2.2 jettison.

2   This insurance covers general average and salvage charges, adjusted or determined according to the contract of affreightment and/or the governing law and practice, incurred to avoid or in connection with the avoidance of loss from any cause except those excluded in Clauses 4, 5, 6 and 7 or elsewhere in this insurance.

3   This insurance is extended to indemnify the Assured against such proportion of liability under the contract of affreightment 'Both to Blame Collision' Clause as is in respect of a loss recoverable hereunder. In the event of any claim by shipowners under the said Clause the Assured agree to notify the Underwriters who shall have the right, at their own cost and expense, to defend the Assured against such claim.

EXCLUSIONS

4   In no case shall this insurance cover

    4.1   loss damage or expense attributable to wilful misconduct of the Assured

    4.2   ordinary leakage, ordinary loss in weight or volume, or ordinary wear and tear of the subject matter insured

    4.3   loss damage or expense caused by insufficiency or unsuitability of packing or preparation of the subject matter insured (for the purpose of this Clause 4.3 'packing' shall be deemed to include stowage in a container or liftvan but only when such stowage is carried out prior to attachment of this insurance or by the Assured or their servants)

    4.4   loss damage or expense caused by inherent vice or nature of the subject matter insured

    4.5   loss damage or expense proximately caused by delay, even though the delay be caused by a risk insured against (except expenses payable under Clause 2 above)

    4.6   loss damage or expense arising from insolvency or financial default of the owners managers charterers or operators of the vessel

    4.7   deliberate damage to or deliberate destruction of the subject matter insured or any part thereof by the wrongful act of any person or persons

    4.8   loss damage or expense arising from the use of any weapon of war employing atomic or nuclear fission and/or fusion or other like reaction or radioactive force or matter.

5   5.1   In no case shall this insurance cover loss damage or expense arising from unseaworthiness of vessel or craft, unfitness of vessel craft conveyance container or liftvan for the safe carriage of the subject matter insured,

            where the Assured or their servants are privy to such unseaworthiness or unfitness, at the time the subject matter insured is loaded therein.

5.2   The Underwriters waive any breach of the implied warranties of seaworthiness of the ship and fitness of the ship to carry the subject matter insured to destination, unless the Assured or their servants are privy to such unseaworthiness or unfitness.

6   In no case shall this insurance cover loss damage or expense caused by

6.1   war civil war revolution rebellion insurrection, or civil strife arising therefrom, or any hostile act by or against a belligerent power

6.2   capture seizure arrest restraint or detainment, and the consequences thereof or any attempt thereat

6.3   derelict mines torpedoes bombs or other derelict weapons of war.

7   In no case shall this insurance cover loss damage or expense

7.1   caused by strikers, locked-out workmen, or persons taking part in labour disturbances, riots or civil commotions

7.2   resulting from strikes, lock-outs, labour disturbances, riots or civil commotions

7.3   caused by any terrorist or any person acting from a political motive.

DURATION

8   8.1   This insurance attaches from the time the goods leave the warehouse or place of storage at the place named herein for the commencement of the transit, continues during the ordinary course of transit and terminates either

8.1.1   on delivery to the Consignees' or other final warehouse or place of storage at the destination named herein,

8.1.2   on delivery to any other warehouse or place of storage, whether prior to or at the destination named herein, which the Assured elect to use either

8.1.2.1   for storage other than in the ordinary course of transit or

8.1.2.2   for allocation or distribution,

or

8.1.3   on the expiry of 60 days after completion of discharge overside of the goods hereby insured from the oversea vessel at the final port of discharge, whichever shall first occur.

8.2   If, after discharge overside from the oversea vessel at the final port of discharge, but prior to termination of this insurance, the goods are to be forwarded to a destination other than that to which they are insured hereunder, this insurance, whilst remaining subject to termination as provided for above, shall not extend beyond the commencement of transit to such other destination.

8.3   This insurance shall remain in force (subject to termination as provided for above and to the provisions of Clause 9 below) during delay beyond the control of the Assured, any deviation forced discharge, reshipment or transhipment and during any variation of the adventure arising from the exercise of a liberty granted to shipowners or charterers under the contract of affreightment.

9   If owing to circumstances beyond the control of the Assured either the contract of carriage is terminated at a port or place other than the destination named therein or the transit is otherwise terminated before delivery of the goods as provided for in Clause 8 above, then this insurance shall also terminate unless prompt notice is given to the Underwriters and continuation of cover is requested when the insurance shall remain in force, subject to an additional premium if required by the Underwriters, either

9.1   until the goods are sold and delivered at such port or place, or, unless otherwise specially agreed, until the expiry of 60 days after arrival of the goods hereby insured at such port or place, whichever shall first occur, or

9.2   if the goods are forwarded within the said period of 60 days (or any agreed extension thereof) to the

destination named herein or to any other destination, until terminated in accordance with the provisions of Clause 8 above.

10 Where, after attachment of this insurance, the destination is changed by the Assured, held covered at a premium and on conditions to be arranged subject to prompt notice being given to the Underwriters.

CLAIMS

11   11.1   In order to recover under this insurance the Assured must have an insurable interest in the subject matter insured at the time of the loss.

      11.2   Subject to 11.1 above, the Assured shall be entitled to recover for insured loss occurring during the period covered by this insurance, notwithstanding that the loss occurred before the contract of insurance was concluded, unless the Assured were aware of the loss and the Underwriters were not.

12   Where, as a result of the operation of a risk covered by this insurance, the insured transit is terminated at a port or place other than that to which the subject matter is covered under this insurance, the Underwriters will reimburse the Assured for any extra charges properly and reasonably incurred in unloading storing and forwarding the subject matter to the destination to which it is insured hereunder.

This Clause 12, which does not apply to general average or salvage charges, shall be subject to the exclusions contained in Clauses 4, 5, 6 and 7 above, and shall not include charges arising from the fault negligence insolvency or financial default of the Assured or their servants.

13   No claim for Constructive Total Loss shall be recoverable hereunder unless the subject matter insured is reasonably abandoned either on account of its actual total loss appearing to be unavoidable or because the cost of recovering, reconditioning and forwarding the subject matter to the destination to which it is insured would exceed its value on arrival.

14   14.1   If any Increased Value insurance is effected by the Assured on the cargo insured herein the agreed value of the cargo shall be deemed to be increased to the total amount insured under this insurance and all Increased Value insurances covering the loss, and liability under this insurance shall be in such proportion as the sum insured herein bears to such total amount insured.

            In the event of claim the Assured shall provide the Underwriters with evidence of the amounts insured under all other insurances.

      14.2   Where this insurance is on Increased Value the following clause shall apply:

            The agreed value of the cargo shall be deemed to be equal to the total amount insured under the primary insurance and all Increased Value insurances covering the loss and effected on the cargo by the Assured, and liability under this insurance shall be in such proportion as the sum insured herein bears to such total amount insured.

            In the event of claim the Assured shall provide the Underwriters with evidence of the amounts insured under all other insurances.

BENEFIT OF INSURANCE

15   This insurance shall not inure to the benefit of the carrier or other bailee.

MINIMISING LOSSES

16   It is the duty of the Assured and their servants and agents in respect of loss recoverable hereunder

      16.1   to take such measures as may be reasonable for the purpose of averting or minimising such loss,

            and

      16.2   to ensure that all rights against carriers, bailees or other third parties are properly preserved and exercised

            and the Underwriters will, in addition to any loss recoverable hereunder, reimburse the Assured for any charges properly and reasonably incurred in pursuance of these duties.

17   Measures taken by the Assured or the Underwriters with the object of saving, protecting or recovering the subject matter insured shall not be considered as a waiver or acceptance of abandonment or otherwise prejudice the rights of either party.

AVOIDANCE OF DELAY

18   It is a condition of this insurance that the Assured shall act with reasonable despatch in all circumstances within their control.

LAW AND PRACTICE

19   This insurance is subject to English law and practice.

NOTE—*It is necessary for the Assured when they become aware of an event which is 'held covered' under this insurance to give prompt notice to the Underwriters and the right to such cover is dependent upon compliance with this obligation.*

APPENDIX 8

INSTITUTE WARRANTIES
(1 July 1976)

1   Warranted no:
    (a)   Atlantic Coast of North America, its rivers or adjacent islands,
        (i)   north of 52° 10′ N Lat and west of 50° W Long;
        (ii)   south of 52° 10′ N Lat in the area bounded by lines drawn between Battle Harbour/Pistolet Bay; Cape Ray/Cape North; Port Hawkesbury/Port Mulgrave and Baie Comeau/Matane between 21st December and 30th April both days inclusive;
        (iii)   west of Baie Comeau/Matane (but not west of Montreal) between 1st December and 30th April both days inclusive.
    (b)   Great Lakes or St Lawrence Seaway west of Montreal.
    (c)   Greenland Waters.
    (d)   Pacific Coast of North America its rivers or adjacent islands north of 54° 30′ N Lat, or west of 130° 50′ W Long

2   Warranted no Baltic Sea or adjacent waters east of 15° E Long:
    (a)   North of a line between Mo (63° 24′ N Lat) and Vasa (63° 06′ N Lat) between 10th December and 25th May bdi.
    (b)   East of a line between Viipuri (Vyborg) (28° 47′ E Long) and Narva (28° 12′ E Long) between 15th December and 15th May bdi.
    (c)   North of a line between Stockholm (59° 20′ N Lat) and Tallinn (59° 24′ N Lat) between 8th January and 5th May bdi.
    (d)   East of 22° E Long, and south of 59° N Lat between 28th December and 5th May bdi.

3 . Warranted not North of 70° N Lat other than voyages direct to or from any port or place in Norway or Kola Bay.

4   Warranted no Bering Sea, no East Asian waters north of 46° N Lat and not to enter or sail from any port or place in Siberia except Nakhodka and/or Vladivostock.

5   Warranted not to proceed to Kerguelen and/or Croset Islands or south of 50° S Lat, except to ports and/or places in Patagonia and/or Chile and/or Falkland Islands, but liberty is given to enter waters south of 50° S Lat, if en route to or from ports and/or places not excluded by this warranty.

6   Warranted not to sail with Indian Coal as cargo:
    (a)   between 1st March and 30th June, bdi.
    (b)   between 1st July and 30th September, bdi, except to ports in Asia, not West of Aden or East of or beyond Singapore.

INDEX